Advance Praise for *India and Her Futures*

'A brilliant, thoughtful critique on contemporary affairs, recording history as it happens. A must-read for young India, a refreshingly unique historical perspective, always ethical and relevant.'

Aruna Roy

'Gopalkrishna Gandhi has long been a redoubtable conscience keeper of our Republic, striving to keep India, in his gentle yet unflagging way, from error and worse. It was to enlighten and enrich – intellectually, culturally, ethically and politically – the citizens of our Republic that he wrote these essays.

Lyrical in their prose and resounding with cadences both historical and deeply personal, these essays offer a tantalising glimpse of his thoughtful, erudite, insightful, and creative personality. Yet above all, they reveal his heart, suffused with that priceless quality that is his greatest civilisational and familial bequest: *insaaniyat* – both humanity and humaneness – so often missing in India today.

Ultimately, Gopalkrishna Gandhi's *India and Her Futures* is not only a resounding testament to his intellect but a tender yet compelling summons to our better selves – both as Indians and as human beings.'

Shashi Tharoor

'Gopalkrishna Gandhi stands as a towering public figure in India, because of his exemplary integrity, courage and commitment to social justice. As the pieces in this collection vividly demonstrate, he is also an exceptionally gifted writer, one of the few who, in this age of extremes, is able to chart a path of sanity, empathy and goodwill.'

Amitav Ghosh

India and Her Futures

India and Her Futures

Essays

GOPALKRISHNA GANDHI

BLOOMSBURY
NEW DELHI · LONDON · OXFORD · NEW YORK · SYDNEY

BLOOMSBURY INDIA
Bloomsbury Publishing India Pvt. Ltd
Second Floor, LSC Building No. 4, DDA Complex, Pocket C – 6 & 7,
Vasant Kunj, New Delhi, 110070

BLOOMSBURY, BLOOMSBURY INDIA and the Diana logo
are trademarks of Bloomsbury Publishing Plc

First published in India 2025

Copyright © Gopalkrishna Gandhi, 2025

Gopalkrishna Gandhi has asserted his moral rights to be identified
as the author of this work in accordance with the Indian Copyright Act, 1957

All rights reserved. No part of this publication may be: i) reproduced
or transmitted in any form, electronic or mechanical, including
photocopying, recording or by means of any information storage or
retrieval system without prior permission in writing from the publishers;
or ii) used or reproduced in any way for the training, development or
operation of artificial intelligence (AI) technologies, including generative
AI technologies. The rights holders expressly reserve this publication
from the text and data mining exception as per Article 4(3) of the Digital
Single Market Directive (EU) 2019/790

ISBN: HB: 978-93-61316-77-7; eBook: 978-93-61310-22-5
2 4 6 8 10 9 7 5 3 1

Typeset in Adobe Garamond Pro by Manipal Technologies Limited
Printed and bound in India by Thomson Press India Ltd

To find out more about our authors and books visit www.bloomsbury.com
and sign up for our newsletters

For sale in the Indian subcontinent only

To
Divya and Amrita

Contents

Introduction   xiii

    PART I   FRENEMIES AND NEIGHBOURLINESS:
                INDIA AND HER NEIGHBOURS

1. How Rajiv and Benazir Shaped Nuclear Restraint   3
2. If That Door Should Shut Now   6
3. This War Cloud Has a New Shape   9
4. A People of an Emerald Isle, Waiting with Doosras   14
5. Civil Warriors   18

    PART II   HOME AND THE WORLD: INDIA AND ITS PLACE
                 IN THE WORLD

6. Turkey, Syria and the Real Threat Beneath India's Feet   25
7. Spot the Tremors   28
8. The New Teacher   31
9. A First Is a First   35
10. An Unasked Question   39
11. Taking a Giant Leap for a New Ethics in Outer Space   42

    PART III   FORGOTTEN HISTORIES OF INDIA

12. Living with the Birds   49
13. Four Deaths, the Right to Life and the Jayaprakash Principle   53
14. Lessons from History for the Balasore Tragedy   55
15. Buddhadeb Bhattacharjee: Interpreter of Tagore to Presidents   58
16. Towering Presence   61
17. That Mushroom Cloud   64

18.	Two Centenaries	68
19.	Old Lessons	72
20.	The Anniversary of a Divide	75
21.	The Gandhis, Mandelas and Kings of Today	79
22.	When India Was Turned into a Vast Prison House	83

PART IV INDIANS WHO BIRTHED INDIA

23.	A Song Sung True	89
24.	A Comrade, Not Acolyte, of the Mahatma	98
25.	A Designer of Cultural Gardens	103
26.	M.S. Subbulakshmi: The Song Celestial	106
27.	Vajpayee: The BJP's Star, and His Own Person	112
28.	A Message from Gandhi to a Very Troubled World	115
29.	The Scorching Truth of Rushdie's Ordeal	118
30.	Dadabhai Naoroji: A Leader Who Served India and Britain	120
31.	Great Arcs of Resonance: A Tribute to Pandit Ravi Shankar	123
32.	S. Radhakrishnan: A Man of Egoless Impartiality	126
33.	In Nehru's Death, a Precedent for Rectitude Was Set	129
34.	Unusual Flower	132
35.	Eternal Verities	135
36.	The Favourites	139
37.	Badshah Khan: The Man, the Mission	142
38.	As Suitable as Ever	150
39.	The Right to Be Oneself	153
40.	Gandhi's Songs	156
41.	Warm, Vital, Restless	160
42.	At Point-Blank Range	164
43.	A Chronicle Foretold	167
44.	Honoured Guest	170
45.	Standing Tall, Together	173
46.	Marching Along a New Path	177
47.	Message from the Martyrs of Jallianwala Bagh	180
48.	Sardar Patel: Truth and Hype About a Leader	184
49.	Only Half Our Story	187

PART V THE IDEAS OF INDIA

50. Ink That Protects the Sanctity of Elections — 193
51. A Call to Treat India's Prisoners Fairly and Humanely — 196
52. We Owe Our Freedom to the Salt of Our Earth — 199
53. On Reality of Caste, Bihar Holds a Mirror — 201
54. Uphold the Lofty Ideals Symbolised by the Tricolour — 204
55. Crafting an Ethical Mode of Governance for India — 207
56. Elusive Value — 210
57. A Unified Field of Pain — 213
58. Flag of Conscience — 219
59. A Symbol of Kakayuga — 222
60. At the Heart of the Republic — 225
61. The Essence of Democracy — 228
62. Such a Long Reckoning — 231
63. A Necessary Presence — 235
64. We, the People; Neither Free of Fear nor Fearless — 239

PART VI OUR INSTITUTIONS

65. In an Era of Diminishing Expectations, the Judiciary Gives Hope — 245
66. Three-Letter Status — 247
67. The Architecture of India's Governance — 250
68. The Subtle Influence of India's President — 252
69. Constant Verities — 255
70. Flickering Hope — 259
71. An Enduring Challenge — 263
72. Beginning Once Again — 267
73. Emergency Medicine — 270
74. Silence Is Not Golden: On the Importance of Being Shashi Tharoor — 273
75. The Eyes of the Beholder — 277
76. Why We Need Governors — 280
77. His Excellency the Governor — 283
78. Rescuing Grace from Disgrace — 289
79. Delimitation Fallout Needs No Political Forecasting — 293

PART VI TROUBLE IN PARADISE

80.	National Blind Spot	299
81.	Gone Girls and Boys	302
82.	Righteous Paths	305
83.	Different Challenges	308
84.	Seismic Traumas	311
85.	Gross Valuation	315
86.	Double Whammy	318
87.	Locked Lives	321
88.	Honouring the Word	324
89.	Time for Caution	327
90.	There Is Struggle Ahead	330
91.	Ill Fares the Land	333
92.	Totem and Taboo	336
93.	Civilised Killing	339
94.	Restore India's Heritage of a Shared Peoplehood	343
95.	Bengal Needs No Radcliffe Line of Hatred	347
96.	When Brecht Speaks as Ambedkar	351
97.	India Stares at Water Scarcity	354
98.	Heed This 67-Year-Old Tryst	357
99.	Spread Thin and Wide	361
100.	Mirrors of India	365

Acknowledgements	369
Index	371
About the Author	392

Introduction

THE ESSAY, AMONG THE various genres of literature, is either not taken seriously enough or is forgotten soon after it is read. Poetry and the story – short or long – hold greater sway. Confining this reflection to Indian examples of English writing alone, I can say Vikram Seth's transportingly beautiful poetry and his amazingly engaging fiction, Amitav Ghosh's fantastic novels, Ruskin Bond's eerie stories and Jerry Pinto's works of autobiography and fiction hold and will continue to hold readers' attention in a way essays written by anyone howsoever readable will not.

This is partly because the essay appears, generally, in a newspaper which by its very nature is a one-day reading wonder before it retreats to the newspaper's archives, there to slumber until some researcher seeks it out. And also because now in our digital times the essay appears on screens fleetingly, only to vanish as suddenly as it has come on. Yet, the essay, as an editorial that appears without a name or an article that carries with it a name of some weight or is of compelling interest because of its topicality, no matter how well or little known its author, manages to linger in the mind. Rather like 'left luggage' in a railway station or airport, or 'un-delivered' letters in what post offices used to call 'dead letter box' meant for the 'addressee not found'. The worthwhile essay, like Shelley's 'Cloud', changes but does not die. From being today's top read to tomorrow's cold print and the day after's old stuff and potential wrapping material, it can all but disappear physically yet stay put somewhere within the mind's reading room. The worthless essay of course does not do that. It deservedly chortles into nothingness.

The essay as a genre has always held me captive.

At my school in New Delhi, two unforgettable teachers, Vedvyasji and Awadh Kishoreji, taught us Hindi and English literature respectively. The polymath Rahula Sankrityayan's Hindi essays on his *ghumakkad* (vagabond) journeys, read out to us dramatically by Vedvyasji, who was a skilled theatre-actor, turned us for that brief hour into trekkers in the Himalayas. Slow-moving ceiling fans whirred over our heated heads in Barakhamba Road's Modern School but hearing him read Sankrityayan made us feel the rugged mountains' cold winds on our skins. Awadh Kishoreji was a wizard of a teacher, capable of making the driest of subjects sound interesting and memorable. Snatches from his teaching have stayed with me over the years that have seen him go to his rest and me turn from an uncomprehending boy to an old man. Reading out an excerpt from an essay by Gandhi, Awadh Kishoreji stopped at a Latin phrase in it – *pari passu*. Telling us what it meant ('on an equal footing') Awadh Kishoreji not only cracked an inaccessible phrase but gently opened a window for me into the wonders of that language. He was *sui generis*. Awadh Kishoreji was one of his kind.

In the college in Delhi I studied in, three teachers made an instant and lasting impact on me. The first was an Englishman, the Rev. Jarvis, who was Chaplain at St Stephen's and also taught English literature to undergraduates. The second was W.S. Rajpal. And the third, the nearest thing to an ideal teacher anywhere, M.M. Bhalla. All teachers in college during my time there (1961–1964) were men and had the suffix 'sahib' attached to their names, after a style that went with the college's many studied mannerisms. So, these three were Jarvissahib, Rajpalsahib and Bhallasahib to their students.

Bhallasahib taught poetry and was like a suspension bridge from wherever we were to the beclouded world of the Romantic poets – strong and swaying in a rhythm and with a poetic lyricism of his own. There was something almost unreal about his pedagogy. I say 'unreal' because the way he read and explained Wordsworth's 'The Prelude', Coleridge's 'The Ancient Mariner' and 'Kubla Khan' or Keats' 'Ode on a Grecian Urn' was outside the standard modes of 'covering' those prescribed texts. His unusually expressive eyes would light up – yes, exactly that – and would sometimes well up as he read or recited from memory the lines aloud. He did not need to say much. The way he read out the text was enough to bring the poems to life – disturbingly, entrancingly, bewitchingly. And he did this while being quintessentially Bhallasahib, a product of the soil watered by the five rivers, as Indian as Lala Lajpat Rai or Bhagat Singh. That he was a contemporary of and knew Faiz Ahmad Faiz and Harivansh Rai Bachchan was a matter of side importance. What made Bhallasahib special to us was his total identification with the subject, his at-one-ness with it. He taught either standing or pacing. The classroom was small, but he would manage to find room to pace inside that tight space as he spoke. And he would stop near each student and peering into his eyes – we were all just-out-of-school boys imagining we were grown men – say what he wanted to say in a decibel only slightly higher than a whisper. Bhallasahib's classroom lectures were oral essays.

Of a totally different cut of sartor was Rajpalsahib. Rumour had it that he had changed his name from Ramsden to Rajpal shortly after India became independent and that even Ramsden had a precursor – Ramsadan, a three-name transformation in step with history. Be that as it may or may not,

Rajpalsahib was all that an Anglicised Indian of good taste could or would desire to be – smart enough to look well dressed, but not so smart as to seem dandy. Come winter and even as the college lawns would suddenly sprout roses, Rajpalsahib would be clad in a tweed coat of the finest trim with sleeves with leather patches at the elbows. Wearing shoes of the finest design to match, he was someone P.G. Wodehouse's Jeeves would approve. Rajpalsahib taught us the essays of Joseph Addison, Francis Bacon and Robert Louis Stevenson with aplomb. Seated and be-gowned by an archaic college practice, he looked like a senator. And sounded like one. So strong was Rajpalsahib's advocacy of Bacon's great stature that his essays 'Of Truth' and 'Of Death' have been inked into my mind. This was because Rajpalsahib, while reading from Bacon, made us feel he was Francis Bacon, Attorney General and Lord Chancellor of England, and we were subjects under King James I. Bhallasahib's identification with Wordsworth or Coleridge was a fluxion of his teaching with the sublimity of his subject; Rajpalsahib's was of his own personality, of which he had a rather good opinion, with the stature and status of his subject. When Rajpalsahib read out Bacon's great line (from 'Of Truth'): 'There is no vice that doth so cover a man with shame as to be found false and perfidious…' he managed to make all in the class despise lying and liars. And when by vocal emphases, employing well his deep voice, he read (from 'Of Death'): 'Revenge triumphs over death; love slights it; honour aspireth to it; grief flieth to it; fear preoccupateth it…' he ironically brought death to life.

Jarvissahib was, well, Jarvissahib. If the bicycle was this priest-cum-teacher's favourite mode of transport, skipping or traipsing was what his walking gait looked like. As the college's chaplain he wore the priest's white robe, which was more off-white than white from the dust that it picked up, and when he came to the class, the robe would fly and dance in the air even on the stillest of still days for the reason that Jarvissahib turned the air around him like a turbine does the waters surrounding it. And his preferred mode of entering the classroom was not through its only door but through its only window. Jarvissahib would slide over its low sill and, unworried about the full length of his legs coming into view during this bit of acrobatics, land inside like an egret on a lake and commence the lecture. With amazing sensitivity to language, style, nuance and meaning he would then take us into the subject. Jarvissahib taught us the *Essays of Elia*, written by that most sensitive of writers, Charles Lamb, originally for *The London Magazine* in the 1820s. Every line, every word was read out like a bedtime story to a child that will not sleep, for the story will not let him. Jarvissahib inflected each word, emphasised phrases, punctuated pauses, in sheer enjoyment of the thought or expression, and resume. I will not forget Lamb's 'South Sea House' as read out by Jarvissahib, who would at times close his eyes after a phrase had moved him. The old trade house in London stood before us as he read '…The moths, that were then battening upon its obsolete ledgers and day-books, have rested from their depredations, but other light generations have succeeded, making fine fretwork among their single and double entries. Layers of dust have accumulated (a superfoetation of dirt!) upon the old layers, that seldom used to be disturbed, save by some curious finger…' and then explained the meaning of the word superfoetation – two foetuses in the uterus – signifying a multiplicity of the layers of dust on the tomes.

Jarvissahib made his class aware of the sensibility of this great man – Lamb – who had, while retelling the plays of Shakespeare in prose with his sister Mary, chosen the Tragedies for his labours leaving the Comedies to his sister who was afflicted by disturbances of the mind, which were in the end to end her life. More, Jarvissahib revealed to us the immense value of the mode of the essay, precursor to the ephemeral newspaper article, and its even more transient cousin, the column. No Charles Lamb, no Jarvissahib for me. No Jarvissahib, no 'sense' in me of the beauty of the good essay, the pearl-in-the-oyster of the thoughtful article, the 'moment-in-a-word' and 'word-in-a-moment' of the topical column.

I dedicate this compilation to my teachers in my school and college for showing how the genre of essays can manage to hold the attention of the reader even under the great competition offered by the highest poetry and the most arresting fiction.

Around the time I was learning from these teachers, the hallowed stars of English journalism in India, *The Statesman*, *The Times of India*, *The Indian Express* and *Hindustan Times*, were giving us essays in the shape of editorial columns of the highest quality. We did not have access to *The Times* or *The New York Times*. We had barely heard of *The New Yorker* or *The Saturday Review*. But reading Sham Lal, Pran Chopra, Kishan Bhatia, S. Mulgaokar, Inder Malhotra, S. Nihal Singh, Khushwant Singh, B.G. Verghese and Kuldip Nayar was to come to learn of what was happening around us but also to come to prize the genre of the essay-column. They wrote grippingly, independently, truthfully and, therefore, memorably.

Newspapers in India's various states appearing in the country's different languages were often ahead of India's English essayists as opinion-makers, with Bengali, Hindi, Malayalam, Marathi, Tamil and Urdu taking the lead. No surprise there considering that a generation earlier Munshi Premchand himself, without doubt the greatest modern writer in Hindi, was a columnist and journalist, as was the peerless martyr to India's secularism, Ganesh Shankar Vidyarthi. Premchand himself was greatly influenced by Maxim Gorky, whose fiction and non-fiction writings have somewhat obscured his essays. Premchand died within days of Gorky's death in 1936, attending a memorial meeting for the Russian despite his very serious and, as it turned out, fatal illness.

Jayaprakash Narayan will be remembered as a political phenomenon, a socialist and democratic icon, who showed a tightly mailed fist to the British Raj and later, another firmly clenched fist to Indira Gandhi's emergency rule. I celebrate him for both those roles but also for another articulation of his personality and activism – the power of his essays and political tracts. These bring powerfully to mind the extraordinary essays of George Orwell, among which, three essays – 'Shooting an Elephant', 'A Hanging' and 'Reflections on Gandhi' – are particularly valuable for us in India. The last named is in my unimportant view about the best assessment of the Mahatma, as objective as it is sympathetic and written without a fragment of care on its traction either among the subject's devotees or his detractors. Who can fail to be carried by his line 'One feels of him that there was much he did not understand, but not that there was anything that he was frightened of saying or thinking.'

Frightened of saying or thinking.

That about sums up a great many conditions across the world, India included. But it also serves to point to the great exceptions to that condition. I regard one among them to be absolutely the greatest: The Russell–Einstein Manifesto was issued in London on 9 July 1955 by Bertrand Russell in the high noon of the Cold War. It spoke in carefully worded terms of the dangers humanity faced from its most horrendous creation, nuclear weapons. Eleven pre-eminent intellectuals and scientists signed it. Albert Einstein, who had played a role in the development of the first atom bomb, signed it shortly before his death that very year. Calling for a conference of scientists who would assess the menace of weapons of mass destruction, it said something the whole world was meant to hear. It said in six simple words what six tomes would not be able to better: Remember your humanity and forget the rest.

The essay and its less elevated cousin, the newspaper article, be it of the long-form commissioned type or a calendared column, are vehicles for saying what one is thinking, and doing so hoping to be heard but not panicking over the greater possibility of being ignored. The traction of an essay lies in the urgency and vitality of its subject and the fluency and force of its expression. When one or both of these are missing, the essay might as well not be written. But when both are present they can make the essay well worth the ink that rolled over it.

I have the desire to do well by the genre of the essay but lack the fight that gives the attempt some punch. A strange impersonator of humility makes me choose the less strong word over the tougher one, the milder turn of phrase over that which says it straight. This is misplaced courtesy. My essays suggest with a tentativeness, rather than say what they want to say emphatically. An acquaintance has told me and, somewhat uncharitably, some common friends of ours that M.K. Gandhi would be unhappy with what this grandson of his has written (or not written). I agree. That he would be no less unhappy with that gratuitous criticism is another matter.

I have also not followed a certain practical tip given to me by another veteran of essay-writing, C. Rajagopalachari. Speak as you think, he said, and write as you speak. I think timid, speak soft, write mild. If despite this what I have written has been published with interest by some newspapers and even fetched me words of appreciation, it can only be because of what my English essay teachers taught me about that great mode.

Exceptional practitioners of that mode exist in India today, of whom I cannot but mention out of sheer fraternal pride my elder brother Rajmohan Gandhi.

Before I conclude this prefatory essay, I need to make one thing clear: I did not offer a selection of my columns to the publisher of this book. Bloomsbury asked me if I would like to have a compilation done of some of my newspaper columns and other occasional pieces of writing.

Unsure if this was a good idea, I took some time to consider it. When I conveyed my acceptance of the suggestion, it was for the reason that even if such a book were to advance no purpose of great moment or serve any cause of apparent worthiness, it would bring to possible attention the possibilities that lie in the genre favoured by Premchand, Pinto, Gorky, Orwell and the 11 scientists of world stature in 1955.

PART I

Frenemies and Neighbourliness: India and Her Neighbours

1

How Rajiv and Benazir Shaped Nuclear Restraint

ASIF ALI ZARDARI RECENTLY took over as President of Pakistan. His wife, Benazir, has been dead, assassinated, and remains buried for 17 years now. Thirty-six years ago, in 1988, not many outside Pakistan had heard of Zardari. But he had just become what Royals would call 'consort,' and a figure to watch in Islamabad. His wife, the 35-year-old Benazir, had just become prime minister of Pakistan. Not many in India knew much of her either except as the stunning-looking, very shy daughter of Zulfikar Ali Bhutto accompanying her father to Simla in 1972, where the then President of Pakistan signed the celebrated agreement with Prime Minister Indira Gandhi.

Neither country was nuclear in 1972, when the two heads of government signed the pact (even as Benazir scooped up all photo ops in Simla), though there were enough bomb-*walas* in the policymaking lobbies of both countries. No one, least of all Z.A. Bhutto and Indira Gandhi, would have thought that his daughter and her son would be prime ministers of their countries, both having the capacity to make nuclear bombs.

Mani Shankar Aiyar's just-out nugget of a book on Rajiv Gandhi (*The Rajiv I Knew*, Juggernaut, 2024) has much going for it, but what I have found to be of more than a memoir value in it is the author's description of the former prime minister's thoughts and actions on nuclear weapons. On this subject, Rajiv was his grandfather's grandson more than his mother's son. He loathed the idea of India disembowelling itself to make the nuclear bomb which would maim and kill millions. A nuclear war cannot be won, he believed; a nuclear war should not be fought. But if Pakistan and China have the wretched thing, can India fold its hands over its chest and put a ring of olive leaves on its head? It cannot. So, must it blindly follow suit?

'He once told me', writes Aiyar, '"You know, Mani, if Pakistan does really have the bomb, even I cannot stop India from going down the road to nuclear weapons."' In another telling conversation, Rajiv told him, 'Well, you see, India and Pakistan both already have the bomb.' Aiyar was puzzled. Rajiv explained. 'The Canadians have gifted them to us. We have the Bhabha Atomic Centre reactor in Bombay and the Pakistanis have the CANDU reactor in Karachi. All that it would take for devastating nuclear explosions that would destroy both our commercial capitals would be for kamikaze pilots from either country to fly an aircraft straight into the reactor of the other.'

This was not nuclear science fiction. This was not Arthur C. Clarke talking. Nor an anti-nuke activist standing on a dealwood box in Hyde Park. This was the prime minister of India, a grandson of Jawaharlal Nehru, despiser of all war, and, therefore, of nuclear war, thinking aloud. Not in panic, not in morbid hallucination, but in full possession of his powers of cogitation. He was, of course, a pilot; so, he knew what he was saying, aeronautically. For him, kamikaze was no frame from a Japanese animation during World War II. It was something as real as anyone sitting in a pilot's seat on any old aeroplane can do. And we should remember this was visualised and said way before 9/11.

Reading this, I recalled with gratitude the late prime minister and his visit to Islamabad over the last two days of 1988. Benazir Bhutto had just taken over. The visit to Islamabad was for a South Asian Association for Regional Cooperation (SAARC) summit. But the visitor being the prime minister of India and the host, the prime minister of Pakistan, it had to be about the two countries. Asked by Benazir 'spontaneously', but in reality, after due preparations by both sides, to spend some extra hours after the summit for bilateral talks, much progress was made to improve the prospects for peace between the two sides and reduce the risks of violence. Swift action ensued.

One of these was the signing, on December 31, 1988, of the Agreement on the Prohibition of Attack against Nuclear Installations and Facilities. I see that agreement as an answer to Rajiv's vivid visualisation of the kamikaze-type attack on reactors. Signed by Humayun Khan, Benazir Bhutto's foreign secretary for Pakistan, and K.P.S. Menon, Rajiv Gandhi's foreign secretary for India, the Agreement bound both parties to refrain from 'causing the destruction of or damage to' any nuclear installation or facility in the other country. The term 'nuclear installation or facility' was specified to include atomic reactors. This propelled Rajiv Gandhi's thought into intent and action. An operative part of the agreement was that both countries would exchange, on January 1 each year, a list of their nuclear installations and facilities.

Incredible for our times of suspicion, secrecy and solecisms, this exchange of lists has taken place unerringly year after year for the last 33 years. It has been done without a single year missed, under the governments of Rajiv Gandhi, V.P. Singh, Chandrashekhar, P.V. Narasimha Rao, A.B. Vajpayee, Manmohan Singh and Narendra Modi. Likewise, through all the vicissitudes of politics in Pakistan from the era of Benazir Bhutto right through to the present time when her husband is the President once again. The lists were exchanged this year, on January 1, as well.

Why should one be so thankful and so happy over this? For the reason that the agreement (which I would like to think of as the Khan–Menon Agreement) shows that both countries regard their nuclear installations and facilities as something that should not form part of any designs for war. 'We have the means for that dead-end war but we will not use them' is not as good as not having them, but is better than having them and reserving the right to use them in any way we like whenever we choose to. That is to say, while both countries are now nuclear weapons countries, we still do not want to become nuclear blasters-of-each-other-and-others. It is important, strategically and civilisationally, for there to be such an agreement binding the two countries to self-restraint, no less than a no-first-use agreement.

But there is another and very important reason why the Khan–Menon Agreement should be cherished. Our exchanging lists, with the latitudes and longitudes for each site being described, should be with the knowledge that each of these installations is or can at any time be on the radar of non-State players that can 'destroy or damage' any of them and paralyse either or both countries, with no war happening.

'We already have the bomb,' Rajiv Gandhi told Aiyar, very rightly, when we did not have the bomb. And the Khan–Menon Agreement was the answer. Now, when Pakistan has just got a new dispensation to take control over its nuclear installations and facilities, it could well be the time for Prime Minister Narendra Modi to visualise and propose starting a new bilateral initiative for nuclear self-restraint. And thereby moving the world nearer to the goal of what Rajiv Gandhi wanted – a time-bound, phased, verifiable action plan for universal nuclear disarmament.

(*Hindustan Times*, March 20, 2024)

2

If That Door Should Shut Now

Aडdditional Solicitor General Tushar Mehta has made an important statement before the Supreme Court ('India Can't Be Refugee Capital: Govt.', *The Hindu*, February 1, 2018). Whether he intended it to or not, it contains a vision, a vision of India. Mr Mehta presented that vision in terms of what India should not be.

Responding to a plea by Rohingya refugees in India, Mr Mehta said in the Supreme Court last week: 'We do not want India to become the refugee capital of the world.' He went on to say to the Bench headed by the Chief Justice of India that if the Rohingyas were given refuge, 'People from every other country will flood our country.' And, he added: 'This is not a matter in which we can show any leniency.'

Four positions can be distilled from those observations: 'We' speak for India; that India does not want refugees; people from 'every other' country are likely to flood India; we will not let India become the world's refugee capital.

The 'we'

This article is not on the Rohingya's case upon which we must trust the Supreme Court to pronounce as the great Sanskrit dictum suggests, '*dirgham pasyatu ma hrasvam*' (look far ahead, be not short-sighted). It is on the Additional Solicitor General's observation on India which is so important as to merit – demand – analysis.

To start with the important opening word in his remark, 'We'. Does he intend to use 'we' in the Constitution's sense of 'We the people…'? I doubt it, for only Parliament would feel mandated to use that expression. And even if the Lok Sabha or the Rajya Sabha were to pass a resolution, they would in all likelihood use 'this House', rather than 'we'.

A law officer, when he uses 'we', has to mean those who have the power, the prerogative and the privilege to instruct him in the matter before the court. But in the statement in question being about India's very personality, the 'we' has to go beyond the knot of individuals who have conferred on a particular brief. It has to convey the thinking of the government as a whole.

A departure

That brings us to the second position taken by him, namely, that refugees will hereafter be unwelcome in India. If that is indeed the government's thinking, then we have been given a major modification in the vision of '*bahujana hitaya bahujana sukhaya*,' where vouchsafing the good of the many and the happiness of the many is a ruler's dharma, with *lokanukampaya* – compassion for the human being – governing state action. It reverses the ancient tradition of the *janapada* being not just the home for its *jana* but a sanctuary for all in need of *ashraya*, refuge – *sarva lokashrayaya*. It is perhaps this ethos that helped persecuted Zoroastrian migrants from Central Asia settle in and around Surat around the 16th–17th centuries to maintain their religious tradition.

Old texts, tenets and traditions apart, the Additional Solicitor General's statement marks a departure from modern India's experience in the matter. By the new yardstick, independent India's giving *ashraya* in 1947 to over 7 million refugees, mostly Hindu and Sikh, from the newly created state of Pakistan was wrong. And, by the same token, Pakistan should have sent back another 7 million and more refugees, mostly Muslim, who left India for Pakistan. By that logic, the Dalai Lama should never have been given refuge in India nor the nearly 1,50,000 Tibetans who have come to India during the last 50 years. And, by the same logic, India should have used force, in 1971, to drive back the estimated 10 million men, women and children seeking shelter in India from genocide in East Pakistan. Tamils fleeing Sinhala intolerance, now said to number 1,00,000, should have been driven back over the Palk Strait to Sri Lanka, not offered even temporary *tanjam*. Afghan refugees, now numbering 10,000, should, by that principle, never have been given space in India, nor should Baloch political dissidents be given *panah* today. Individuals like U Nu when he exited from Ne Win's regime, Sheikh Hasina when she came to India in self-exile, and several political figures from Sri Lanka and Afghanistan should, by that principle, have been bolted out, Taslima Nasreen never allowed to step foot in India.

Were Nehru, Shastri, Morarji Desai, Indira Gandhi, Rajiv Gandhi, V.P. Singh, Chandra Shekhar, Narasimha Rao, Deve Gowda, Inder Kumar Gujral, Atal Bihari Vajpayee all naive or worse in not closing India's doors to shelter-seekers? Were they unpatriotic? And were the people of India, in understanding the ethos of *ashraya*, equally mistaken?

The Additional Solicitor General's remarks have amounted to saying 'we' now have a new vision, a new perspective, a new philosophy of India that does not, will not, open its doors to the refugee. In fact, it has closed its doors to refugees and to refugee-hood itself.

Now, this is not just a passing opinion on a transient matter but a rock-hard position concerning India and the human condition of nobody-ness, of homelessness, of statelessness that seeks refuge. In terms of the statement of the Additional Solicitor General, sanctuary or *ashraya* (Sanskrit), *panah* (Urdu), *sharan* (Hindi), *tanjam* (Tamil) are no longer to be India's attributes. 'Back you go!', 'Out!', are to be our answers to any refugee at our door.

Seeking refuge

The third proposition, namely, that India is in danger of being flooded with refugees 'from every other country' must cause astonished disbelief. Is the world pining for refuge in India? There is as much risk of India becoming the world's refugee capital as there is hope of India becoming the world's tourist capital. Common sense — a strong Indian trait — would tell us that only those in India's neighbourhood facing the dire prospect of victimisation or death want India's sanctuary. The same common sense has, for a cousin, another sense, an uncommon Indian sense, of seeing the urgency, the sheer panic, that is caused by victimisation and ethnic hate. And that enables us to see the heartlessness and the hollowness of the fourth proposition, namely, that we will not let refugees into India.

If a neighbouring country, out of political spite, 'or on account of race, religion, political opinion', were to force Hindus out of its borders and into India, we would be right in giving them *ashraya*. And we would be right to demand world condemnation of the outrage.

Keeping our land and sea frontiers open for massive numbers of people to cross over is hugely problematic. And terrorists sneaking in as refugees with sinister designs constitute a grim reality. But when has India been spared of troubles that come 'not as single spies but in battalions'? We, as a nation, cannot be so amnesiac, so altogether aphasiac, so opaque to history as to say no refugees, none at all, will hereafter be allowed to enter our territory.

Non-refoulement and international law are neither my expertise nor my theme here. The human condition is. And its most tragic experience — fear of persecution, of the furious chase, the flying bullet. William Blake wrote about two centuries ago: 'Each outcry of the hunted hare/A fibre from the brain does tear.'

India has not let the hunted hare die at its door. And if that door should shut now, a fibre from our collective brain must and will tear.

(*The Hindu*, February 5, 2018)

3

This War Cloud Has a New Shape

OUR CONSTITUTION SHARES SOMETHING with Leo Tolstoy. 'War and peace.' Those three words, written exactly like the title of his classic novel, comprise Entry 15 in the Union List of our Constitution. In mindscapes as ordinary as mine, this simply means that the Union of India, and the Union of India alone, can decide when to declare war, when to return to peace.

We are almost at war. 'Almost' because war has not been declared by the Union government or the President who, contrary to popular belief, is not 'Supreme Commander of the Armed Forces' but in whom the supreme command over our armed forces vests. The point of this quibble is that the President in declaring war (if and when he does) acts on the aid and advice of the council of ministers headed by the prime minister.

Wars, declared or undeclared, in India or by India are the work of the prime minister of the day. That is the first thing about any 'India war'.

A short history of India's wars

We have been at war five times before. And all but once with the same country, Pakistan. In 1947–1948, 1965, 1971, 1999. Was war 'declared' in all those four cases?

War could not be formally declared in 1947–1948 which was Prime Minister Nehru's India–Pakistan war; there was no time. The second India–Pakistan war, Prime Minister Shastri's war, also started on August 5, 1965, without a formal declaration of war.

The 13-day, third India–Pakistan war of 1971, Prime Minister Indira Gandhi's war, started officially when on the evening of December 3, 1971, the Pakistani Air Force (PAF) struck 11 airfields in our north-west, including Agra. Addressing the nation over All India Radio that evening, she said the PAF air strikes were a declaration of war against India, and the Indian Air Force responded with initial air strikes that very night.

In the last of the series, in May–July 1999, the Kargil war of Prime Minister Vajpayee, unleashed by Pakistan soldiers infiltrating into the Indian side of the Line of Control (LoC), took us by utter surprise, even disbelief. We were in the war before we could declare it. Declared in terms of Entry 15 or not, all four were wars. And they were wars linked for all time, for the better or worse, with the prime ministers of the day.

We are now on the threshold of war. Prime Minister Modi's war. Tolstoy's phrase in the Union List beams red to show danger, green as if to say, 'Go Ahead'. As citizens of India, we must trust that such a war, if it does take place, will be justified, will be fought clean, and will put cross-border terrorism in its place.

The results and questions

But before that happens, and while there still is time, we have to ask ourselves: What did the four previous wars achieve?

In the first of the India–Pakistan wars in 1947–1948, estimates say, Indian losses were 1,500 killed and 3,500 wounded, and Pakistani losses were 6,000 killed and 14,000 wounded. Nehru's army taught Pakistan a tough lesson but with international pressure mounting and Governor General Mountbatten turning internationalist, Nehru agreed to a ceasefire. Pakistan gained roughly a third of the former state, a net gain for the new nation. India retained a truncated Valley, Ladakh and Jammu. Who won, who lost that war?

In the second war, the fatalities were 3,000 Indian soldiers, 3,800 Pakistani soldiers. India held Pakistani territory in solid bulk, Lahore being but a knuckle away from Indian control. But the Tashkent Declaration, signed by Prime Minister Shastri and President Ayub Khan, got Indian and Pakistani forces to pull back to their pre-conflict positions, pre-August lines. Who won, who lost?

In the third war, in 1971, what did India win and Pakistan lose? India won self-confidence, Pakistan lost East Pakistan. India won Bangladeshis' appreciation, Pakistan lost their companionship. In the process, Pakistan had 8,000 killed and 25,000 wounded and even victorious India had 3,000 dead and 12,000 wounded. In the Simla Agreement, Zulfiqar Ali Bhutto agreed to recognise an independent Bangladesh, even as Indira Gandhi agreed to return all the more than 90,000 Pakistani soldiers taken prisoner by India in the 13-day war. Bangladesh today is friendly to India. But this does not mean that it will always be inimical to Pakistan. Who won, who lost?

Estimates differ wildly but it is believed that in the Kargil war of 1999, Pakistan lost close to 1,000 soldiers and India 550, many of them senior officers. Pakistan had to abandon the Indian points it had got hold of.

It would be sobering to acknowledge the net gains of the four wars that could be termed 'positive'. One, thanks to India's active reflexes, Pakistan has understood that its provoking of India by crossing the border or the LoC does not, and will not, work for it.

Two, thanks to India's active and pro-active reflexes, Bangladesh is on the South Asian map, a permanent rebuff to the Two-Nation Theory.

Three, the Tashkent Declaration (1966) and the Simla Agreement (1972) have shown war as wrong-headed, peace the only condition for the two neighbours to live with each other. Prime Minister Vajpayee's readiness for a dialogue with Pakistan both before and after Kargil, and Prime Ministers Gujral and Manmohan Singh striving for a détente have been influenced by Tashkent and Simla, the latter being cited in narratives more than the former because it is a signed and ratified agreement.

Are these three results of the four wars active on India–Pakistan minds today? They are not.

All that's changed.

We should remind ourselves that two Indians – Lal Bahadur Shastri and Indira Gandhi who were no wimps – signed parchments in which the following was said:

> The prime minister of India and the President of Pakistan agree that both sides will exert all efforts to create good neighbourly relations between India and Pakistan in accordance with the United Nations Charter. They reaffirm their obligation under the Charter not to have recourse to force and to settle their disputes through peaceful means. (Tashkent Declaration, January 10, 1966)
>
> The Government of India and the Government of Pakistan are resolved that the two countries put an end to the conflict and confrontation that have hitherto marred their relations and work for the promotion of a friendly and harmonious relationship…respect for each other's territorial integrity and sovereignty and non-interference in each other's internal affairs. (Simla Agreement, July 2, 1972)

Prime Minister Vajpayee's nod for an agreement on a ceasefire on the LoC in 2003 carried Tashkent and Simla forward. This was the first time that India and Pakistan agreed to a ceasefire that covered the International Border, the LoC and the Siachen Glacier in Jammu and Kashmir.

What is the difference between the time when Nehru, Shastri, Indira Gandhi and Vajpayee followed the 'War' prerogative in our Union List with the 'Peace' prerogative in the same and agreed to what they agreed to, and now?

Terror was known then, terror is known now, but in more ferocious and ingenious avatars. And in both countries, intolerance has come to be anointed.

That – intolerant frenzy – is being excavated by hawks to fuel a war psychosis even before war is declared or erupts.

In Pakistan, hawks in the military and clergy have found in terror groups their best grime-handler. In India, Hindutva has found in Pakistan-harboured terror groups their best friend-in-enemy's garb.

Fuelling hatriotism

Terror and Hindutva do each other's work for them. They offer to a credulous and suspicious public in both countries an alternative patriotism, which is hatriotism – hatred of the other country, its majority religion. The two have a common enemy: liberal secularism, pluralism, concord. They use a common weapon: incitement. They use a common fuel: fanaticism. They would die without the other. They feed on and feed each other's mistaken, misguided, misleading nationalisms.

India and Pakistan are being drummed into war-mindedness, not in the sense of a readiness to face war should it happen, but in the sense of wanting a war. This is the difference.

George Perkovich said as far back as 2003 – in the Vajpayee era – 'Pakistanis cite the RSS and VHP as proof that Hindus are out to destroy Muslims and, of course, Pakistan. The RSS and VHP, of course, use the prominence of Islamist parties and terrorist organisations in Pakistan as proof that Muslims are evil…The only way for India to liberate itself from Pakistan is through pluralist liberalism, not cultural nationalism.' He can say, and we should say to ourselves, the same today.

But we should do more. We should trust our prime minister, whose mind is so difficult to fathom, to remember what Shastri, Indira Gandhi and Vajpayee did in 1965, 1971 and 1999, respectively, but also how they followed that up with moves that placed war in the doghouse.

This is not to exculpate terrorism. It is to not oblige it by overreaction and self-destruction. M.K. Narayanan's sage advice in these very columns two weeks ago must be heeded by New Delhi.

There is no such thing in war, declared or undeclared, as tit for tat, and that is that. Surgical strikes can be expected to be followed by post-surgical complications. Who will pay for them? Those who gloat over the 'fitting reply'? Certainly not. Those who describe that as 'the rise of a new India'? Most certainly not.

Soldiers, brave-hearts, trained to fight and be prepared to die fighting, will fight the war if it comes. And we will, as we must, honour them. But while they do their duty by war, we must do ours by peace. Remembering that 'War and Peace' are one single entry in the Union List, we – you and I – must fight another war. And that is the war against war mongering, a war against the psychology that glorifies war, that makes nuclear warheads of our minds. We must step out of the queue for sectarian hatred and line up with that for secular intelligence. We must declare war against the un-entered Entry that seeks to displace 'War and Peace', which is 'War and Polarisation'. We must expunge it.

(*The Hindu*, October 4, 2016)

4

A People of an Emerald Isle, Waiting with Doosras

GEORGE BERNARD SHAW VISITED Ceylon in 1948, skipping India altogether. So much for the ego of the island's massive neighbour. But that was not all. In a letter to India's Prime Minister Jawaharlal Nehru, the unpredictable playwright wrote: 'I was convinced that Ceylon is the cradle of the human race because everybody there looks an original. All other nations are obviously mass produced.' Anthropology was as far from Shaw's brain as the razor from his beard. But in this observation he had hit upon both a human truth and a Lankan verity.

The emerald isle's people have traditionally been seen in terms of ethnic groups. The categorisation has its uses, as, for instance, in understanding the demographic weight of sections of its population such as given in this latest figure (Census of 2012): Sinhalese 74.9 per cent; Sri Lankan Tamil 11.2 per cent; Sri Lankan Moors 9.2 per cent; Indian Tamil 4.2 per cent; others 0.5 per cent ('Moors' being a quaint Lankan way of describing, a la Shakespeare and Othello, the island's Islamic population).

But identity-clustering can be very self-depriving for a nation.

Muthiah Muralitharan is one of the 4.2 per cent of Sri Lanka's population called Indian Tamils. '[B]orn in Kandy…to a Hill Country Tamil (Malaiyaha Tamizhar) Hindu family of tea plantation workers, the eldest of the four sons born to Lakshmi and to Sinnasamy Muttiah who runs a successful biscuit-making business, he is a grandson of Periasamy Sinnasamy who migrated from south India in 1920 to find work on Ceylon's tea estates.' But Murali is also the fast-bowling spinner of spinners who sends the ball as only he does, with a menacing sneer to match, and 'has taken more wickets in international cricket than any other bowler'. You cannot get more original than that.

The Sinnasamy family is part of the large group of agricultural labourers that began coming into the island from the drought-ravaged and poor districts in southern Madras over a 100-year period, from about 1830 to 1930. As the plantations and the island's export earnings from the plantations, especially tea, grew, the labourers' numbers grew too. Did their incomes and educational and health scores grow proportionately?

They did not. And here, the single-minded and unrelenting work put in by another 'original' Indian Tamil leader and head of the Ceylon Workers' Congress, the late S. Thondaman, made a difference. He was a 'fast-bowler' of his own kind. His ability to inspire and mobilise his people gave them voice, gave them self-respect. More than that, it made them feel they mattered as persons, individuals.

And there was the issue of citizenship. After 10, 25, 50, 100 years, were they Ceylonese or Indian or a bit of both? Nehru told India's Parliament on April 9, 1958, 'They are or should be citizens of Ceylon.' He had the moral authority to do so, given the Congress-led Parliament's record in the matter of affirmative action to ameliorate India's debasing caste system.

Today, all that is history. The Sirimavo–Shastri Pact of 1964 and the Sirimavo–Indira Gandhi Pact of 1974 saw the translocation of a large number of Indian Tamils to India, a procedure Nehru would have surely resisted. The repatriates are now part of the fluctuating fortunes of India's underemployed, self-employed and unemployed wage-searching masses. But the stateless and futureless situation of the Indian Tamils on Sri Lanka's plantations has ended. The bulk of Indian Tamils on Sri Lanka's plantations are now citizens of that country, with voting rights.

More and more of the young among the Indian Tamils now are seeking avenues of work outside the estates, like Murali's father did, with reasonable success. On-estate issues remain, in terms of deficits in housing, medical and educational standards. And in ergonomic norms. And, there are political aspirations of the Indian Tamils in Sri Lanka that call for remedial action as well. These, as identified by participants in a 'Malaiyaham200' event organised by the Katugastota-based Institute of Social Development include retention of the proportional electoral system, power sharing at the central, provincial and local government levels, the re-vesting of human settlements in the plantations with the State (not the estates) and being recognised as villages so that government schemes and services as also land rights can flow equally to the community.

Changes that are needed

But casting a forward gaze, the Indian Tamils of Sri Lanka now need the following five important changes to be made by them and for them: First, to start being seen as distinct and equal Lankans with huge and unique professional expertise making a major, indeed critically important, contribution to their country's economic well-being.

Second, to have their land-based climate-dependent profession protected against the now almost certain threat of adverse and erratic weather conditions.

This calls for urgent, in fact, emergency mitigation strategies not just in the interest of plantation labour but also of the plantations themselves, and therefore of Lanka's economy.

Third, to have their work sites, work cycles and work styles readied to face the real possibility of COVID-19's variants and other pandemics, especially zoonotically triggered ones, revisiting the plantations. It is vital to obviate the crippling disruption that shattered plantation aspirations over the virus's two waves by dips in export, in prices.

Fourth, to ensure that this sector is not left vulnerable to policy-related adversities such as those that were created by the ill-conceived ban on chemical fertiliser some months ago which hit tea estates in the gut, and to make it creatively equipped to respond to the gradual but globally discernible change in tea tastes, away from the current black tea pattern towards green and herbal teas.

Fifth, and most important now, to recognise the global opportunities, and equally the challenge, that artificial intelligence (AI) is opening for the community. The opportunities are, among others, helping predict weather and, using drones to help make planting, de-weeding and de-infesting near perfect if not zero-defect operations, and using algorithms to transform the future of the plantation sector. Authentication has been cited as one area where AI will confer a boon. Labels can and do misrepresent facts. Traditional methods can fail to see adulteration or to spot 'spent leaf' in bags of mixed tea. '100% X or 100 % Y' may be only 10 per cent or 20 per cent or so. AI will tell the true from the fake. Algorithms detecting fraud, calibrating flavour through sensor technology and chemometrics are going to transform the industry. But will AI cut employment on estates? Could AI, in a short space of a few months, displace hundreds of thousands now working on the island's hill slopes? Will AI, in some unregulated brain and in some frenzy of corporate rivalry, tamper with tea or coffee preferences and generate a spasm of craving for something that replaces tea and coffee and makes the tea bush or coffee plant objects in museums of antiquated forest produce? This is not about science fiction, but about AI's flip side. Is anyone in Sri Lanka or elsewhere, thinking of this? Are plantation labour unions? They must.

If Sri Lanka's plantation workers, in a measured but audacious move, were to be made part of the creation and development of an AI university situated in the central highlands and specialising in algorithms for the plantation sector, their originality as individuals and genius as persons could work not so much for their own as for Lanka's good. The 4.2 per cent have been generators of wealth for Sri Lanka, themselves remaining in want. The time has come for them to be harbingers of change, themselves leading – and regulating – the change.

The author of Pygmalion was an AI drone buzzing over the island's future, spotting not Eliza Doolittle–like originals who could speak a zero-defect English but women and men spinning their individual destinies with doosras waiting to fly.

(The Hindu, June 21, 2023)

5

Civil Warriors

INDIA CAN AND WILL ferret terror out with its arms and soldiers in action, not as some wild beast but with the precision pointedness of Neeraj Chopra's unbigoted and un-deflected javelin.

Janab Asaduddin Owaisi, the head of the All India Majlis-e-Ittehadul Muslimeen and member of the Lok Sabha from Hyderabad, has, over the years, said things I cannot be in agreement with. And there is much about his politics which rather mystifies me. But he said last week something I am not just in agreement with but which resonated with the admirer of Sardar Patel in me.

Referring to the trolls targeting the foreign secretary, Vikram Misri, following the government's announcement of the ceasefire with Pakistan, Owaisi*sahib* said, 'Mr Vikram Misri is a decent and an honest hard-working diplomat working tirelessly for our Nation. Our civil servants work under the Executive. This must be remembered and they shouldn't be blamed for the decisions taken by the Executive or any political leadership running Watan-e-Aziz.'

As our first home minister, Sardar Patel, in the October of 1949, spoke in the Constituent Assembly on draft Articles 311 and 314 of the Constitution, which afforded a modicum of protection to the civil services. Some members had spoken harshly of the role of the Indian Civil Service (ICS) under the Raj, terming it as unpatriotic. Said Sardar Patel: 'I wish to record in the House that if during the last two or three years most of the members of the Services had not behaved patriotically and with loyalty, the Union would have collapsed. If you have done with it and decide not to have this Service, I will take the service with me and go. They will earn their living. They are capable people.'

The foreign secretary, Vikram Misri, had been trolled viciously, his patriotism brought into question, the privacy and sanctity of his home life threatened. It was a shameful thing. And why? Had Misri not done India, Indian diplomacy, and India's spokespersonship proud with the maturity and high impact with which he reported developments in the four days' undeclared war impeccably? Had he not spoken in a splendid combination of exceptionally good English and equally deft Hindustani? But above all, in the language of truth? I do not know if anyone in Pakistan was allowed to watch and hear Misri and his two outstanding companions – Sofiya Qureshi and Vyomika Singh – speak from their briefing panels. If they were, they would have got a sense of India's tenacity and more: India's veracity. And it would be no surprise if warmongers and India-haters in Pakistan had pitched into these three stunning spokespersons. But it was not some sour Pakistani but some Indians who trolled Misri, and then a minister in Madhya Pradesh, letting his discretion fly, made an unacceptable comment on Sofiya Qureshi! Our diplomats and civil servants doing 'wartime duty' are civil warriors, non-uniformed soldiers, who, along with our uniformed brave-hearts, strengthen the nation's resolve to defend its integrity.

Civil service and foreign service associations lost no time in raising their voice of dismay and protest at the way the foreign secretary has been attacked and the courts of the land, no less, called upon the minister to apologise, which he did very quickly.

Had Jawaharlal Nehru as prime minister and Patel as deputy prime minister heard a member of their secretariat spoken of in the terms used by fellow Indians for Misri, or the way Qureshi had been described, they would have risen to the person's defence reflexively and memorably in and outside the legislature. For much more than a person's credentials are involved in such a slander. The ethos of the civil service, of our administrative and diplomatic structure, of our defence forces, is involved. To take a swipe at them at a time like this is to weaken our defence, our preparedness, our solidarity. It is to amuse and please those who want India weakened.

And so I found Owaisi*sahib*'s statement admirable. His use of the phrase of Persian origin used equally in Arabic, *Watan-e-Aziz*, meaning Dear Motherland, was also something I warmed to.

That our Dear Motherland is mother to all her children, irrespective of caste and creed, should be obvious to the plainest intelligence. But the plainest intelligence unfortunately keeps company, in our *Watan-e-Aziz*, with the meanest of minds such as extends the trolling mechanism to a person in unspeakable grief like Himanshi Narwal, whose 26-year-old husband, Vinay Narwal, a naval officer, was among the victims of the barbaric terrorist shoot-out in Pahalgam on April 22. The couple had been married for less than a week and were on their honeymoon. Himanshi, through her grief, urged people not to target Muslims or Kashmiris and was she hailed? No, she was trolled! She was saying what the wisdom of India was saying, namely, do not play into the hands and the designs of terrorism, which wants India to break out in communal combustion, burning our national equilibrium. Get at the terrorists, not innocents, get at the perpetrators of the evil who chose their victims, one by one, religion-wise, and killed them in cold blood. Do not copy those vile beings. Spot and get the terrorists, each of them, and their masterminds, not innocents. Show the world India is a giant not just in weaponry but in its intelligence and integrity. It is a behemoth; it is not a brute. It is a civilisation, not the caricature of a nation.

Also unspared was Neeraj Chopra, our precision-prince, the javelin-genius, whose freedom from bigotry irritated some.

Our defence forces have done us proud. Our political leadership and administrative-diplomatic services have raised our flag sky-high. And we the people of India, described in the Sanskrit version of the Constitution of India's Preamble lyrically as *Vayam Bharatasya Janaaha* and in the Urdu as *Hum Hind/Bharat ki Awaam*, have shown the very restrained responsibility, the measured focus, like Neeraj's javelin, that are needed to tell terrorists that their gory days are numbered. India can and will ferret terror out with its arms and soldiers in action, not as some wild beast but with the precision pointedness of Neeraj Chopra's unbigoted and un-deflected javelin.

I will conclude with what Margaret Bourke-White, the great photographer who was in India at the time of Partition, has written on a martyr of martyrs, Maqbool Sherwani (1928–47):

> Mir Maqbool Sherwani had been a co-worker of Sheikh Abdullah in the democratic movement, and like Abdullah, he had preached the need for religious unity in the fight for people's rights...When the tribesmen invaded Kashmir and terrorized the countryside, Sherwani, who knew every footpath in the Valley, began working behind the lines, keeping up the morale of the besieged villagers, urging them to resist and to stick together regardless of whether they were Hindu, Sikh, or Muslim, assuring them that help from the Indian Army and People's Militia was on the way. Three times, by skilfully planted rumours, he decoyed bands of tribesmen and got them surrounded and captured by Indian infantry. But the fourth time, he was captured himself. The tribesmen took Sherwani to the stoop of a little apple shop in the town square of Baramulla, and the terrified townspeople were driven into the square in front of him with the butts of rifles. Knowing Sherwani's popularity with the people, his captors ordered him to make a public announcement that joining Pakistan was the best solution for Muslims. When he refused, he was lashed to the porch posts with ropes, his arms spread out in the shape of a cross, and he was told he must shout, 'Pakistan Zindabad: Sher-i-Kashmir Murdabad.' It was a curious thing that the tribesmen did next. I don't know why these savage nomads should have thought of such a thing unless their sight of the sacred figures in St. Joseph's Chapel on the hill just above had suggested it to them. They drove nails

through the palms of Sherwani's hands. On his forehead, they pressed a jagged piece of tin and wrote on it: 'The punishment of a traitor is death.' Once more, Sherwani cried out, 'Victory to Hindu-Muslim unity,' and fourteen tribesmen shot bullets into his body.

Gandhi's diligent biographer Pyarelal writes in his biography of the Mahatma, *The Last Phase*, 'But within 48 hours of the cold-blooded murder, his dying prophecy was fulfilled, and the raiders were driven out of Baramulla with the Indian troops in hot pursuit.'

And with pride in every Indian soldier, diplomat and civilian who was engaged in the war for justice, and will, whenever called upon to do so, let us say with Sardar Patel that their patriotic duty is what is keeping our Union from collapse and keeping our ill-wishers in firm check.

(*The Telegraph*, May 18, 2025)

PART II

HOME AND THE WORLD: INDIA AND ITS PLACE IN THE WORLD

6

Turkey, Syria and the Real Threat Beneath India's Feet

A RAZOR'S EDGE SEPARATES life from death. *The Kathopanishad*, a conversation between Nachiketa and Yama, the god of death, uses the Sanskrit phrase for that edge – *kshurasya dhara*. This edge has a seismic equivalent in the fault lines between the 15 log-jammed tectonic plates on which the Earth's crust sits. These lines can sleep for decades, centuries even, so quietly that their existence is forgotten by those who are not geologists or seismologists. Which is a huge majority of us. Until they stir and shake, and then mutilate, destroy and kill whatever lies on and along those lines, those razor edges.

No one knows this edge, this *dhara* today better than the millions of Turkish and Syrian survivors of the earthquakes that devastated those two countries on February 6. With 40,000-odd people dead and the numbers mounting, their people felt the razor's edges come murderously alive that day. They were asleep when the first quaking happened after 4 a.m. at 7.8 on the seismic scale of 0 to 10. A second, measuring 6.7, followed 11 minutes later. The third came like an accomplice of the first, nine hours later, decimating whatever lay on or around those fault lines, those razor's edges.

These tectonic plates and the fault lines at their intersections keep moving, ever so silently, even as they sleep, exactly as human tissues keep growing even as we slumber.

India which has the Indian plate pressing on to the Eurasian plate, which sculpted the Himalaya by colliding, has a similar razor's edge right along the great Himalayan arc, stretching from Kashmir to the Northeast. It is asleep as I write this, but perfectly capable of rousing from sleep, and stirring and shaking and killing even as you, dear reader, read this.

Are we aware of what this means?

Many who live in Uttarakhand and other places along or below the great Himalayan arc know this. They have been jolted and maimed and seen their kin killed, time and again. But even they, like all living beings, believe life manages to overcome death, that the chances of long stretches without any earthquakes are greater than the chances of an earthquake occurring. And, as for others who are outside and beyond the zones of danger, the reality of those razor's edges is pure theory.

This is dangerous innocence. It must end. Seismologists tell us that our two great tectonic plates have now slept enough and that the built-up pressure inside their folds is itching to find release. This may not happen for a long time. It may happen now. The chances of it happening now in the Garhwal–Kumaon region are too serious to be ignored.

Are we ready for that rude experience?

Far from it.

Is it too late?

Certainly not.

The Government of India has shown what fast reflexes mean in the speed with which it rushed aid to Turkey and Syria. But the earthquakes in Turkey and Syria have done us through and with their torment, a great favour by asking us to wake from our sleep before the fault lines wake from theirs. The earthquakes of February 6 have reminded us of the real and imminent danger that lurks beneath our feet.

We have a ministry of earth sciences – a great felicity. And we have a National Disaster Management Authority – another vital asset. What we do not have is public awareness, public participation and public backing for earthquake preparedness. It is time this is generated and we the 'people' are involved in our seismic safety.

How is this to be done?

I believe this can only be done in the way our involvement was enlisted in response to the COVID-19 pandemic, and with the nation's political and medical leadership helming the process.

I would say, using the vocabulary of the virus surge, that the seismic surge has not started but its rumblings are clear. Just as epidemiologists were heard, if not fully heeded, in 2021, seismologists should be heard and heeded in 2023. And since we are still ahead of the actual strike, we have a distinct advantage this time.

We must bring the existing seismic zonation up to date if that is required. If not, we need to make it known to the public, loud and clear. The zones high on the risk gradient need to know where they stand (and where they may fall). This means that there has to be a seismic mapping of risk factors such as vulnerable buildings, relocation of people living in precarious dwellings and inaccessible tracts (especially in hill regions), schemes for fast-tracking rescue, relief and rehabilitation, with blueprints for helipads, camps and first aid, zone by zone. And also, a hard look wherever needed, at installations such as reactors and dams situated in high-risk zones. Above all, we must reboot our architectural mores to make earthquake-proofing the norm.

Doing all this will be difficult and expensive.

Not doing it will be…We can ask Turkey and Syria how the *kshurasya dhara* works.

(*Hindustan Times*, February 17, 2023)

7

Spot the Tremors

I WRITE THIS AT a time when the world is aflame with two wars – Russia vs. Ukraine and Israel vs. Hamas-propelled terrorism from Palestine.

The Office of the United Nations High Commissioner for Human Rights has reported that as of October 8, 2023, there have been a total of 9,806 civilian deaths as a result of Russia's actions against Ukraine with 17,962 people injured. Without doubt, as the human rights office tells us, the 'real' numbers could be higher.

Israeli air attacks on Gaza have left at least 4,200 Palestinians dead and over 12,000 wounded. On the 'other side', since the war began, the number killed in Israel has reached 1,400, with 2,800 wounded. This is about the actual theatre of war. Israel's asking some one million Palestinians to leave northern Gaza ahead of an expected ground invasion of the territory under Hamas control has led the UN to warn Israel that such a mass exodus would be – *would be*, not *could be* – 'calamitous'.

'Forget about food,' Nebal Farsakh, a Palestinian Red Crescent Society spokesperson, said on October 13, 'forget about electricity, forget about fuel. The only concern now is just will you make it, if you are going to live.' The Hamas commander, Mahmoud al-Zahar, has chillingly claimed that Israel is just the initial target and that 'the entire 510 million square kilometres of Planet Earth' will be under its control.

By the time this column of mine appears in print, we would know how the UN's warning, its apprehension, and al-Zahar's claim have shaped. I write this hoping, praying, that the UN's warnings will be heeded by the four parties in the two wars and by their war-backers so that the dance of death, made so perilous by the nuclear weapons hovering on those wars, abates.

This column today is about our being ready – India and the world being ready – for some fearsome things that we are going to face, inescapably, unavoidably, inexorably.

And they are, to quote Farsakh again, about '…will you make it, if you are going to live.' To adapt her words further, 'Forget about food, *bijli, pani*. Forget about the price of petrol, of gas. Think of how you are going to survive. Just that – survive.'

The first threat to our safety concerns, artificial intelligence – both as a worry and as a wonder.

A Calcutta-based IT professional, young enough to be my son but old enough to have a son of his own, studying for a double master's in Europe on 'History in the Public Sphere', writes to me to say: 'The entire software development industry will not be the same after a few years. Most of the code will not be handwritten but generated by the generative AI models. A large percentage of coders will most likely lose their jobs.'

This is dire.

Are we prepared for that? Will the change take a few years or just about a couple of years? How will that change impact our lives, our security, our very ability to survive?

Codes and coders and jobs apart, is the world ready for the use of AI in global war by state and non-state players? A Reuters report dated October 10 says: 'In May, Israeli Defence Ministry Director General Eyal Zamir said the country was on the brink of becoming an artificial intelligence "superpower", using such techniques to streamline decision-making and analysis.' The same report also ponders if Hamas was able to pierce that 'iron dome' of Israel's security with AI-resistant technologies and techniques in its arsenal. Is Al-Zahar's threat an indication that it counts among its allies, AI? And AI being world property now, and a global plaything, will other countries and agencies like those based in or working out of Lebanon, Qatar and Egypt use their AI against Israel's AI, buttressed by NATO's AI in the coming weeks? Will there soon be something like a war AI and a peace AI, the first hosting and the second halting mass deaths?

The second threat is not about anything artificial. It is about something as real as living organisms.

The jury will never 'return' with a clear verdict on whether the COVID-19 pandemic was wholly and 'innocently' the work of a self-generative virus or whether some laboratory had a perverse hand in its arising and spread. Both hypotheses need responses. But even if no faceless villain caused it, human arrangements, human mismanagement, human callousness – in other words, all of us – have certainly created conditions for that natural arising and spread. Zoonotic disease is bred in the crazy zoo of human inefficiency and ignorance at best and human callousness and greed at worst. There is nothing to show that the world has learnt any long-term lessons from the COVID-19 horrors. India certainly seems to regard the pandemic as gone when its essential core has only taken a weekend off. And that 'zoo' flourishes in every town, city, marketplace and abattoir. It thrives in the mindlessness of congregations, rallies. Can AI be used to sense where diseases are incubating lethally?

The third threat is also about nature but again, like COVID-19, not only about nature. Human agency, our agency, is involved as well. It has to do with the earth's crust on which we are situated. The pressure on the Indian plate has been building up and it requires no seismologist to tell us that the frequency of earthquakes in the higher seismic zones in India is increasing.

A Turkey-like quake is more than likely. Nothing can prevent it. But are we prepared for it? Take one look at any of our cities and towns. The way they have grown does not invite earthquakes but it does invite danger when the earthquake occurs. 'Ninety per cent of the existing buildings are based on old technology and most of them are non-engineered structures, especially in rural areas,' Major General M.K. Bindal, the former executive director at the National Institute of Disaster Management, ministry of home affairs, has said (PTI, updated February 12, 2023). 'It is a massive work to convert the old, non-engineered structures that do not adhere to seismic codes, like in Delhi, into earthquake-proof buildings,' he adds and tells us honestly and scientifically, 'a massive exercise is needed to map out each and every existing building (in the high-risk areas).' A tall order. But the challenge is taller. And the more vulnerable for being taller.

But there is great news. We are told, 'An AI-driven tool was 70 per cent accurate in predicting earthquakes a week before they happened, during a seven-month trial in China,' scientists report. The outcome was a weekly forecast in which the AI successfully predicted 14 earthquakes within about 200 miles or 320 kilometres, of where it estimated they would happen and at almost exactly the calculated strength.' ('Earthquake-predicting tool driven by AI shows 70% accuracy, new research reveals', PTI, last updated: October 7, 2023). The international competition was held in China in which the University of Texas (US)-developed AI came first out of 600 other designs. Are we in India going to use AI to prepare us for the earthquakes that seem to be waiting to hit us?

I know nothing of that science but only know that it is more powerful than anything the world has known. Will mastery over it belong to those that wage wars or will it belong to those who wager on peace and its purpose – a planet at peace with itself?

We have never been on the brink of a global catastrophe like this. And we do not seem to realise it.

(*The Telegraph*, October 22, 2023)

8

The New Teacher

IT IS ABOUT 21 now, not 20.

Our prime minister's announcement at the New Delhi G20 Summit that the African Union is now in the grouping has got far less attention than it deserves. The European Union is the only other 'group' member. But Europe with 50 countries is not in its entirety in the EU, which has 27 members. Whereas the whole of Africa with all its fully sovereign 54 countries or 55 counting is in the African Union (AU). And so all of Africa has now entered the G20, morphing it into the G21. The host-leader deserves congratulations for enabling this tectonic shift in the grouping's composition and character. I call it by that seismic name, for it is nothing less than that, a metaphoric movement of the African plate into the G20 crust.

By that one stroke, the whole of Africa can now join and shape G21 deliberations on matters affecting life on earth, like climate change mitigation, sustainable development, and the global economy. This is only right. But what is only right does not always happen as it should. It happens when, to use Victor Hugo's immortal phrase, its time has come.

Its GDP (PPP) of $8.05 trillion (2022 est.) is less than India's $13.033 trillion (PPP; 2023 est.). Africa is, according to Wikipedia, 'the least wealthy continent per capita and second-least wealthy by total wealth…' Africa's entire population (1.39 billion) is less than India's. Among continents, Africa has the lowest teledensity and the smallest number of computers in the world. And it has, over the centuries right up to our times, been riven by inter se conflicts, secessionist and separatist battles, civil wars, riots, massacres, belying the image conjured by the Organisation of African Unity and the AU, of a united continent at peace with itself.

And, yet, as the site where the human species originated and where, ironically, the world's population today is the youngest (the median age in Africa in 2012 was 19.7 as against the worldwide median age of 30.4), Africa as a whole, a single entity, deserves the title of 'the earth's human cradle'.

If I may be permitted a personal note here. Way back in 1996–1997, I was working in Pretoria, and when I first heard the new South Africa's national anthem beginning with *Nkosi Sikelel' iAfrika*, which means 'God save Africa', I was astonished. God was being asked in South Africa's national anthem to save Africa, not South Africa. No country's commemorative song in Asia or Europe would seek divine blessings for the continent on which it is situated.

It would be necessary to take the inclusion of the AU in the G21 by Prime Minister Narendra Modi as a recognition of the pan-African entity and identity and thereby facilitate funding by the wealthier members of the G21 to build human capital, infrastructure and sound health regimes. This will also mean the G21 doing its best to address Africa's crippling external debt, trade imbalance, and low capital inflows. Information technology and the knowledge revolution through the internet should no longer pass Africa by. The G21 must help end Africa's isolation from the world's advance.

All this will not be a favour done to the AU but a step taken by humanity for 20 per cent of the world's land area and 18 per cent of the world's population. And if that happens, India and Modi in G20/21 2023 can derive some satisfaction over the AU joining G20 during India's helming of the group.

But aside from what Africa must gain by the AU joining the G20, certain distinct gains can accrue to the new G21 and, thereby, to the world, as a result of the African augmentation of the powerful grouping.

The first of these is through the AU's experience in inter-country conflict resolution in Africa and its peacekeeping operations conducted sometimes with and sometimes independently of UN peacekeeping as part of the G21's mandate for sustainable development, which can only happen in a conflict-free environment. I am not suggesting here that these AU exercises have been a success story. They have sometimes been that, oftentimes not. The idea is that Africa's failures as much as its successes through the AU-led interventions for peace should be turned to for similar initiatives elsewhere in the world.

The second and, in my view, the most important gain for the G21 by the AU joining it will come in the form of a recalling of the 1996 Treaty of Pelindaba. This is one of the most underestimated treaties of modern times. Pelindaba, in uranium-rich South Africa, was the venue of apartheid South Africa's partially constructed atomic bombs. And Pelindaba is where, after President Nelson Mandela decided to 'roll back' that programme emphatically and irreversibly, he chose to convene a pan-Africa summit to establish a nuclear-weapon-free zone on the African continent. The conference agreed, with 43 signatories, through the African Nuclear-Weapon-Free Zone Treaty, as the Pelindaba Treaty is called, to 'prohibit the research, development, manufacture, stockpiling, acquisition, testing, possession, control or stationing of nuclear weapons, as well as the dumping of radioactive wastes'. This was historic. With the Pelindaba Treaty, after outer space, Antarctica and the seabed, Africa became a rare nuclear-free zone in and around the earth. Significant for the G21 is the

Pelindaba decision to 'promote individually and collectively the use of nuclear science and technology for economic and social development' and, to this end, 'undertake to establish and strengthen mechanisms for cooperation at the bilateral, sub regional and regional levels'.

Nuclear disarmament is not on the G21 agenda. But in any initiative for sustainable development, it cannot shut its eyes to the existential hazard posed by the nuclear arsenals of the world's nine nuclear weapon states. Pelindaba tells us how Africa has faced the challenge of those hazards in its immediate environment – the continent of Africa. But now has come the chance for the G21 and through it for the world to see, within the G21 mandate, a living African example and to enlarge that example.

South Africa's veteran diplomat, Abdul S. Minty, said in the Conference of Disarmament (CD) on September 1, 2011: 'While the threat to humanity posed by chemical and biological weapons has long been recognised, which led to the banning of these weapons of mass destruction through negotiations in this very body, the achievement of a world free from nuclear weapons remains an unfulfilled promise and elusive goal.

'If the indiscriminate destruction and vast humanitarian consequences posed by weapons of mass destruction is unacceptable, then the continued retention of the nuclear weapons option surely cannot be justified or maintained. It is also clear that the only absolute guarantee against the use of such weapons is their complete elimination and the assurance that they will never be produced again.

'We are convinced that neither the possession of nuclear weapons nor the pursuit of these weapons can enhance international peace and security. The primary responsibility for undertaking the necessary steps for the elimination of nuclear weapons lies with those states that continue to regard nuclear weapons as central to their security.'

The G21, in which the leading nuclear weapon states sit, should know that with the induction of the AU the Pelindaba Treaty leaps beyond the continent of Africa to tell the world, to quote Ambassador Minty at the CD again: '…global security is not achievable when enormous financial and other resources are still being diverted towards the acquisition of more and more destructive capabilities…'

And very significantly, he said then: 'We believe that common threats can only be effectively addressed through enhanced international cooperation and strong international institutions that can respond to our collective security concerns. Our approach in this forum should therefore be one that addresses common security concerns rather than that of certain blocks, regions or security alliances.'

The G21 must ponder these words. It will not be easy for it, with its nuclear load, to do so. But now that the AU is in its midst, can it avoid doing so? And can the AU avoid saying so to its new colleagues?

Africa is entering the G20 to make it the G21 not as a late admittee but as a new teacher. If the G21 hears and learns from the collective wisdom of Africa, a new anthem could well be heard – '*Nkosi Sikelel' iG-21*'.

(*The Telegraph*, September 24, 2023)

9

A First Is a First

BARACK OBAMA NEEDED TO become president of the United States of America. Not just the US but the world too wanted to see an African–American president at the helm of its most powerful democracy. Did Obama make a great or even a good president? The question will be asked in early evaluations of his presidency. And most answers will be far from complimentary. His pre-election views on war will be judged against what he sanctioned in Iraq and Afghanistan. His promise on Guantanamo's concentration camp will be matched against reality. And the Nobel Peace laureate will be asked if he did what he said he would on nuclear disarmament. Yet, the fact of Obama will loom over the facts of his presidency. A first is a first. A decade or more on, Obama may get a more favourable comparative appraisal than now. And the record of his successors might help him.

Hillary Clinton seems close, closer than ever, to her goal. And even if the US vote is divided, most of world opinion wants to see the US install its first woman head of state. If she wins, the question will be asked: Will she make a great or even a good president? Her record as secretary of state will be scanned in fine resolution. And Libya will hover over her image like a ghost. Yet, the fact of a gender chasm having been closed will prevail over all thoughts, by and large, giving her 'first' a resounding cheer.

Will the American woman have come into her own? Five 'American women' came to mind. Two are fictional, the other three, historical.

The first, Topsy, was and remains for me the complete heroine of *Uncle Tom's Cabin*. The anti-slavery novel written in 1852 by Harriet Beecher Stowe (1811–1896) has been upbraided in modern assessments as being condescending. They are harsh about the depiction of the submissive Uncle Tom whose belief in Christian love and, consequently, his seeming meekness have led to the derisive adjective, 'Tomist'. It is easy to be radical, retrospectively. Tom is almost a sepia figure, but not Topsy. The little slave girl is the great tool of the novel, which was itself a great tool against slavery in the political imagination of abolitionists. Google tells us of an apocryphal story about President Lincoln towering over the diminutive Stowe, saying, 'So, this is the little lady who started the great war?'

If the book became the best-selling novel of the 19th century and the second-best-selling book after the Bible in the next, it is not a little because of that wisp of a girl, Topsy. When asked if she knows who made her, Topsy professes ignorance of both God and a mother, saying 'I s'pect I growed. Don't think nobody never made me.' Topsy is a sharp arrow in equality's quiver. If I had not known of her at school, I would not have understood Rosa Parks in university. Will November 8 be a winning day for her?

The second fictional woman is Blondie. Heroine of the eponymous cartoon series created by Chic Young, Blondie is ageless and deathless. A pair of perpetually surprised eyes which can swing from joy to exasperation represents her quick brains and her good heart. Smart, alert Blondie is the woman neighbours would trust with their pouch of heirloom coins, friends with their confidences. She is her husband's world, her son's sanctuary, her daughter's very heartbeat. Born the same year as Walt Disney – 1901 – Chic Young survived Disney by seven years, dying in 1973. Disney is an icon, Young is real. Blondie's hilariously naive husband, Dagwood Bumstead, who thrives on 'mountain-high' sandwiches that he loves making and eating while slouched on a sofa, is contrasted by the clear-headed and sure-footed Blondie. She has her viewers – of whom my friend, the brilliant mathematician and physicist Anand Doraswami, is about the most passionate – in thrall. Blondie personifies middle-class common sense. Will November 8 be her day or will war mongers change Blondie into a fearful, suspicious woman who votes for walls, drone strikes, for everlasting combat between an imagined 'us' and 'them'?

The third, Katherine Mayo (1867–1940), is perhaps India's most hated American. Described as a researcher, historian and political writer, she has achieved notoriety as a racist and white supremacist who opposed independence for Roman Catholic Philippines and Hindu–Muslim India. Her *Mother India* (1927) reads like what it is: the work of an Indophobe. Gandhi famously and accurately described it as 'a drain-inspector's report', and she said some frankly brutal things about Gandhi. But despicable as it is, vicious in its aim and deeply troubling in its impact, *Mother India* is a book every Indian must read for the bitter truths it contains about our drains. The treatment of Indian womankind by its men lies at the heart of the book. It tears, excoriates, lacerates; it hurts, it burns. But then, India through the ages has done precisely that to its women. The Child Marriage Restraint Act 1929, known as the Sarda Act (after its largely forgotten but pioneering sponsor, Harbilas Sarda), passed on September 28, 1929, fixed the age of marriage for girls at 14 years and for boys at 18 years. This seems absurdly inadequate.

But, again, it is easy to be radical retrospectively. No Sarda Act in 1929, no legislation setting 18 years for girls and 21 for boys today. The act was most certainly influenced by the impact of *Mother India* on Indian opinion. Mayo will never be forgiven by India, but she has written her name across the evolving story of gender justice not just for India but everywhere. She inflicted wounds on a man's world on behalf of a brutalised womankind. She was a first, a conflicted first, but a first.

The fourth, Margaret Sanger (1879–1966). The American birth-control activist, sex-educator, nurse and writer knew her India. Consider what I was told were her own words:

> Their religion makes it an Indian woman's highest duty to have children. The more she has the better she likes it. One highly educated Indian man said to me, 'Why, Mrs Sanger, you can do nothing. We all admit that birth control is the only answer to India's population problem, but the women themselves don't want it.' I was sure they were wrong. Just two days after I arrived in Bombay, I went to the chawls, the long rows of tenement houses where the city's mill-workers were crowded together in small dark rooms. Children, their naked little bodies bone-thin, played in the streets or sat listlessly in the shadow of the buildings. Mothers stared with inert eyes. Almost everyone had a baby or small child on her hip. I knew that of every 1,000 children born in Bombay, 298 die. I know that it has been estimated that 100 of every 1,000 mothers in India die in childbirth. I looked at these poor, worn out women, at their undernourished, undersized children. 'Ask this mother how many children she has,' I said to the social worker who accompanied me, and pointed to a woman in a ragged sari, squatting on the street, holding a baby in her arms. 'Six,' was the answer. 'And how many dead?' I asked. 'Five,' she answered. 'And how many more do you want?' I pursued. She threw out her hands in a pathetic gesture. A look of fear came into her tired, lined face: 'Please god, no more!' No Bombay man can again tell me that women of this city, or any city in India, do not want information that will free them of the dread of bringing children into the world to rob those they already have of food and clothing and care of the very breath of life.

Sanger is unrivalled. The fifth, Pearl S. Buck (1892–1973). For generations of Indians this American novelist has been a window into China. *The Good Earth* (1931) is not a book sinologists would carry to lectures or historians add to recommended reading or sociologists to optional reading. But the novel will be read, reread, regardless, always, and enjoyed as timeless, fascinating fiction. As a human document, it has the ring of truth in it, if not the 'thing' of academic study. Even if the novel had not won the Pulitzer (1932), or the novelist the Nobel (1938), Pearl Buck would have been for readers across the world a great educator, a stirrer of interest in things beyond the narrow confines of nationality and citizenship. China comes alive in Buck. You feel its famines in what William Blake would call the 'fibres of your brain'. You feel its loves, its griefs, its longings, its despairs. Pearl Buck has breached an impenetrable wall. For those who have read *The Good Earth*, O-Lan and Wang Lung are as real as Sarbojaya and Harihar in Satyajit Ray's cinematic rendering of Bibhutibhushan's *Pather Panchali*. The scene in which Wang's son brings home stolen meat and, furious, Wang throws the meat on the ground as he does not want his sons to be seen as thieves places morality on a pedestal. But then when O-Lan calmly picks it up and cooks it, it brings sanctimonious morality down to the threshold of life's reality.

Topsy, Blondie, Mayo, Sanger and Buck are tough prototypes. They show that transformational change comes not by self-righteous affirmations of identity but by action, not by the accident of genetic addresses but by the choices of directions and destinations.

(*The Telegraph*, November 7, 2016)

10

An Unasked Question

SAMUEL MOORE'S TRANSLATION OF *The Communist Manifesto* is the most widely known of its English versions. Friedrich Engels helped Moore with the exercise and oversaw its publication in 1888, 40 years after the original, jointly authored by Karl Marx and Engels, had appeared in German. Scholars must know, but I do not, whether the *Manifesto*'s opening head-quote, now a slogan of slogans, appearing just beneath the title, was written by Marx or by Engels. Perhaps it was written by neither, but retrieved from an earlier work. But Engels must have most certainly approved Moore's powerful rendering of it in the language of Shakespeare: 'Workingmen of all countries, unite! You have nothing to lose but your chains. You have a world to win.'

I was reminded of the three-line preamble to that work of almost Biblical status when news came of the death of Hugo Chavez Frias.

If there is anyone outside of processions, *michhil*s and *bandh*s who could have been energised by a slogan of the Left, it was the late president of the Bolivarian Republic of Venezuela. I have seen the clenched fist raised by members of the 'Party' self-consciously and even apologetically, except at mass rallies or at the funerals of comrades where solidarity is natural and sloganeering and gestures of camaraderie, at home. But, irrespective of where he was, and what was happening around him, Chavez would have raised his right fist first, and then waved both his hands in a trance of exhilaration on hearing even the first syllables of that piece of revolutionary literature.

His one and only visit to Calcutta – a 24-hour affair – took place on March 5 and 6, 2005, within three months of my having joined duty in that city. State visits are not frequent in Calcutta and a certain uneasiness over how it was to be handled was apparent at the Writers' Buildings and at Raj Bhavan. But Chavez was not the kind of State guest we need have really worried about in terms of protocol compliance or formalities. He was the very embodiment of 'workingmen', their broken chains, their unity and self-assertion. Chavez wanted to see Calcutta's socialist exuberance. Calcutta wanted to see a leftist star. Neither was disappointed.

That very morning, at an event where prizes were being given to police personnel, the then Chief Minister, Buddhadeb Bhattacharjee, made a speech – the first I was hearing him give – in which he asked the police to be friends of the people and a foe to criminals irrespective of 'who they are'. To me, this meant that he wanted the police to be totally impartial and be un-swayed by the political affiliations of the accused, an admirable doctrine. It was with this glad thought in my mind that, a few hours later, I went to the airport to receive the visiting dignitary. I had seen pictures of the Bolivarian leader but I was surprised by the way health and vigour seemed to be bursting from the man's enormous bulk. The ceremonies were quickly over, with Chavez on a clear 'high' and the chief minister not quite able to keep pace. But the mismatch was soon rectified.

At a mammoth rally that evening, at the Rabindra Sarovar Stadium, Chavez held forth for a considerable length of time in Spanish. A wonderful young interpreter, detailed, doubtless, by the ministry of external affairs, did his best to render the sonorous words into equally lilting Bangla. Applause and cheers followed almost every other sentence until a difficulty arose. Chavez decided to recite, in Spanish translation, Tagore's '*Chitta jetha bhoy-shunya*'. The audience knew the original by heart, by training, by instinct. The brave interpreter, however, was trying to put the Spanish translation into his own Bangla, with hilarious results. Calcutta would have preferred to hear Chavez's Spanish rendering of the famous work untranslated rather than hear it done in an improvised Bangla. Jeers rent the air. Taunts tore into the interpreter. Chavez was thrown off guard. Have I said something wrong? Have I committed a *faux pas*? He stopped, looked at all of us, seated beside him, in wide-eyed wonder. That is when Buddhababu rose. Asking the president of Venezuela to restart the poem, he said he would recite the poem line by line, from the original Bangla of Tagore's composition, from memory. I have not heard too often the kind of deafening applause that now replaced the jeers. As a visibly relieved Chavez resumed his recitation, a supremely self-confident chief minister completed it. By the time Buddhababu reached '*Bharotere shei svarge…*' the gathering of at least 20,000 was delirious.

And I, too, I must confess, was not unexcited. Here was a visiting mass leader, being interpreted by another mass leader, the chief minister of West Bengal, in front of a mass of humanity. More, 'my' chief minister was one who had just a few hours earlier said something that was so admirably civilised, namely, that the police force was the 'people's friend' and was to make no distinction between ruling party sympathisers and others.

A State banquet for visiting dignitaries is *de rigueur*, and a scarlet red president can be no exception. But neither he nor the chief minister was really interested in food, of which elegant portions remained uneaten on their cold plates. Chavez would not stop talking through the many courses, the same interpreter translating his Spanish into English for the chief minister's and my benefit. Complimenting Chavez on his Rabindra Sarovar speech, I asked him at what age he had made his first speech. 'Ah,' he replied, through the interpreter, 'when I was eleven...' And he added he remembered what he said in that speech. Unlike many politicians, particularly from our part of the world, he was not coy with the hostess. Holding my wife Tara's hand, he said, 'You remind me of my mum,' a compliment she has not forgotten. Effective informality overtook the formal setting of the banquet which ended up being a very chaotic success.

Chavez was no intellectual, unlike his effective host in Calcutta. But if Buddhababu knew his Tagore, I do not doubt that Chavez knew his Simon Bolivar, and was more than aware of the political philosophies of Salvador Allende and Che Guevara. Noam Chomsky, among contemporary thinkers, influenced him. His great quote of 2010 recalls Moore's translation of the *Manifesto*'s head-words: 'Rousseau said, "Between the powerful and the weak all freedom is oppressed. Only the rule of law sets you free." That's why the only way to save the world is through...a democratic socialism...giving power to the people...it is not the government of the rich over the people, which is what's happening in almost all the so-called democratic Western capitalist countries.'

Chavez's stout defence of national sovereignty against economic co-options and political hustling will be remembered with approval and even admiration. As will his passion for education and his sense of Latin America's unity. But his apologist support of Muammar Gaddafi and Syria's Bashar al-Assad will leave question marks.

Why is it that so many of the great mass movements of the world – with great exceptions like those in India and South Africa – have, on getting entrenched in power, become so hated and reviled, their leaders turning into figures of fear rather than of inspiration, their political organs turning into bywords for rough handling and terror hordes? Why does the idealism of a mass movement, when it enters the plaster cast of government, forget the value of internal debate, participatory processes? Why does a slogan become a shibboleth? Why does courage, when robed in office, become authoritarian? And why does a spartan, when rebellious, become a gourmand for power, when enthroned? Why does the *chitta* that is *bhoy-shunya* when in the streets, no sooner than it is installed in office, wield that very *bhoy* like a baton?

These are not questions that Hugo Chavez could have answered, but they are questions that must be put to the Chavez 'type', socialist and non-socialist, for idealism must be redeemed from its debasings.

(*The Telegraph*, March 10, 2013)

11

Taking a Giant Leap for a New Ethics in Outer Space

THE ITCH TO GET there first and fast is human. Being competitive is part of the human's survival instincts.

The urge to plant one's flag there before the other flag-bearer does is human too. It is part of the human's political instincts.

Some 11 decades ago, in 1910–1912, both itch and urge were quivering in the northern hemisphere. Robert Scott, a 43-year-old British naval officer, was preparing a daring expedition to the South Pole. Around the same time, a Norwegian explorer Roald Amundsen, about four years younger, was planning a bold ice-drift to the North Pole. On learning of dubious but loud claims by two Americans, Frederick Cook and Robert Peary, Amundsen lost interest in that destination; it had been reached. But the South Pole beckoned. While others had fringed that continent of ice, no human foot had stood on the southern-most point of the earth.

Setting foot on the South Pole

Scott and Amundsen knew of each other's target and goal. But observing due courtesies all right, they raced to it. Scott and his men with dogs and horses, Amundsen with his dogs and sledges. Amundsen and his five companions, with 16 surviving dogs, got there on December 14, 1911, 34 days before Scott and his team of five did. Planting the Norwegian flag there, Amundsen felt fulfilled, as he should have. He named their South Pole camp Polheim, meaning Pole-home, in Norsk. And he renamed the Antarctic Plateau as King Haakon VII's Plateau, after his monarch. Scott and his team were to perish on the Pole, having been caught in foul weather.

On exploration's success scrolls, Amundsen is placed on top; in legend and lore, Scott has for all time outpaced his Norwegian rival. Any race has its victories; some have ironies, besides.

In 1939, Norway laid claim to a vast area of Antarctica which it called Dronning Maud Land, or Queen Maud Land, after its reigning Queen, wife of King Haakon. This area covers about a sixth of the entire continent. There followed another Norwegian claim to Peter I Island, which is about 450 kilometres off the western side of the Antarctic peninsula.

Britain had been outdone by Norway on the South Pole. But she was not going to be out of the race for territorial claims over Antarctica. Nor others. And now, apart from Norway the first South Pole 'arrivee' and claimant, Britain the second South Pole 'arrivee' and claimant, there are five others who have sharply defined areas on Antarctica which they regard are 'theirs' – Australia, Argentina, Chile, France and New Zealand. So Antarctica has seven flags flying on their own 'Antarctic territories'. How are these seven tracts of Antarctic ice over which flags of different stripes fly, then, different from colonies of the imperial era? They are different. There are no subject people there, no 'native' residents, who are being denied freedom, no resources are being drained out from there to the 'mother country'. But then why were the seven on that inhospitable continent at all?

Regulation and Antarctica's well-being

With the International Geophysical Year (IGY) in 1958 seeing many players becoming active in Antarctica, and fears of Cold War rivalry taking unexpected turns, United States President Dwight D. Eisenhower convened in 1959 an Antarctic Conference of the 12 countries active in Antarctica during the IGY, to negotiate a treaty. When Argentina proposed that atomic explosions be banned in toto on Antarctica, the US objected, saying only those tests that were carried out without prior notice and consultation should be banned. The USSR and Chile supported the Argentine proposal, leading the US to agree and take the negotiations forward.

In the present times when satellites can pick up any activity that is suspicious, none of them can do anything questionable there. They will be found out. But even before the world developed its sky-eyes, the early Antarcticans had to share their space with others if only to justify their own. Argentina, Australia, Belgium, Chile, France, Japan, New Zealand, Norway, South Africa, the Soviet Union, the United Kingdom and the United States – 12 countries – had established over 55 Antarctic research stations for the IGY, and they had to make the Treaty accord full acceptance to two basics: freedom of scientific research in Antarctica and the peaceful use of the continent. An indirect consensus emerged for demilitarisation as the treaty prohibited nuclear testing, military operations, economic exploitation, and further territorial claims in Antarctica. Today there are 54 parties to the Treaty, with 29 having consultative status, India with its own station on Queen Maud's Land being one of those 29, that have 'demonstrated their interest in Antarctica by carrying out substantial scientific activity there'. Close monitoring systems are in position to regulate the activities of the countries with a presence on Antarctica in order to maintain its ecological integrity. But the fact that there are around 66 scientific stations in Antarctica, 37 being occupied year round, the remainder closing down for winter and some 4,000 people through the summer months and about 1,000 over winter each year living on it, in my opinion, compromises its well-being. Is the work being done for humanity's good from there sufficient grounds for the present and future footprint of humanity on its climatically challenged surface? But this article is not about the earth's South Pole alone.

The earth's seas and ice are different from the sky and its spheres but we know that there has long been an Antarctic-type race in outer space between the powers which have perfected, with great toil and at great expense, to penetrate it and go higher and higher, faster and faster, than their several peers. And the world has been all too aware of the need, dire and pressing, to prevent an arms race in outer space.

An agreement that is about restraint

Even as the earth's South Pole drew Amundsen and Scott to it, the moon pulled Russia's Luna-25 lander and India's Chandrayaan-3 to it. The Indian vehicle reached its destination, but the Russian was not so fortunate. And just as the world's engagement with Antarctica led to a treaty, so does the Moon Agreement adopted by the General Assembly in 1979 in resolution 34/68 (elaborating on many of the provisions of the Outer Space Treaty) provide that space-probing humanity's dealings with the moon should be used exclusively for peaceful purposes; that its environment should not be disrupted; that the United Nations should be informed of the location and purpose of any station established on it. The agreement states that the moon and its natural resources are the common heritage of mankind and that 'an international regime should be established to govern the exploitation of such resources' when such exploitation is about to become feasible. The Moon Agreement is far-sighted. Something of the world's experience of Antarctica and the working of the Antarctic Treaty informs it. The Moon Agreement is a self-regulating covenant of restraint. It anticipates human appetites for turf, for control, for the urge to get there first, flag and all, and dig in.

Pride and exhilaration over the Chandrayaan-3 achievement, entirely natural, must now be followed by a mature policy on the future of India's earth-borne plans on the moon. To put it differently, as an earth-pioneer on the moon, India must, by precept and practice, set the pace for the earth's agenda on the moon and of the moon's future as a partner with the earth.

As a partner, not as property. As a collaborator in science, not a colony in subjugation. The Moon Agreement must be taken to its next logical stage. Prime Minister Narendra Modi's statement – 'The success of Chandrayaan-3 is not just India's alone but it belongs to all of humanity' – was wise and responsible. Following up on that, he can now do the world's space missions great service. He can do so now by taking the initiative to craft a declaration of the fundamental rights of outer space. And thereby inaugurate a new ethics for human activity in outer space, including, very pointedly, the earth's responsibilities towards outer space debris. This new ethic must make the non-militarisation of outer space a non-negotiable covenant. The Outer Space Treaty and Moon Agreement now need aligning not just with the latest advances in space missions but with a moral compass to the stars.

India cannot afford to be among those who may want to scramble for outer space hegemonies over what is not just the common heritage of humankind but that of a larger cosmos.

(*The Hindu*, September 21, 2023)

PART III

Forgotten Histories of India

12

Living with the Birds

'WILD LIFE? THAT IS how we refer to the magnificent animals of our jungles and to the beautiful birds that brighten our lives,' Jawaharlal Nehru says in his foreword to E.P. Gee's *The Wild Life of India* (1964) and goes on to wonder what the animals and birds think of man. He doubts if the wild world's appraisal can be very complimentary.

Nehru's scepticism is shared by Salim Ali, the widely respected ornithologist who turns 85 on November 12. Described by K.P.S. Menon in *Delhi to Chungking* (1947) as 'looking more and more like a bird', Salim Ali views matters outside his chosen field with the astonishment of a bird, surprised by human intrusiveness. Salim Ali uses the words 'astonished disbelief'. The disbelief is usually over man's inability to see the obvious.

E.P. Gee has said that Salim Ali 'is a most useful companion to have on an expedition for when he is there one need not look up his very fine books to see which bird you have seen or for other details. His remarkable memory and long years of experience in every part of India can give you all the answers and a lot more besides.' A non-naturalist bureaucrat by profession, I have found a 'lot more besides' birds in Salim Ali as I have had the good fortune to meet him in Tamil Nadu in the autumn of 1975.

He was born in Bombay 85 years ago, and his links with the north-west coast have continued since. For centuries that area has known men – and birds – coming up to it from other shores.

Last year when Salim Ali was in Kandy, I happened to accompany him to the famous botanical gardens at Peradeniya. Seeing one of the intricately patterned orchids there, Salim Ali stepped back and asked: 'Now who do you think designed these?'

*

The conversations with Salim Ali that I had the opportunity of joining in were refreshing. I wrote to him recently to ask if he would put down some of the answers he had given to my queries so that there could be a record. It was not without some hesitation that he agreed. Here are some of the questions and answers.

Question: Mahatma Gandhi influenced your uncle Abbas Tyabji. You had met Mahatma Gandhi and Jawaharlal Nehru more than once. Could you say something about those meetings?
Answer: I vividly recall my first meeting with Gandhiji in 1917, not long after his return from South Africa. My brother Hamid Ali, then in the ICS, was Assistant Collector in Godhra district (Gujarat) and while on tour he was trying a case in which a village patel was charged by the government with disloyalty or sedition or something of that sort, and Gandhiji had come to give evidence in his defence. We were under canvas, and I remember my brother bringing him into the dining tent for tea after the court sitting. Though Gandhiji had not yet acquired his Indian aura, I was thrilled to meet the man who had earned such worldwide reputation for his anti-segregation and humanitarian work in South Africa. The thing that had impressed me most about him was his unassuming simplicity and his humour. I am allergic to pomposity in any form, and a firm believer in the saving grace of humour. Therefore I have high admiration for one who is not obsessed by the sense of his own importance and can sometimes laugh at himself. This is a trait that I admire most in the British character.

At one time the Nehru family were frequent summer visitors to Mussoorie where my uncle Abbas had a house for escape from the Baroda heat, and the two families often shared their pleasures together. When out of jail, Jawaharlal Nehru was also usually there. He was keenly interested in nature, especially wildlife and birds and outdoor activities as trekking and mountaineering. It is chiefly on this plane of common interests that our contacts ran. Later, as Prime Minister he was our last resort in saving the Bharatpur Waterbird Sanctuary (then the Maharaja's private duck-shooting preserve) from vandalisation by the local politicians who wanted to 'punish' the Maharaja for his 'past misdeeds'. Two other well-known birdwatchers – Horace Alexander and General Sir Harold Williams – also friendly with Jawaharlal, were associated with me in a joint appeal to him to save the sanctuary. There was immediate positive response…

With Jawaharlal I never talked politics. The only time I tried to do so was on one of my occasional visits to him in the local jail while I was living in Dehra Dun. He said to me: 'I am sick of talking politics and it would be refreshing to talk of something more interesting for a change.' These may not be his exact words. Then we had interesting chats about the birds he had been watching around the jail in which his brother-in-law and cell mate, Pandit, often joined.

During his prime ministership I deliberately kept away from Jawaharlal Nehru as much as possible lest it be suspected that I had axes to grind. However, I now realise that this was a tactical blunder because with his sympathetic backing much could have been done to conserve the wildlife and forests. This is a subject which invariably gets low priority from blinkered dry-as-dust politicians. I have become wise and reversed my attitude and find that with Indira Gandhi – a knowledgeable birdwatcher in her own right and also, like her father, deeply concerned with nature and environment – it pays.

Q: Like Nehru, you are a man of science although not a scientist in the technical sense of the term. Could you bear with a non-scientific question? Does your association of a lifetime with the study of a species of non-human life – birds – lead you to repudiate man's separateness from the rest of nature? Or do you believe him to be apart from the rest of nature, fulfilling instincts other than those of hunger, procreation and self-preservation?
A: At the outset I must perhaps shock you by confessing that I am an out-and-out philistine and non-believer in anything that savours of the ultra-sensory or occult. Therefore I firmly believe that man is no different from any other animal – endowed with the same basic instincts, impulses and behaviour patterns as other animals, only with a more highly evolved brain which enables him to think and act rationally while at the same time presuming to arrogate to himself, by 'Divine Right' as it were, a dubious superiority over lesser creatures. If you have not seen it, and ever get a chance to do so, I would strongly recommend a superb film classic entitled *Ape Super Ape*, which illustrates in a beautifully graphic way how man's emotions, instincts and behaviour are basically the same as of lower animals only somewhat refined as we choose to consider them. I am afraid I am a babe in the woods where philosophy is concerned and deem it futile, for instance, to sit cross-legged on a mountaintop and contemplate on the navel or worry about the hereafter or concepts for which there is no rational basis for believing or disbelieving. What I realise is that our present life is the only time when we are at the driving wheel, as it were – when we have the power to consciously regulate or control our own actions, and consider it a gross misuse of that potential to 'waste' our life in pondering over abstruse conjectures and abstractions for which we (at least I) find no satisfying basis. In short I am what some would call a 'dyed-in-the-wool' materialist, but not necessarily a wicked one. From the tangible scientific evidence around me, I see no difficulty in believing that man has evolved from lower being through the process of natural selection as postulated by Darwin and refined by subsequent scientific discoveries, and that essentially he remains a super ape.

Q: Jospeh Needham, the biochemist-historian, has said: 'Man is not merely a flask of amino acids, but a whole lot of other things.' Would you not concede there is a non-material factor in man that marks him out from the rest? How would you 'place' man's aesthetic and moral faculties? Would you say they arise in his more highly evolved brain?

A: Not being of a philosophical bent, I must admit that I have never given specific thought as to whether the higher faculties of man, such as the aesthetic and moral, arise in the brain. Although I believe that the brain is the main centre of all perception and sensitivity, and the ultimate fons et origo of all our faculties which in turn are moulded by it, I do not maintain that this is the only moving force. There is certainly, it seems to me, something like conscience (or inner voice, as I think Gandhiji called it) of whose origin I will not presume to seek or offer a rational explanation. Unless we are much mistaken there is a similar aesthetic and moral sense also in animals, not often outwardly perceived by humans until it shows up visibly, as for instance in the Bower Birds of the Australian region. Here the male scrupulously clears a piece of ground, builds upon it a bower of twigs and decorates its interior with deliberately chosen bright-coloured objects often collected at considerable distances from the structure, obviously for the delectation of the female. Or, take our own black-throated weaver bird. At a given stage of the nest-construction (by the male only) – the stage at which the female exercises her choice from among several competing nests – the male daubs a little wet mud on it and sticks petals of gay coloured flowers, obviously to appeal to the aesthetic sense of the prospecting female and attract her to the nest.

Q: To go back to Nehru, he shared your scepticism of the more visible forms of a religious life and your faith in the scientific temper. But your position is more rigorously rationalistic. Consider Nehru's observation '... there is no natural conflict between free will and determinism. Life is both. Life is like a game of cards. You have no control over the hand that is dealt you. The hand corresponds to determinism. The way you play the cards corresponds to free will.' Would you exclude belief in the 'dealing of a hand?'

A: While the question of 'a hand being dealt one' goes a little over my head, I do believe that a hand *is* dealt out to each one of us – the outcome of inherited genes, I suppose, over which we have no control and which, for convenience, we call destiny or 'kismet'. But being possessed of free will I believe it is possible for humans to give direction to this destiny to a limited, though considerable, extent. In other words (using the analogy of the dealing of a hand), to play our cards to differential effect.

(*The Sunday Statesman*, November 1, 1987)

13

Four Deaths, the Right to Life and the Jayaprakash Principle

THE PURPOSE OF THIS column is to retrieve from the pages of history four episodes, among countless, of illnesses contracted by Indian prisoners and their subsequent deaths.

The first three are of Indians in South Africa, imprisoned for participating in satyagraha campaigns between 1908 and 1913 for fundamental civil rights and self-respect.

'Sammy' Nagappen was a young indentured labourer from the Madras Presidency. Imprisoned in 1909, he was sentenced to hard labour. Nagappen was made to work, in Mahatma Gandhi's words, 'as a prisoner on the African veldt in the bitter cold of winter, in the early morning when there was no sun'. One can imagine the young lad with DNA that intended him for a life under the Tamil sky, unable to withstand the South African chill and, what is more, labouring in it. Even after he took ill, Gandhi says, Nagappen 'still held on…' Released when death seemed imminent, Nagappen died on July 6, 1909.

Harbut Singh, 75, was an indentured labourer from the United Provinces. He was jailed at Volksrust in 1913, with Gandhi. The Mahatma records that the man was '6 feet tall and of noble carriage'. Gandhi asked him why he had opted to participate in the satyagraha at that age with all the risks involved. The doughty Indian said: 'In the evening of my days, I am content to pass the rest of my life in prison to deliver my countrymen.' Singh died of pneumonia on October 5, 1914.

Valliamma, a Tamil girl of 18, was arrested for participating in the march and jailed with Kasturba Gandhi, among others, in Pietermaritzburg, with hard labour. She was released when she was ill. Gandhi, just out of prison, went with his associate, Henry S.L. Polak, to see her. '…we lifted her with the greatest care on to her carpet and tended to her.' Valliamma died on February 22, 1914.

On the same date, but in 1944, Kasturba Gandhi died of grave illness in prison in Poona. The House of Commons was informed on March 2, 1944,

'...She was receiving all possible medical care and attention, not only from her regular attendants but from those desired by her family.' To this, Gandhi responded: 'The deceased herself had repeatedly asked the Inspector General of Prisons for Dr Dinshaw Mehta's help...Again the regular physicians Drs Nayar and Gilder made a written application for consultation with a Dr B.C. Roy of Calcutta...The Government simply ignored their written request and subsequent oral reminders.' The House of Commons was also told that no request for her release was received by the government, to which Gandhi asked: 'Would it not have been in the fitness of things if the Government had at least offered to her, me, and her sons, to release her?' And then said: 'The mere offer of release would have produced a favourable psychological effect on her mind. But unfortunately no such offer was ever made.'

Jayaprakash Narayan, imprisoned after the infamous Emergency was proclaimed in 1975, was released when his health collapsed. His release and subsequent medical attention, painfully slow as they were in coming, saved his death, not very long thereafter, from being attributed to his imprisonment.

The government's prerogative to prosecute is not to be questioned. Nor the court's to punish. But this much can and needs to be said: No undertrial or convict should be rendered vulnerable and susceptible to disease or morbidity with the condition reaching the point of becoming fatal. He or she must, on sickness being verified, get medical aid promptly and professionally with the prospect of supervised release. The right to life demands this. No detention or sentence is meant to run concurrently with illness. A sick detenu's right to medical attention with the release on bail under a bond, if asked for and found to be justified, amounts to a principle, no less: The Jayaprakash Principle.

(*Hindustan Times*, July 20, 2021)

14

Lessons from History for the Balasore Tragedy

THE BALASORE TRAIN TRAGEDY which killed at least 288 people, mostly poor and crammed into unreserved bogeys, has shaken us. But it has also done something else that brings a couplet from the *Tirukkural* to life:

> As swift as the arm that saves one's vesture from slipping
> Is the help of a friend when it comes at the moment of reckoning

In a speed that artificial intelligence could note with tutelary admiration, several agencies from the Union government, the railways, the defence services, governments of states from where many of the stricken passengers hailed, private institutions and above all, locals, as the people of the region are called, moved like the Kural's swift-moving arm to help save lives, reduce pain, and give to the life-lost the dignity in death they deserved.

For one of my generation, the scene unfolded memories of two railway accidents that occurred in 1956 during the tenure of Lal Bahadur Shastri in the railway ministry. In September that year, a disaster occurred on Central Railways in Mahabubnagar, erstwhile Andhra Pradesh, resulting in the death of 112 people. And in November, on Southern Railways in Ariyalur, then Madras State, another accident left more than 140 dead.

The Ariyalur accident occurred in the dim hours of predawn when it was raining torrentially. The Madras–Tuticorin Express was over the bridge of the Marudayar river when the first seven of the train's 12 bogies jumped off the rails and plunged 15 feet down into a deep ditch, leaving some bogies standing perilously on the bridge and the remaining safe. Of the seven, four were third-class compartments including one reserved for women. The first of these had 63 pilgrims from north India headed for Dhanushkodi.

Why did this happen? What and who was responsible?

These questions were to be asked but the immediate need was rescue. And it came then, too, with the speed of the Kural's hand. Shastriji was at headquarters but O.V. Alagesan, the deputy minister for railways, was in Madras, about 170 miles away. Hearing the news on the radio, he rushed to the site with senior officials of Southern Railways. By evening, under Alagesan's watch, 104 bodies had been extricated and moved to a cement factory nearby for identification.

Communication systems then were not what they are now. No mobile phones but ordinary land-phones and the humming of sleepless telegraphy in extraordinary transmissions enabled Southern Railways to tell the world within hours, for instance, that the entire crew of three consisting of the driver, Mr G. Doraiswamy, and two firemen, Mr M. Muniswami and Mr A. Kothandapani, were killed on the spot but the chief guard and under guard were safe. Reading that communiqué now, I am humbled by the use of Mr before the three names given. That title immediately invests the three with human dimensions – a family grieving, an office bereft, a rare learnt skill extinguished. Today, 67 years on, it is not unlikely that some of the seniors in the families of those three and of the scores of others killed are still with us and remember the trauma. And contemporary digital technology enables newspaper offices to attend to their old issues and educate us on the events of the time. As do that remarkable mint of archival gold often called the Hansard, namely, the records of Parliamentary debates.

Prime Minister Jawaharlal Nehru had declined to accept Shastri's resignation after the Mahabubnagar accident but very reluctantly accepted it when Shastri gave it after Ariyalur, in order to make the point that government should not be seen as status quoist when a tragedy like this occurs. Parliament was taken aback by the resignation's acceptance, with many members from the Opposition urging Shastri to stay on. I have found the debate on this in the Lok Sabha on November 27 and 28, 1956, fascinating for what it says of the political culture of the time.

K.M. Vallatharas, a member of Parliament (MP) from the Praja Socialist Party (and the Krishak Mazdoor Praja Party) elected from the Cauvery basin area initiated the debate and said there could be no better substitute to Shastri, but demanded that local officials should be 'at least placed under suspension'. Frank Anthony, the nominated member representing the Anglo-Indian community that had strong links with the railways, expressed 'deep sadness' at the minister's resignation and said it would be reducing accountability to an 'absurdity' if the responsibility for railway accidents was to be traced back to the minister. Maharaja Karni Singh of Bikaner said Shastri was a 'man of action' and 'a giant in the matter of honesty and integrity', and should take back his resignation in the interests of the railways and the nation. A.K. Gopalan, the fiery doyen of the Communist Party from Malabar, went beyond the subject of the minister's resignation and said what was needed was 'a shake-up, a real and good shake-up in the entire railway administration'. That was what he called perspective.

Shastri's reply as the former minister who would not take his resignation back, is a text that should be read and reread by each and every employee in the railways, and every regular traveller on the railways, but also by others, especially those in public life, but for the transparency of its truthfulness and the voltage of its ethics. He refused to blame those 'lower down', defended the Railway Board with passion, and placed everything in perspective in these words: 'There are two very important elements in these accidents. One is the human factor. There are various regulations laid down and yet a driver might pass against a signal…The second factor is the fury of nature…'

Those two – the human factor and what may be called factors beyond human control – should not be cited to explain away lightly any accident of the kind that Mahabubnagar and Ariyalur witnessed in 1956, and we have just done in Balasore. Shastri referred to them to give the Lok Sabha some perspective but he took the responsibility on himself.

What does railway minister Shastri's action show? And what do the reactions of MPs of that time show? This – that in the life of a nation when tragedies occur, one needs to react to them with the immediate reflexes described in the Kural, but also take, when the rescue stage is over, a view that includes that of a microscope and a telescope. And give no room in the reactions to politics – either of blame or of denial. Neither Shastri nor Alagesan nor the Railway Board nor any arm of the government flaunted the action taken to rescue the victims. They regarded what was done as duty, dutifully performed. Investigations were ordered but as earnest searches for causes, not witch-hunts for the culprit. No attempt was made by the government to minimise culpability. No attempt was made by the Opposition to become witnesses for the prosecution.

Uchharangrai Navalshankar Dhebar, Congress president at the time, said that Shastri's resignation was 'an act of self-effacement' and 'would rank as a landmark in the annals of democracy'. But almost no one at that time demanded resignations.

To self-efface is not easy, to deface another not so difficult.

(*Hindustan Times*, June 17, 2023)

15

Buddhadeb Bhattacharjee: Interpreter of Tagore to Presidents

I F THERE WAS ONE political leader whom his people knew without being able to unravel, one they admired but without becoming anything like 'close' to him, one who was cherished as one might cherish a work of surpassing art, it was Buddhadeb Bhattacharjee.

He was minister for information and culture in Jyotibabu's cabinet when I first met him. He had been described to me sometime prior to that by a woman journalist I greatly respect for her discernment as 'a singularly handsome man' and, as he received President K.R. Narayanan (in whose office I was then working), I could see she was right.

Looks have to do with an inner self no less than how 'one looks'. As Buddhababu accompanied President Narayanan on a visit to Jorasanko, his mind sparkled, almost with the excitement of a university student. I could see he knew his Tagore.

'I have often wondered,' the President said, 'has Tagore used the phrase "In this haven of freedom let my country awake"…or "heaven of freedom"?'

A gentle smile flashing across his face, Buddhababu took no more than a second to say, 'Heaven, not haven', and then proceeded to recite the immortal verse in its original.

Some six years later, President Hugo Chavez of Venezuela came visiting India and, of course, as any communist leader visiting India would, he came to West Bengal. By then I was working in Kolkata, entirely courtesy of Buddhababu for it was he, as chief minister, who had asked Prime Minister Manmohan Singh to send me to its Raj Bhavan.

At a giant rally in the city, Chavez recited the same iconic poem in Spanish and his interpreter, a sincere Bengali, struggled to render the poem from the Spanish into Bangla.

The mass of humanity present knew the poem well and became impatient with the interpreter. It did not want to hear an 'anyhow' rendering of the work in Bangla; it wanted the genuine thing.

Buddhababu, seated quietly to a side, then rose, and telling Chavez something in his ear, proceeded to the mike and, replacing the interpreter, recited '*Chitta jetha bhoyshunyo*' from memory.

The concourse erupted in joy. And Chavez was thrilled – his Spanish rendering was being restored to Bangla.

Buddhadeb Bhattacharjee was an artist in politics, a curator of public discourse and debate. Had he not been impacted along with his generation by Marx, and had he not joined politics, he would still have been a man of few words and very restricted hand gestures but would have commanded the field he occupied – which I believe would have been academia.

He would have been an ardent student, a wonderful teacher, with students who would have hung on his every word – few and far between as those would have been – looking for deeper meanings.

And with wisps of tobacco smoke surrounding his elegant head of first black, then grey and then white crown, he would have been the toast of any campus.

There is one other field he would have been a master of: directing high art cinema.

He once told me, 'Don't go to see any Bengali film without asking me. I will tell you which to go to, which to avoid. Some of them are plain rubbish.'

As a film director, he would have towered. His films would have had character, psychology, humanity. Above all, they would have had engaging dialogue – in short sentences. And he would have stuck to black and white. Colour, he would have said, is bogus. He loved to use that word – 'bogus' – for persons and things.

But it is India's and Bengal's great good fortune that he chose to be in politics where his transparent sincerity, his patent integrity and his total commitment to his ideology made him more than an asset – a treasure. Throughout my five-year tenure in the state, I had in Buddhadeb Bhattacharjee a chief minister I could respect, trust, and work with in mutuality.

The sharp conflict between us over Nandigram was to threaten the cordiality with which we started out; it could not and did not in the slightest reduce my respect for him and my admiration. But even in the white heat of Nandigram, I understood that such negativity as had crept into our equation was driven by the politics of compulsions and obligations.

I cannot forget two episodes. I once told him that a certain party functionary whose reputation was hurting the government should be sacked by him. 'My party is the Communist Party. It is not a Nazi party. We do not work like that. We have procedures.'

I could think of some stern procedures adopted by the Communist Party of India (Marxist) but I was sobered by his reply. It is another story that the person concerned was to betray him and his party later.

And once when I saw that he was clearly unhappy with my statements on Nandigram, I said to him, 'Buddhababu, you can ask for another Governor, your party is in alliance with the Congress. That is how you were encouraged to ask for me to be posted here. You can in the same way ask for another Governor.'

He was silent for a while and then said: 'I will not do that. I am not such a person.' What could be more civil than that?

As a committed Marxist, a loyal member of his party, a steady soldier of the Left, he remained an independent thinker, judging people and observing processes from the standpoint of what was *bhadra, bhalo*. Something in him revolted against all that was in poor taste.

As governor and chief minister, we frequently exchanged letters, official, needless to say to each other. Mine would be longer than necessary. His shorter than they need have been.

Once Buddhababu asked me which year I was born and, when I said, '1945', he merely said, 'I was born in 1944.'

More need not have been said. He was older, so he knew the world that much better.

I cannot conclude without saying something in partial modification of what I have said at the start of this tribute. There was one person who understood him and whom he understood and was really close to – Anil Biswas, almost exactly the same age as him. The day Anilbabu died, something in Buddhababu closed up. One needs a thought-partner in life. He now had that only in Meeradebi, his remarkable wife.

Leaving his family behind would have torn Buddhababu's departing heart. But then he being he, he would not have shown it.

'*Ayyo*,' I said when I heard of his demise. That Tamil word says it all. *Ayyo*, pity us, dear Time-Keeper, for you have bored a deep hole into our country's civility.

(*The Telegraph*, August 9, 2024)

16

Towering Presence

Just around the same time that news came of our very singular Chief Justice of India, D.Y. Chandrachud, making a visit, with his wife, to the Somnath temple in Gujarat, I was absorbed in a favourite activity: reading up old diary notes of mine to see what I was doing 10, 20, 30 years ago around the date of my reading them. And I was amused to find 'Somnath' occurring in my diary for January 2005.

I too was travelling in January 2005, and with my wife. We had come to Calcutta just about a month earlier that year on what was to be a memorable five-years' stay which did include some places of worship, notably Dakshineshwar. But on January 21, 2005, we had gone by train not to a temple city but to Bolpur on our first of several visits to that town and to Santiniketan at the invitation of the former MP of Bolpur and the then Speaker of the Lok Sabha, Somnath Chatterjee. He had set up a cultural complex in Bolpur, not surprisingly named 'Gitanjali', and he had done me the honour of asking me to inaugurate it. The towering, large, convivial Marxist leader was at the railway station to receive us. Going by his appearance alone, anyone unfamiliar with him would have said this was a prosperous merchant, owning a few mills, and once owned several rolling acres of fertile land until the Left Front government took over almost all of them under land reforms schemes. Such a person would not have associated him with membership of the Communist Party of India (Marxist). 'Welcome, Rajyapalji,' he said, with a twinkle in his eye, as we alighted from the train. Sixteen years older than I, the '*ji*' in his greeting had more humour in it than protocol. And with that started a conversation that proceeded the whole day, educating Tara and me on Bolpur's history, on Santiniketan (of course), but most pertinently on Tagore. Now, there is virtually not a single Bengali I know who does not know her or his Tagore with an immediacy, an ardour amounting to a passion. But Somnathbabu's knowledge of the great Bard's oeuvre was 'something else'. He spoke of Tagore's influence on him from his childhood days as having been foundational, making his Marxism seem almost like a detachable overlay. He could, of course, cite from Tagore's poetry with reflexive ease.

Did being Somnath have any impact on the leader? I would not know. Was he Hindu at heart, atheist of mind? I would not know. More pertinently, I did not care. Somnath Chatterjee was a warm human being who had dedicated his life to social justice. Would the great deity at Somnath want more of any human bearing his name?

I could not but marvel at my host's intellectual integrity – having stayed clear of the Hindu Mahasabha beliefs of his distinguished father, Nirmal Chandra Chatterjee, and then not allowing his firm grounding in Left politics to come in the way of his aesthetic and literary affiliations. He was, I could see, first, the elected representative in the Lok Sabha of the people of Bolpur and, second, Speaker of that House, a position which seemed so clearly for him to make him the shared asset of the whole House. How a person, the same person, can be true to his personal belief systems and be rigorously objective in the discharge of public office was exemplified by Somnath Chatterjee. He was Marxist enough to found a memorial lecture in Parliament honouring the great communist leader, Hiren Mukherjee (a series inaugurated by Amartya Sen that has unfortunately fallen into desuetude), but once in his high seat, he was the Hon'ble Speaker whom his own party could not take for granted and all MPs could trust to be impartial. This scrupulous objectivity led to an expulsion from his party when, in 2008, defying his party's whip to all its MPs, he opted to not vote against the Manmohan Singh government and continue to preside over the House as a neutral Speaker.

Once an MP is elected Speaker, her or his party must forfeit all claims on that person's political affiliation, and the Speaker must slough off all partisan raiment. Somnath Chatterjee exemplified this principle, and though that cost him his place under the Marxist sun, it established a most wholesome nostrum.

My diary entry for January 21 is about the second Somnath, also of Left persuasion, Somnath Hore, the master sculptor who lived in Santiniketan. When Tara and I called on him, he was in bed but totally 'with it'. He took my breath away when, bending, he dragged out from under his bed a work of his. I will excerpt my diary entry: 'Call on Somnath Hore. At 84 he is clear of mind and speech. He shows me a piece of sculpture in black bronze. It depicts a human, an animal – dog – a tree, a bird, all dead, killed by a nuclear bomb. It is powerful beyond words, a masterpiece. Who am I to compare the Greats but I feel the composition is ahead of Picasso's *Guernica*. Talking of the nuclear plan, he says, "We are mad." And then he gives us a rare gift – another sculpture by him – of a Hindu and Muslim united in death. I cannot check my tears at his generosity. I say to him, "I do not deserve this", to which his daughter says, "How do you know?" I cannot respond to that.' The piece reminded me of those Hindus and Muslims and Sikhs who risked their lives saving men and women from the hands of marauding men of their own faith, some of them dying in the process.

The piece which he called the 'Nuclear Winter' showed a stark desolation, in which specimens of human, animal, bird and plant life all lay dead, mute in joint annihilation. There was a chill to the work. A freeze that was also searing. The piece was not large, no bigger than a small suitcase's size, and would have been a great work to place under a glass case for visitors to see. On returning to Calcutta, I wrote to Natwar Singh, the then minister for external affairs, suggesting that the Government of India acquire it or the UNO be encouraged to do so. Art does not have the same draw for foreign affairs as security does, and the idea did not go further. I should, I now realise, have written to the first Somnath, Somnath Chatterjee. He would have acquired it for Parliament House, I am sure.

The two Somnaths who filled my January 20–21 of 2005 were men of what can only be called 'human values' and skills to match. In our singularly cold and calculating times, these two examples of 'Somnath' from Bolpur–Santiniketan come, in Tagore's great phrase, like *karuna dhara*, a shower of mercy.

(*The Telegraph*, January 21, 2024)

17

That Mushroom Cloud

TWENTY-FIVE YEARS AGO, IN the month of May in 1998, India conducted five nuclear bomb test explosions at the Indian army's Pokhran Test Range. They are known as Pokhran II. The first of these, on May 11, coincided with Buddha Jayanti.

That was bizarre.

Could the Great Indian Establishment, then headed by Prime Minister Atal Bihari Vajpayee, not have avoided that date?

Bombs and the Buddha do not go together.

But why should it have avoided that date? After all, the very first such test, known now as Pokhran I, was also conducted on Buddha Jayanti – May 18, 1974. More, it was code-named by the Great Indian Establishment of the day, headed by Prime Minister Indira Gandhi, as Smiling Buddha.

If the daughter of Jawaharlal Nehru, an ardent admirer of the Buddha, did not have the sensitivity to see the incongruity of conducting a nuclear test on Buddha Jayanti, then there is no reason why Atal ji should have worried about the coincidence of his Pokhran tests and Buddha Jayanti.

Atal ji was, if anything, more honest. He spoke the truth about the test. He did not say that it was a peaceful device that had been exploded. He knew it to be and had it described as what it was: a nuclear bomb tested successfully.

And the country as a whole celebrated the achievement. Our embassies abroad and the Indian diaspora generally were elated. 'We can now hold our heads high' was the sentiment underlying the euphoria.

I was working then for the President of India, the wise and brave K.R. Narayanan, as his secretary. I knew he was in favour of India going nuclear. That was his considered belief and I could only respect it in the position of a seasoned diplomat and scholar of international affairs. He was reading some official papers seated in the Mughal Gardens when I went to him with the news of the test as conveyed over the phone to me by Mr Brajesh Mishra, the national security adviser. That incredibly able diplomat and strategist had apprised President Narayanan earlier, in complete confidence, about the intended tests. So, this news was not unexpected.

Nonetheless, the president was visibly pleased and straightaway wrote out a statement: 'This event is a major breakthrough in the realm of national security. I extend my felicitations to all the scientists and technologists who have made this possible and say to them – India is proud of you.' The Opposition Congress hailed the event as '…a national achievement of which the nation is proud'. The former prime ministers, I.K. Gujral and Deve Gowda, too, lauded the tests.

After the news had become official, I rang a cherished friend of mine and said, 'We have burst the crackers…' Shocked, he said, 'No! No!' I went later that evening with him and my wife to the sublime Buddha shrine adjacent to the Lakshminarayan Temple, better known as Birla Mandir, on New Delhi's Reading Road for a few moments of quiet reflection. I could, of course, see the Buddha smiling but it was a curious smile that seemed to say, 'Mankind is bent on suicide; yet some will strive with diligence to draw it away from that path.'

Way back in 1957, a British Quaker called Harold Steele had come to India to get a ship that he could sail in to get to the Pacific Islands to be blown into smithereens. Blown up? Precisely that, under hydrogen bombs that Britain was testing there. Steele, with other like-minded people, was appalled that this should be done, unmindful of the radiation which the tests would subject humans to in that zone. I sat in during a meeting Steele had with my father, a newspaper editor at the time. What was discussed, I cannot remember but Steele's clean-cut face and his determined jaw made an impression on my 11-year-old mind that has not gone away. Steele's mission came to naught due to lack of funds and official obstruction, but I was not surprised to read much later that Steele had, apart from meeting my father, been received by Nehru in New Delhi. Steele was to record: 'Mr Nehru wished me well and his whole bearing and attitude of speech showed he was not opposed to my mission.'

Nic Maclellan in a study of Steele has this to say: 'Harold Steele's dream of sailing a boat into the middle of the Pacific nuclear test zone went unfulfilled, but his vision inspired many others. In 1958, US pacifist Albert Bigelow planned to sail the *Golden Rule* from California to Enewetak Atoll in the Marshall Islands, to disrupt the US military's test series codenamed Operation Hardtack. When Bigelow's yacht was seized by the US Coast Guard off Hawai'i, a former US naval officer Earle Reynolds took up his voyage, and sailed the yacht *Phoenix* to waters off Bikini Atoll. Reynolds, his wife Barbara and children later sailed to the USSR to protest against Soviet nuclear testing.

'More than a decade later, the rusting fishing trawler *Phyllis Cormack* was renamed the *Greenpeace*, and sailed from Vancouver in 1971 attempting to halt US nuclear tests in the northern Pacific. Greenpeace activists and other mariners aboard the *Vega*, *Fri*, *Rainbow Warrior* and other vessels bedevilled the French state in the waters off Moruroa Atoll until France's nuclear testing program ended in 1996...Harold Steele's tradition of moral witness and "bodies on the line" had taken root in the Pacific – a lesson learnt by a new generation of climate activists.'

Today, one does not hear voices from civil society talking of the nuclear threat or, for that matter, of biological and chemical threats to the world. Disarmament is a piety in conference agendas. And, of course, there is no voice from the world of scientists and physicists anywhere near that of J.R. Oppenheimer, Kenneth Bainbridge, Bertrand Russell and Albert Einstein or Joseph Rotblat, the leading light of the Pugwash Movement, who warned the world of the peril of a nuclear pile-up, in the great Russell–Einstein Manifesto of July 5, 1955. (The Pugwash Conferences on Science and World Affairs sought to work to reduce the danger of armed conflict.)

The risks of nuclear devastation caused by war or terror or error as outlined by Martin Rees, the great astrophysicist, are one great exception. Speaking about his book, *The Final Century*, Rees says: '...[W]e have to go back to what happened in the post-War era, post-World War II, when the nuclear scientists who'd been involved in making the atomic bomb in many cases were concerned that they should do all they could to alert the world to the dangers. And they were inspired not by the young Einstein, who did the great work in relativity, but by the old Einstein, the icon of poster and t-shirt, who failed in his scientific efforts to unify the physical laws. He was premature. But he was a moral compass – inspiration to scientists who were concerned with arms control.'

On this 25th anniversary of Pokhran II, some contrarians among us might think why today, when the risks of mass extinction are far, far greater, the moral compasses amid us to warn of those are so much fewer. Why should we have Pokhran after Pokhran in India but not one Pugwash? The scientists that were identified as having made India proud are known. But are there any among that community who can claim to be of the Einstein, Russell, Rotblat league? For the record, it must be said that Professor M.S. Swaminathan lent distinction to the Pugwash body by serving on it.

The Buddha in our history now embodies *dukkha* in the shape of the ground quaking from nuclear explosion after nuclear explosion. Agni is not the ancient fire god who sanctifies, but a missile. Prithvi not Mother Earth, but also a missile. In a park that I regularly walk in are some of the finest botanical specimens one can find anywhere. Also, replicas of these missiles. And tanks. No one notices the trees. Everyone flocks around the missiles and the tanks. Especially children, whose parents then take pictures of them saluting the war machines.

Will any of them ever get to hear of Indian opposition to war? Of Indian protests for peace? It is not as if there are no brave-hearts who wage that war on war and fight that peaceful fight for peace. But they are few and are not taken seriously.

Nuclear, biological, chemical and cyber weapons further fortified by the as yet only dimly perceived risks of artificial intelligence, can unleash misery upon us.

Grim as this prognosis is, the Buddha at Birla Mandir saying through a curious smile '…some will strive…' makes me believe that individuals, including scientists in Japan and Germany (countries which were placed under war constraints after World War II), South Africa (which reversed its nuclear weaponisation programme) and India, will pioneer an initiative towards comprehensive disarmament.

(The Telegraph, July 23, 2023)

18

Two Centenaries

HAD THEY NOT DIED at 81 and 55 respectively, two Indians would have turned 100 this year. And their centenaries would have been celebrated with enthusiasm – but by very different sets of people. As indeed, they are being organised, now, in their memories.

No two persons could have been more different from each other than the bare-headed, bush-shirted Marxist, Indrajit Gupta, and the be-turbaned, bejewelled maharaja, Jayachamarajendra Wodeyar of Mysore. They were as contrastive as a sickle and a sapphire or a hammer and a diamond-encrusted walking stick.

And we can be certain that they hardly knew each other. They are, in fact, unlikely to have ever met. They could have done so, ironically enough, in England. Indrajitbabu completed his Tripos at King's College, Cambridge under the spell of the Marxist powerhouse, Rajani Palme Dutt, just as the young maharaja-to-be arrived in Britain to meet and get to know artists and writers. But they missed each other by a few months. Their paths were not meant to intersect in India. Indrajitbabu was no habitué of concerts of classical music over which the maharaja presided with natural flair. Correspondingly, the maharaja was never a member of the Lok Sabha to which the Communist leader was elected 11 times and, as the senior-most member of Parliament, was its pro tem Speaker, time and again. If they did ever actually meet, by chance, anywhere at all, we can take it that they exchanged nothing more than formal pleasantries, lapsing thereafter into silence.

And yet, history, culture and politics link the two exact centenarians, uncannily, through three distinct pathways.

First, through Moscow. For Indrajitbabu, the capital of the Soviet Union was the secular equivalent of a Mecca. The influence of Marxism which started in London, through Palme Dutt, streamed into the inspiration that the Communist Party of India, founded in 1920, had received since the time of the Second World Congress of the Communist 3rd International held that very year. For Jayachamarajendra too, Moscow was a pole star. And that came about through an altogether different cosmology: Western classical music. The core of that inspiration was Moscow-born and then London-based composer, Nikolai Medtner (1880–1951). Medtner became, for the young royal, a soul-drenching inspiration, leading him to finance the recording of a large number of Medtner's compositions and then, not stopping there, to go on to found a Medtner Society in London, in 1949. Medtner's 3rd Piano Concerto, Google tells us, is dedicated to Jayachamarajendra.

Second, Quit India. For very different reasons and from very distinct backdrops, both 'CPI's – the Communist Party of India and the Chamber of Princes of India – opposed the Gandhi-led Congress movement of 1942. Indrajitbabu, as a loyal and policy-bound member of the Communist Party, stood with his party which opposed Quit India as it was directed against Britain which, in alliance with the Soviet Union, was fighting Hitler. Jayachamarajendra, crowned Maharaja in 1940, as a loyal and protocol-bound '21-gun salute Prince', opposed the same movement in his state, emphatically, with other princes, in total solidarity with the British Raj in the war effort. The two CPIs found themselves, in 1942, in the same trench, albeit in different parts of it.

Third, in the wake of India's Independence, both Indrajitbabu and Jayachamarajendra, for very different reasons, got 'stamped out' together. This was not about them as individuals but about the institutions to which they belonged. The government of independent India, but more specifically, the deputy prime minister and home minister, Sardar Vallabhbhai Patel, banned the Communist Party of India in a rage of indignation after the party's call, in its Second Congress led by B.T. Ranadive, for an armed struggle. And the princes were, of course, famously and deftly, made functus officio by him, in the calm of self-confidence, through the integration of their territories into the Indian Union. To adapt 'Jack and Jill', sickle, hammer, sceptre and crown, all four, came tumbling down and were made compliant with the new democratic State.

Communists are ideologically rooted, shaped and committed. But they are not robots. Marx and Engels, Lenin and Trotsky, Mao Zedong and Zhou Enlai, were ideological kin, not identical twins. Josef Stalin can be left to describe himself. As were, in India, M.N. Roy and S.A. Dange, B.T. Ranadive and P. Sundarayya, E.M.S. Namboodiripad and Jyoti Basu, A.K. Gopalan and Harkishen Singh Surjeet, Lakshmi Sahgal and Aruna Asaf Ali. But who could fail to be struck by their individual personalities? All of them wrote on the same page but using type-fonts that were their very own.

Born on March 18, Indrajit Gupta (1919–2001) was 'Sunny' to his parents, 'Comrade' to his party, 'Sir' to deferential younger MPs across party divides and to admiring officials who worked for him when he was briefly, but memorably, India's home minister. Choosing his responses to match the context, he was always himself. Brusque, even gruff with the facile, fatuous or facetious even from among his own circle, he was gentle and considerate towards all, including political adversaries. He could question his party line without flouting it. As India's first, and so far only Communist home minister, he opposed a move by the then governor of Uttar Pradesh to terminate the state's Bharatiya Janata Party-led government, for the step was constitutionally open to question. And he told Opposition MPs criticising him: 'If I were in your place, I would have done the same.' In our times when unnamed donors can contribute to uncountable election expenses, Indrajit Gupta will be remembered for the key recommendation of a committee on election reforms that he chaired: 'The names of donors should be invariably declared.' His sense of justice came from communism, his sense of fairness came from himself.

Except in 45 out of the world's 195 countries, royals are an extinct or rapidly extinguishing order. They are a living archive, a breathing monument, half sepia, half colour, uncomfortable with the past, uneasy about the future. And their present? It is difficult. If a fool, a prince, be he an incumbent or 'ex', occasions no surprise. If a debauch, no shock. But should she or he have, as indeed so many royals have, like all humans, their own uniqueness, a spark of talent or the gift of a skill, a personality of their own, they cause some disbelief and get to be dismissed as the exception that only...and so on.

Born almost exactly a hundred years ago, on July 18, Jayachamarajendra Wodeyar (1919–1974), the 25th and last Maharaja of Mysore, was exceptional. His large and strong frame looked like a granite sculpture. 'Majestic' as an adjective never had a more natural subject than this monumental king with a broader than usual forehead, a brocade turban completing the larger-than-life effect. He had exceptional attributes going for his mind, of which sound political sense ranked high. Having been loyal to the British Raj, his signing of Mysore's Instrument of Accession to independent India, was swift. Moving from being Maharaja to Rajpramukh and then Governor of the merged and reorganised Mysore state, Jayachamarajendra was also Governor of the neighbouring non-royal state of Madras. But if this Prince is remembered today it is for something that was his own personal achievement, his own individual attainment: his *vaggeyakara*'s passion for composing tunes and lyrics. Jayachamarajendra composed a significant number of songs in both the Carnatic and Hindustani traditions. But it is the fate of gifted princes to have their gifts seen as borrowings. The extraordinary novelist, R.K. Narayan, has this to say of Jayachamarajendra: 'The so-called compositions of the Mysore Maharaja were actually composed by Vasudevachar. The Maharaja would call Vasudevachar and say I want these phrases from the Devi Ashtottram and the composer would do his bidding.' Unconditional admirer as I am of

Narayan as a writer and human being, I have to say that his assessment of the composer-king is certainly entertaining but unfair.

What do the synchronising centenaries of an outstanding Indian Marxist and an exceptional Indian maharaja tell us today? This, that the individuality of its people, their contrasting affiliations, their passions are the soul of our republic, not monochromatic sameness trying to pass muster as unity. And that two seemingly unconnected Indians connect us today to that truth.

(*The Telegraph*, July 21, 2019)

19

Old Lessons

ONE HUNDRED AND SEVENTY-FIVE years ago, when Queen Victoria was two years into her reign, Calcutta had for the occupant of its stately Government House, George Eden, the First Earl of Auckland. Remembered very negatively for disastrous campaigns in Afghanistan and the de-throning of Dost Mohammed, Governor General Auckland is recalled, in gentler colours, as the bachelor brother of two gifted sisters – Emily Eden, the novelist and painter of colonial India, and Fanny Eden, the author of a delightful journal, *Tigers, Durbars and Kings*.

This, however, is written not about those grand and exotic proceedings but about something else, of far greater moment to the world of the mind, that was happening at that very time, with another bachelor Briton, who was to leave an impress on the mind of India rather more abidingly than the rulers of his time.

That man, all of 19 years, set sail that year – 1839 – from England to the southern coast of India. George Uglow Pope (1820–1908) was an Englishman of Canadian descent and had been bitten deep by the India bug that led some unusual men to journey to that far land and preach the Gospel to the 'Indian heathen'. But this Christian missionary's India fascination had another, unusual, twist to it. One might call it a sense of expectant wonder that completely outstripped his commitment to the New Testament.

Almost without exception, every missionary learnt the 'native language', if only to make communication tasks that much easier. But young Pope wanted not just to learn Tamil but see if some jewels unknown and unimaginable to a European mind lay in it. And so on board the ship, he began to learn Tamil with what can only be called appetite. I do not know what book or tattered notes were available to him on that voyage, but grapple with the strange new and magnetic language, its script and its spirit, he did. So diligent was his study and so fruitful that when he landed in Sawyerpuram, near Tuticorin, in 1839, he was able to 'reply' to a welcome address in Tamil.

George Uglow Pope was to stay for nearly half a century in the Tamil country (and finally in Bangalore) before returning to England. During this period he saw as many as two dozen governors of Madras come and go, including the fascinating Mountstuart Elphinstone, rumoured to have been 'sent off to Madras because Queen Victoria had fallen in love with him. Elphinstone, in turn, fell in love with no queen but the 'Queen of Hill Stations', the Nilgiris, building for himself a cottage in those 'blue hills'. Pope also saw nearly 20 governors general of India in and out of their Calcutta manor, including Dalhousie, who changed India's political face through his Doctrine of Lapse as also the face of the Crown Jewels in London through his capture of the Kohinoor and his gifting of it to Queen Victoria. Pope would have heard the rumblings of the Great Revolt of 1857, the massacres in merciless numbers of British residents in upper India, and of Indians in malicious numbers, after it.

George Pope lived through those events, grew from youth to middle age and entered old age in the Tamil-speaking world doing all that he did and was meant to do for his Christian mission. But also doing something no one asked him to, no one expected him to, and no one else could have done with anything like his elan – translate into English the formidable Tamil epics – the *Tirukkural* (in rhymed verse), the *Tiruvachakam* and the quatrains of the *Naladiyar*.

Pope had, before him, the extraordinary example of Costanzo Giuseppe Beschi (1680–1742), the Italian Jesuit and, briefly, dewan to Chanda Sahib, whose work under the Madura Mission had been accompanied by his path-finding translation into Latin of the *Tirukkural*, almost exactly a century before Pope's English rendering.

A brief description would be needed here, for the *Tirukkural*-unfamiliar, of that spectacularly important work. 'Kural', in Tamil, means 'small'. This classic of 1,330 compact, concise, rhyming couplets, each 'containing', in Pope's words, 'a complete and striking idea expressed in a refined metre', was written by a single author, known not by his name but by the title given to him – Tiruvalluvar. Described by Pope as 'undoubtedly one of the great geniuses of the world', Tiruvalluvar was a weaver who in today's political parlance would be called Dalit. He lived in Mylapore, Madras, sometime between the 2nd and the 5th centuries BCE. His translation of the Kural is in three sections, or Books, the first on righteous living, the second on statecraft and the third on conjugal love.

Which of these three subjects drew Pope to the Kural? None of them by themselves did, but the work in a totality did, the totality of life. Pope, in his introduction to the translation, quotes M. Ariel: '[I]ts author addresses himself, without regard to castes, peoples, or beliefs, to the whole community of mankind...in the austere metaphysical contemplation of the great mysteries of the Divine Nature, as in the easy and graceful analysis of the tenderest emotions of the heart.'

That Tiruvalluvar knew how exactly kings, ministers, officials and councils of State fare, comes in the delightfully timeless section that Pope translates as 'Not to Dread the Council': 'By rule, to dialectic art your mind apply/ That in the council fearless you may make an apt reply.'

A similar one from the section called 'The Correction of Faults': 'Faultless the king who first his own fault cures, and then/ Permits himself to scan the faults of other men.'

Tiruvalluvar's advice to the ruler on how to take criticism from his ministers is so wise as to never be accepted. Pope translates it as: 'What power can work his fall, who faithful ministers/ Employs, that thunder out reproaches when he errs.'

Tiruvalluvar's understanding of statecraft is canny and Pope sets it out in vivid English. But it is in his translations of Tiruvalluvar's section on love that the missionary surprises us by what seems to come from his own knowledge of the subject in the manner of John Donne: 'Let her, whose jewels brightly shine, aversion feign/ That I may still plead on, O night, prolong thy reign!'

And 'A "feigned aversion" coy to pleasure gives a zest/ The pleasure's crowned when breast is clasped to breast.'

I do not know if anyone knows what George Uglow Pope's love life was about, if it was about anything at all. But like anyone born to flesh, the 19-year-old could not have turned 29, 39, 49 and so on without something called Eros knocking at his church-bolted door. A mischievous thought occurring to me has Emily and Fanny Eden visiting the south, meeting G.U. Pope at the crest of his study of *Tirukkural Book III* on Love, both falling in love with him, to the consternation of their brother, the governor general. It also has young George, wanting to dodge them, going away to the Nilgiris, and immersing himself, hermetically sealed, in Tamil scholarship.

This 175th anniversary of Pope's arrival in our country, anticipating other ordained priests like Charles Freer Andrews and Verrier Elwin, in his unconditional love of India and in his reverence for India's literary and cultural legacies, serves to tell us two things: one, scholarship is about scholarship, not about nationality, ethnicity or indeed any identity other than that of the true scholar. Two, scholarship must pursue its goals un-deflected by 'the world outside'.

(*The Telegraph*, June 1, 2014)

20

The Anniversary of a Divide

THIS YEAR, THE 70TH anniversary of India's independence is also the 70th anniversary of India's partitioning. The division was not neat. It was a giant, bloody mess. Uprooted from their homes, some 14.5 million human beings – Hindus, Sikhs, Muslims left the new Pakistan for India, or India for the new Pakistan.

They left in terror, travelled trembling, and 'arrived' traumatised to a ramshackle refuge. A new and powerful word moved from the small print of the English lexicon to everyday Indian speech: refugee. The very rich and the ridiculously poor were refugees together. One had left a manor, another a hut. Both begged together for food, shelter, medicines, clothes – and dignity. All these took time coming. The only immediate relief was that the claws of abduction, loot and death were no longer upon them.

Rejoicing and mourning

Estimates vary but some of them tell us that at the lowest about 2,00,000 and the highest about 2 million human beings were butchered in the process. The Government of India claimed that 33,000 Hindu and Sikh women had been abducted. The Government of Pakistan claimed that 50,000 Muslim women had been abducted.

Life stood divided, death stood partitioned.

Refugees seethed in rage.

On this anniversary, we should remember that 1947 was one part independence, one part dismemberment, one part triumph, one part tragedy. Unimaginable, indescribable tragedy.

'Tomorrow we will be free from bondage to the British,' said Gandhi in Calcutta on the eve of the new dawn. 'But from midnight tonight Hindustan will be broken into two pieces. So tomorrow will be both a day of rejoicing and of mourning.' There was much celebration in the city, great camaraderie.

The euphoria was short-lived. Sixteen days into Independence, on August 31, at about ten at night, a fuming mob of Hindu youths came to where he was staying in the Muslim quarter of Beliaghata, looking for his Muslim hosts to attack and perhaps kill them. It was Gandhi's day of silence.

He was unwell, tired and preparing to leave the next morning for Noakhali, by now in East Pakistan, to assuage Hindu families traumatised by the murderous attacks on them. The youths started breaking things, hurling stones at lamps and windowpanes.

They ran into the rooms looking for their 'targets'. 'What is all this?' Gandhi asked the rampaging crowd, breaking his silence and walking into the mob. 'Kill me, kill me, I say. Why don't you kill me?' A posse of military police arrived and dispersed the crowd. But riots flared in the city. The next day, Gandhi cancelled his Noakhali visit and went on a fast.

'For how many days?' Abha Gandhi asked. 'Until peace is established I shall take nothing but water.' By the fourth day of the fast, Calcutta was quiet again. Later that night some of the riot-instigators came and surrendered their weapons – rifles, cartridges, bombs.

In Delhi shortly thereafter, he saw the same mayhem again. Another fast ensued, another calm. In his prayer meeting on January 20, 1948, as he spoke, a small bomb – they later called it a gun-cotton slab – detonated. There was some commotion. '*Suno, suno* (listen, listen),' he said to the congregation, '*kuchh nahin hua hai* (nothing has happened)...*agar sach kuchh ho jae to kya karoge* (if something were to really happen, what will you do)?' And then asking the gathering to stay calm, he got his associates to begin singing the Ramdhun. All India Radio has recorded the entire sequence, with the sound of the explosion distinctly audible.

The 'bomber' was 25-year-old Madanlal Pahwa, a refugee from West Punjab. He was spotted by a woman, appropriately named Sulochana (the good-eyed), and a police team soon arrived and took the young man into custody. When asked later if he thought Pahwa's was just 'the harmless prank of an irresponsible youth', Gandhi said it was not.

'Don't you see there is a terrible and widespread conspiracy behind it?' He was right; Pahwa was integral to the conspiracy which was to hit its target 10 days later. That was the temper of the nation 70 years ago. Hate, brutality, violence both sudden and also calculated. It was the season of vengeance, of retribution. It was the season of dank suspicion, of hooded conspiracies.

So, does the 70th anniversary of the birth of independent India which is the 70th anniversary of the death of undivided India as well, admit of any celebration?

Of course it does, for ridding ourselves of the yoke of colonialism was unquestionably a triumph. Seeing the imperial power out of our lives was a matter of rejoicing. Watching Jawaharlal Nehru unfurl the Tricolour on the Red Fort was 'very heaven'.

We must and will celebrate that and more – the advance of India on the path of economic self-reliance and prosperity, electoral democracy and the rule of law. But we cannot afford to forget the price at which that independence came. Not just because it was a heavy levy but because we are paying that cess even today. And it may be called the Two Nations Theory Cess.

The Two Nations theory had two celebrated articulators: Vinayak Damodar Savarkar of the Hindu Mahasabha and Mohammed Ali Jinnah of the Muslim League. Their perspectives were different, their purposes divergent. Savarkar believed Hindus and Muslims were two nations living in their distinctness within an un-harmonised India but he did not want a division. Jinnah believed Hindus and Muslims were two separate nations that needed to be in two separate nation states.

The Muslim League's advocacy of the Two Nations theory reached its purpose by the formation of Pakistan 70 years ago. What of the counter goal of a Hindu Rashtra?

Bedrock position

For some three generations over the last 70 years, India has been a plural society with a secular government committed to the idea that religion has no business with government and government has no interest in religion.

Has that bedrock position been officially reversed? No, it has not. But it stands undermined.

Those connected historically and culturally to the idea of a Hindu Rashtra are, today, promulgating their passionately held philosophy in different ways, dispersed incidents, apparently unconnected, in ways that make a Muslim feel fearful, a Christian feel as light as a leaf that can be blown off by a single majoritarian breath, a liberal feel vulnerable, a dissident feel targeted. They serve to make the cattle-trader afraid, the non-vegetarian at his meal declare it is not, please, Sir, not beef. They go to make the journalist feel hesitant, the farmer feel betrayed, the Dalit and the tribal feel insecure. Above all, anyone hurt by administrative wrongdoing or dismayed by state policy feels afraid to say so for: if you are against the government, you are against the nation.

Fear is abroad, like an invisible fume that you do not see but know that it surrounds you. And know, too, that it can ignite in your face.

The great American thinker Thomas Jefferson said: 'We may consider each generation as a distinct nation.' A new generation of Indians, a new distinct nation, is marking the 70th anniversary of our independence in an idiom and with a vocabulary which has nothing to do with the freedom struggle. It is making 'the differently disposed', both outside and within the Hindu fold, its target. And its equally active counterpart in Pakistan, going for 'the other' both within and beyond Islam, is not its adversary but its twin. Their religion is not Hinduism or Islam, it is Separateness.

On the 70th anniversary of Independence and Partition we must resist a second partitioning of India, of its versatile ethos, through an invisible surgery, performed by the knife of discord moving under the numbing anaesthesia of fear.

(*The Hindu*, June 16, 2017)

21

The Gandhis, Mandelas and Kings of Today

WE CANNOT CELEBRATE MAHATMA Gandhi today nor Nelson Mandela nor Martin Luther King Jr without inviting their immediate and stern reprimand.

All three would say, each a bit differently from the other: 'If you are gathered to celebrate us, stop right here. If you are gathered to think with us, then listen. Not to us or to those who speak in our names but to your consciences, for that is all we did. We did look back to our heroes and heroines, we did celebrate their anniversaries, but only in order to look more clearly at the world around us and into the future that beckoned. India is a free country today, the colonised world is gone. South Africa's sharp, bruising chains of apartheid iron have snapped. The US, with its Civil Rights Act in place, has made slavery a thing of the disreputable past. It has gone on to elect a distinguished President, Barack Obama, from among people who did not, until very recently, even have the right to ride in a bus on a seat of their choice. But are you – Indians, South Africans, Americans – a happy and contented people?'

They would ask us this question in anxiety and in pain. We know the answer.

The gluttony of a civilisation

India, South Africa, the US, and the whole world are in the grip of the vicious virus that goes by the name of COVID-19 but are in reality in the grip of the gluttony of a civilisation that is disembowelling the earth of its resources and is hunting down the earth's life forms to gratify its craving for commercial profit. There is a wild animal market in every city and town and, more significant than that, within each of us who are not among the poor, in the shape of a callous disregard of life and the sanctity of due proportion.

The 'crown' of the novel coronavirus microbe is not different either in its human origins nor its inhuman effect from the giant plumes that rose over the embers at Hiroshima and Nagasaki. Its victims are like those of the bomb: innocent human beings, invariably poor and marginalised.

Blaming China's opacity or Nature's insentient actions shifts our own guilt for the willed depredations of the human species' powerful segments. Nature is not taking it out on us. It has caught our hegemons destroying what we are meant to respect, to nurture. Zoonotic pandemics are modern powerhouses' most diabolic, if unintended, creation, after our fabrications of nuclear, chemical and biological weapons and the propensity of nation states to practise custodial torture. Albert Lutuli's and Mandela's South Africa has signed and ratified without any objections or reservations the United Nations Convention Against Torture. Abraham Lincoln's and Martin Luther King Jr.'s US has done so with reservations. Rabindranath Tagore's and Gandhi's India has signed but has not ratified the Convention Against Torture. What would those two men have had to say about this? Is something about torture more valuable to a state than its outright abolition?

George Floyd's dying words, 'I can't breathe', rival Martin Luther King Jr's living words, 'I have a dream'. That Floyd's words were uttered when the world was breathing through masks, inhaling with fear, expiring in despair has given us a chilling picture of the human origins of the crisis that we have brought upon ourselves.

A long walk home

Gandhi was thrown out of a train on the night of June 7 in 1893, in Pietermaritzburg. That train journey changed the course of colonial history. Trains have captured India's headlines today – only very differently. Not by someone being thrown out of one of them but by millions bundling themselves into them. They are all migrant workers, exactly as Gandhi himself was in South Africa, except that he was a lawyer with a solid income and in a different country. These migrant workers were locked out of livelihoods and of ways of travel in their own country but in a far distant part of it when a lockdown was imposed to contain the spread of the virus. While for the upper class of society lockdown meant staying home, watching films, baking, eating, doing stationary exercises and staying one metre away from one another, for these millions it meant the sudden disappearance of wages or work, of every security and, ironically, because they were now obliged to stay cooped up in their tiny dwellings, it also meant overcrowding, inhaling others' exhalations for hours together. So they moved on foot, no matter how far they had to go, just to get back home. And for the reason that they were breaking the lockdown rules, they were pushed back. Until it dawned on those who mattered that these fellow human beings had to get home to stay home. And trains were deployed. Too few for too many, they saw the opposite of social distancing. I believe the Railways when they say that as many as 80 migrant workers who died on these trains died not due to infection or starvation. I want to believe that, for I trust the Railways and the government to speak the truth. But even the Railways do not say these persons did not die.

We are thinking of heroes today. May I speak of a little heroine? The indefatigable documenter of rural livelihoods in India, P. Sainath, and his colleagues Pushpa Usendi-Rokade, Purusottam Thakur and Kamlesh Painkra tell us: Jamlo Madkam was a 12-year-old from the tribal Muria community of Chhattisgarh who went with others of her village to Telangana to work on chilli farms. When the lockdown was announced she was told her work had stopped and she might as well leave. So, with others the little one walked. Over three days and 140 kilometres she walked, and when she was just 60 kilometres from her village and could walk no more, collapsed and died. The virus did not kill her. She was thrown out of no train. But she was thrown out of opportunity, pushed out of life. No government, no politician, no employer but the whole lot of India's consumerist population, we, did that.

Will post-COVID-19, the world return to the profligate misuse of its natural inheritance? Will it learn any lessons from the deaths of thousands? If the way in which the upper classes are hailing relaxations of the lockdown is any indication, the old story seems set to be back. After all, only those dying and meant to die, die.

Rays of hope

And yet we must not on this day let hope down. Rajmohan Gandhi has reminded us of Li Wenliang, the Wuhan doctor who first sounded the world about the virus that he had found in patients and then himself succumbed to. Li had been pilloried for having started a rumour and disrupted social order. He is now receiving honours. 'I think there should be more than one voice in a healthy society,' Li said before dying.

There are Lis among Indian, African and American doctors, nurses, lab assistants, police and guards, and there are many who are speaking up not only against racism but against what Sainath has described as classism, a new form of callous elitism. Protesters in the US and in England and Australia and elsewhere saying 'I can't breathe' are not doing so in Gandhi's or Mandela's or King's name. But they are doing exactly what Gandhi, Mandela and King were doing. They are, in fact, Gandhi, Mandela and King. Together with Li and Floyd and Jamlo, they are saying we are with them. We are them.

This is the edited text of a speech made online by the writer on June 7, 2020 for a commemoration of June 7, 1893 when Mohandas K. Gandhi was expelled from the train at Pietermaritzburg station. Two others who spoke with him were Ndileka Mandela, head of the Thembekile Mandela Foundation, and Clayborne Carson, History Professor and Director of the Martin Luther King Jr. Institute, Stanford University. David Gengan, Chairman of the Pietermaritzburg Gandhi Memorial Committee, which hosted the programme, moderated it.

(*The Hindu*, June 12, 2020)

22

When India Was Turned into a Vast Prison House

ON THE 50TH ANNIVERSARY of its promulgation, falling on June 25, the horrors of the national Emergency (1975–1977) will be recalled by just about everyone as the darkest period in post-Independence India. The Emergency regime's abuse of power, its brutal suppression of democratic opposition and muzzling of free thought and expression will be excavated from the past, roundly and rightly rebuked. The ruling establishment will cite the Emergency's excesses, and the Indian National Congress will not deny the venality of those excesses. Indeed, it cannot. But it will also respond by asking the government, 'What about yours?' In the slanging match that might ensue, the lessons that need to be learnt from its horrors may well get lost.

For me, the horror of all the horrors of the Emergency was that India had become a vast prison house. Fear gripped the political class, the intelligentsia, the business community and the media. During the Emergency, it has been estimated that 34,988 people were arrested under the Maintenance of Internal Security Act and 75,818 people were arrested under the Defence of India Act and Rules.

As a 30-year-old junior officer in the Tamil Nadu cadre of the IAS, I felt like I was suddenly imprisoned myself, unable to speak my mind without looking over my shoulders, for walls had overnight acquired ears, corridors eyes. Newspapers were under the strictest censorship, and the radio relayed only government-sponsored news.

Word came through, nonetheless, of Jayaprakash Narayan, the country's tallest leader, having been woken up at three in the morning and taken to jail, and his saying, as he was being moved, *'vinasha kaale vipareeta buddhi'* (as perdition nears, the ruler loses his mind). National leaders like Morarji Desai, Atal Bihari Vajpayee, L.K. Advani, Charan Singh, Chandra Shekhar, were all taken in. As were student leaders including Prakash Karat and Sitaram Yechury of the CPM, and Arun Jaitley of the BJP. George Fernandes was captured after some months of being underground. His supporter Snehalatha Reddy was thrown into prison, tortured and died shortly after, while on parole. P. Rajan, a student at the Regional Engineering College, Calicut, was arrested by the police in Kerala on March 1, 1976. He was tortured to death in custody. His body was never found.

This sequence, transposed over what I had learnt of jailings during the British Raj, made the prison the ugliest symbol of the State for me. It also made the prison something I wanted to see and get to know in the course of my work as a civil servant. Had I become a district collector, that chance would have come to me organically. But as it happened, that coveted position eluded me in my career in the IAS. I came to see the inside of a jail only years later when, working in West Bengal, I did what Prime Minister Manmohan Singh asked all governors to do. I visited correctional homes, as jails were by then called.

In one, a bearded young man came up to me and said in Hindustani: '*Huzoor,* I am a Pakistani. I wanted to visit Ajmer Sharif for a *minnat* (vow). I got a visa and came. But my mistake was I came alone. I was detained on the suspicion of being a terrorist. I want to make no request or complaint to you. I only want to thank you. By arresting me and putting me in this jail, India has done me a favour. I have found a copy of the Holy Quran in the library here and have read it for the first time from beginning to end…' I did not know what to say to him. Was he being ironic, sarcastic, genuinely appreciative? In any case, he was being totally intellectual.

In another correctional home, as I was leaving, completely torn by the spectacle of elderly women sentenced for dowry killings, and by a section cruelly called *pagal* ward (ward of the mad), I was accosted by a young Bengali inmate. '*Saer,*' he said breathlessly, in Bangla, 'Our library here… it needs a regular supply of good new books.' He could have been a final year student in any of our universities.

In yet another, the inmates made a plain request: 'Can we have, just for the day, Sir, a TV installed to enable us to watch the Wimbledon Open?' This was done, to the great delight of the set there that might have included murderers, rapists, thieves. But all of them were for that day, tennis fans no different from other free followers of Rafael Nadal and Roger Federer. We who are 'out' do not know the story of those who are 'in'.

India is under no Emergency today. But is the horror of Emergency horrors, the jail, call it by whatever name, not a grim reality? Are there no political detenus in India today? Is the threat of imprisonment not active in our political economy? The 50th anniversary of the promulgation of the Emergency should respect history, not serve politics.

The Congress has a truly golden opportunity to offer an unequivocal and unstinting apology for each and every transgression committed in the course of that Emergency, across the gamut of human rights, political norms, legal nostrums. Would it be too much to expect the Congress president to call on arguably the senior-most living ex-prisoner of the Emergency era, Advani*ji*, and offer him a personal apology? He should do this not as the president of the party that was in power during the Emergency, but the party that led India to freedom. And the government has a golden opportunity to do something beyond recalling the Emergency's horrors.

What may that be?

It can announce a chapter-turn in India's penological history by releasing all so-called political detenus, and by saying detaining persons for their political views, when not accompanied by incitement to violence, or hatred, will henceforth not happen. More, it can alter for all time, our prison profile, turning our jails into serious centres for state-of-the-art correctional services across physical and mental counselling, personality therapy, reorientation, where there is no question of custodial torture, where prisoner-on-prisoner violence and perversions are erased, where in-jail crimes with outside collaboration, especially in drug abuse, are a thing of the past. Above all, it can put life into the amendment of the Code of Criminal Procedure (CrPC), which by Section 436A (new Section 479 of the Bharatiya Nagarik Suraksha Sanhita), allows for the release of undertrial prisoners on bail after they have served half of the maximum sentence prescribed for their alleged offence, provided it is not a capital offence (punishable by death or life imprisonment). Seventy-five per cent of the inmates of our scandalously overcrowded correctional homes are undertrials, most of whom are very likely innocent.

The practice of releasing prisoners on anniversaries is an old and respected tradition across the world. The Government of India will show by tangible deed its abhorrence of the imprisoning spree that marked the Emergency if it startles the nation by this radical reform.

(*Hindustan Times*, June 21, 2025)

PART IV

Indians Who Birthed India

23

A Song Sung True

HER NAME RESPONDS WITH images. O.P. Sharma has a lovely photograph of her. A 'late' Kamaladevi, picture-daters would say. She is seated at a table, her hands stretched across it. The round face is lined with scars of battle. The Salt March of 1930, for instance. A thousand footsteps on the sand are etched on that face. And a smile washes over them, like the waves at Dandi might do. As you look at the picture more closely, you see a chin of extraordinary determination and eyes of a rare penetration.

But it is the hands that grip you. Strong-veined and profusely, almost ostentatiously, bangled. Who says courage and beauty do not go together, she seems to ask. They cannot but. I am proud to be a woman and I celebrate the beauty of womanhood, the whole frame can be heard saying. Let no one, absolutely no one, take beauty to suggest weakness, no fear! And to proclaim womankind's strength, I will assert its femininity, not ape men. My working, writing, and creating hands will proclaim them.

Then there is the black-and-white footage of her fanning a pot of boiling saltwater. The quirk of 8 mm speed-filming gives her hands, bangled again, an extra verve. With each wisp goes a wisp of imperial hubris. Each sedimented salt crystal makes swaraj tactical. Kamaladevi is in that frame the satyagrahi incarnate. But she is not to be typecast! Not in that scene, not anywhere else.

In Mangalore, where she was born on April 3, 1903, father, mother, elder sister and Kamaladevi constituted a rather small family, for those days. It was there, in the verdant garden home of her Saraswat parents – Ananthiah Dhareshwar and Girijabai – that Kamaladevi first saw, touched and began to move the multicoloured beads on the abacus of her sensibility. Her memoirs (*Inner Recesses Outer Spaces*, Navrang, 1986) tell us that the twinkling of the *mrigasirsha* star which heralds rain, the onset of showers in the month of *shravana* and the worship of the *tulasi* plant became a continuum for her, signalling the reassurance, if any, as needed in that fecund part of our western ghats, of the creative principle of life. Kamaladevi's narration of her childhood is no idle amble down a memory footnote. I had not heard it explained anywhere until I read her autobiography that *mrigasirsha* is so named because the rains it heralds are such as to make the *mriga* (deer) bend its *sirsha* (head) down under the torrent.

For Ananthiah, a district collector, nationalist politics was taboo. But even in her teens, Kamaladevi made her own decisions. Nobody was to give her taboos. In this, she was clearly influenced by her mother, 'a feminist with a very strong consciousness about women's rights'. In 1910, when Kamala was seven, Ananthiah died, leaving no will. Her stepbrother claimed the entire estate and offered a subsistence allowance to Girijabai. This the self-respecting widow declined to accept and decided to support her daughters by herself.

For those times, this was no ordinary resolve. It steeled the young girl in adversity and resoluteness. But certain customs Girijabai could not resist. By the custom of the times, Kamala was given in marriage while in her early teens – and not surprisingly, was widowed not long thereafter. What could that 'status' have meant to a child? In a less enlightened home, it could have meant an irreversible eclipse. But Girijabai's home was different. Kamaladevi studied, passed her Senior Cambridge and was encouraged to pursue her interests which were clearly taking her towards the arts and theatre. She moved to the intellectual capital of the South – Madras.

Around that time her path crossed that of Harindranath Chattopadhyay. A musical genius, the young Bengali had poetic and histrionic talents that could only have been matched by those of his sister, the Bulbul-e-Hind, Sarojini Naidu. Kamaladevi and Harindranath found that they had shared interests and decided to marry, affronting the orthodox not just because this was, in her case, a remarriage but by its cross-regional nature. Spurred by a joint vision, this did not deflect them. 'When poet-musician Harindranath and I teamed up it was for a sharing of dreams and ambitions to devote ourselves to create a new theatre in India,' she writes in her memoirs.

But the real theatre of the times was not under arc lights or on stage. It was being played out under the sharp daylight of non-cooperation. Kamaladevi was but 16 when she happened to be in Bombay and attended a mammoth meeting addressed by Mahatma Gandhi. Chowpatty was 'a sea of heads', she recalls, and being there she felt the power of the Mahatma's appeal. She was enlisted into politics that day, I should imagine.

What drew Kamaladevi into that vortex was more than the self-evident political compulsion of the cause. It was the strange mix that Gandhi was offering of political regeneration and constructive renewal. Kamaladevi and Harindranath met the Mahatma and Rabindranath Tagore at Santiniketan. 'Tagore felt that personality can be built up through music,' she records. Whereas Gandhi said it was 'to be built up through craft – the use of hands'. Harindranath, restless by temperament and peripatetic by choice, wanted to go to England and savour its world of letters and theatre. Kamaladevi joined him there and enrolled in Bedford College, London, to read sociology and economics.

But after a brief spell she returned home. Not because she would not have made a success of an academic course in London but because her mind was in India. She enrolled in 1924 for volunteer work – no simple badge-pinning work, let us remember, but everything that needs to be done at a mammoth gathering – at the Belgaum Congress. The session was a historic one, presided over by Gandhi himself. The Mahatma had been a volunteer in earlier Congresses himself, when still relatively unknown. Nothing was too menial or too 'high' for a volunteer. Kamaladevi's presence did not go unnoticed. How could a Sakuntala have gone unnoticed! And especially when her Dushyanta, Harindranath, was as prone to short-term memory loss as the hero of Kalidasa's epic. A drama troupe started by the two had been most successful, with 'Abu Hasan', the play Harindranath wrote when he was 18, showing to packed halls in Bombay. Another, 'Discovery of India' showing the progress of Indian civilisation from 5,000 BCE to contemporary times had also captured popular imagination. Their son Ram had a role in that production. So here was a stage heroine boarding the nationalist train.

Within two years Kamaladevi was in the thick of mainstream politics. In 1926, elections had been called to the Madras Provincial Legislature, and just on the eve of polling it was announced that women too could contest. Margaret Cousins, educationist wife of the Irish poet and playwright James Cousins, prevailed upon Kamaladevi to do so. She decided to file her nomination as an Independent, as Congress had already closed its lists. With no time available, and no resources of any kind, her debut was foredoomed. And fail it did, but with the astonishingly small margin of 51 votes! Her 'defeat' was in fact a victory and was hailed as such. She had made a point – that in the man's world of elections a woman could take men on as their equal.

The Congress invited Kamaladevi to become a member of the party the very next year and organise a volunteer corps in Madras, which she did with the kind of 'to-the-manor-born' ease she was to become celebrated for in public life. In 1927–1928, Kamaladevi was elected to the All India Congress Committee, the citadel of political participation. But the citadel was not so pleasing! Not to her, anyway. She found the status of women needed to be safeguarded even there, in the very core of the freedom movement.

As batches of volunteers began to be identified for the salt satyagraha in 1930, she learnt that women were to be excluded from the enacting of that historical moment. Never awed, she went to the Mahatma. 'The significance of a non-violent struggle,' she put in, 'is that the weakest can take an equal part with the strongest and share in the triumph.' The point was conceded. Kamaladevi was one of the first to break the salt law. 'Even as I lit my little fire to boil the salt water, I saw thousands of fires aflame, dancing in the wind. The copper pans sizzled in laughter while their bosoms traced the white grains of salt and the heat lapped up the last drop of water.'

I do not think Sarojini Naidu could have improved upon her sister-in-law's description. 'Hail Deliverer!' are the words which the Nightingale of India had uttered, as the Mahatma bent to pick up his fistful of salt at Dandi. Kamaladevi was at that time making a double point. The salt law needed to be broken and it needed to be broken by the sons and daughters of India, together.

Even as Gandhi was arrested, so was Kamaladevi along with hosts of others, the magistrate saying she had been responsible for more people breaking the law than anybody else! She was incarcerated at Yeravada, Poona, in the first of her many jailings which were to extend to a period of five years during different periods of the struggle. Five years are, today, thought of exclusively in terms of Lok Sabha terms and governorships. She clocked a different kind of quinquennale.

In the 1932 Civil Disobedience movement, she shone as a star. By now Harindranath and Kamaladevi were pulling in different directions. He was a musical bee, humming his winged way in a garden of many flowers. She was the sole lotus in the garden pond – sublime when she was closed for him, sensational when not, as in the plays they did together. But the lotus's decision to bloom or remain inaccessible was the lotus's. The bee had no part in it. They parted. He, to explore other harbours and manorial hothouses. She, to remain firmly rooted in her deepening concerns. Harindranath performed and performed brilliantly. Kamaladevi just was.

There was something naturally anti-pomp in Kamaladevi. Anti-pelf and shall I say, anti-chandeliers. Her charisma glowed from a simple oil-wick in an earthen lamp. And strangely the wick remained soot-free. Naturally, she was drawn to the socialist ideal, going counter to 'insider' sentiment in the Congress. Becoming a founder–member of the Congress Socialist Party (CSP) in 1934, she was elected president of the CSP at its Meerut session in 1936. Elections took place in 1937 to the provincial legislatures and Congress won eight out of 11 provinces, notably in Madras where Kamaladevi had done so much work. Rajaji was to be the premier of Madras. Many illustrious Congressmen were for the first time inducted into office.

I have recently come across a fascinating letter written April 5, 1937, the Mahatma to Jawaharlal Nehru, then president of the Congress, on the subject of women in the higher reaches of the Congress of the times. I excerpt it:

> Kamaladevi was travelling with us from Wardha to Madras. She was coming from Delhi. She came to my compartment twice and had long chats. At last

she wanted to know why Sarojini Devi was excluded (from the Congress Working Committee), why Rukmini Lakshmipati was being kept away by Rajaji (from the Madras Ministry), why Anasuya bai was excluded, and so on. I then told her of my part in her exclusion, and told her almost all that I could remember of the note I wrote for you on that silent Monday. Of course, I told her I had no hand in Sarojini's exclusion at first or inclusion after. I told her also that Rajaji, so far as I knew, had nothing to do with L's exclusion. I thought you should know this.

Now that was Kamaladevi at her typically determined and assertive best. Nobody was allowed to ignore womankind. Not when womankind was not ignoring the struggle. And if that meant boarding the Mahatma's compartment between Wardha and Madras, and obtaining from him a point by point clarification, which then had to be shared with the Congress president, so be it. World War II broke out two years later and Kamaladevi addressed the Mahatma another letter, which must rank among the most important in India's political discourse on the war. Quoting it in extenso, Gandhi wrote an article on her intervention in the *Harijan* of October 9, 1939. One part of that letter of Kamaladevi is memorable: '…if England and France have the right to rule over large tracts and big nations, then Germany and Italy have an equal right. There is as little moral justification in the former countries crying halt to Hitler as there is in what he calls his rightful claims. That there is a third view the world hardly seems to think, for it rarely hears it. And it is so essential that it should find expression: the voice of the people who are mere pawns in the game. Neither Danzig nor the Polish corridor are the issue. The issue is the principle on which the whole of this present Western civilisation is based; the right of the strong to rule and exploit the weak.' Kamaladevi was telling Gandhi, not very gently, that in his opposition to the Hitlerian aggression, he and the Congress were letting Britain get away too easily.

Gandhi commented in his article:

I agree with Kamaladevi's analysis of the motives of the parties to the war. Both are fighting for their existence and for the furtherance of their policies. There is, however, this great difference between the two: however incomplete or equivocal the declaration of the Allies are, the world has interpreted them to mean that they are fighting for saving democracy. Herr Hitler is fighting for the extension of the German boundaries, although he was told that he should allow his claims to be submitted to an impartial tribunal for examination. He contemptuously rejected the way of peace or persuasion and chose that of the sword. Hence my sympathy for the cause of the Allies.

In 1941 she toured the USA, making a deep impression on the Roosevelts and numerous others by her candid countering of British propaganda against the Indian national movement. She also visited China and Japan, and while in Japan roundly criticised the Japanese aggression on China.

Sanctimoniousness was something she had no time for. Words devoid of sincerity were verbiage, action which was not genuine, hypocrisy. So if the Congress could not contain her, nor could the mantra of socialism. It had to prove itself in the actuality of daily life. Having been in the forefront of the Quit India movement in 1942, she became a member of the Congress Working Committee in 1946. Anyone would have expected her to gravitate from there to the Constituent Assembly. Kamaladevi declined. She had taken to politics as a vocation! She was to turn down other offers. Saying 'no' came almost as an aesthetic exercise to her. She had said that most effectively to an aesthete of aesthetes after all – Harindranath himself.

Kamaladevi's signature, incidentally, became a wonder to behold. Few signatures have its elegance. Though separated from Harindranath she had retained his surname. But the 'C' in capitals and the following 'h' in her signature intersect, making a cross, a crossing-out. I find that flourish of her carefully held pen deeply symbolic. She did nothing without thought. A ministership of state came her way very early on after Independence. 'If Rajkumari Amrit Kaur, very rightly, should be of cabinet rank, should I…?' Only this time, she did not seek to interrupt the prime minister's train journeys. The modes of leaders' travel had also changed! Kamaraj, then chief minister of Madras, wanted her to be governor of his state and sounded Nehru. 'Ask her,' the prime minister told the chief minister, 'If you can persuade her, what can be better!' Nehru knew, Kamaraj understood, that Kamaladevi's ambitions were not for office.

After 1947, Kamaladevi turned her attention increasingly to crafts, to the use of hands, the natural passion which had been whetted in her by Gandhi and by a valued friend, G. Venkatachalam. Setting up the Central Cottage Industries Emporium and heading the All India Handicrafts Board for a number of years, Kamaladevi became a synonym for crafts. But not for the acquiring and flaunting of objects made by hand. That she left to the 'cultivated' classes of Delhi.

She meant by crafts the makers of those objects, their needs and the nurturing of their genius. For her, handcrafted objects were not an elite interest, though that too she did not exclude as a natural aspect. For her, crafts meant a continuum between the maker and the user of those objects, not unlike that between *mrigasirsha, sravana* and *tulasi*.

Kamaladevi came to know innumerable craftspersons intimately. And she discovered talent among city-breds in the matter of crafts promotion.

L.C. Jain, whose acquaintance she had made earlier in the matter of refugee rehabilitation, brought his formidable talents of marketing and distribution to her cause. Craftspersons thanked her for her assistance, of course. But more, they thanked her for her understanding. The World Crafts Council sought her out. And she travelled the world, meeting artists – her natural constituency – and writers, thinkers.

Kamaladevi probably had more friends in the outside world among its true 'greats' than anyone not in high office in India. The Roosevelts, De Valera, Generalissimo Chiang Kai Shek and his wife, Chou En-Lai, Oppenheimer – all came to know and respect her personally. Kamaladevi told me once of how an All Important Person had looked right through her at the Central Institute of Education in New Delhi, only to be told within days by a visiting prime minister that she wanted 'to see Kamaladevi more than anyone else in Delhi' – and then being invited by the same Mightiness to a meal in honour of the visitor and being hugged ostentatiously!

She visited Sri Lanka, as Chairman of the Sangeet Natak Akademi, when I was working there, in 1978. Her visit was regarded in that country as that of an Indian stateswoman. She was better known there than many then or later in high office in India. She had first visited the island in 1931 with the Nehrus – Jawaharlal, Kamala and young Indira. Apocrypha grow like mildew around the famous. I was told by Minnette De Silva that the Kandy of 1931 was agog with rumours of Kamala Nehru strongly disapproving of her husband's taking the other 'lotus' a-rowing in Kandy lake! And Kamaladevi was also remembered in Sri Lanka for her later visit in the early 1940s to help the Lanka Sama Samaj Party 'build up'.

In her 1978 visit, she did not stop with visiting the high and positioned. Her hosts, High Commissioner Thomas Abraham and Meera Abraham, had drawn up a fine itinerary for her. But she found time to include in it visits to the homes and huts of little-known mat-weavers, potters, painters and writers, travelling in a bumpy jeep I was able to offer her. 'Do you know if Manjusri is still alive?' she asked me. I had not even heard of Manjusri at that time. Inquiries were made and the great artist of Sri Lanka's temple paintings and decorations was traced and brought, in an ecstasy of joy, to meet Kamaladevi. Years later, when I was back in Sri Lanka, Manjusri's son, now an acknowledged artist himself, remembered that meeting of his late father and Kamaladevi. And Chitrasena, the Lankan dancer, recalled her as 'the greatest Indian name after Gandhi and Nehru'.

All this is not to say that Kamaladevi was a beloved goddess always and everywhere. She was not. There were many who found her hard, difficult, impossible to persuade or correct when she was in error. In the iciness of her relations with the remarkable Aruna Asaf Ali, the 'fault' was not that of the heroine of 1942 alone, surely. And in her lack of warm understanding between the creative and much misunderstood Pupil Jayakar.

Kamaladevi's reserve amounting to coolness certainly played a part. Especially when it came to judging people, she was human enough to make mistakes, serious ones, of assessment. She could be taken for a ride. And many tried to do just that.

As the years advanced, and Delhi's long shadows of indifference crept over her evenings at India International Centre, she became easy prey to the passer-by's idle curiosity and even naughtiness. She could be made to play favourites – easy and disastrous in the world of the performing arts over which she reigned as Chairman of the Sangeet Natak Akademi. Never dizzied by applause or dismayed by its absence, she was nonetheless susceptible to the insidious effects of Delhi-bile. She saw through games soon enough. But only after they had caused her distress and her causes, harm.

Kamaladevi was human enough to be greatly pleased when she was asked if she would accept the Padma Vibhushan. 'I am getting it for my contribution to Letters!' she said with barely concealed joy. Some years later when the President of the day most appropriately conferred the Bharat Ratna to Aruna Asaf Ali, Kamaladevi was not alive. If she had been, the Gods of Equity would have been displeased. It would have been like conferring that highest award to Latabai Mangeshkar before Subbulakshmi.

Kamaladevi had said no to office and power, but not to public life. Her interest in causes such as those of the tribal communities of India, of refugees and of children, was great. But great as it was, her interest in them had to be subordinated to her care for individuals. When towards the end of her days she came across the case of two boys, one of whom happened to be a Hindu and the other a Sikh who were picking berries somewhere near the Punjab border between India and Pakistan and strayed absently into the 'wrong' side of the border and were locked up, she took up the matter with President Zia ul Haq. Her letter worked, and within a few days the boys were back home. But not before they came to her personally to say thanks. Everyone else had just seen the reports in the papers and turned the page, perhaps with a tch, tch.

I remember about the same time seeing Kamaladevi in tears. 'This girl,' she said, 'Anshu Saxena, has had acid thrown on her face and on her torso by a bunch of hoodlums in Meerut.' I did not know quite how to respond. 'You cannot imagine what that can mean to a girl.' And then tears were repeated with rage and resolve. 'Those men have to be given the hardest punishment there is for such an offence. But more than that I want to raise enough money to see that the girl gets the best reconstructive surgery there is. Will you help me, Gopal?' Many people helped, not because they would have 'even otherwise', but because after she had spoken to them, they saw the 'case' as a human being's traumatic experience. Among them was the then President of India, R. Venkataraman, who wrote out a handsome cheque and sent it to her with the spontaneous seriousness of something due from a diligent Roman to Caesar. Truth is a big word. So misused. And made so common. But if there is one word I would associate with Kamaladevi, it is that word.

Decades earlier, Kamaladevi's mother had told her the truth: 'Taste the tiny drop of its essence and you will continue to linger on it...' Kamaladevi did that. She lingered on what seemed to her to be true and just. Its tiny drops, one by one. Be it Sarojini's exclusion, the ordeal of two berry-pickers, Anshu Saxena's torment. Or the dry and howling cataract of our neglect – India's and particularly male India's neglect – of those who ought not to be counted as 'weak' but are. To all these she extended her hand – the use of her hand – as Gandhi had told her. A strong-veined and bangled hand which seemed to say 'you know, these bangles...they have been made by a remarkable couple I know in the deep of Madhya Pradesh...'

In Kamaladevi's equation with Gandhi there was space for candour, with Nehru for firmness, with Jayaprakash for compassionate understanding. Her nationalism had room for a global outreach, her socialism for individual expression. Her work for women came from within. It came from her as the *sravana* breaks over Mangalore, spontaneously and torrentially. It is my conviction that had she lived some more years, Kamaladevi would have organised a nationwide movement in support of women's issues and become something of a national lodestar once again, even as Jayaprakash Narayan did in the late 1970s. And perhaps with the same disillusionment?

(*Seminar*, August 2004)

24

A Comrade, Not Acolyte, of the Mahatma

ACHARYA J.B. KRIPALANI, WHOSE birth centenary occurs today, belonged to that part of the subcontinent – Sind – which has given our country its name: Hindustan or India. Proud of Hindustan or his roots in the Sind, devoted to the Sindhi language and possessed of the brave 'frontier spirit', Acharya Kripalani brought to bear on the national movement something of his stark province's tenacity of purpose, a strength to bear hardships with fortitude and, above all, an inexhaustible resource of the spirit.

Kripalani was first roused to significant political action by the Bengal Partition. The authorities of a college in Karachi spotted the rebel in him. When the principal of the college made a slighting reference to Indians as 'liars', Kripalani and his fellow students immediately organised a strike. This was his first taste of direct action. He then shifted to Wilson College in Bombay and Ferguson College, Poona. Both institutions watched him, warily. He was a student apart from others and yet capable of drawing others to him. History had clearly reserved Kripalani for public life.

It is not widely known that of all the front-ranking leaders who joined the freedom struggle in response to Gandhi's call, Kripalani was the first – the very first – to have met the Mahatma. That first meeting (in Santiniketan) was no casual encounter but a meeting of the minds. Indeed, of the hearts. The year was 1915. The Acharya was then a professor of history in a college in Muzaffarpur, Bihar. He has recalled:

> I was introduced. I greeted him in the old traditional Indian style with folded hands. He returned the courtesy with a broad welcoming smile. He invited me to sit by him and straightaway entered into conversation. The talk on both sides was personal. There was no mention of politics at this first meeting. But from his occasional gaze at me, I thought he was trying to know me and measure me. I too on my side was doing the same. Today it may appear presumptuous for a young man to talk in terms of taking the measure of Gandhiji. But it must be remembered that in those days Gandhiji was not the Mahatma that he became afterwards.

Kripalani served for a while, thereafter, as private secretary to the redoubtable Pandit Madan Mohan Malaviya, founder of the Benares Hindu University, who was also the Congress president at that time. But the call of Gandhi was insistent. A little later, when Gandhi set up his new Satyagraha Ashram at Ahmedabad, Kripalani saw its prospectus. He was attracted to it and, at the same time, bewildered by it. Gandhi had specified therein that if man used superfluous buttons on his shirt or coat, he would be 'stealing'. Kripalani writes:

> I thought if a person was so hopelessly unrealistic there is no point making any suggestions to him. He might establish his Ashrams in the Himalayas rather than in Ahmedabad, the city of mill owners. Thus, I dismissed Gandhiji from my thoughts.

But, as Kripalani has himself conceded, Gandhi was not one to be so easily dismissed. And certainly not by Kripalani who, beneath all the sarcasm, was himself a man of deep affections and a steady idealism.

Gandhi's burning passion to secure justice between man and man and group and group began to exercise a powerful influence over Kripalani. He saw that Gandhi was working for a pervasive social transformation in India and not just a political change. This appealed to the teacher of history. The authorities were keen to dispense with Kripalani's services in the college, and Kripalani, on his part, was absolutely ready to join Gandhi's Champaran campaign. Kripalani had realised that the Indian population had been roused by Gandhi as though by a miracle to cast off their fear and become conscious of their own and the nation's destiny. He saw how Gandhi, when he was working for the removal of political injustice, worked simultaneously for the removal of injustice among the people. Champaran was the launching pad for a series of movements where Gandhi put his sociopolitical beliefs to the test.

Gandhi was, at that time, in a formative stage of his political evolution. While his social and philosophical views were already advanced, Gandhi's politics were yet to acquire definition. This process called for dialogue; it called for discussion. Above all, it called for an intelligent, frank and trustworthy interlocutor. In the words of the Sufi poet Jalal-ud-din Rumi:

> It's not the Way I talk of, I seek him
> Who'll walk the Way with me:
> It has been said, first the Comrade,
> then the Way.

It was as if Gandhi, looking for a comrade with whom to tread the new path, had been helped by destiny to find Acharya Kripalani.

During the Champaran campaign, Kripalani and Gandhi went out on long walks during the course of which they held discussions on political and philosophical matters. Kripalani could not quite comprehend the Mahatma's theory of passive resistance. He argued that whatever might have been Gandhi's experience in South Africa, it would be impossible to achieve the freedom of India through non-violence. Kripalani, with his usual candour, told the architect of satyagraha that while Gandhi had legal knowledge he lacked knowledge of history. There is no instance in history, the professor told the Mahatma, in which a subject people had achieved their freedom without the use of some violent force. But Gandhi was not impressed with this argument. He explained his point of view to Kripalani from day to day. Gandhi then gave Kripalani the historical argument that India was the most non-violent country in the world. Kripalani countered by saying that Indian history was a series of wars, big and small, and wondered how India could be regarded as more non-violent than other countries. Their viewpoints differed thus although there was no gainsaying that Kripalani had already become Gandhi's trusted colleague.

The teacher of history soon realised that he had himself been taught something. Kripalani has recorded:

> It was in after-years when again and again I thought over what Gandhiji had said that I could understand his point of view. I saw that a superficial view of Indian history would show that India was as much involved in wars as any other country from the times of the Ramayana and the Mahabharata. But a penetrating study of Indian history, especially of the people, would show that the Indians were less prone to violence than people elsewhere… Not only did I reread Indian history but also I reviewed human history from the point of view of non-violence. I found that as people advanced in culture and civilisation, their institutions became progressively non-violent.

Kripalani's frankness and willingness to accept a correction appealed to Gandhi who wanted not acolytes but associates in his struggle: not camp-followers but colleagues, who could help him understand situations and help him to plan and execute his great vision for free India.

Given his background in education, Kripalani was encouraged by Gandhi to take up, in 1922, the principalship of the Gujarat Vidyapith, Ahmedabad, which had been set up as a National University for the benefit of those who had quit government-run educational institutions. He thereby became a source of inspiration and revolutionary enthusiasm for several generations of students. A khadi shawl draped loosely over his spare frame, tall, and absorbed in thought, Kripalani inspired both respect and affection. Kripalani's scholarship, his unusually frank observations and his total and transparent honesty endeared him to all students.

But while people and places could win Kripalani's affiliation, they could never bind him down. When in 1927 Gandhi wanted every member of the executive body of the Vidyapith to sign a pledge to the effect that he would be non-violent in thought, word and deed, the Acharya declined. Kripalani said that his moral evolution did not justify his signing such an absolutist pledge. Such was Kripalani's honesty. Here was a case of someone who knew what ahimsa meant and who enjoyed the complete confidence of the greatest votary of ahimsa, proclaiming his own insufficiency in ahimsa. There can be no doubt that Gandhi appreciated Kripalani's principled stand.

Leaving the Vidyapith, however, was only leaving one department of the Gandhian revolution to enter another. Kripalani joined soon thereafter the Gandhi Ashram in Meerut, which was to become a premier khadi organisation. Here Kripalani, who had hitherto been only a teacher and a principal, displayed great and almost unsuspected organisational skills in providing self-employment through khadi to tens of thousands of underemployed villagers, especially women.

The year 1934 was momentous for Kripalani. Engaged in earthquake relief operations in Bihar, he met Sucheta Mozumdar whom he was to marry in 1936. And then in the same year, his politics saw an upswing. Gandhi reasserted that year that he stood for India's complete independence. The Gandhian movement was once again placing political work high on its priority. Dr Rajendra Prasad became the Congress president and, at its Bombay session that year, the Acharya was chosen to be general secretary. He was to hold that post continuously for 12 years – until 1946.

For those 12 years, Kripalani and his office secretary, Sadiq Ali, were the centre of the organisation. Kripalani was general secretary under a galaxy of Congress presidents: Dr Rajendra Prasad, Netaji Subhas, Jawaharlal Nehru and Maulana Azad. His turn came, on the eve of the transfer of power, to become Congress president himself. It was Kripalani's privilege to head the great organisation when India won its freedom. But not for much longer thereafter. New equations were being forged after August 15, 1947; new balances were attaining equilibrium. The office of the Congress president – 'Rashtrapati' as it had indeed been known during the struggle – naturally came to be overshadowed by the new arrangements. Kripalani felt that the office of Congress president ought to continue to exercise the earlier weight. This was not found to be possible. Kripalani tendered his resignation. Characteristically of him, Jawaharlal Nehru offered Kripalani a place in the Union cabinet as well as a governorship. But Kripalani said no, thank you, to both.

Founding the Kisan Mazdoor Praja Party, leading the Praja Socialist Party, sitting in Parliament as an Independent MP, touring, writing, speaking with devastating sarcasm, Kripalani personified democratic dissent. On his part, Jawaharlal Nehru, democrat of democrats that he was, initially left Kripalani's constituency uncontested by the Congress. Kripalani was given a front seat by the Speaker in Parliament though, technically, this privilege did not automatically belong to an Independent MP. But Kripalani was a fighter. He demanded a fight – and got it, sometimes losing it as in North Bombay in 1962 to the brilliant Krishna Menon and sometimes winning it as in the Amroha by-election the very next year.

His speeches were scintillating. 'We have become a nation of live corpses,' he used to say, 'without a purpose or dynamism since Independence.' Requested, in the early seventies, to unveil a plaque at the spot in Madras where Gandhi had first visualised the 1919 all India hartal and where, ironically, a five-star hotel was coming up, Kripalani said to an abashed audience: 'Whatever Gandhiji touched, he turned to gold. We practise a contrary alchemy!'

Shortly after Kripalani had turned 90, this writer once asked him, 'Dada, how come you do not use a walking stick?' Came the reply, 'Because I have a short temper!' Friends and foes alike ducked to avoid his verbal missiles. But he had, really, no foes. His political antagonists respected Kripalani's independence; they respected his integrity.

The 1970s saw dismay and disappointment play musical chairs with India's destiny. In 1978, worn and dejected, Kripalani announced his retirement from public life. In a statement issued then he said:

> I have tried to serve the nation for the last 72 years with whatever ability God has given me. It has been a labour of love. I had no connection with any government before or after Independence. As human creations, I consider all governments imperfect, only some less so than the others...

His wife Sucheta, herself a woman of extraordinary capacity and commitment, had predeceased him.

Assisted by his loyal secretary N. Krishnaswamy, Kripalani continued to read, to answer mail, meet friends and travel. His last journey was to Ahmedabad. There, where he and the Mahatma had conversed on so many occasions, in March 1982, the brave warrior was recalled by time. Recalled just as he had been originally billeted – a soldier in the service of the nation, unadorned by decorations save the seal of a conscience at peace with itself.

Crossing the frontier between life and the hereafter, Kripalani could well have said of the fabric of his life, with the mystic poet:

Das Kabir jatan se odhi / Jyon ki tyon dhar dini chadariya

(*The Telegraph*, November 11, 1988)

25

A Designer of Cultural Gardens

THEY FLOCKED TO HER official residence, ma'am-ed and propitiated her when she was perceived to be one of the zodiac. But with Indira Gandhi's end, word went round that the new stellar formations did not include Pupul Jayakar. That was not quite the case, but it sufficed for New Delhi's fawners of power. They fled now from her vicinity, speaking in I-told-you-so tones of her imperiousness and misjudgments. The house which had needed until then to be stretched out into its garden spaces for visitors, shrank to its core: her drawing room of which the magnetic centre was an oil painting of a sharp-chinned and white-haired man, everyone assumed to be Jiddu Krishnamurti. Official entertaining was replaced now by home meals for close friends in her private dining room.

'I have more time to read now and, hopefully, to write...' was how Pupul looked at the change. A book on Indira Gandhi had suggested itself earlier and she went about the task of writing it with vigour. Interviewing people – friends and adversaries of her subject – on tape, she also investigated her own memory and perceptions of her slain friend. 'We were very close and have discussed many, many things, people ... I can't really put those in ... On the other hand ...' Her tiny hand, with a silver ring shaped like the radiant sun, shook in the air as she explained her predicament.

J. Krishnamurti and the Dalai Lama were in Delhi around the time of Indira Gandhi's assassination and were to have met, at Pupul's instance. That could not happen; the trauma and the mayhem that followed had changed the environment for such a meeting. The following year, Krishnamurti's health began to fail. I was Secretary to Vice-President Venkataraman at the time. He too was an admirer of that philosopher of unconditioned awareness. Pupul kept me posted, for the Vice-President's information, of the phases in Krishnamurti's glowing sunset. When the ashes were brought from Ojai in the US to Delhi, Pupul had the urn kept under a flowering tree in her garden – a tree he had spent many hours under when staying with her. One part of Pupul ceased to care for life thereafter. She continued with her writing, of course, and went on to complete the Indira book, as well as a new one on Krishnamurti.

But in a crucial sense her life now became residual. Except, perhaps, when she revisited the Krishnamurti Foundation's Rishi Valley school at Mandanapalle and spoke to the bright, questioning students there. And except, too, when she 'threw herself' into the Krishnamurti centenary celebrations. The meeting between JK and the Dalai Lama had not worked out in 1983, but His Holiness came to Madras for the centenary celebrations, a very special gesture.

Other involvements also remained strong: her reflexes remained alert. But a new stillness had taken possession of her after Krishnamurti's death. New, because she had always had a certain special stillness to her, an inner rootedness which would not be overpowered by anything. But this new stillness was different. It contained a readiness to depart from life. After changes of government in the early 1990s, Pupul returned to Bombay. 'That is where I belong, although I have been in Delhi for years now. Bombay is a more real place.' Pupul returned, in a sense, to the days when she had been herself, her sharp, observant self. An observer, not an organiser.

Pupul Jayakar's organising abilities had always been regarded as formidable. From the turbines of her mind she could generate the energies of a dozen organisations. Her first 'public' undertaking had started with the collection drive for the Kasturba Gandhi memorial fund – in 1944. That was also her first substantial interaction with the Mahatma. When Pupul arrived in his presence, she was not wearing the mandatory khadi. Die-hard Ashramites were quick to bring this to Gandhiji's notice. 'Never mind,' he said to them, 'she can wear when she prefers; it is what she is doing that matters.'

Pupul was not the one to change her personality in order to be more acceptable in any situation. Her interest in India's handweaving tradition was a natural corollary to this. Gifted with a pachyderm's memory – and its unpredictability of mood – she carried an undrawn handloom map of India in her brain. Be it fibre, dye, pattern of weave or print, Pupul knew where and how to plot it on that map. Martand Singh's almost *purva-janmic* identification with the same subject made him an invaluable pillar of support for her. Rajeev Sethi's restless creativity gave him a similar role. 'They are my right and left hands,' she once told me.

'Cultural czarina' is a title which the media gave her, factually if also cynically. And she did not contest the description for there certainly was something in Pupul Jayakar that would cut a swathe in any crowd she walked into. Not every woman wearing her chunky rings or handsome saris or with her wonderfully coiled grey plaited bun had that effect. An imperiousness Pupul certainly had, but her brand of it came not so much from a desire to control (she needed to control a great deal) as from a confidence, not always justified, that what she was doing was right. Alongside her overpowering mien was a simultaneous humility, when it came to interacting with 'real' artisans and artistes. I have seen her talking to weavers and musicians with a respect that was no different from that she showed to the Mitterands and Kosygins of the world.

Even when some of her close friends disagreed with her, as for instance on the Emergency of 1975–1977 and when she sanctioned the spectacular and spectacularly expensive Festivals of India – she did not waver. 'The Festivals are helping our crafts, our artisans, our artistes, as nothing has ever before,' was her answer. Was she aware that middlemen and contractors were helping themselves too? Perhaps she did not know, or did not mind, as long as some tangible gains accrued to the arts and artistes.

For some of us who held the incomparable Kamaladevi Chattopadhyay in great esteem, it was no wonder that the two were, as the poles, a universe apart. To try to bring them together would not be difficult, it would be futile. For Kamaladevi, the regeneration of India's craft traditions was part of a regeneration of the aesthetic life. Beauty, Kamaladevi would say, is not something apart from life but part of its day-to-day rhythms. Pupul's vision was different. For her crafts and handweaves were an endangered species to be sought out and cultivated. If Kamaladevi was a Sakuntala in Kanva's wild growing *tapovana*, Pupul was a Roshanara – a designer of cultural 'gardens' with musical fountains and topiary.

Likewise, there was a gulf between the home-ground training provided to performing artistes by Rukmini Devi Arundale and the platforms given to them by Pupul. And yet, both were needed, the teacher and the presenter. These three – Kamaladevi, Rukmini Devi and Pupul Jayakar – were three powerful rivers: the first two originating from the Gangotri of the Indian renaissance – free-flowing and laden with the nutriments of India's cultural alluvium. The last – Pupul – arose from a catchment in the hinterland and also became a powerful river, but with this difference, that the river in her had been 'captured' midstream in a hydel dam of governmental make. From this dam, she caused a very different, high-voltage and official electricity to be generated. To the earthen lamp of Kamaladevi and the *kuthuvilakku* of Rukmini Devi, Pupul was a chandelier of many iridescent crystal droplets.

Pupul Jayakar like the late G. Parthasarathi, the late K.S. Shelvankar, P.N. Haksar and H.Y. Sharada Prasad, belonged to a small but special constellation that shone in the firmament of Indira Gandhi's sky with its own light. There were many other 'stars' and meteors in that sky that lived on a shallow and borrowed reflection. In her departure, a powerful and questing intelligence, at once proud and humble, authoritative and soft, self-willed but uncompetitive, has crossed over to the beyond. As Pupul Jayakar yielded to the Hand that starts, regulates and stops the beating of the human heart, we can be sure she did so in the knowledge that endings and beginnings are not what matter, rather the things – large and small – contained between those two over-estimated points.

(*The Hindu*, April 7, 1997)

26

M.S. Subbulakshmi: The Song Celestial

EGMORE. MADRAS. THE YEAR is 1925 or thereabouts. Veena Shanmukhavadivu, the eminent Carnatic instrumentalist from Madurai, takes her child-daughter to the home of her friend Veena Dhanammal, the renowned exponent of the same art from Tanjore. The two *vainikas* from Madurai and Tanjore respectively, enjoy reputations as formidable as the majestic spires in their home towns.

Shanmukhavadivu knows her daughter is unusually gifted: she has a voice that sounds like temple bells. But fond mother though she is, Shanmukhavadivu is also a believer in standards. She would value her distinguished contemporary's assessment of her daughter's talent. Dhanammal observes that the child has an unusual shantham (tranquillity) on her face and asks her to sing. She does so with some trepidation. Dhanammal listens raptly and when the song is over, compliments the girl on her 'susvara' (pure intonation). Dhanammal then prophesies: 'This girl has a bright future.'

Madurai Shanmukhavadivu Subbulakshmi steps out into a world which is to call her 'MS' for short, 'MS' for ever.

Speaking half a century later at the 1968 conference of the Music Academy, Madras, MS said, 'In my case my mother was not merely my mother, she was also my music teacher...Both as my mother and music teacher I prostrate before her and pray for her soul force to come to my aid.'

It is significant that MS invoked her mother's soul-force. Not her artistic genius (which she inherited naturally) but that inner spirit which made Shanmukhavadivu's music sublime.

We do not quite know when it was that MS arrived at what may be called her philosophy of music. To start with, Sangeeta Vidwan Srinivasa Iyengar of Madurai commenced MS's music tuition. Breaking a coconut before starting the first lesson, he taught her 'up to the stage of varnam'. Thereafter, the mother took over. There were long, exacting sessions, the veena functioning as a standard-setter.

Progress was rapid. By the time she was 10, MS began to accompany her mother at public performances all over the presidency, Shanmukhavadivu playing the veena as the main artiste, Subbulakshmi providing vocal support. Narayana Menon, the distinguished musicologist, records: 'During those early days mother and daughter made a delightful combination. I remember one such concert quite clearly in Trivandrum in 1931. Soon the young girl was to blossom forth into a soloist in her own right. By the time she was 17, MS was giving major performances at institutions like the Madras Music Academy....'

MS was now the main artiste, Shanmukhavadivu providing instrumental support. The beauty of her voice and the purity of her rendering made MS's concerts an unalloyed delectation. There was in that voice a quality that is best described in the Tamil word *ganeer* or the Hindi *goonj*. The two words are untranslatable into English but can perhaps be approximately taken to mean resonance: the resonance of a gong. And then there was the unusual purity of her *ucchaara*. The *sahitya* (text) of any song was rendered by MS with the same accuracy as the notes.

'What were the main compositions and ragas that you rendered in those days?' MS was asked recently. 'Mainly the compositions of Ayyarvaal (Tyagaraja); not many compositions in Tamil...All the major ragas, Sankarabharanam, Todi, Kalyani....'

MS's extraordinary stage presence became as much a matter of admiration as her bell-metal voice. The corkscrew ringlets beside her doe eyes, her Vinaya and her ability to lose herself in her song – all these had a magical influence on her listeners.

One August in 1931, T.T. Krishnamachari was taken to an MS recital at Soundarya Mahal, Madras. He had not heard the prodigy before. In a Tamil article written for *Ananda Vikatan* years later, TTK recalled: 'The singer on the stage was a tinily built young girl. But on her face, I could see a radiance (prakasam).'

The poet Subramania Bharati once said, 'If there is radiance in the heart, there will be radiance in the voice.' An inner glow began to characterise MS quite early, setting her apart from the rest, her seniors and her repertorial superiors. A glow that seemed to touch her voice and made it incandesce.

Laurels came thick and fast. Persons of that generation remember the young MS sporting medallions received by her at various concerts. The musical cognoscenti as well as others, drawn by the sheer quality of her voice and the shantham which Dhanammal had noticed, flocked to listen to her and to see her. Moved by the transcendental effect of her music, a listener penned the following versification:

> Minakshi, goddess at Madurai, smiled
> At genuflecting worshippers beguiled

> By bells and shimmering camphor
> Into the mazes of metaphor.
>
> A singer of unsurpassed renown
> Came one humid eve to town
> In effervescent rusting silks divine
> To sing before Minakshi's shrine
> Men a gathered, each other nudged
>
> The women, craning, their heights begrudged
>
> To catch a glimpse or note of song
> Uncircumscribed by the throng
> They saw the orange of her shortsilk flame
> Its pink, subdued, the lighting blame.
> One trained a sidelong searching squint:
> 'Look, how the gems of her nose-stud glint!' Another at her jasmines sighed
> And a whiff thereof to capture tried.
>
> The novitiate tufted priest forgot
> Duties his Seniors had taught
> As in the chambers of his mind
> (To dreams and visions much inclined)
> The singer's and Minakshi's eyes
> Did momentarily synchronize.

Not surprisingly, MS was requested to accept roles in the newly burgeoning world of black-and-white talkies. Those were days when playback singing was not in vogue, artistes being selected for all-round talents of which music was an important one. MS was offered roles which would do justice to her musical talents. *Sevasadan*, produced and directed by the late director K. Subrahmanyam, and *Sakuntala* saw her play memorable roles. It was at that point, in 1940 that MS married T. Sadasivam, the dynamic Gandhian constructive worker and freedom fighter. Sadasivam brought to the just-launched vessel of MS's life the steadying support of a ballast as well as direction. Featuring MS in a memorable celluloid version of the life of Mirabai and producing the film both in Tamil and Hindi, Sadasıvam secured for MS a national audience.

Furthermore, by casting her in a role that brought out her *manobhava*, Sadasivam, in a sense, completed the work of Shanmukhavadivu. The mother had helped MS discover her gift of *sangita*; the husband helped MS discover her gift of *bhakti*. *Meera* was a success even before the filming was over. A small but talented cast (which, incidentally, included MGR in the minor role of Jaimai) worked on the film at Madras and also went to the North for location shooting. One of those to be captivated by the film and by MS was Sarojini Naidu. Mrs Naidu spoke of 'the beauty of her voice, the magic of her personality, the gracious clarity of her heart'.

'*Kaatrinile Varum Geetham*' was rendered by MS in the Tamil *Meera* with wafting notes, and was a sensation. In turn, the *Meera* songs in Hindi, such as the lyrical '*Main Hari Charanana Ki Dasi*', the ecstatic '*Paga Ghunghuru Re*' and the moving '*Yad Ave*' took the North by storm. MS soon became something of a social exemplar, with several parents naming their daughters 'Meera'. Interestingly, a particular aquamarine shade of Kanjeevaram silk came to be called 'MS Blue' after the colour of a sari she frequently wore.

A few weeks before the assassination, MS and Sadasivam visited Mahatma Gandhi at Birla House, New Delhi. The Mahatma, anguished by the discord among the principal communities of India as he then was, heard MS sing *Meera* bhajans with intense attention. Later, at that evening's prayer congregation, Gandhiji told her, 'Subbulakshmi, *Ramdhun tum gao*.' This daughter of Tamil Nadu then led the residents of Delhi in singing the other Hindi prayer song, with which Gandhiji's name is inextricably linked.

The MS legend has grown simultaneously with the list of her concerts. Accompanied by Radha Viswanathan and Vijaya Rajendran and a carefully selected team of instrumentalists. MS has given some two hundred 'benefit' recitals thus far. Doubtless, the list will grow. Simultaneously, she has been giving regular recitals. recordings, and has been singing at special occasions by request.

Her Carnatic repertory has deepened, with assistance from the late Musiri Subramania Iyer and Sri Semmangudi Srinivasier. Compositions of the trinity of Carnatic music apart, she invariably includes in her recitals devotional pieces composed by Annamacharya, Arunachala Kavi, Purandaradasa, Svati Tirunal, Papanasam Sivan. Likewise, bhajans of Mirabai, Bhattadri, Tulsidas and Narsinh Mehta rendered by her in the major Indian languages, give MS's recitals a pan-Indian character. Her singularly chaste recordings of the morning incantation of the Tirupati hills – the *Suprabhatam* – and the *Vishnu Sahasranamam* are played daily in thousands of homes.

MS is appreciative of the decorations and awards received by her: Padma Bhushan (1954), Sangita Kalanidhi (1968), the Magsaysay Award (1974), Padma Vibhushan (1975) and several honorary doctorates. But she wears them all ever so lightly.

Singing has become for MS a sacrament. Her voice can still reach dizzy octaval heights to a burst of applause from her listeners. But the real appeal of her concerts now lies elsewhere. It lies in the surpassing quality of their soul-force – the phrase she had used in the context of her mother.

Be it the Edinburgh International Festival of Arts (1963), the United Nations Day concert in New York (1966), the Festival of India at London (1982), Paris (1985), Moscow (1987), be it any *sabha* at Madras or the sanctum of her own private shrine room at Nungambakkam, Madras, when MS sings, she is in communion. If the Mahatma was deeply moved by MS's rendering of '*Vaishnava Jana To*' and '*Hari Tuma Haro*' so was an agnostic, Jawaharlal Nehru. Stirred by MS's music, Nehru gave MS the appellation 'Queen of Song', describing himself as 'a mere prime minister'. Then again, each time Jiddu Krishnamurti visited Madras in his later years, MS sang for him. Krishnamurti would sit in the middle of the small invited gathering, listen attentively – and observe.

A haiku describes the song of a flying bird as 'white'. MS's music has a multidimensional quality to it. One hears it and – sees it. The graduated ascent of her *alapana*, step by step as if to a hilltop shrine, its wayside pauses, resumptions, and the ecstasy of arrival, are an experience which transforms the listener into a pilgrim. Even those like the writer of this article who can claim no knowledge of Carnatic music, are enabled to uncover the *raga bhava* in each rendering, unmistakably. The *raga bhava* and, if one may coin a phrase, the *raga chitra*. When, for instance, in her rendering of Arunagirinathar's piece...*raga senchuruti*, MS sings the lines:

> *Deepa mangala jyoti*
> *Namo namah*

Even a sightless listener can see a lamp being lit somewhere between the singer and the audience. Even an agnostic, hearing her render '*Chandrashekharam Aasraye*' can see the figure of the Sage of Kancheepuram form itself, hand upraised in blessing over the radiant head of this singer-devotee.

Subbulakshmi and Sadasivam are now a *rishi dampati*, an ascetic twosome. They have an almost yogic detachment from the affairs of the world. A poignant song written in Tamil by Chakravarti Rajagopalachari, '*Kurai Onrum Illai*' (No Regrets Have I), which she renders with great feeling in her recitals, sums up the state of MS's mind.

Regrets if ever MS had any, have been subsumed in her self-surrender, through music, to the Divinity she worships. Aspirations, if ever MS had any, have been sublimated in the rapture with which she shares her faith with her listeners.

Eyes closed, her small frame swaying ever so slightly, her hands sculpting the air, Madurai Shanmukhavadivu Subbulakshmi transcends the stage that she sings from, transcends her audience, transcends even her own music. She goes beyond all these to that sun-dappled margin of Man's consciousness where, like creatures of the wild at a watering hole, he may slake his thirst.

To such a one we can only offer the tribute from the *'Guru Dasakam'*
Namasye chitta shuddhaye

(*The Indian Express*, March 12, 1988)

27

Vajpayee: The BJP's Star, and His Own Person

WHEN KRISHNA DEVI PRESENTED to her husband the school teacher Krishna Bihari Vajpayee, this day in 1924, a son, they must have wished the best and the most blessed for him, but could not have guessed his future. Or that of Gwalior where they were living, or of India. They could not have guessed by a long shot that the rulers of the fort-crowned principality, the Scindias, would one day cease to be rulers, would become part of a free Indian Republic's new polity where elected representatives of the people, not kings, would govern the land in the name of the people. They could not have imagined that the newborn would one day be someone the Scindias would look up to, would need, would stand with, stand against, only to stand with him again. And with him rising taller and taller with each passing year, each election, each decade.

But they would not have been surprised to find Atal Bihari absorbing the history and cultural ambience of a place which had faced and repulsed an attack by Mahmud Ghazni in 1021, been captured by Iltutmish in 1231, staying under Muslim rule till the Tomars gained control of it, inaugurating what was locally regarded as its golden age. There is such a thing as the atmospherics of one's child mindscape. Atal Bihari knew, certainly, of the musical genius Ramtanu of Rewa, better known as Tansen, who attended a music school at Gwalior and was to become one of Akbar's navaratnas.

A Tansen, I feel, slipped quietly into Atal Bihari's psyche – with aesthetic genius, a sense of measured melody, infused like in the great man's *dhrupad* with a thoughtful and carefully calibrated delineation of idea and expression and that genre's gentle but undeniable strength. As Tansen was in Akbar's court, his own person, so was this youth going to be in whatever he was to do, though in an organisation, bound by its rigid nostrums, its set views, its unalterable coda.

Atal Bihari was all of 14 going on 15 when, in 1939, he joined the Rashtriya Swayamsevak Sangh (RSS), a 'cultural' organisation, but with an unmistakeable political voltage. He was 94 going on 95 when he died, on August 16, 2018.

He had remained connected to that 'address' all his life. But connected with a thread that was his own, drawn from his own mind.

Atalji had been in politics, therefore, counting from 1939 to 2018, for 80 years.

In politics, throughout; in power briefly.

He was minister for external affairs (1977–1979) for some two years and then prime minister over three spells, for a little over six years (1996, 1998–2004), which makes a total of eight years. Eight out of 80 is a modest score. But a significant one, for being prime minister of India, is an extraordinary achievement.

Far more significant, in my view, are the 72 years that he spent in politics, but not in power or, to put it differently, when he was, so to say, outside office and inside the Opposition. Can the pre-Independence RSS be described as 'Opposition'? Not strictly, for it did not oppose or challenge the Raj as the Congress was doing. But it was opposed to the Congress, which was the leading and growing political force at the time. He was, like his chosen organisation was at that time, a naysayer.

After 1947, he was, of course, frontally, in the Opposition. Of the five decades that he was in Parliament, he was in the Opposition for four and more, as a Bharatiya Jana Sangh (BJS) member of Parliament, indeed, its star. And in that role, the role of a dissenter of distinctive sparkle, an opponent with his particular style of speaking and debating, as an occupant of the Opposition's bench in the Lok Sabha and the Rajya Sabha with a personal charisma that won friends across the political divide, Atalji became what he became – a national figure who was his party's ornament, but, more, his own person.

He had a ghar – the BJS and then the BJP, in which he resided with several others. But he also had a gharana – of which he was the creator, the practitioner, of which he was the sole occupant. If I was to give his gharana a name like Gwalior, Agra, Atrauli-Jaipur, Kirana, Patiala, to mark its flavour and its strength, I would not choose a place but a position and call it the Gharana Maryada – of dignity, decency, decorum and honour. One in which there is a sense of what is right, what is not right, what is done, what is not done.

From the Opposition's ranks, he never spoke a word that hurt, though it reached its target. He never made a point at the other's expense, never wanted to win a debate or even an argument. Jawaharlal Nehru on the treasury benches and he on the Opposition bench exchanged friendship with frankness, courtesy with candour. Atalji as minister and prime minister defended his policies with ardour but never said a word that could injure the maryada of a single Opposition leader or party.

Atalji could, therefore, say what he said in Parliament at Nehru's death in the most melodic and moving Hindi, which translates poorly as: 'The sun has set, we now have to find our way with the help of star-dust' – dhrupad at its highest. But there was also a tough political message in his obituary speech: 'His [Nehru's] way of carrying his opponents with him, that sajjanata, that mahanata will perhaps be difficult to come by in the near future…'.

(*Hindustan Times*, December 25, 2021)

28

A Message from Gandhi to a Very Troubled World

A BUST OF MOHANDAS Karamchand Gandhi is to be installed at the United Nations (UN) headquarters on December 14. The Secretary-General of the UN, Antonio Guterres, and our Foreign Minister, S. Jaishankar, are going to be present at the ceremony.

There is something very apposite about this, something very right because, though born in India, educated in England, and 'made' in South Africa, Gandhi has long belonged, for decades, to the common causes of humanity and the imperilled world. That this event is coinciding with India's rotational presidency of the UN's Security Council is of but passing relevance. That this should happen at a time when the world is teetering on the razor's edge of dire dangers is what gives it salience.

Five of these dangers stand out, menacingly.

One, a horrendous war between a behemoth of a nuclear State and a country much smaller, but backed morally and materially by other behemoths, three of them nuclear States themselves.

Two, some 1,500 nuclear weapons, which an act of error, terror or stealth can explode on us before we can say Happy New Year.

Three, the very real possibility, of which a post-COVID-19 world is but dimly cognisant: the horrifying possibilities of germ warfare.

Four, adding to the dangers of chemical and biological ogres, a dirty new gnome prowling about in the shape of cyber terror which can disable vast sections of human society and lurk behind it, its parent, artificial intelligence's twin, robotic malevolence.

Five, a climate crisis that is very likely to see water and food dry up at an unprecedented scale in the very near future, alongside bizarre acts of nature taking swipes at littoral States, drowning them in our collective cauldron of greed.

Gandhi's spirit has already been on that magnetic site in the shape of another stunning work of art. We, in India, are not really aware of the name of the Swedish sculptor Carl Fredrik Reutersward (1934–2016). His powerful creation is called, simply, Non-Violence. It is a bronze gun that is cocked, and yet, because its barrel is tied in a knot, cannot, will not, shoot. It is strength, self-curtailed. The masterpiece was installed in 1988 at the UN headquarters by then secretary-general Javier Pérez de Cuellar.

That work of art has been choreographing the self-curtailment of all weapons and their wielders who seek to intimidate, dominate and decimate. The knotted gun has been showing how much superior peace is to victory, which, unlike victory, does not humiliate, does not mutilate, does not annihilate any adversary. In a sense, Gandhi has been speaking through it, of how violence perpetrated from behind the shield of armour is utter cowardice, apart from being utter evil. He has been showing how the non-violence of the brave is far superior to the violence of the coward.

But now he is entering the rare portals of the UN in his own likeness. Doubtless, the greatly articulate and honest speaker that he is, Guterres will speak words that rise to the occasion. (He said memorably only the other day that, 'the world is on a highway to climate hell'.) As will our minister for external affairs.

But may we spare a moment to ask ourselves what Gandhi may himself say, if, by another incredibility typical of him, he is surrealistically present? It may be something like this:

Mr Secretary-General, Honourable Shri Jaishankar, Excellencies.

Being here on the grounds of this great organisation, I feel both happy and sad. Happy, because I can see people from all parts of the globe gathered here as one family, but sad to recognise great and deep discord among its members. Not just discord, but what is worse, distrust. I believe in trusting. Trust begets trust. Suspicion is foetid and stinks. He who trusts has never yet lost in the world. The UN has not lost the world. But has it won the world?

I must also own that I feel both honoured and embarrassed by the occasion. I feel honoured, because in placing here the bust of an Indian who regarded himself as a farmer, a weaver, a cobbler, and one among the lowliest of the low, this world organisation is recognising, in these times where material success is worshipped, the down and out. But I am also embarrassed because I think it is a waste of good money to spend it on erecting a clay or metallic statue of the figure of a man who is himself made of clay.

Seeing here, the beautiful sculpture of the knotted gun, I am reminded of the moment when walking to my prayer, I saw a gun. It was almost the last thing I saw before a great white light took me to my Rama, who to me represents truth. I learnt to invoke Rama from my saintly mother and an equally saintly woman who worked in our home, whenever darkness gripped me. The knotted gun tells us in our dark times to tie up hatred and fear into a knot. Believe me, it takes more courage to knot up a gun than to fire it. I should know.

You have all assembled here to listen to the words of the secretary-general, and those of India's foreign minister, not mine. But I will crave your indulgence to mention three persons none of you may have heard of – Ganesh Shankar Vidyarthi, Sachin Mitra and Smritish Banerjea. They were all young men, killed during the insane riots that accompanied the partitioning of India, while trying to stop frenzied mobs from attacking and murdering each other. They had families to support, ambitions to fulfil. Yet, they plunged themselves into the fire with no hatred, no anger, only calm. Fear did not figure in their dictionaries.

I want to ask the nations represented here: Are you willing to sacrifice your egos, if not your lives, for the love of peace? Is there, in your governments or in your societies, a single man ready to die without hatred in his heart in an attempt to pacify rioting crowds and prevent nuclear terror and war? Is there any government that is ready to say it will start to dismantle its death machines unmindful of others not doing the same? Any government ready to say it will not just join, but lead the world in reducing our fouling up of the planet's air and its fragile surface? And, most important – any government that will atone for wrongs done out of sheer pride of race, religion or out of naked greed for more territory or power? Does 'sorry' figure in your dictionaries?

And so, when I heard you, Mr foreign minister, say, 'Over the last 75 years since Independence, India has mostly used force defensively, almost always within its own borders,' I was glad for its simplicity and honesty. Countries cannot threaten or attack others. Whilst they must resist aggression by force if necessary, they should know their doing so will have moral authority only if they have not disfigured their records by similar intentions or acts of their own.

Mr Secretary-General, I thank you for your patience and wish you and this great organisation Godspeed.

(*Hindustan Times*, December 11, 2022)

29

The Scorching Truth of Rushdie's Ordeal

I WAS BROUGHT UP on Tulsidas's *Sri Ramcharitmanas*. My father read the whole text out to me *chaupai* by *chaupai*, *doha* by *doha*, not leaving out the *sorathas* and the *chhands*, some of which he sang aloud, as instructed in his childhood by his father.

On the grounds of the Theosophical Society in Chennai, where my wife and I walk regularly, there is a small stone image of Hanuman, surrounded by foliage. He has the most gentle and benign visage, and with his palms brought together in a namaskar, he looks like he may have once been part of a set that included Rama, Sita and Lakshmana. But now he stands by himself there, blessing anyone who may choose to seek his benediction. I stop for a moment before this stone image each time I pass it and repeat the lines from the *Hanuman Chalisa* that I have heard sung in the golden voice of M.S. Subbulakshmi:

Nasey rog harey sab pida
Japat nirantar Hanumat bira
(Demolishes disease, annihilates suffering, He, In those who chant his name unceasingly.)

On Saturday, August 13, when I crossed the statue, I prayed intensely and spontaneously for Hanuman to come flying with the magical herbs of healing to someone who I know only through his stature as a writer and as a man of exceptional courage under stress. As I did so, the life and work of Salman Rushdie passed through my mind's eye as in the footage of some deep tragedy.

That the author of *Midnight's Children* should be battling for his life as the 75th anniversary of that defining hour is upon us makes Rushdie a figure in history. He has moved from the columns of literature to the casements of history. From being a gripping chronicler of the freedom and Partition of India, he has become a direct player in the subcontinent's life after the night of August 14/15, 1947.

At the time of writing, all I know with the rest of the world is that Rushdie has been taken off a ventilator and is recovering, a day after he was stabbed as he prepared to give a lecture in New York.

He is undergoing, for no reason other than for being who he is, what an estimated 1 to 2 million who were attacked and who died, did, during the Partition riots of 1946–1947. They were attacked and they died just for being Hindu, or Sikh or Muslim. Among them were those that were old, those that were young and those that were mere infants. And women. At the hands of men who were not Hindu, Sikh or Muslim so much as they were brutes, they suffered what was worse than assault. I need not elaborate.

'Rushdie must not die' is the thought that has seized millions across the world. Millions, among whom I find my place. He must survive and see that his visualising all that he did in *Midnight's Children* was not just the work of a creative writer, but the visualising by one who was living in his veins and in his brain what he was describing. One who, having been born just a few days before the Independence and Partition of India, was part of that great 'tryst with destiny' as Jawaharlal Nehru so memorably called the dawn of freedom and also the great trauma that enveloped it.

That hundreds upon hundreds of thousands suffered indescribable pain at that time is a fact of history that the children of that midnight or children of those children can come to terms with, howsoever difficult that may be. But that what caused that pain has not gone away, that it lurks in the minds of the vengeful and the violent in all the three countries that were once undivided India, is the scorching truth that Rushdie's ordeal demands we do not forget.

Ramchandra Gandhi, the philosopher-grandson of the Mahatma, once said unforgettably: 'Gandhi was not felled by three bullets. He stopped three bullets in their track.' Truer words have not been spoken, in philosophy's response to history.

Gandhi's assassination was the result of judgment blinded by intolerance.

The attack on Rushdie comes from the same source.

We don't have a Bernard Shaw or an Einstein to put in words the fearful truth of our traumatic witnessing. But we do not need eloquence to respond to them. We need honesty – and the courage for that honesty – to see that the greats of history apart, it is innocents who will suffer, who will pay a price they do not deserve to, if intolerance is not checked and stopped from becoming violent.

Our innate dislike of hate and violence must prevail over the attempts of those, no longer few, who wish to spread them on our subcontinent. As Rushdie wages his battle against his wounds, we hold our breaths in faith in the freedom we won 75 years ago.

(*Hindustan Times*, August 15, 2022)

30

Dadabhai Naoroji: A Leader Who Served India and Britain

ON THE DAY RISHI Sunak rose to the prime ministership of Great Britain, a long-time Parsi resident of London, Rusi Dalal, mailed me to say this historic event happened in a year that rhymes with another Indo-United Kingdom (UK) landmark moment.

This year, 2022, marks the 130th anniversary of the election, in 1892, of the first person of Indian origin to the House of Commons. Dadabhai Naoroji (September 4, 1825–June 30, 1917). Hailed as the Grand Old Man of India, Naoroji was a Parsi by birth, a Mumbaikar by upbringing, a teacher (of Gujarati) by calling, a scholar by aptitude, an economist by training, a philosopher by natural bent, a Londoner by extended domicile, a politician by instinct, a leader by history's design. And what a leader!

Dinyar Patel's masterly biography of the great man, *Dadabhai Naoroji: Pioneer of Indian Nationalism*, tells us how the 67-year-old Indian who made a name for himself as one of the founders of the Indian National Congress in 1885, and a Liberal politician, contested the Holborn seat the very next year.

Holborn, a strongly Conservative area, defeated the Indian liberal. The then Conservative prime minister, Lord Salisbury, famously or, rather, notoriously said that Britain was not yet ready to elect a Black man. The description offended all men and women of taste in both countries. But Naoroji was undeflected from his aim to enter Parliament in London and speak for the underdog, for women (who had not yet got the vote), for the elderly, for Irish Home Rule, and the end of Britain's economic exploitation of its largest and most populous colony, India.

Naoroji, who had already served as the second president of the Indian National Congress (from 1886 to 1887) and was going to do so again, from 1893 to 1894 and 1906 to 1907, not only found no contradiction but a felicity in being politically active and 'office-holding' in both countries.

In 1892, he moved to the largely working-class constituency of Central Finsbury, and defeated, very narrowly, the Conservative candidate. Naoroji was elected to the House of Commons by three votes (some estimates put the margin, post-recount, to five) giving Naoroji the hilariously accurate and alliterative moniker of 'narrow majority'. To be strictly accurate – something Naoroji's rectitude would demand – he was the second member of Parliament (MP) of Asian descent, coming after the Eurasian MP David Ochterlony Dyce Sombre, who was unseated for bribery during his campaign in Sudbury, Suffolk, nine months after getting elected.

Before his Finsbury win, Naoroji met a young student of law in Inner Temple, 23-year-old Mohandas K. Gandhi, and either left an everlasting impression or had an everlasting impact on the future leader. He also met another aspiring lawyer then enrolled at Lincoln's Inn – 16-year-old Mohammed Ali Jinnah, who was to serve for a while as Naoroji's secretary. Jinnah had the distinction of hearing Naoroji's maiden speech in the House of Commons from the Visitors' Gallery.

As a Liberal MP in the House of Commons between 1892 and 1895, Naoroji made more than a mark. He cut a swathe of influence with his eloquence, his punctilious regard for factual documentation, his deep study of Britain's draining of Indian wealth, and his complete freedom from racial bias, sectarian tilting, and personal animosities. By all that he so forcibly argued in Parliament, Naoroji came to represent, vicariously, the mass of humanity that his mentee Gandhi termed as 'India's dumb millions'.

Conservative in terms of party affiliation and conservative in terms of political belief, Sunak has little in common with Naoroji other than an India-touched firstness. But there can be no denying the aptness of Dalal's enthusiastic mail about the India-descended 42-year-old becoming prime minister and India-born Naoroji becoming MP in rhyming years – 1892 and 2022.

We rejoice in Sunak, in the fact of him, as we did in the fact of Kamala Harris on that half-Tamil United States (US) national becoming the vice president of the US. But no one can envy the young man. Angela Rayner, deputy leader of the Labour Party, said: 'Rishi Sunak has been crowned by Tory MPs. He has no mandate and the British people have had no say.' And, in her sharp tweet, she sign-posted 'general elections'. If Sunak has indeed been crowned, it is a crown of thorns. He has an economic mess to clear.

But he has to do things beyond setting Britain right. Most importantly, he has to do something that needs not just the fire of youth but the light of truth to address the globe's climate crisis.

Naoroji's seminal *Poverty and Un-British Rule* appeared in 1901. It turned 'British' from a noun to an adjective, challenging the country of his adoption to give 'being British' a moral height by stopping the immiseration of its great colony, India. At the COP27 summit in Sharm el-Sheikh, Sunak has a great opportunity to announce British decisions which, by example, and not just promises, can slow down the polluting and heating up of planet Earth.

Sunak's is, like Naoroji's, a narrow majority. But if the Grand Old Man of India, despite that handicap, could challenge Britain to be British and do right by India's political economy, so can the new prime minister challenge Britain to give a great 'British' lead to do right by the world's climate.

(*Hindustan Times*, November 5, 2022)

31

Great Arcs of Resonance:
A Tribute to Pandit Ravi Shankar

THE GEORGIAN BUILDING ON Mayfair's South Audley Street, which the short-tempered but far-sighted V.K. Krishna Menon had obtained for the High Commissioner of India on a ninety years' lease, now houses its Nehru Centre.

The Centre is readying itself for Jawaharlal Nehru's birth anniversary. There are to be no speeches, no placings of flowers (the bust, ordered from Delhi, is yet to arrive), but there is an air of preparation, a quiet bustle, for something special that is to be experienced. Aziz Ahmad Saheb, a North London-based calligrapher, puts the finishing touches to a white signboard on which he has drawn in gentle tones the words: 'Jawaharlal Nehru, November 14, 1889 to May 27, 1964. Recital by Pandit Ravi Shankar.' When thanked for his virtually honorary artwork, he says '*Yeh to meri khushnasi bhi hai*' ('It is my good fortune to have been asked to do this work').

Surinder Singh, a wizard with tools, has put together a sturdy new wooden stage for the performance in the Centre's theatre. He and his brother have sawn away for many hours on planks which Surinder has chosen with care. The professional pride of Punjabi workmanship stands exemplified in their product. He also does the stage lights, creating three pools of glowing amber that settle on the stage and on the walls behind it like as many suns at twilight. We are in the heart of high-tech London. But this expertise is Indian. And it is first class. That, one tells oneself, is what Indian skills are all about.

Pandit Ravi Shankar is to arrive in an hour. He will check the sound system, practise (does he need to?) for a while before the audience arrives, and then play for an hour. But the man with the sound 'system' – another bearded strong-armed son of the Punjab – has not yet turned up. We have another aspect of India there. A car sent to fetch the maestro, we realise, has left quite a while ago and so he should be here any minute. But as of now, there are no mikes, no amplifiers with us. Little bubbles of panic rise in the Centre's psyche. An alternative PA set is quickly sent for. The services of Kumar, the High Commissioner's *asthana-vidwan* on electrical matters, is turned to, like a trusty family general practitioner when the specialist fails to deliver. The tranquil Bengali assures us he will get the equipment in a matter of minutes. After what seems an age, both systems arrive – together! The young sardar explains in his London accent: 'Thought I noo my wye roun'ere but y' know ...' He shrugs his muscular shoulders, heaving the stuff up just in time. This too is India, Indian serendipity.

From the brink of assured collapse, the situation is retrieved. The system is just about up when the car drives in. The driver had been given an incorrect address and had therefore spent over half an hour looking for the house.

He kept looking for Osborne Square instead of Osborne Street. Raviji says smilingly, without the slightest reproach, 'That is why we are behind time.' I do not – dare not – tell him that the delay has saved the Centre much embarrassment. Had Raviji arrived on time, he would not have found the sound system in position. We take him, Sukanyaji and little Anoushka (who is to accompany Raviji on the tanpura) to the theatre. The sound system is tested and found to be 'perfect'; the lights too 'excellent'. Raviji tunes his sitar and plays for a few moments. As the trial notes from his instrument suffuse the hall, flow through the doorway like invisible mist on to the stairway, we ponder the significance of the moment.

What is he thinking of, this samrat of Indian music, as he tunes his instrument? I tell Shireem Isal, the very quiet, very able administrator of Raviji's programmes in Britain, of my days at school with Shubhendra or Shubho as Raviji called his son. He was very musical at school, Shubho was and I, anything but. He could play the sitar, sing. Neither of us was particularly good at books, preferring wanders in the school's ample grounds to study. We crossed over and over again aimlessly. And Shubho, quietly one autumn day, had now done the final crossing. Raviji had seen and placed me as 'Shubho's friend'.

This is to be Raviji's first recital after Shubho's going. The checking over, with very few words said, he goes to get ready for the programme.

The hall fills up. The chairs first, and then the floor. The High Commissioner arrives with his wife. Kathleen Raine the poet-philosopher comes with her granddaughter, followed by George Harrison and his wife. Rupert Snell, the scholar-teacher of Hindi and Braj at the School of Oriental and Asian Studies is there, as is the distinguished poet and teacher of Bengali, William Radice. The London-based sitar player, Nishat Ganguly, comes as does the talented young sitarist Nishat Khan, a son and student of Ustad Imrat Khan and nephew of Ustad Vilayat Khan. Baroness Shreela Flather, the Indian-born member of the House of Lords, and her husband are there among scores of Londoners. Raviji has brought the different colours of the Indian rainbow

– Hindu, Muslim, Sikh, Christian, Parsi and Jaina – together under a British sky, on London's cosmopolitan soil.

As Raviji is conducted from the green room, he tells me about Abhishek Kaushal, who is to accompany him on the tabla. 'He is my protégé ... is protégé the right word? Or you could introduce him as my shishya!' On reaching the hall, Raviji needs a path to the stage. The floor-seated audience has left no aisle! And so he is conducted along the room's edge to the platform amid respectful applause. There is a hidden anxiety in the applause. It seems to ask: 'Has he overcome the harsh demands of time?' A brief word of welcome ('Not more than a few seconds long', he has requested) is offered while he tunes their tanpuras for Anoushka and Archana Rajan. That done, and the tabla tested, Raviji becomes still for a moment. Still, and yet still journeying. Walking on another aisle, through another crowd, a crowd of memories, to a raised clearing of the purest contemplation. And then from that hushed centre, Raviji commences his recital. He plays the raga Poorvi, transporting the audience eastwards on the wings of the raga's uncompromising grammar. And once he has reached his destination, the fretwork cannot hold the vibrations down. Grammar yields to poetry. Each percussive touch releases great arcs of resonance, linking the player with the listener and both, with aquifers of primordial sound. At the climax of the raga's ascent, Raviji's arm goes up like a flag unfurled. There is a detonation of applause which has more to it now than respect. It has celebration. The celebration of a man who blended talent with tapas. And of a man who has paid Time its dues with such elan as to make it look like a revenue collector before the Jagirdar who has just gifted his estate away.

(*The Hindu*, April 4, 1993)

32

S. Radhakrishnan: A Man of Egoless Impartiality

TEACHERS' DAY OR SARVEPALLI Radhakrishnan's birthday was on September 5. So, writing this column about our philosopher-president may be a little late. But the weeks and months before he relinquished the office of the President of India on May 13, 1967, and immediately after, merit, in this 75th year of our Independence, recapitulation independently of the birthday.

Shortly before he left Rashtrapati Bhavan, his stature soared higher than its already great height. His re-election to a second term seemed almost certain. But in his Republic Day eve broadcast that year (1967), Radhakrishnan spoke his mind. Calling the past year, which had been through a crippling drought, the worst since Independence, he said: '…even after making allowance for all the difficulties of the situation, we cannot forgive widespread incompetence and the gross mismanagement of our resources'. The Opposition used the observation in the rallies that were taking place for the elections that year. The Congress won but was mauled. The Opposition to the Left and the Right declared their support for a second term for Radhakrishnan. But his equation with Prime Minister Indira Gandhi, not surprisingly, ran into difficulties. And soon, it was clear that though Congress president K. Kamaraj was emphatically in favour of Radhakrishnan, the prime minister seemed inclined to favour the vice president, the distinguished Dr Zakir Husain.

Radhakrishnan was not one to press his case and soon made it clear that he wanted to retire. Derek Hill, an outstanding portraitist, was commissioned to create a painting of the statesman for All Souls College, Oxford. The work, which hangs in that college library, shows the withdrawn yet happy resignation on his face.

Having demitted office as India's second president, he retired to what was effectively his home town, Madras, as Chennai was then called. The scholar-teacher in him chose not to linger in New Delhi, seeking sanctuary in one of Lutyens' bungalows through the patronising indulgence of the incumbents of high office. As vice president for 10 years (1952–1962) and then as president

(1962–1967), he had seen and understood the Capital for all it is and has been – the pavilion of power and its shadow plays.

With his priceless and countless books, his son (the historian Sarvepalli Gopal) and his daughter-in-law, 79-year-old Radhakrishnan returned to 'Girija', the gracious home he had built way back in 1934 in Mylapore, by the sea on the Marina. He had made it when he was vice-chancellor of Andhra University and hoped to serve Madras's provincial government as director of public instruction. Instead, he was denied the position, an Englishman senior to him in the Indian Educational Service being appointed to it – just as well for him. He was now returning to it as a former head of the Indian State, who had gained worldwide recognition and one who, as Rashtrapati, had brought a rare distinction to that office, seeing three prime ministers into office – Jawaharlal Nehru, Lal Bahadur Shastri and Indira Gandhi. And two wars – the Sino-Indian war of 1962 and the India-Pak war of 1965, the first giving India deep trauma and the second a sense of victory and vindication.

Madras welcomed its Telugu son with warmth. Chakravarti Rajagopalachari, older by a decade, and a former incumbent, as Governor General of India, of the house Radhakrishnan had just vacated in Delhi, sent him a welcome message. Saying he need not lavish fresh praise on Radhakrishnan as he is venerated already, Rajaji quoted Shakespeare from 'King John':

> To gild refined gold, to paint the lily,
> To throw a perfume on the violet,
> To smooth the ice, or add another hue
> Unto the rainbow, or with taper-light
> To seek the beauteous eye of heaven to garnish,
> Is wasteful, and ridiculous excess.

But the emptiness of retirement soon took over. S. Gopal writes in his amazingly objective biography of his father: 'A succession of grey hours took the place of years of public recognition and acclaim.' Then, in September 1968, not long after his birthday, he suffered a stroke.

By the time he heard of the Templeton prize for Progress in Religion being given to him, his formidable mental powers had gone into a region where none could reach.

Every governor, vice president and president of India may with benefit ponder these words of his biographer-son Gopal: 'In his five years as the country's president...the people learned to look to him as the impartial guardian of the public interest, befriending and advising the government but also capable if need be of standing apart from it.' And this without transgressing the letter or spirit of the Constitution.

Constitutional authorities should be impartial guardians, capable of standing apart from the government if need be.

Who or what determines that 'need be'?

Egoless impartiality.

(*Hindustan Times*, September 10, 2022)

33

In Nehru's Death, a Precedent for Rectitude Was Set

THE CRISIS INDIA FACED on May 27, 1964, was unprecedented. Jawaharlal Nehru, our prime minister, had been unwell since January of that year, after a stroke in Bhubaneswar, where he was attending a Congress session. And all who saw him during the intervening months found him unwell. Harivansh Rai Bachchan, the great Hindi poet – a translation into English of whose masterpiece, *Madhushala*, Nehru contributed a memorable foreword to – noticed something unusual: On the dew-laden lawn of his home at Teen Murti, New Delhi, Nehru's walking feet left two impressions. One foot left the marks of feet, each separate from the other. The other foot drew a line, as it dragged itself.

India was debilitated as a result.

But it was not disabled.

On May 23, Union Home Secretary V. Viswanathan sought to meet the Secretary to the President, Subimal Dutt. The two civil servants were seasoned officials, both from the Indian Civil Service. Viswanathan would become governor of three states, and Dutt, who had been Nehru's foreign secretary (1955 to 1961), would become India's first high commissioner to Bangladesh.

One can imagine them conferring in the imposing hush of the Secretary's room in Rashtrapati Bhavan with controlled but real concern. Viswanathan told Dutt something the latter was not unaware of. But he was now hearing it from the most authentic and credentialed voice. The prime minister, Viswanathan said, was not well.

This was information, but on a matter of the highest importance. But more, it came with the concomitant request that the President should give thought to what would need to be done 'in case there was a vacancy in the office of the prime minister'.

Viswanathan and Dutt had not held the offices they had held in the past, nor the ones they occupied at that point, without learning what weathering means. Concerned they were, in fact, deeply worried. Panicky, they were not. They knew that the matter was urgent, grave. But they were taking time by the forelock. Nehru was ill, very likely dying. And as life lingered yet, something called contingency planning had to be done. No coyness was allowed there, no delay.

Message conveyed by high Malayali to high Bengali, the matter was left for the holder of the tallest office in the land, the great Telugu master of Sanskrit, the Veda, the *Itihasa*, Bradley and Adi Sankara, the best-known commentator on the *Gita*, President Sarvepalli Radhakrishnan, to respond to. Radhakrishnan had no precedents to go by, true. But he had the profundity of wisdom to turn to, the reflexes of his intelligence to actuate. No prime minister of India had died in office, no vacancy had so far occurred in the station.

Radhakrishnan had written in *The Hindu View of Life* (1927): 'The cards in the game of life are given to us. We do not select them. They are traced to our past karma, but we can call as we please, lead what suit we will, and as we play, we gain or lose. And there is freedom.'

Now, Radhakrishnan had the freedom that came with his responsibility and the prerogatives that devolved on him with his discretion to lead his 'suit'. The one difficulty he faced was the deep sorrow he was feeling over the condition of a man who was not just his prime minister but also a thought-partner, a valued friend with whom friendship was frank and conversation candid.

His son and biographer Sarvepalli Gopal was there with him, in Rashtrapati Bhavan, and Radhakrishnan and Gopal must have talked about the crisis and its imminent deepening. Gopal writes in his brilliant biography of his father that the President acted quietly and, without either delay or fuss, decisively.

Since the Constitution did not contemplate a situation where India was without an elected prime minister, no vacuum, he figured, should be allowed.

He decided that he would swear in the second senior-most member of the cabinet, Gulzarilal Nanda, as prime minister, as soon as possible if Nehru died.

When the vacancy did arise, he told a dazed Nanda that he would swear him in as prime minister that afternoon, and he did. He also made it clear to Nanda that this was an interim arrangement, to end as soon as the Congress Legislative Party (CLP) elected its new leader.

Radhakrishnan knew, as did all political observers, that Nehru's most credible successor, and one Nehru seemed to have anointed in one way and another, was Lal Bahadur Shastri. But propriety demanded that the CLP take that call.

In the hand given to India by destiny, another stalwart – incidentally like the President, also from the south of the Vindhyas – bestirred himself. K. Kamaraj, now Congress president, and Radhakrishnan enjoyed a close rapport. Strong as a granite hill, he conferred with Radhakrishnan and of course with Congress seniors, and saw to it that the stature enjoyed by Shastri was quickly converted into support without any wrangling.

Election yes, squabbles no. And on June 9, through a veil of sighs, Shastri assumed office as India's second prime minister, but with no hood of doom covering the change-over.

Atal Bihari Vajpayee, then in the Rajya Sabha, paid a condolence tribute in his unique Hindi that belongs to the annals of literature, not the Hansards of legislature. He said, with Nehru gone, 'The sun has set; we will now have to find our way about with the aid of starlight.'

An effulgent orb sun had indeed set, but the night that followed gave us the starlight of duty to guide us through the dark.

Recalling these transactions, on the 58th anniversary of Nehru's passing, we may tell ourselves that Viswanathan, Dutt, Radhakrishnan and Kamaraj did what their duties told them to do without any ego goading them, nor any motive other than doing one's duty, and without being prevented by anyone else from doing so either.

Power was seen as trust, its transitions as the processes of a hand dealt to us to use with respect, not ambition.

Respect. That was the operative emotion. With trust as its turning key.

Fear there was, but only of one's conscience.

Nehru was not a man of religion. But he was a man of conscience. S. Gopal has given in the same book what I believe is the best description of Nehru's 'within': 'Nehru was…a reverent agnostic, without religious faith but with a religious feeling.'

All those men had and showed respect. Viswanathan and Dutt demonstrated respect for prudence where procedures did not exist, Radhakrishnan for sheer propriety where no precedent existed, Kamaraj for robust common sense where no convention guided, and Shastri, with the humility of the good, respect for destiny.

Along with Vajpayee in his seat on the Opposition benches, all of them were egoless instruments of Bharat's *Bhagya Vidhata*.

In an unprecedented situation that they were in that day in 1964, they set a precedent for rectitude in public life.

(*Hindustan Times*, May 27, 2023)

34

Unusual Flower

IT HAS TO DO with the fact that Kamala Harris (b.1964), the vice president of the United States of America, is fighting for that country's highest office.

It has to do with that, else the name, Kamala, derived from the Sanskrit for 'lotus', which is our national flower, would not be occupying my thoughts as it has been these last few days.

This column is about those whose name is Kamala. Many readers, not some, but many, may groan and exclaim: Has the man no sense of priorities? Absurd, they would say, an absurd subject. They would be right, of course. But the human mind is notorious for being just that – absurd. The etymology of 'absurd' says it comes from the Latin, *absurdus*, meaning incongruous, out of tune. Being 'in tune' is standard. Being out of tune, like the celebrated crack in S.D. Burman's singing voice, can be a not entirely unwelcome change. So, despite several competing 'issues' of vital urgency demanding a columnist's attention, I have let 'Kamala' prevail.

The first Kamala that came to my mind's recall was Kamala Nehru (1899–1936), immortalised, ironically, by the words in her husband Jawaharlal Nehru's dedication of his *An Autobiography* (1936) – 'To Kamala who is no more.' The book had been written over many months preceding but published just after Kamala died. Theirs was an uneasy marriage, partly because the Nehru household was very different from the simpler background of the Kauls that she came from. Her closest friend was Prabhavati Narayan (1904–1973), whose own marriage to the revolutionary, Jayaprakash Narayan, cherished as 'JP', was not without tensions for the opposite reason. It was he who had to do the difficult adjustments. 'Adopted' by Kasturba and Mohandas Gandhi, Prabhavati had been reared in the *ashramic* tradition of celibacy – no recipe for marital bliss. A sheaf of letters written by Kamala to Prabhavati over the years of their *abhinna* (inseparable) friendship, was handed over, in his typical trusting generosity, after Prabhavati's death, by JP to Kamala's daughter, Indira Gandhi. They are not in the public domain.

Kamaladevi Chattopadhyay (1903–1988), after whom, we are told, Kamala Harris's mother named her daughter, was born between Kamala Nehru and Prabhavati Narayan, both of whom she knew well. And apart from being famous as a woman of uncommon intelligence, independence and even insouciance, Kamaladevi was the best MP, cabinet minister, ambassador, governor, vice president and president India never had. Reason: she did not lobby for those positions and when sounded out for some of them, 'couldn't care less' for the offers. Apart from the best this-and-that she was not, the list of the great things she was included being a dancer, a catalyst for India's artisanal integrity, a champion of gender justice without any cultivated slatternliness, a socialist without the ism, a Congresswoman apart from the herd. But she too was, like Nehru's, Harindranath Chattopadhyay's very differently wired wife. So different from her husband (who was five years older and lived two years longer) that one hesitates to use the term, 'wife', for her.

The third Kamala to come to mind is not just the most beautiful of all Kamalas I have known of or known but, with Rajmata Gayatri Devi of Jaipur, one of the most beautiful women I have beheld. Kamala Markandaya (1924–2004), who would have been 100 this year, wrote a clutch of novels centred on India, from her gentle but not always consoling perch in London. I saw her first in that city when I was 11 and she 32. Her great novel, *Nectar in a Sieve*, (title drawn from Coleridge's eponymous poem with the line: 'Work without Hope draws nectar in a sieve,/ And Hope without an object cannot live.') had just come out, making waves. I saw her last, once again, in London, where I was working, when I was 51 and she a stunning 72. By this time, another dozen novels by her had been published, all of them of the highest quality but not as successful as her first, and she was now almost as silent as she was beautiful. Other novelists and novels had hit the market which had hit new technologies of promotion and marketing. *A Silence of Desire* (1960) was – is – a high-class work, about, at its core, marriage. A bureaucrat with the very likely name of Dandekar suspects his wife of disloyalty – nothing new! – as he notices her going away quietly on afternoons. But he is soon chastened by the knowledge that a tumour caused her to go on those afternoons to a witch doctor for a cure. By 1994, when she still had 10 years ahead of her, Kamala Markandaya said to me she was curtailing her visits to others. A private person always, she was now a recluse. Coleridge's lines seemed to imbue her inner life.

Another Kamala I cannot forget spelt her name without the middle 'a' – Kamla. Her married surname was Chaudhry which, as the scholar of medieval and modern Hindi, Rupert Snell, tells us in his remarkable new book (*The Self & The World*, Rajkamal, 2024) 'has more than twenty variations'. But Kamla Chaudhry (1920–2006) had no 'variations'; she was singular in every way.

Married to a civil servant, she should have had what is the stuff of nuptial blessings – 'a long and prosperous married life'. But Khem Chaudhry, as Wikipedia tells us, was murdered one night 'as the couple slept' in the north-western province where he was posted. A letter from Tagore, who had known her as a young student at Santiniketan, saved her from despair and she decided to study psychology in the United States of America and work, which is when another singular person, Ahmedabad's most famous son, the astrophysicist, Vikram Sarabhai, came into Kamla's life. Giving her a prized and tough responsibility at Ahmedabad Textile Industry's Research Association, Vikram, who was married to the famous dancer, Mrinalini Sarabhai, embarked on a beautiful and original equation with Kamla. The word for relationships in Hindi is *rishta*. The novelist, Amrita Pritam, has said famously '*rishton ko koyi naam nahin de sakta*' (you cannot give relationships a name).

R.K. Laxman, the brilliant cartoonist, was married twice, serially, and to a Kamala each time. The first Kamala (b. 1924) to be Mrs R.K. Laxman, 'Baby' and, later, 'Kumari' Kamala the celebrated dancer, turns 90 this year. My generation remembers her with admiration. After his divorce, Laxman married his niece, a writer of children's books, also a Kamala – a felicity of which one might tell the great man, adapting his pocket cartoon's title, 'You Said it – Twice.'

I will round off with a Kamala whom our generation has not seen. Daughter of the polymath, Sir Asutosh Mookerjee, this Kamala (1895–1923) was given in marriage at the age of nine, only to be widowed within a year. Remarkably for those times, Sir Asutosh had Kamala married again at age 13, only to be widowed yet again within a year. Kamala was herself to die at age 28. Sir Asutosh's agony recalls Lear's indictment of death in Shakespeare's great tragedy about his daughter, Cordelia.

The story of the great Calcuttan's daughter has to bring to mind the agony of Abhaya's parents in Calcutta and Sunil Chatterjee's heart-churning rendering of Lear's lines: '*Keno ekti kukur-er, ekti ashwar-er, eedur-er-i thakbe jibon, aar tumi…aar tumi…shudhu niswas rohito?*'

All names are precious, Kamala among them. I have lingered on it for the persons it evokes in me and their stories which are not just about them but about life.

(*The Telegraph*, September 22, 2024)

35

Eternal Verities

ALL THE VIOLENCE THAT has marred our bilateral relations and all the mutual trust erosion that has occurred notwithstanding, I believe Prime Minister Modi cannot but want concord, not discord, with Pakistan.

Posthumous conferrings of the Bharat Ratna have, with one or two exceptions, occasioned the thought in me: 'Why could the honouring not have been done in his lifetime?' The ones announced last Friday of those on the late M.S. Swaminathan and the two former prime ministers, Chaudhary Charan Singh and P.V. Narasimha Rao, have not been exceptions. But that response apart, they reminded me of the very first Bharat Ratna that was conferred posthumously.

President Sarvepalli Radhakrishnan was woken up at 2 a.m. on January 11, 1966 to be told that Prime Minister Lal Bahadur Shastri had died of a heart attack in Tashkent two hours earlier. For one who is 78 himself and in none too great health, to be startled by such an interruption at that hour is no simple thing. But Radhakrishnan was no ordinary man. Apart from the fact that he had in Yezdi Gundevia, of the ICS, an ace secretary and in Sarvepalli Gopal, a historian son who gave him immense, if also inconspicuous, strength, the philosopher head of State had a mind that had been honed by years of discipline to be poised, unruffled and – awake. Radhakrishnan moved swiftly to summon the senior-most cabinet minister, Gulzarilal Nanda, and swore him in as acting prime minister with the clear understanding that the CLP, which commanded a majority in the Lok Sabha, would have to elect its new leader very soon. His priority as president was to ensure that India would not be without a prime minister.

It was after his duties by the Constitution had been done that the president sat down to grieve for the man he had sworn in as prime minister only 18 months earlier upon the death of Jawaharlal Nehru. Lal Bahadur, as he called his prime minister 17 years younger than himself, had done the nation proud by helming a decisive victory over the aggressive forces of neighbouring Pakistan only a few weeks earlier. As one in whom the supreme command of the Indian armed forces was vested, President Radhakrishnan knew what that victory meant.

Asking, in those wee hours of that January day, for a radio broadcast to the nation to be arranged at 8 a.m., he prepared the address within his uniquely puissant mind. Said President Radhakrishnan to his fellow citizens in his speech: 'I had once or twice, spoken to Lal Bahadur about the greatest distinction we have in our gift of Bharat Ratna and I had decided to announce this award on him on the Republic Day. I do so now with a sad heart and confer on him the Bharat Ratna posthumously.'

When the president had spoken to the prime minister 'once or twice' about the Bharat Ratna, it was obviously in the context of it being conferred on him for the extraordinary victory achieved under his leadership in the war. We do not know what Shastri's response to the presidential sounding was, but we may assume that it would have been consistent with his temperament – extreme self-denying humility. Shastri knew how the nation had hailed the armed forces for their stellar performance in repelling the aggression and how his own standing among the people of India had zoomed. As Shastri himself said to a senior writer, from a time when watching the mandatory documentaries put up by cinema houses before the start of the main film they laughed at the diminutive successor to Nehru, they now clapped thunderously whenever he appeared on the screen. Shastri knew that. He would yet have, most likely, put off a direct positive response to President Radhakrishnan.

But now he was gone.

Radhakrishnan's posthumous conferring – the first ever – on the former late prime minister was, however, not just on one who had won a difficult war but on one who had won a fraught peace. Radhakrishnan said in his address: '…the conflict with Pakistan in the Rann of Kutch and in Jammu and Kashmir shocked our people. A united national effort was put forth to withstand this attack and Lal Bahadur took the leading part in these matters. He went to Tashkent to conclude an agreement with Pakistan. The effort and the strain brought about his end. He died pledging our two countries to work for peace and friendship, forgetting the bitterness of past years.'

And there followed a rumination as only befits a philosopher-president. But Sarvepalli Radhakrishnan, renowned professor of comparative religion and author of what is perhaps the most acclaimed commentary on the Bhagavad Gita, was also the supreme commander of the armed forces of India. He was doubtless of that role of his when he said: 'There can be no military solution to our problems. We should both realise that if we conquer our foes by force we enhance enmity and hatred. If we conquer them by understanding and attain goodwill we attain peace and goodwill. A peace based in repression and fear can only be temporary, while it will be lasting if it is based on moral force and truth.'

The challenges in waging peace faced today by Prime Minister Modi belong to a different order from those that Shastri faced in Tashkent.

India and Pakistan at that time had no nuclear weapons. Terrorism, as we now know it, had not raised its sinister head. Today, it would be hard for any president to say what Radhakrishnan said then. But there is such a thing as eternal verities and we should not forget that Prime Minister Modi, following the initiatives of the prime ministers, Narasimha Rao, Vajpayee and Manmohan Singh, went the extra mile to come to an understanding with the then prime minister of Pakistan, Nawaz Sharif. All the violence that has marred our bilateral relations since that early move by him, and all the mutual erosion of trust that has occurred notwithstanding, I believe Prime Minister Modi cannot but want concord, not discord, with Pakistan.

Whatever be the other considerations that weighed with him in recommending to the president a posthumous Bharat Ratna for the former prime minister, Narasimha Rao, I would like to tell myself that the late prime minister's several meetings with Nawaz Sharif at different venues to come to a concordat and his path-breaking Border, Peace and Tranquility Agreement with China have something to do with it. I would like to believe that somewhere within its folds, the posthumous parchment to Narasimha Rao holds a recognition of the place of negotiation without bitterness in the conversations of our foreign policy.

Will the first posthumous Bharat Ratna to Lal Bahadur Shastri be seen in that perspective? It is very difficult to say it will, especially with the elections just concluded in Pakistan blurring the political scene there. But for precisely the reason that an unstable polity in Pakistan and an increasingly vengeance-minded society in India are bad news for peace, we must hope the instincts displayed by Prime Minister Modi in his first prime ministership will find another chance. I said a few sentences ago that no president of India today can speak like President Radhakrishnan spoke on January 11, 1966. I need to correct that. President Droupadi Murmu in her Republic Day-eve address to the nation last month quoted the Buddha, as Radhakrishnan might have, as saying: 'Not at any time are enmities appeased here through enmity but they are appeased through non-enmity. This is the eternal law.' I find something exquisitely apposite about a daughter of India's tribal heritage in the part of India where Ashoka saw the futility of war and enmity speak to us of the Buddha's wisdom.

The natural question, 'Why was the Bharat Ratna not given to P.V. Narasimha Rao in his lifetime?', is less important than 'Will the "greatest distinction in the gift of our Bharat Ratna" that Radhakrishnan spoke of encourage a posthumous life for peace in our weaponised and terror-ridden subcontinent?' M.S. Swaminathan was president of the Pugwash conferences from 2002 to 2007, working with other scientists for a world free of nuclear and other weapons of mass destruction. His Bharat Ratna has to remind us of the very real threat of annihilation through error, terror or outright war that has its hood spread over the Indian subcontinent.

(*The Telegraph*, February 18, 2024)

36

The Favourites

FICTION? WHOEVER HAS TIME for it now? When we can barely make time to get at facts, fiction stands little chance. And there is also this added complication (or, if you like, simplification): one gets so much fiction, pure make-believe in the guise of facts, that the real thing – literary work of the creative imagination – is not missed.

And, yet, when the other day I came across on my granddaughter's shelf an attractive volume of Ruskin Bond's short stories for children and took it down just to get a flavour of the man's work, I knew I had been smitten. I could not put the book down, devouring story after story, every single one of them, and finding with each such 'visit' something I had missed earlier. For the time I was his captive, his world of the hills became my world, his characters in it, the population of my mindscape. Melaram the postman, who is devoured by a leopard, Professor Lulla, the retired pedagogue, with a morbid obsession with funerals, including of those he scarcely knows, and who is also surprised (and eaten) by another pair of sawed jaws, Dukhi the grim gardener, the father whose brief life is depicted with the simplest but most affecting strokes of the pen, the un-named stepfather who is portrayed without a single word of disfavour, but who the reader cannot but hate with intensity, became the most important people in my life during that captivity. The jungle streams where the little boy protagonist dives into for swims, the hillsides, the skies and the trees compose an ecology that no brush can paint, no camera can shoot.

His way with ghosts in his spooky tales is a gift. When a strange boy talking to the protagonist at night suddenly lets the light fall on his face which has no mouth, no nose, no eyes, you are with a ghost. The real thing. 'Mr Bond, do you believe in ghosts?', he was once asked by an interviewer.

'I do not believe in ghosts,' he had replied. 'But I see them all the time.' Spookier than that you cannot get! Bond is the soul of fiction, the heartbeat of suspense in storytelling.

Reading Ruskin Bond (b. 1934) for the first time in my 77 years, I said to myself, 'You are lucky, you fool, to be reading a fiction writer of the highest calibre who is right here, alive, at 88, and not in some attic of novelists long dead and gone into the mouldy shelves of antiquarian books in a library no one visits.'

And it occurred to me that in the world of Indian writers of English fiction, we have some truly great names of men and women who are with us, right here, in our times, our contemporaries. We must halloo them.

Too often, far too depressingly often, do we see obituaries that make us feel and say, '*Ayyo*, why did I not know her when she was alive!' Far too often have I felt on reading a touching tribute to the just-dead person, 'What a good man…Wish I had known of him when he was there with us, when I could have rung his doorbell and asked "Sir…May I come in…Only if I am not obtruding…?"'

Let me just list a few such novelists, writers of stories, who are *hayyat* not *marhum* and may they stay that way, please God, for years and years more.

Nayantara Sahgal (b. 1927) must head that list. I first heard of her when her memoir, *Prison and Chocolate Cake* (1954), made its appearance. I was nine, at school. The title gripped me, as did the book. It was her first book, followed about a decade later by another in the same genre, *From Fear Set Free* (1962). After that there was no looking back for this publicity-shy daughter of the legendary Vijaya Lakshmi Pandit. Novel followed novel, with the sequence being counted still, *The Fate of Butterflies* (2019) bringing up the rear. Nayantara writes in a unique rasa. You cannot call it sad, for it has so much humour in it and you cannot call it fun, for it has pathos – in a way the realisation of destiny would. It also disturbs you, makes you worry, makes you fear but in indignation, not weakness. *Butterflies* is not for the lily-livered.

Vikram Seth (b. 1952) is about genius, sheer genius. There is no other description for this man's oeuvre. He entrances like the Everest towers, or the Taj bewitches. I first read him outside fiction, in his travelogue, *From Heaven Lake* (1983), that took me into Sinkiang and Tibet in a way a physical journey would have but more: it took me there *with him*. And him being Vikram Seth. I had to read everything that was to come from his pen thereafter, poetry, biography, anthology but his three novels above all: *The Golden Gate* (1986), *A Suitable Boy* (1993), *An Equal Music* (1999). To read Vikram Seth is to experience the source of things as also their *finis*. There is something in his writing that reminds one of the brilliance of Pandit Ravi Shankar with the sitar. Need more be said?

Amitav Ghosh (b. 1956) with his one dozen novels, each more riveting than the other, more intricately woven, more mind-boggling and soul-scorching, is a samrat of fiction-writing. Reading *The Shadow Lines* (1988) made me a fan forever. Ghosh reminds me of the great sitarist, Ustad Vilayat Khan, whose mastery of that instrument was reflected in the way he walked – like an emperor. He writes with the elan of one who is in control, in charge, enthroned.

If *Em and the Big Hoom*, published in 2012, was the only thing that Jerry Pinto (b. 1966) ever wrote, his place in the world of fiction would be assured. Other than this work I have read few things, whether in Indian or non-Indian writing in English, that are so moving, so deeply stirring of one's within. Why am I saying 'few things'? Why am I playing so stupidly 'safe'? Have I not been moved to the depths by Em? Have I not the guts to say, 'I have read nothing so moving'? The searing honesty of that work makes me chastise my own reticence and acknowledge the oceanic surge of this writer's sensibility which, coming as it does with the gift of laughter, so as to say Pinto is the Pandit Kumar Gandharva of Indian writing in English.

Premchand's, Bibhutibhushan's, Kalki's, Thakazhi's and Mahadevi Verma's India will, I do not doubt, produce fiction greater than that coming from its English pens. My selecting these five writers in English from our time is only to say how utterly grateful I am for my luck in being alive at the same time as the five out of many others that I have described. And to say, too, I lament the loss of R.K. Narayan, of Khushwant Singh, of Kamala Markandeya – all of whom wrote English fiction of world class without bothering about whether they did or did not. But I rejoice in the knowledge that I am alive at the same time as these five. And in times when fiction is increasingly to be got in what is presented as truth.

(*The Telegraph*, December 18, 2022)

37

Badshah Khan: The Man, the Mission

KHAN ABDUL GHAFFAR KHAN, the monumental leader and guide of the Pakhtoons, shares with Khwaja Ahmed Abbas, the writer, and Salim Ali, the ornithologist (both of whom passed away recently), besides their Islamic inheritance, an exemption from all prejudice – ethnic, religious or any other. All prejudice, that is, except a prejudice against hypocrisy.

Ghaffar Khan's 'passport' age is 97. His real age? Popular belief has placed him at over a hundred, seating him thereby at the head of the table of surviving Greats from the freedom struggle. But this has also made him something of a Rip Van Winkle, who has had to rub his eyes in disbelief at the turns history has taken on either side of the Khyber Pass.

Fortunately for him, Ghaffar Khan's sense of humour is as strong as his sense of justice. He has been able thereby to let an inner smile check his tears, a burst of sunshine to dispel the clouds of anguish on his deeply lined brow.

Ghaffar Khan's life has, in fact, been a continuous alternation between hope and disappointment. The fifth child of the chief Khan of Utmanzai village in Peshawar district, his early life was a series of false starts. Seeking to join the army he gave up the idea when, on a visit to a friend in the army, he saw him being grossly insulted by a British officer of lower rank. Entering next the Aligarh Muslim University, he gave up the course when his father suggested that he go to England to study engineering. That opening too was not in Ghaffar Khan's kismet, for his mother, who had already seen one son (Dr Khan Saheb) go abroad, did not like the idea of parting with her younger son. And so it transpired that this scion of a Frontier chieftain's family remained in close proximity with the people whom he was destined, in time, to lead.

Ghaffar Khan did not, however, settle down to the life of quiet which 'pacified' tribals were expected to lead. Imbued with the Aligarh spirit, he discovered an interest in education. Government schools sat unconvincingly on the North-West Frontier Province's (NWFP) terrain, appealing neither to the Pathan's head nor to his heart. The local maulvis, dissatisfied with the schools run by the government, were nevertheless unable to offer constructive alternatives.

Ghaffar Khan busied himself with the setting up of national schools in the region as an alternative to government schools. The idea caught on.

This was also the time when India was warming up to the Rowlatt Act agitation. News of the pan-Indian movement reached the NWFP and its leader-in-the-making. A seam in Ghaffar Khan's consciousness seemed to have been touched and awakened by the development, alchemising his being. Responding to the signal, he called a meeting at Utmanzai on April 6, 1919 which was attended by over a hundred thousand Pathans – a huge gathering by any standard. It was this congregation that gave him the appellation of Badshah (king). Much more than an honorific was involved in this – a new responsibility, a new commitment. Badshah Khan has described the event thus: 'There was no overt action of satyagraha. The fact of our having had this meeting was quite enough for the authorities. Though I was arrested, there was no kind of trial. I was asked if I was a "Badshah of the Pathans". I said I did not know it, but I knew that I was a servant of the community and that we could not take these Bills lying down. The jirga that waited in deputation on me used all kinds of threats and all kinds of specious arguments..... I remained adamant and so there was nothing for it but to arrest me with a number of others.'

Badshah Khan was taken to jail handcuffed, and had fetters on throughout the imprisonment. He was a big-made man, weighing nearly 100 kg, and the authorities were hard put to it to find a pair of fetters to fit his legs. When they did put one on him, the leg above the ankle bled profusely. The die had been cast.

Word of this young Pathan leader's personal courage and his inexhaustible stamina travelled eastwards, to the villages, towns and cities of India. Badshah Khan attended his first Congress session at Nagpur in 1920 and threw himself into the khilafat movement. Thereafter, he and the freedom struggle intertwined. Indeed his participation in the movement came to be regarded as axiomatic, like that of Gandhiji. No Congress session was complete without him and his brother Dr Khan Saheb. It was with the surge in Badshah Khan's personal reputation that the plains began to learn something direct, something authentic, about the Frontier Province. Until then, it had been regarded as a hazy transborder land which had served as a conduit for invaders heading towards the plains of India and over which the 'Russian menace' perpetually loomed. Popular misconceptions had also held sway. India's traditional view of the NWFP was that it was generally (with the inaccuracy of all generalisations) the *sarhad* (frontier) from where the ubiquitous Pathan moneylenders came to charge usurious interest and commit acts of individual violence, only to make a quick getaway back to Peshawar, Kabul or thereabouts beyond the reach of the law. Badshah Khan changed all that. By the late twenties the NWFP began to stand for something quite distinct – the home of a people who had made the fight for freedom their own, suffering much more than others in the process.

As Badshah Khan became increasingly involved in the national movement, he absorbed and completely interiorised the new political concept of non-violent direct action.

A cynic might ask: Was not satyagraha the 'in' thing then and is it a matter of surprise that Badshah Khan too adopted the prevailing credo? Satyagraha had, indeed, suffused the national imagination at that time but, in their adherence to it, different people had differing motivations. Most found it a good instrument. The Congress organisation itself adopted it because it was seen to work. Jawaharlal Nehru writes of satyagraha in his autobiography: 'We had accepted that method, the Congress had made that method its own, because of a belief in its effectiveness.' Badshah Khan's response, however, was altogether different. For him satyagraha was not just a political modality but a new system, a way of life that seemed to demand of him more – much more – than allegiance. It demanded an inner transformation.

Badshah Khan belongs to the world of Pathans who have always been known, as Dr Zakir Husain once observed, 'for their skill in the use of arms, for the risk they took with their lives, and the impunity with which they took other lives'. A hardening of muscle, spirit and even of conscience is only natural in a war-inured people. For one of such a class, the doctrine of ahimsa was not just a new methodology but a new metaphysics. But Badshah Khan, as an individual and as a Pathan, already possessed two subliminal ingredients of a satyagrahi – the self-respect of the truthful and the truthfulness of the self-respecting.

A model prisoner

Even in his very early incarcerations, this quality was evident. Mahadev Desai tells us in his remarkable study of Badshah Khan, 'Two Servants of God' (1935), that the Pathan leader was a model prisoner. He would brook no breach of jail discipline, would expect or accept no favours and would not compromise on principle, though there were officials who would accommodate him and go out of their way in relaxing the rigours that they were bound to impose on him under the rules.

Badshah Khan also had in him an innate feeling of propriety, which made him a somewhat shy person. Asked about this, he referred to the aquifers of his religious faith. 'It is my inmost conviction that Islam is *amal, yakeen, muhabat* [right conduct, faith, love] and without these, one calling himself a Musalman is like sounding brass and tinkling cymbal. The Koran-e-Shareef makes it absolutely clear that faith in One God without a second and good works are enough to secure a man's salvation.'

To Badshah Khan adopting satyagraha was, therefore, an arrival, the journey having begun much earlier. He was able to bring to his work, effortlessly, a measure of Gandhiji's moral dimension. And if the gathering on the slope lands of Utmanzai had called him 'Badshah', the people of India spontaneously came to look upon him as 'Sarhad-e-Gandhi', the Frontier Gandhi.

By founding the order of the Khudai Khidmatgars or the Servants of God, he achieved what seemed virtually impossible. A non-violent Pathan? The term seemed almost contradictory, an illusion. But the course of events proved the contrary. After Gandhiji's arrest in the wake of the salt satyagraha in May 1930, the whole nation convulsed in protest. The government unleashed a series of the severest measures. Badshah Khan led the Khudai Khidmatgars' campaign.

Acharya Kripalani has recorded in his biography of Gandhiji (1970) the experience of the brave Pathans under Badshah Khan: 'The worst repression was resorted to in Peshawar in the North-West Frontier Province on the non-violent Pathans, the Khudai Khidmatgars. After Ghaffar Khan's arrest, batch after batch of non-violent satyagrahis – men, women and children – marched forward to face the shooting. They bared their chests and defied the authorities to do their worst. In Peshawar the shooting went on for hours, killing a large number of people.'

Prof. Sumit Sarkar tells us ('Modern India,' 1983) that though according to the official communiqué 30 were killed, non-official estimates ranged from 200 to 250. The satyagraha had another remarkable sequel to it. A platoon of the Garhwal Rifles (Prof. Sarkar records), comprising Hindus, refused to open fire. 'We will not shoot our unarmed brethren because India's Army is to fight India's enemies without. You may blow us from the guns, if you like,' they declared before their court martial later. Many of them got 15 years of imprisonment. There have been few examples of transcommunal solidarity scaling heights such as this.

Unparalleled success

This was a textbook victory for satyagraha. Badshah Khan said of his experience: 'The unparalleled success of the experiment in my Province has made me a confirmed champion of non-violence. God willing, I hope never to see my Province take to violence. It may be I may fail and a wave of violence may sweep over my Province. I will then be content to take the verdict of fate against me. But it will not shake my ultimate faith in non-violence which my people need more than anybody else.' He told Gandhiji: 'Whatever may be the case with other Provinces, there is no other way of salvation for the Pathans except through non-violence..... Your movement has instilled fresh life into us.'

The truth was that Badshah Khan had also instilled fresh life into Gandhiji's movement. A province – and a Muslim-majority province at that – devoted to the Congress's creed of non-violence, fighting with exemplary discipline and devotion for swaraj: this was almost a dream situation. The 'Red Shirts' as Badshah Khan's followers were called (after the brick-red hue of their locally woven khadi uniform), acquired a nationwide reputation.

A man is known by the company he keeps – and also by the company he does not. Badshah Khan and communal organisations were anathema to each other. Neither the extreme Muslim elements nor organisations like the Hindu Mahasabha were comfortable with him. The Mahasabha actually supported the government's ban on the 'Red Shirts'. But his stock in the nation continued to rise. How deeply Badshah Khan's crusade had affected the Indian mind, conscious and subconscious, is illustrated by a 1932 experience of Nehru in the Dehra Dun jail. He notes in his autobiography: 'In the heat of a summer afternoon I dozed off, and I remember having a curious dream. Abdul Ghaffar Khan was being attacked on all sides and I was fighting to defend him. I woke up in an exhausted state, feeling very miserable, and my pillow was wet with tears. This surprised me, for in my waking state I was not liable to such emotional outbursts.'

The elections of 1935 saw a most memorable success for the Congress in the North-West Frontier Province. And that, after a most frustratingly difficult campaign. The Khan brothers had been externed from the province and thereby prevented from taking part in the campaign. Dr Khan Saheb 'led' the campaign in absentia. Nehru too was not allowed to campaign in the province, while many prominent Muslim Leaguers were. Despite this, Dr Khan Saheb won a resounding victory, capturing 21 of the 36 'Muslim' seats, all the six 'Hindu' seats and two of the three 'Sikh' seats.

Pyarelal writes in his book *Thrown to the Wolves* (1966): 'In September 1937, a Congress Ministry was formed in the Frontier Province under Dr Khan Saheb's premiership, and the outlaws of yesterday became the party in power. But Badshah Khan, the fakir, did not stand for election; nor did he join his brother's Ministry. Convinced that nothing but non-violence, as inculcated by Gandhiji, could elevate his people and raise them to their full moral stature, he chose the steep and stony path of service instead.'

Badshah Khan invited Gandhiji to tour NWFP in 1939. Dr Khan Saheb was the premier. Travelling through the mountain fastnesses of that region, Gandhiji complimented the Pathans for their success with satyagraha.

The Muslim League, however, did not take kindly to its defeat and did everything to deprive the Pathans of their success. By 1940, Jinnah, the Quaid-e-Azam, and the League had proposed the formation of Pakistan on the basis of the 'Two-Nation' Theory. The Muslims' homeland was to comprise areas where they enjoyed numerical preponderance, stradcling Punjab, the NWFP, Kashmir, Sind and Baluchistan. (The League later added Bengal and Assam to the list.) The Khan brothers rejected the Two-Nation Theory spontaneously, emphatically and totally. But events took their remorseless course.

Communal violence broke out in the towns and cities in India. Gandhiji was a study in anguish. Pyarelal records: 'In January 1947, Gandhiji sent for Badshah Khan to join him, when from Noakhali he set out on his mission of peace and mercy in Bihar. Here Badshah Khan's dignity, poise, rock-like firmness and abiding faith in the essential goodness of human nature and God stood out like a shining beacon in the tempestuous darkness of the night. Photographs have immortalised the two Gandhis – Frontier and Mahatma, Muslim and Hindu – watching their dreams crumble into physical and human debris. With Pakistan a reality, Badshah Khan asked his friend on June 3, 1947: 'So Mahatmaji, you will henceforth regard us as Pakistanis, aliens, will you not?' Gandhiji replied, 'Khan Saheb, non-violence knows no despair. It is the hour of your trial..... You can declare that Pakistan is altogether unacceptable to you and brave the worst. What fear can there be for those who are pledged to do or die?' To his companions he said about Badshah Khan, 'The sight of his grief wrings my heart. But if I were to give way to grief, brave Pathan though he is, it will break his heart.'

Gandhiji then suggested to the Viceroy, Lord Mountbatten, that he should ask Jinnah, now that he had got his Pakistan, to 'woo' the people of the Frontier Province, including the ministry in power, 'to become a province of Pakistan with perfect freedom to frame their own provincial constitution'. Pyarelal tells us that Mountbatten spoke to Jinnah but to no purpose. Thereupon, with the concurrence of the Congress leaders, Gandhiji proposed that since Jinnah had refused to woo the Pathans, Badshah Khan should, by the same token, make an attempt to woo Jinnah and the Muslim League. Accordingly, on June 18, Badshah Khan at a meeting with Jinnah at the latter's residence, in another effort to arrive at a settlement with him, told him that they were quite willing to join Pakistan, provided (i) it was on honourable terms; (ii) in case Pakistan, after Independence, decided to stay on under British domination, the Pathans in the settled districts or in the tribal areas should have the power to opt out of such a dominion and form a separate independent state; (iii) all matters concerning tribal people should be settled by the Pathans themselves, without the interference or domination of the non-Pathans.

Strikes no chord

But this too struck no chord in the future Governor General of Pakistan. His dreams of a free and united India shattered, Gandhiji even lost interest in his old and oft-repeated desire to live up to 125. On the day the League's rejection of the Frontier Gandhi's proposals was received, Gandhiji is reported to have become restless. 'I cannot cease thinking of Badshah Khan even when [I] have ceased to desire to live up to 125 years,' he remarked. 'Badshah Khan is a prodigy.' Gandhiji added. 'For such a person there can be no defeat..... I am sure he will shrink from no sacrifice but will die serving the Pathans with his last breath.' The faithful Pyarelal informs us that Gandhiji then tried to sleep but after a while he again opened his eyes and said, 'No, I cannot..... The thought of him has robbed me of my sleep.'

A plebiscite on the limited choice of joining India or Pakistan was forced on the North-West Frontier Province. The Congress high command protested but did not force the issue. The NWFP Congress finally decided to boycott the plebiscite. Today, 40 years later, not many in India or Pakistan remember that if in 1947 the NWFP went to Pakistan, it was by the decision of just 9.52 per cent of the total population of the province. The rest, that is 90.48 per cent, of the Pathans had not spoken their minds.

Badshah Khan has spent the four decades after Partition among his people, the Pathans, who continue to love and venerate him. There were spells of separation too, when the Government of Pakistan, not surprisingly, put him in prison. Prison, of course, was not a new experience for him. The loss of liberty did not worry him. But the loss of identity did. The North-West Frontier's Pathan had never been 'just another Indian'. Now he was not even that.

Whether in jail or out of it, whether in Pakistan or on his trips to Kabul and, later, to India, Badshah Khan continues to command respect. No one could ignore him. No one listened to him either. But is that not the fate of the human conscience? Known to be 'there', it is a channel that is rarely tuned in to and seldom for long.

Anguished and disappointed as he was, Badshah Khan remained, nonetheless, entirely free from bitterness. Forgiveness is an attribute of the brave. He had once told the late Kamal Nayan Bajaj: 'The Congress leaders had assured us that they would never accept Partition.....but they accepted it..... The Congress leaders thought that by accepting Partition they would have peace, the hatchet would be buried for good. But how can you expect love to sprout from the seeds of hatred? What has been founded on hatred has to be sustained also by hatred.' Bajaj asked Badshah Khan if his creed of love embraced Pakistan also. The answer was an instruction in civilised behaviour:

'Yes, I have no quarrel with the people of Pakistan. My heart aches for them. They, too, are God's creatures like the poor suffering folk anywhere else. I pray for them that God may vouchsafe to them courage and faith. My quarrel is with the rulers, and with the wrong system of rule. I pray for the rulers also that, inspired by the spirit of love and service, they may appreciate those who follow that path and cooperate with them.'

It was a measure of Badshah Khan's transcontinental stature that as he lay comatose in July 1987 in the intensive care unit of the All-India Institute of Medical Sciences, New Delhi, before he was flown to Peshawar, his callers included, apart from India's leadership, the Ambassador of Pakistan in India and a delegation of political personalities from Afghanistan. Crippled by a stroke, he sank steadily into deeper and ever deeper levels of unconsciousness. But his broad chest heaved, nonetheless, with the strong breathing one associates with a long-distance sprinter or a swimmer. Pathan that he is, Badshah Khan was negotiating his journey through the coma on his own terms.

Nor are the Fates leaving him alone. As always, they are set to frustrate his intent. 'You go your lonely way as is your wont; we shall take the rest our way as we always have,' they seem to be telling him. 'Violence and arson rock North India' screamed the newspaper headlines when Badshah Khan was in the Delhi hospital. The dailies also informed the readers that Badshah Khan was 'battling for his life'. The sentence keeps going round and round in one's mind. Battling for his life? That is an accurate description. Yet there is something wrong about it. And then, like one of Badshah Khan's sudden smiles, comes the realisation. Facing at last the frontier of all frontiers, Badshah Khan is battling, yes, but not for his life. In this strife-torn, trigger-happy, mad, mad world, he is battling for the dignity of human life.

(*Frontline*, September 5–18, 1987)

38

As Suitable as Ever

VIKRAM SETH'S *A SUITABLE BOY* will, in the next few months, 'finish' a quarter century. When it was launched, in March 1993, there was a general expectation that the modern 'epic' would win that year's Booker. It did not and many thought publisher hype about the prize being 'a certainty' worked against it. I am not sure of that nor particularly sorry that 'Booker Prize Winner' has not been the book's selling tag. The book stands on the strength of its fictional veracity.

Fictional veracity? Is that not an oxymoron? Not if one reads *A Suitable Boy* as a story based on many real-life experiences that went into making India.

What has surprised me is that the story did not become a tele-serial or a film in a mix of English and Hindustani. I can imagine a Merchant Ivory film based on it with some stunning songs by Gulzar or Javed Akhtar. Anita Desai's *In Custody* became a great film around the same time that *A Suitable Boy* appeared, with some powerful poems of Faiz Ahmad Faiz sung in it, becoming that film's very life.

One can never tell with films but my hunch is that had it become such a film with some of Vikram Seth's own poems set to music in it, *A Suitable Boy* would have been more than a box-office hit. Like Mehboob Khan's *Mother India*, its strong political core would have made a difference to a whole generation's sense of India's destiny. And it would have taken Seth's sensibility from its English domicile to its original home – among the people of Hindustan, with all their complications, contradictions and tragedies.

But this column is not about Seth's outstanding novel.

It is about Vikram Seth's place in India today.

And of the place of one like Vikram Seth in today's India.

But, before going into that, the question needs to be asked: Who is Vikram Seth? What exactly does he stand for, represent?

Famous for his novels as he is, and will always be, Vikram Seth is, in the essence of his being, a poet. And that makes him a person who needs and cherishes being alone. '…I am so lonely, so content' is a one-line autobiography of his. He is complete being himself. He is his uniqueness, his uniqueness is him.

And what is his uniqueness?

More Indian than any Indian one can know, he is yet not of India. He therefore has been and remains for us, his fellow Indians, '*hazir bhi, aur ghayab bhi* (invisible and yet, right here)'. Now, that makes him an enigma. The traveller from China to India in his amazing travelogue *From Heaven Lake* (1983) was Indian. His homecoming at the end of that gripping book is that of a Delhizen. But in his altogether sui generis novel in verse, *The Golden Gate* (1986), there is not a trace of India or of anything Indian. A slim collection of the most compelling verse had appeared under the title *Mappings* (1980) earlier, without fuss or much notice thanks to the far-seeing scholar-publisher, P. Lal. Those poems come from a poet who happens to be Indian, not an Indian poet. There – in his un-denominated *insaniyat* – lies Vikram Seth's uniqueness.

The appearance of *A Suitable Boy* in a sense retrieved him for India. And yet the novel remained part of the poetic world of Vikram Seth, in which there was goodness and its exact opposite, good luck and its exact opposite and there was Vikram Seth, leaving those two incompatibles to die in one another's arms, and disappearing thereafter from view.

I can never forget the evening in London in 1993 when he was reading from his mint-fresh novel to an admiring, almost mesmerised crowd. There he was, at the centre of all attention, perfectly at home in it, comfortable in his celebrity-ness and in no hurry to conclude the event. But when it was done, before anyone quite realised it, he put on his cap, his coat and quietly, without a single backward glance, disappeared into the anonymity of that city. As I caught a glimpse of the slight figure turning into a bend down the dark road, I said to myself it was a happy thing to see him be so himself.

Kahan se aye, Vikram Seth, kahan gaye Vikram Seth, yah koyi nahin kah saka hai. Aur is par koyi afsos nahin. Kyunki, jab tak ve samne hain, tab tak ve puri tarah se samne hain, hasne, hasane, khushi bantne, gham bantne jaise, darya-e-dil ki mohabbat dene, jaise aur koyi nahin kar sakta...Par agle kshan ve kahan honge, ve kya karne kya kahne, kisko...yah koyi nahin kah sakta...

[Where Vikram Seth has come from, where Vikram Seth has gone, none has been able to tell. And it has not mattered that this is so. For, as long as he is there with you, he is there, right there, in front of you, laughing and making you laugh, sharing your happiness, sharing your gloom, generous and loving like no one else...Once that moment is gone, he is gone with it, where to no one can know, to do what, say what, who to, none can tell...]

Gayness is an unproclaimed feature of his personality, just as his genius is and his no nonsense-ness. These go with him, as his eyes and his forehead do, both capable of the most dazzling smile and the most chilling scorn. No one may mess with Vikram Seth as a person, as a holder of views. Nothing low, tasteless, vile stands a chance with the author of *All You Who Sleep Tonight*. And that includes illiberalism, bigotry.

What and where is the place for such a Vikram Seth in India today?

It is precarious and it is dangerous.

In the *akhara*s of social prejudice in today's India, purblind custom is making the individual hostage to hypocrisy and patriarchy. In the halls of political posturing, arrogant majoritarianism is taking the measure of Indian pluralism. In the quadrangles of justice, the Supreme Court is told, privacy is not a fundamental right. And in the streets of India, dissent is portrayed as sedition and criticism of State policy, anti-national. A hyper-nationalism rules the communication mogul of our times, which goes by the name of social media. The voice of Indian liberalism, raised at protests, through writing and different forms of advocacy, is spattered with abuse, vile abuse and threats on Twitter and Facebook postings. In Du Fu's words of 1,300 years ago which Vikram Seth has translated with such delicacy: '…we must mind our words, with spies about…'

Thank God for the Supreme Court which has ruled that privacy is a fundamental right. That protects, as I see it, poetry. Not just the poet's verse but freedom's score. Thank God for our still free media which resist threats.

Vikram Seth's place in intolerant India is the place Faiz Ahmad Faiz occupied in intolerant Pakistan. India's beleaguered freedoms, as dusk settles over them, urge that Faiz in him to help it *unchi rakhe lau*.

They say to him, in Faiz's words again, *pas raho…tum merey pas raho…*Stay near me now, just stay very near me.

(*The Telegraph*, September 24, 2017)

39

The Right to Be Oneself

CHITTO JETHA BHOYSHUNNO, UCHCHA jetha shir is impossible to render in English or in any other language. Three taut words followed by three. A breath taken deep, then let go.

That opening line of Tagore's verse in Bangla is a masterpiece of imagery coiled in sound. The poet's own English translation of it, 'Where the mind is without fear and the head is held high' has become world famous. It has overshadowed the original. And yet, those who can read both the original and the translation will vouch for this: like thunder following a bolt of lightning, the English translation comes close to but cannot clasp the brilliance of the original.

The poem, first published in 1910 and later included in *Gitanjali*, stirred the popular imagination both because its language startled and because its meaning empowered. It engendered a sense of confidence and high purpose.

This column, however, is not about *Chitto jetha* but its great comrade: *Swarajya ha majha janmasiddhahaqqa aahe, ani to mi milavanarach*. Five taut words drawn deep in, followed by four aspirated into time.

This line's English version too has become famous, more famous than its original. So much so that no one quite pauses to think if '*Swarajya* is my birthright and I shall have it' was said by Lokamanya Tilak in English or in the language of which he was an absolute master, Marathi. It was indeed spoken by Tilak in his mother tongue, one hundred and one years ago on June 1, 1916. The venue was Ahmednagar, the purpose: spreading the cause of home rule. Tilak had spoken in a similar vein in Ahmednagar the previous day as well, and in Belgaum the previous month.

The British Raj moved against Tilak swiftly, charging him under Section 108 of the Criminal Procedure Code for disseminating – orally – seditious matter punishable under Section 124 A of the Indian Penal Code. The case against him was that, by saying what he did about swarajya, Tilak had committed sedition. It became what is commonly called a *cause célèbre*. Was asking for swarajya seditious? More, what, indeed, was *swarajya*, and what was sedition?

Defending Tilak was a lawyer who knew not one word of Marathi or its parent, Sanskrit. But he knew the meaning of Self Rule and Home Rule, and knew what sedition meant. Most pertinently, he also knew and respected Lokamanya Tilak as a patriot and a man of honour. The lawyer was none other than M.A. Jinnah, the future leader of the movement for Partition and founder of Pakistan. Jinnah had, in 1908, failed to have Tilak acquitted in a sedition case that led to his six-year incarceration in Mandalay. But this time he was not going to fail. In his brilliant biography of the Quaid-e-Azam, written in the most chaste Hindi (*Jinnah: Ek Punardrishti*, Rajkamal, 2005), V.K. Baranwal writes: 'Through his legal contentions and powerful arguments Jinnah was able, this time, to win Tilak an acquittal from the charge of sedition and release from detention.'

In *Emperor versus Bal Gangadhar Tilak* of November 9, 1916, Judge Batchelor of the Bombay High Court gave a historic judgment (which he delivered with another judge, Shah J., concurring eloquently) in which he said: '…it is, I think, reasonably clear that in contending for what he describes as swarajya his object is to obtain for Indians an increased and gradually increasing share of political authority and to subject the administration of the country to the control of the people or peoples of India. I am of opinion that the advocacy of such an object is not per se an infringement of the law…'

Jinnah had been as '*bhoyshunno*' as Tilak in the case. His defence carried conviction with the judges, Batchelor and Shah. Tilak's legendary words, 'Swarajya is my birthright,' vindicated by the court, became a rallying flag for the aspirations of the 'peoples of India'. And the flagstaff had Jinnah's name etched firmly on it. *Janmasiddhahaqqa* was Marathi. Jinnah's endorsement was in the King's English. Most citations use the Sanskrit '*adhikar*' over '*haqqa*', but that is linguistic cleansing, not ascriptive veracity. I accept the reference which has Tilak say '*janmasiddhahaqqa*' – why should Marathi and Urdu not go naturally together? The distinguished jurist, A.G. Noorani, and the political analyst, Sudheendra Kulkarni, have written about this little-known but invaluable Tilak–Jinnah link.

Is wanting a say in decision-making, wanting to be heard without hindrance, voicing opposition, dissenting, the same as sowing hatred against the State and destabilising the nation? The judges, Batchelor and Shah, showed the difference 100 years ago in *Emperor vs Tilak,* with Tilak being defended by Jinnah.

But what of now? The prosecution can be expected to be prosecutionist and the defence to be defensive, but what of judges? A judge may act with Batchelor's and Shah's care as to an individual's motivation but then, he may not.

One hundred and one years after the historic Batchelor and Shah judgment, we face a piquant fact: logjammed in competing nationalisms, India and Pakistan are using the same law, the same provision, inherited from the same source, namely, the British Raj, to strengthen their sinews for tackling dissent under different names. Punishable with imprisonment for life, sedition is defined as bringing or attempting to bring into hatred or contempt, or exciting or attempting to excite disaffection towards the government. Hatred, contempt and disaffection are not objectively patent. They are not like robbery, rape or murder. They inhabit the field of subjective interpretation, ideological posturing.

Are we in India, Pakistan (and Bangladesh) today, as nations and a people, moving towards a situation where the fear of the 'sedition law' will curb dissent, honest, law-abiding, non-violent dissent, from expressing itself? In two outstanding lectures delivered over April and May, this year, namely, the M.N. Roy Memorial Lecture in New Delhi and the Lawrence Dana Pinkham Memorial Lecture in Chennai, the former chief justice of Delhi High Court and chairman of the last Law Commission, Ajit Prakash Shah, has described the position lucidly. In the Roy lecture, he said: 'Even if one is eventually acquitted of sedition, the process of having to undergo the trial itself is the punishment – and more importantly, the deterrent against any voice of dissent or criticism. The enforcement or the threat of invocation of sedition constitutes an insidious form of unauthorised self-censorship by producing a chilling effect on the exercise of one's fundamental right to free speech and expression.'

On this anniversary of Tilak's '*Swarajya* is my birthright' call, we will do well to remember three things: one, swarajya is about the right to be oneself. Two, that right has to be exercised non-violently, without hatred but unequivocally. Three, as far as the exercising of this right is concerned, Tilak and Jinnah are on the same page. As are Tagore, Gandhi, Nehru, Patel, Ambedkar, Subhas Bose, Khan Abdul Ghaffar Khan, Rajagopalachari, Azad, Periyar, Namboodiripad. Their religions – or agnosticisms – were their personal affair, their languages, cultures, cuisine different, but in their faith in human rights and republican values, they were and remain together. And so must their 'peoples' be: *chitto – bhoyshunno, shir – uchcha*.

(*The Telegraph*, June 4, 2017)

40

Gandhi's Songs

IN THE COURSE OF a public conversation in Chennai, Vidvan T.M. Krishna asked me if Gandhi had any music in him. I was unsure of the answer then, but going through some Gandhi-related writings recently has shown an unexpected presence of music in that life of hectic preoccupations – a presence, not in spite of the preoccupations, but in a mutually sustaining bond.

The recitation of texts is not quite music but, nonetheless, it is nearer to singing than it is to speaking as this reference in his autobiography to the twilight days of his father, Karamchand or Kaba Gandhi, shows: 'He had not read religious texts but…had begun to study the *Gita* and every day, during his puja, he would recite, in a high pitch (*unchesvare*), a few slokas from it.' And the following, translated from the original Gujarati, connects father, mother and son musically: 'There came to our place around that time itinerant showmen. Shravana carrying, by means of slings fitted from his shoulders, his blind parents on a pilgrimage was one of the pictures painted on glass I was shown. The agonising lament (*vilap*) of the parents over Shravana's death is still fresh in my memory. The tender verse (*lalitchhand*) moved me deeply and I played it on a music box (*vajun*) that my father had procured for me. I liked learning to play musical instruments.'

The *S.S. Clyde*, in September 1888, took a very shy Gandhi to London to study for the Bar. The experience of travelling in a liner included something unexpected: 'There were musical instruments in the streamer. I every now and then played upon the piano.' Wanting to become an English gentleman in London, the freshly arrived Gandhi got himself a chimney top hat, an evening suit, a gold pocket-watch chain. But what of culture? He writes in the autobiography, 'I started to learn to play the violin so that I could get a sense of the notes and beats. Three pounds went into the purchase of a violin and some more to its learning.' But the '*moha*' did not last long. He ruminated, 'Was I going to spend the rest of my life in England? How was my dance-learning going to help me back home? The violin I can learn to play when I return. I am here as a student. I should acquire but one asset: learning…

I took my violin to my violin teacher. She was most understanding. She said she would try to sell the violin for whatever value it fetched.'

The violin he could, and did, abandon. But the deep impress of the '*lalitchhand*' that little Mohan had heard as a child was to stay with him and work with him over the years of his evolution from an essentially shy student in London to an assertive attorney in Durban, and then from the author of passive resistance in South Africa to the role that led him to be called 'Mahatma'.

On February 10, 1908, Mir Alam, a Johannesburg-based Pathan who had placed his trust in the anti-finger-impressions campaigner Gandhi, got rattled when the same Gandhi came to an understanding with Smuts under which the fingerprint law for 'Asiatics' was to be repealed in return for voluntary fingerprinting. Mir Alam struck all but lethal blows on Gandhi. 'I fell down,' Gandhi has recounted 'with the first blow which was delivered with a stick…' Gandhi lost consciousness and Alam, who was then joined by other assailants, stopped only when they thought Gandhi was dead.

The Baptist minister, the Reverend Joseph J. Doke, and a friend who was present saw the whole thing and took the fallen man immediately to his home nearby where, on regaining consciousness, Gandhi asked, 'Where is Mir Alam?' Doke told him that he had been arrested with the other attackers. 'They should be released,' Gandhi said. Gandhi records that, a little later, he asked if Doke's little daughter, Olive, would sing for him a hymn he so loved, Cardinal Newman's 'Lead, Kindly Light'. Doke asked Olive to stand by the door and sing the hymn in a low tone, which she did. Gandhi never forgot that 'entire scene' and Olive's melodious voice rendering: 'Lead, Kindly Light, amidst th'encircling gloom; /Lead Thou me on! /The night is dark, and I am far from home…One step enough for me.' The hymn, along with others from Christian music and several bhajans from the different languages and faith traditions of India, were put together by the Sabarmati Ashram, under Gandhi's watch in the *Ashram Bhajanavali*, the first and probably the only cross-religion hymnal anywhere. It includes the '*Ramdhun*', of course, ascribed to Tulsidas, which Mohandas was to electrify with the addition of '*Ishvara Allah tere naam*'.

In the winter of 1931, on his way back from the Second Round Table Conference in London, which had collapsed on the Hindu–Muslim and Hindu–Harijan divides, Gandhi stopped in Villeneuve de Chillon to call on the philosopher and musical savant, Romain Rolland. The aesthete has written, '…after the prayers, Gandhi asked me to play him a little of Beethoven. I played him the Andante of the 5th Symphony. To that I added, "Les Champs-Élysées" of Gluck – the page for the orchestra and the air for the flute. He is very sensitive to the religious chants of his country, which somewhat resemble the most beautiful of our Gregorian melodies, and he has worked to assemble them. We also exchanged our ideas on art, from which he does not separate his conception of truth.' That was one of Gandhi's rare engagements with music for music's sake.

The next year took place Gandhi's 'epic fast' in Poona against separate electorates for the depressed classes. The fast ended with B.R. Ambedkar agreeing to the alternative of reserved seats under the still-operative Poona Pact. Tagore was present at this climactic moment. As life revived in the fasting man, Tagore sang his '*Jibana jokhono shukae jae* (Where the heart is hard and parched up, come upon me as a shower of mercy)…'

Some 15 years later, by which time Tagore was gone and a free India was being born, death stalked Gandhi again. In a tense Calcutta in the August of 1947, Gandhi moved from Sodepur, his customary place of stay, to Hyderi Manzil, Beliaghata, the Calcutta suburb where Muslims lived in large numbers. Among his hundreds of visitors, mostly self-invited, was the 27-year-old Juthika Roy. 'My mother and I made obeisance,' she has recorded, 'he touched our heads and asked us to sit down using sign language as he was observing silence…Then as he went to the next room, I sang bhajans without the help of instruments. When he came back I stopped singing and he flashed a broad smile…'

Only a few days later, a Hindu mob all but killed him. Manu Gandhi records the scene of August 31, 1947: 'It was ten o'clock at night. There were only three of us in the whole building, Bapuji, Abhaben and I…The boys [outside] soon increased in numbers. They started breaking things. Stones were hurled at lamps and windowpanes, shattering them. The boys wanted to catch and kill our Musalman hosts. Bapuji came out…"What is all this? Kill me, kill me, I say…why don't you kill me?" and with these words he tried to rush amidst the crowd…Military force arrived and dispersed the crowd… Ministers, including the Chief Minister Prafullababu, came and told Bapu they would arrest the Hindu Mahasabhaites. "You should not arrest them…," he said. "Ask them what they want, peace or riots…"'

The riots he feared, miming those of August 1946, broke out in the city. Gandhi went on fast. He was 78 and frail beyond words. Some 70 hours of that ordeal later, peace limped back to the scenes of murder and mayhem. Only after the Governor, Rajaji, sent word that tension had ceased in the city and all was now quiet, did Gandhi, his voice sunk to a whisper, said that he would break his fast. He did so by sipping a glass of diluted orange juice handed to him by H.S. Suhrawardy, the principal target of Mahasabhaite fury. Suhrawardy broke down and bowed before the Mahatma as all present sang, spontaneously, Tagore's '*Jibana jokhono shukaye jae*'.

Gandhi moved on almost immediately thereafter to Delhi, which was being rocked by sectarian murders. Amid all the torments, visitors, invited and uninvited, flocked to Birla House to see him – 31-year-old M.S. Subbulakshmi among them. At the evening prayer there, when the '*Ramdhun*' was to start, Gandhi said to her, 'Subbulakshmi *tum gao, tum shurukaro...*' Another fast ensued, another peace followed. A lasting peace? No one could say then, no one can say today. On January 29, 1948, Pyarelal writes, 'Gandhi mused why politicians who had toiled and sacrificed for freedom's sake, and on whom now rested the burden of independence, were succumbing to the lure of office and power.' And then, Pyarelal says, in a tone of infinite sadness Gandhi repeated a verse of Nazir, the celebrated Urdu poet of Allahabad, '*Hai Bahar-e-bagh duniya chand roz...*': 'Short-lived is the splendour of Spring / In the garden of the world, / Watch the brave show while it lasts...'

The next day, on the way to the gathering where he was to lead the congregation in singing *Ishvar Allah tere nam sabko sanmati de Bhagavan*, his chest, throbbing with the prayer of music and the music of prayer, stopped three bullets in their track. Gandhi's music was didactic. But then his life was god-bound.

(*The Telegraph*, October 2, 2016)

41

Warm, Vital, Restless

SAINT TERESA...THAT MAKES YOU somewhat distant, Mother Teresa. It places you, warm, vital, restless, in a cold glass case with wax candles all around you. Sainthood turns you, the owner of a thousand wrinkles, into a doll of the smoothest plaster. It turns you, a woman with the brow of care on your forehead, into a caramel éclair.

Popular reckoning says the Catholic world has had, roughly, 10,000 saints, each of them with a set smile, a fixed halo, hands raised in everlasting blessing. These come from 'back then', from the early days of Christianity. Of the 'properly' canonised ones, that is, those who have been so titled by the Pope, a more exact number is given – 810. And so, Ma Teresa, you are now moving the Vatican 810 to the fine count of 811 and the 10,000 to a rough 10,000 and more.

You never heard Earl Grant's 'Number Fifty-Four', did you? No matter. Let me rejig it for you to say that as a saint you now make

A full 10K more/
In a waxen case/
With a waxen roof a waxen base/
Don't turn a waxen bore!

Now that you are a saint you will wear a halo of wax sticks and you will shed, in public view, viscous tears. 'Whoa!' they will exclaim, 'A miracle!' And the multitudes will throng. From Skopje, where you were born, to Calcutta where you died, from Brasília to Manila, the 2.4 billion Christians the world over (33 per cent of its population, no less), of which around 1.27 billion are Roman Catholics (17.8 per cent) and non-Christians no less, will crowd centres of your Missionaries of Charity and seeing the cracks on your waxen images will shout: 'See her veins, her throbbing veins! She is alive, the Saint! Saint Teresa lives!' Grown-ups mimic their grandchildren.

But seeing it 'all in all', let me say, Ma Teresa, that your canonisation is a wonderful thing to be happening, particularly now. The scholar-priest, Reverend Father Adrian Mascarenhas, has put it thus: 'The significance of the canonisation is that St. Teresa stands for a Church that is spontaneous in its response to human suffering – a message that is also close to the heart of Pope Francis – a Church that acts, that intervenes, that gets involved, without asking questions or making distinctions, a Church that is basically on a rescue mission to those whose lives have been shattered.'

I value your canonisation for that, Ma, and for these three supplementary reasons: first, it has brought to our forgetful society a new awareness of your incredible life. Second, it has brought a new attention to Christian India. Third, it has given a pause, brief though it may be, to the tsunami of majoritarianism overtaking our country.

To focus on the first reason first, you remember the day you were driven up the capacious forecourt of the Rashtrapati Bhavan where India's First Citizen resides? You emerged from the car, almost weightless, smiling through those creases on your face, looked with a practical gaze at the presidential palace, and said: 'This building will do nicely for our work.' Mother Teresa, going to be beatified, to become a saint, you were also a woman who had a certain job as well, albeit honorary – that of a space manager – so many sick to so many square feet, so many cribs to not so many square feet. You were a working woman with children to look after, old children and small children, with little money and less time. You were the very personification of millions of overworked and under-acknowledged mothers.

Now, for the second reason for celebration.

Your canonisation gives India the chance to deepen its knowledge of Christian India. Your becoming a saint should bring back to our collective mind the fact that but for that emancipator of India's womanhood, Raja Rammohan Roy (1772–1833), powerfully influenced by Christianity, India would have been burning widows, including little 'widowed' girls for another two centuries. The Raja was from our East. From our West, Pandita Ramabai (1858–1922), the Sanskritist and Christian, showed that India's girl-child was brighter than the lout who claimed superiority over her, and so she must go to school, college, become a harbinger of change. From our Tamil south, the Kumarappa brothers, J.C. (1892–1960) and Bharatan (1896–1957), provided the much-needed intellectual leavening to the movement for *swaraj*, even as in Kerala, George Joseph (1887–1938) led the freedom struggle there with inspirational grit, while Mangalore-born Reverend Jerome D'Souza (1897–1977), Jesuit priest, impacted the thought processes of our Constituent Assembly transformationally.

'Don't leave out the North,' you will point out, Ma, and you will be right. I almost did, but that is because the North tends, despite itself, to dominate and I dislike domination. Amrit Kaur, brave rajkumari of Kapurthala (1889–1964), as a woman, a Christian and a Sikh–Christian at that, personified resistance as a freedom-fighter, modernisation as an educationist and was India's first health minister. She it was who inaugurated mass immunisation and family planning in our society controlled by superstition and quackery.

You never dabbled in statistics, Ma. 'Numbers?' you may well say. 'The only numbers I know are of the dying.' But we need to know that there are 27.8 million Christians in India (1.16 per cent of the world's Christians, and around 2.3 per cent of the population of India). Of these, 17.3 million are Catholics (around 1.4 per cent of the world's Catholics, or 1.55 per cent of the population of India).

Christianity has spurred education with Anglo-Indians in the lead, bolstered medical care with missions driving it, as few others have. In 1869, Wellesley Bailey, a young Irish teacher in Punjab, saw a row of huts inhabited by persons with serious deformities. Shocked to learn that they were suffering from leprosy, Bailey was to recall: 'I almost shuddered, yet I was at the same time fascinated, and I felt that if there was ever a Christlike work in the world it was to go amongst these poor sufferers and bring them the consolation of the gospel.' That was the beginning of the Leprosy Mission in India. Ida Scudder, Graham and Gladys Staines have carried the work further afield, with other pioneers, many of them non-Christian, doing the same.

What about conversions? Were they not awful things to have happened? Done through intimidation and exploitation, of course they were. You have not escaped the charge yourself, Ma, have you? Did you, while ministering to the leprosy-hit, put a wafer and wine to her or his lips and say, 'Ayesha, you are now Alice', or 'Biman, you are now Basil'? If you did, a thousand pities. But if you did not, shame, a thousand shames, on the accuser for he was doing precious little for Ayesha or for Biman.

Missionaries may have made our Northeast a strong home to Christianity; they have thereby also made India's Northeast that much more at home with India, its 'India-ness', which is so different from Brahminic Bharatiyata or Delhi-centric Hindustaniyat. Conversions are a sorry fact but they belong, in most part, to history. Tendentious non-Christian reviling of Christian conversions is a sorrier fact for it belongs wholly to political opportunism.

'Rainbow nation' is a phrase that belongs to Mandela's South Africa, but if India has tones of many hues in many ways, one has come from non-Indians domiciled here. Despondent India met a counsellor in C.F. Andrews, tribal India a friend in Verrier Elwin, and, above all others, in you, Ma Teresa, destitute India found a redeemer. If all these could come to serve India, we have Jesus Christ to thank.

What of 'the idea of India'? you may ask, saying those words, now so over-used, with some scepticism, which brings me to the third reason for celebrating your canonisation. Jerome D'Souza, that handsome Mangalorean, as a member of the Constituent Assembly, strove for the rights of the minorities to be protected by the Constitution. He was instrumental, along with Harendra C. Mookerjee (1887–1956), who chaired the minorities sub-committee of the Constituent Assembly, in having the right to practise and propagate one's religion included in the Constitution as a fundamental right. Nehru made D'Souza join India's delegations to the general assembly of the United Nations four times.

That was then. We are in the 'now'.

Only the other day, the president of the Bharatiya Janata Party said in Jerome D'Souza's Mangalore: 'It has become a fashion for persons and organisations to question nationalism by invoking their right to freedom of expression.' And he then told his listeners to 'isolate them' (*alag-thalag kar dijiye*). That phrase is about more than 'isolating'. It is about marking out, singling out, differentiating the holy from the…who? Dalits, Christians, Muslims?

Islam is exposed to a thousand questions, all zeroing in on beef, the triple *talaq*, jihad, the Taliban, al Qaeda, Islamic State of Iraq and al-Sham. Christianity, likewise, is unceasingly made to account for the inquisitions, crusades, colonialism, conversions, and even the Holocaust.

So, Ma Teresa, you who made waters thirst for the thirsty, food hunger for the hungry, the rich go a-begging for beggars, now as Saint Teresa, you have yet to do something beautiful for your India. Show it how being Catholic is about seeing Mary as the mother not of the Eastern-most Christian but the Western-most Asian. And show us, please, how pride at being a great democracy must be accompanied by shame at being so vulnerable a republic.

Make us whole, not holy, sainted mother.

Ami tomake pronam kari.

(*The Telegraph*, September 4, 2016)

42

At Point-Blank Range

THE TALIBAN GUNMEN WHO shot their targets, unarmed children, on their heads did so at 'point-blank range'. The heinousness of that act, accompanied by that description of the range, took me back to when, a child myself, I wanted to know what 'point-blank range' meant. The term had been used almost mechanically, without sufficient explanation, to describe the assassination of M.K. Gandhi and was taken generally to mean 'from up close'. We had no Wikipedia in those days but my father, a very facts-scrupulous newspaperman, supplied the detail. When a firearm's muzzle is not in actual contact with its target but is as close as about three feet from the chosen target at the moment of discharge, it is said to be at 'point-blank range'. The gunmen who had stormed the Peshawar school had shot the children, one by one, from that cynical distance. They wanted to be sure that they were not leaving their targets alive.

Other than being unarmed and unguarded, Gandhi had this in common with the slain children: the 79-year-old took the three bullets Nathuram Godse's Beretta M 1934 emptied into him from less than three feet away, from point-blank range. Godse too wanted to take no chances.

Anxiety and incredulousness pulsing in his voice, a friend asked me the other day: 'Could you have imagined, even as of a year ago, that we would be discussing a statue for Nathuram Godse in our country?'

I have imagined many slights of the Mahatma by a Hindutva-powered dispensation but I had not, I admitted, visualised this fancy of a perverse imagination.

It is not as if Godse has been regarded by all hands as a villain, no. Guided by the principle of *audi alteram partem* ('hear the alternative party too'), many have wanted to find out what prompted Godse to murder Gandhi. His testimony, written as well as extempore, before the three-judge bench of the Punjab High Court hearing his appeal, has been regarded by many as exceptional. Godse's belief in 'Akhand Bharat' and his delusionary thought that Gandhi was responsible for the Partition of India reached boiling point when Gandhi, through his last fast, made the new Government of India honour the agreed division of cash assets due to Pakistan. In Hindutva circles, particularly in Pune, Godse has been a cult figure who, by doing what he did on January 30, 1948, ranked in their esteem next only to his mentor, Vinayak Damodar Savarkar.

But this is neither unusual nor misplaced. The urge to be fair, objective and to walk the extra mile to understand the accused's point of view has been part of jurisprudential grace and historiographic civility. Abraham Lincoln's 26-year-old assassin, John Wilkes Booth, has received fair, even understanding attention from biographers of Lincoln and others. He had his beliefs. In a letter written to his sister, Booth had said that African slavery is 'one of the greatest blessings…God has ever bestowed on a favored nation'. And he regarded Lincoln as the reverser of that 'blessing'. Booth's boiling point came when Lincoln announced, after the war had been won, that he was going to give suffrage to the former slaves. Booth's diary entry has this about his victim: 'Our country owed all her troubles to him, and God simply made me the instrument of his punishment.' This is often quoted to show Booth as a man who was driven to do what he did on April 15, 1865. And contemporary records show that many drawing rooms in pro-slavery states had Booth's pictures adorning the walls till well after the war and the assassination had become history.

So Godse has company.

But there is a difference and it is huge.

Barring sympathisers of the Ku Klux Klan and racist freak-groups, no one in the United States of America or anywhere else speaks of Booth as a historical or even a 'personality' counter-point to Lincoln.

This is where our histories converge and diverge.

Racism in the US has had its hidden, even entrenched, adherents. Communalism in India has had its disavowing advocates. But racism has never come close to acquiring power through the ballot in Lincoln's country. Communalism has been more successful in Gandhi's India. It is within point-blank range of Gandhi once again.

Even as a strikingly beautiful statue of Gandhi becomes ready for unveiling in what could be regarded as his 'opposite goalpost', London's Parliament Square, we in India are talking about the rights and wrongs of a statue to his assassin. At one level, a rather facile one, this could be seen as a sign of India's political maturity, its democratic temper. 'We have only come of age,' I can hear a guileless democrat declaim, 'if we can un-agitatedly deliberate on a statue for the murderer of the Father of our Nation.' In actual fact, if we are considering an 'artistic' celebration of Gandhi's assassin, we have 'come of' or into nothing of the kind. We have only come to a sorry pass in our history where the bully scores over the innocent, the tyrant over the peaceable and where a new fascism that feeds on hate seeks to prevail over the Republic of Equality. A new iconism, operating through deft official and political patronage, seeks now to install the visual and textual accoutrement of a democratic oligarchy. The 'statue for Godse' idea is another example, and a particularly sinister one, of the audacity of this oligarchy that exploits our civility and our liberal ethos to further its purposes.

I would concede here that the 'Congress years' in their purblind self-centredness overdid statues and portraits, each more unaesthetic than the other, of Gandhi and, rather more so, of the Nehru sequence of its leaders. The eruption of statues of their political alternatives such as, notably, of Bhagat Singh, Subhas Bose, B.R. Ambedkar and of Periyar E.V. Ramasamy was an inevitable and wholly welcome correction. And was very much part of an evolving historical narrative.

The advocacy of a statue for Nathuram Godse and, more than that, the latitude given to that advocacy by the political power centres of the day, belongs to a different order of political iconography. It forms part of a conscious re-scripting of history, a re-choreographing of dramatis personae to validate that which is morally gross and politically outrageous.

It is my hope – even my 'gut' feeling – that the Government of India will dissuade the Godse-statue advocates from proceeding with their idea. But we may assume that the statue is already 'up', as a bronzed idea.

And the legend under it says: 'At point-blank range to plural Hindustan'.

(*The Telegraph*, January 26, 2015)

43

A Chronicle Foretold

THREE INDIANS WERE DECORATED with the Bharat Ratna in the very first year – 1954 – that the civilian awards were instituted: the elder Statesman, Chakravarti Rajagopalachari, the vice president, Sarvepalli Radhakrishnan, and the Nobel laureate, C.V. Raman. No one said at the time that all three were south Indian, all three Brahmins. Their pre-eminence was manifest. They accepted the decoration with respect and went about their work according to their lights.

All three had a Calcutta connection. CR had served as the first governor of West Bengal, the other two had taught, with distinction and dedication, at the University of Calcutta. *Om krato smara kritam smara*, the Isha Upanishad tells us. The work alone is to be remembered, the work alone.

It is instructive to see, on the anniversary of our Independence, what these men had to say in the midst of and, indeed, from the very heart of their work, about their country, their people.

CR was a prisoner of the Raj in 1921. Holed up in Vellore Jail, he could have been bitter about his jailers, about the imperial power. He could have looked forward to *swaraj* as one might to a dreamlike goal. But no, he did something that surprised his contemporaries then and surprises us now. He wrote in his jail diary: 'We all ought to know that Swaraj will not at once or, I think, even for a long time to come, be better government or greater happiness for the people. Elections and their corruptions, injustice, and the power and tyranny of wealth, and inefficiency of administration, will make a hell of life as soon as freedom is given to us. Men will look regretfully back to the old regime of comparative justice, and efficient, peaceful, more or less honest administration. The only thing gained will be that as a race we will be saved from dishonour and subordination.'

This was a full quarter century before *swaraj* was attained.

Radhakrishnan was a member of the Constituent Assembly on the midnight of August 14/15, 1947 when, with Jawaharlal Nehru, he made a speech of surpassing value. Reminding the nation of 'our national faults of character, our domestic despotism, obscurantism narrow-mindedness, superstitious bigotry', he said almost exactly what CR had said 25 years earlier. Radhakrishnan's words: 'Our opportunities are great but let me warn you that when power strips ability, we will fall on evil days…From tomorrow morning – from midnight today – we can no longer throw the blame on the British. We have to assume the responsibility ourselves for what we do. A free India will be judged by the way in which it will serve the interests of the common man in the matter of food, clothing, shelter and the social services. Unless we destroy corruption in high places, root out every trace of nepotism, love of power, profiteering and black-marketing which have spoiled the good name of this great country in recent times, we will not be able to raise the standards of efficiency in administration…'

That was said at the very moment free India was born.

I do not have access to any comment made by C.V. Raman on the eve of Independence but the following observation of CVR's to young Indians is an agnatic cousin of CR's and SR's: 'Success can only come to you by courageous devotion to the task lying in front of you and there is nothing [of] worth in this world that can come without the sweat of our brow. I can assert without fear of contradiction that the quality of the Indian mind is equal to the quality of any Teutonic, Nordic or Anglo-Saxon mind. What we lack is perhaps courage, what we lack is perhaps driving force which takes one anywhere. We have, I think, developed an inferiority complex. I think what is needed in India today is the destruction of that defeatist spirit…'

Today, those three Bharat Ratnas would have been saddened to see their apprehensions and prognoses coming true. Generalisations are wrong but who can deny that efficiency of administration is not India's best introduction? Who can deny that our elections have brought us a great stature in the world but have also brought corruption? And where is the doubt that the power and tyranny of wealth – CR's startling phrase – rules the land?

Power, political and monetary power, outstrips ability by a long measure. And corruption in high places – Radhakrishnan's astonishingly prescient expression – has disfigured the image of our public life.

As for the sweat of the brow, Raman's ideal, that has long since ceased to be valued, especially in oneself. The concept of hard work, of service, of what used to be called pride in one's work, is now an archaism. Except in our gifted artisans who survive miraculously, in our armed forces, in the body of farm labourers across the country and in a few remarkable professions like those of nurses and teachers, 'work ethic' is a national casualty.

We seek to derive the maximum advantage from the minimum effort. There is a mentality, widespread if not omnipresent, which sees the plodder as a fool, the successful shirker as clever. It only follows that the man or woman who is honest with money is regarded as naive, to be pitied, and the crook who gets caught making illegal money as unlucky. It is the honest politician, by which I mean one who does not encash files, sell favours, turn opportunities of service into ATMs, and there still are many of those, who keeps us in hope. It is, likewise, the exceptional official, doing the work of a hundred, who keeps the administrative machine from collapsing. Thank god there are some such exceptional men and women, still, amid us. But by and large, the surface density of work-shirking, responsibility-dodging, blame-shifting, back-biting, tale-carrying and, alas, palm-itchy laggards has swelled beyond belief. What we are, the State is.

Radhakrishnan also spoke of intolerance.

This trait takes many forms but nowhere more seriously than in politics. Ironically and paradoxically, the denominationally intolerant are being projected as administratively able. Those with a questionable secular integrity are said to be men of unquestionable financial integrity.

The first three Bharat Ratnas foresaw more than ordinary mortals can. But even they could not foresee the self-contradictory piquancy of our predicament today. The liberal Indian, the Indian with a secular conscience, an innately democratic instinct, a value for civil rights, is shown up as effete, a political pansy, whereas the macho rattler of sabres is offered to the nation as its saviour. A country with its work ethic weakened, its abilities outstripped by narrow self-interests, and its domination by the power and tyranny of wealth well-nigh complete, is easily persuaded to say 'give us a benign dictator'. Fascism comforts the sloth of mind, the slow of thought, the valuationally sluggish. Fascism excites the timid, the languid and the bored.

And so, we are seeing rise in the very heart of a democratic but languorous India a poison plume of the most corrosive intolerance. In the coming months the nation will be obsessed with who will 'make it' to the Lal Qila next August 15. That is only natural. But we should be agonising about what kind of flag will be unfurled on its ramparts – the great national Tricolour or one with a skull and crossbones sewn behind it.

(*The Telegraph*, August 15, 2013)

44

Honoured Guest

WE DO NOT REALISE how lucky we are, how profoundly lucky, to have in our midst the rather incredible human being called the Dalai Lama. Two Indians – both naturalised Indians – have won the Nobel Prize for Peace: Mother Teresa and the Dalai Lama. India lost no time in decorating the Saint of Kalighat with the Bharat Ratna, but only after she had got the Nobel. But the Dalai Lama, who won the Nobel in 1989, has not yet become a Bharat Ratna nor is likely ever to become one.

The reason is a five-letter word, China. There is no other. That the fear of displeasing another nation should stand in the way of India officially honouring a person the world honours is a matter of shame.

Our official policy has been unambiguous, since the time Jawaharlal Nehru was prime minister. It has four parts to it, each simpler than the other:

1. The Dalai Lama is India's honoured guest.
2. He is so, as a spiritual figure, not as a political exile.
3. Tibet is a part of China.
4. The Dalai Lama will not carry out any political activities from Indian soil.

He has been our guest now for over half a century. He has not once flouted the civil understanding that he should not say or do anything from Indian soil which could be seen as interfering in China's internal affairs. He has not once embarrassed us. He has done more: he has said repeatedly that he does not want an independent Tibet, that he only wants its cultural and religious uniqueness to be safeguarded. And yet, we are afraid: What will China say?

What can China say? Both India and the Dalai Lama have made it clear that they accept Tibet as a part of China. So, what stops us from giving ourselves the satisfaction of honouring the Dalai Lama, as we have done Mother Teresa?

There the National Democratic Alliance and the United Progressive Alliance governments have been on the same page. And Prime Minister Narendra Modi is not likely to be any different. But the Dalai Lama getting or not getting the

Bharat Ratna is not so important as our knowing the great asset we have amid us in terms of sheer spiritual intelligence. And that is no ordinary asset.

Over two days last month the Dalai Lama convened a meeting of the kind I have never seen before. It was a meeting of religious, theological and philosophical leaders to discuss the subject of inter-community harmony. To call it a Parliament of Religions would be exactly right. And it was pervaded by the spirit of the monk of Belur and the words he spoke in Chicago in 1893.

Those who are so assiduously co-opting his name and charisma today should ponder the words of Vivekananda at the World Parliament of Religions. 'I am proud to belong to a religion,' he said, 'which has taught the world both tolerance and universal acceptance…' Then, going on to say something we should repeat to ourselves a hundred times in India today, he said, 'Sectarianism, bigotry, and its horrible descendant, fanaticism, have long possessed this beautiful earth. They have filled the earth with violence, drenched it often and often with human blood, destroyed civilisation, and sent whole nations to despair…'

The New Delhi hall had persons in every religious garb and style – saffron, blue, black and white turbans, skull caps, tufted heads, scarved heads, beards trimmed and untrimmed, greying, hennaed and black, foreheads with *tilaks* on them and with the mark of the *namaz* on them. There was, of course, the gleaming Parsi hat, contrasting with the soft sufi head-cloth. And there was one venerable religious leader who wore nothing at all.

A good number of them spoke on the subject with a kind of mutuality that was unbelievable. The Dalai Lama sat in the 'audience', listening attentively to each speaker, nodding from time to time. He was visibly moved when a Hindu *dharmaguru* from Varanasi got up even as the head of Ajmer Sharif was speaking, went up to the stage and, as a token of endorsement, presented him a rose. A few people with no marked religious affiliation, like me, were lucky enough also to be invited. If this is how our religious leaders feel, it seemed to me, why should we worry for our plural future?

One example of direct intervention by a *dharmaguru*, I said with some temerity, will do what a thousand speeches will not. How many *dharmagurus* have died while trying to quell a riot? How many *ulema*? And just to drive home the point, I invoked five examples.

The first was from the third week of March, 1931. A savage sort of communal violence had engulfed Kanpur's mixed *mohallas*. Ganesh Shankar Vidyarthi – teacher, journalist, founder of *The Pratap* and president of the Uttar Pradesh Congress Committee in 1929 – did not phone the police. He did not go to newspaper offices to fulminate against communalism. He did not lapse into prayer, wailing or rhetoric. He did just what Gandhi wanted *satyagrahis* to do in communally charged situations. Over four days, Vidyarthi saved the lives of several – hundreds – Hindus and Muslims from the blind fury of the murderous hordes. On March 25, his biographer, Anandi Prasad Mathur tells us, that a man running for his life asked Vidyarthi to save some people who were hiding nearby. Not for the first time that day, Vidyarthi was in the direct line of death – blow upon blow raining on him, sharp instruments piercing his thin frame. Gandhi wrote in *Young India*: 'The death of Ganesh Shankar Vidyarthi is one to be envied by us all…Let this noble example stimulate us all to similar effort should occasion arise again.'

Occasion arose in 1946 – in Ahmedabad, Gujarat. It was July 1, the day of *Asad Sud*, when images of deities are taken out in a *rath yatra*. The city broke into the most ghastly communal riots. Thirty-year-old Vasantrao Hegiste and seventeen-year-old Rajab Ali were colleagues in the Congress. When news came from the suburb of Jamalpur that frenzied mobs were on the rampage there, Vasant and Rajab ran to the spot. They were threatened, but they defied the armed bullies and lay down in the rioters' path to protect their victims. They died, crushed by several murderous feet.

In August and September of 1947, when Gandhi was in Calcutta, the communal frenzy reached new heights. Gandhi moved to one of the city's most turbulent quarters, Beliaghata. Hydari Manzil, where he stayed, was attacked on the night of August 31, 1947, by bloodlust-crazed youths. They took an associate of Gandhi, Bishen, to be a Muslim and were about to kill him when Gandhi confronted them: 'Kill me, kill me I say, why don't you kill me?' The mob melted away. Two brave youths, in their 30s, volunteers of the Gandhi school, Smritish Banerjea and Sachin Mitra, went into the riot-affected areas the next day. Sachin was stabbed while trying to still mob fury on Calcutta's Zachariah Street, while Smritish became a martyr while watching over a peace march.

I was prepared for the religious heads present to be upset when they heard me say that it is men like these, not religious leaders, who have stemmed communal frenzy in India. But they did not react as I thought they would. They were in the Dalai Lama's presence.

What has been happening in parts of Uttar Pradesh in the last few weeks could be 'episodic', could be part of a pattern that is revealing only its tuft. Political leaders fomenting action and reaction go into hiding the moment the 'thing' starts. Religious leaders fall sagely silent. But, should occasion arise, if even one of them says, 'They will have to kill me first,' he would save innocent lives. The Dalai Lama would. But then he is under the 'honoured guest' protocol.

We have to be among the most paradoxical nations. The President of China is personally shown round Gandhi's ashram at Sabarmati by our prime minister. But the Mahatma's most cognate spiritual heir in India today, the Dalai Lama, half a century and more after having become one of us, must remain the gem we will not call by its name.

(*The Telegraph*, October 12, 2014)

45

Standing Tall, Together

I WRITE THIS ON Sardar Patel's birth anniversary – October 31 – which also happens to be the anniversary of Indira Gandhi's assassination.

If I was writing that preceding line last year, or on any year since 1984 until this year, I would probably have put it the other way round.

Probably.

The obscuring of the statesman's birth anniversary by the assassination of India's third prime minister has galled. It has seemed to be so not right, so muddled.

Jumping queues, elbowing someone out, stealing the limelight is the stuff of puerile, competitive politics. A politics we know well. But why should Time, oceanic, deep, vast, encourage the calendar in political one-upmanship?

Neither the Sardar nor Indira Gandhi willed the dates of their arrival and departure.

And yet...

Ever since Sardar Patel died, his birth anniversary has been observed by the Congress with a progressive regression, with an incremental indifference. The Congress can deny this only if it wishes to compete for a prize in incredibility. And the Indian State, for the years that it has been ruled by the Congress, has done likewise. Non-Congress governments at the Centre lacked both time and interest to correct the egregious error.

The most striking neglect took place in 1975, the centenary of the Sardar's birth. Reason: India was under its one and only – so far – national emergency.

India was in a state of utter fear, fear of the 'supreme leader'. No one dared ask her why the centenary of a man so supremely important to us was being passed by virtually unobserved. No one, not even leaders of the Gujarat Congress, dared ask her. Ask her? Why, they would not have dared ask even her home minister.

Now, in 2014, the year the Congress and its allies have suffered the worst-ever defeat at the national polls, comes the Great Correction – a new order of commemoration. And it is as loud in its happening as the neglect was in its not-happening.

I rejoice at this correction. Sardar Patel was not just central to the Congress's struggle for freedom, not just foundationally, definingly, vital to the emergence of India as we know it, but a leader in whose hands the integrity of the nation was safe. And so I feel joy at what is a rectification – something that was needed was being done. It is time, with its fresh knowledge of where it stands in the public's estimation, the Congress realised that it cannot be selective about repaying its arrears of gratitude. It cannot put on its plenary backdrop the cut-outs of the pre-Indira Gandhi greats as a sequence of also-rans, a sepia succession intoned merely for the record. It cannot perpetuate the myth that India is the Congress and the Congress is equal to a particular family. Jawaharlal Nehru, with his sense of history and of basic fairness and decency, would have revolted at that thought.

I believe that Sonia Gandhi does not subscribe to that myth. She is too aware of what can be called simple truths, bare facts, to believe in that myth. But such is the none-like-you, nothing-but-you, we're-sunk-without-you servility in her party that she does not call its bluff. And Dr Manmohan Singh does not believe in it either. But he is too deeply imbued by a sense of something he owes to a party that made him, an 'outsider' and a non-politician, prime minister of India.

It is clear as can be that in this great correction lies a great opportunity for Prime Minister Narendra Modi. In speaking of the Sardar, he appears handsomely non-partisan (Patel was after all a Congress leader), selfless (it is not his own birth anniversary), a good Gujarati (obviously) but no more than the Mahatma was (those two were 'inseparable'), an admirer of Patel's statecraft and of Patel's no-nonsense politics (which is, please note, his own).

This 'use' of Patel by the National Democratic Alliance is the offspring of the disuse of Patel by the Congress. This 'owning' of Patel is a result of the Congress' disowning of Patel. The embrace has followed the cold-shouldering.

Co-option is not less egregious than disinheritance. If in 1975, fearful people flinched from celebrating the Patel centenary, should people now attend Patel's birthday celebrations with another version of fear, fear of seeming to be not conforming?

Sardar Patel was the symbol of integration, not some monochromatic sameness called 'unity'. As Rajmohan Gandhi explains in his biography of the Sardar, his integration policy brought more people into India, including Muslims, than were lost to Pakistan. This was about bringing people in, including them in the rhythms of a new India, not steam-pressing them into some new-fangled conformity. That is what needs to be understood, acknowledged.

But there is more to all this than just one individual's stature and its acknowledgement or non-acknowledgement.

What we are witnessing is a playing out of posthumous rivalries by contemporary adversaries for present and future gain. This may or may not help the adversaries; it is harming us as a people.

Nehru as prime minister, in 1950, was a very confident prime minister at that, but the deputy prime minister was formidable. The nation was with Nehru; Congress MPs were behind Patel.

And yet, a largeness of heart overpowered all other emotions, ambitions. The two leaders made no secret of their differing viewpoints. In letters to each other, both offered to quit, leaving the 'reins' in the other's hands. And both withdrew their impulsive offers. Both walked out of crucial cabinet meetings, only to meet up again and resolve the precipitating difference in the nation's larger interest.

The Sardar, in 1950, was getting on to 75. Crumbled within himself after the Mahatma's assassination, he had already been through a heart attack. At a session of the All India Congress Committee, in Nasik that September, Patel told delegates from Gujarat to 'do what Jawaharlal says'.

And on October 2, 1950, at Indore, Patel said: 'I have been referred to as deputy prime minister. I never think of myself in these terms. Jawaharlal is our leader. Bapu appointed him as his successor and had even proclaimed him as such…It is the duty of all Bapu's soldiers to carry out his bequest. Whoever does not do so from the heart in the proper spirit will be a sinner before God.'

November 14, 1950 was the prime minister's 61st birthday. The 75-year-old deputy prime minister, ill and fatigued, sent him a handwritten greeting. On November 23, the prime minister came calling. 'I want to talk to you alone when I get a little strength…,' Patel said to Nehru. 'I have a feeling that you are losing confidence in me…'

Nehru replied, 'I have been losing confidence in myself.'

By the first week of December, he had lost the will to live. Patel's daughter Maniben heard him repeat Nazir's line, *'Zindagi ka yah tamasha chand roz…'* Doctors told him he should shift to Bombay, where the cold is less severe. To his loyal colleague in the cabinet, N.V. Gadgil, who came to say goodbye, Patel said, 'Make me a promise…I am not going to live…' And then taking Gadgil's hand into his own, 'Whatever your difference with Panditji, do not leave him…'

Rajendra Prasad, who would not have been president but for Patel, Nehru, who may well have left the prime ministership but for Patel's offering to vacate office himself, Rajaji, who was denied the presidentship largely due to Patel's preference for Prasad but retained Patel's affectionate esteem, were all there, and in scarcely concealed tears, as the Iron Man's pyre was lit on December 15, 1950.

Who, in the Bharatiya Janata Party or in the Congress, dare deny this legacy?

For we need to see, in our fractious times, how Nehru and Patel furled their egos and worked together.

We need them to work together again, Nehru to secure our pluralism and Patel to safeguard our integrity. And both to keep us from the coarsening of what can only be called our political *iman*.

A chance is presenting itself, on November 14 this year, for the prime minister to close the divide that is being kept wide open. A chance has come to him to invite the Congress president, not just to join but to lead the official celebration of Nehru's 125th birth anniversary.

That would be a Patel-like thing to do. Vintage Patel.

(*The Telegraph*, November 2, 2014)

46

Marching Along a New Path

I AM YET TO read Laura Dassow Walls's acclaimed 2017 biography of Henry David Thoreau. But from what I have been able to gather, it is kin to Ramachandra Guha's *Gandhi 1914–1948*.

Both books are incredible – for our times. For the reason that both those men seem to belong to another time, a different planet.

Thoreau's essay, 'Civil Disobedience', I am sure, does not find place in Donald Trump's bookshelf. He will just not be able to comprehend the author of *Walden* saying, 'Under a government which imprisons any unjustly, the true place for a just man is also a prison.'

Gandhi's appeal for Hindu–Muslim peace, signed with Jinnah, in the summer of 1947, would likewise not be part of Narendra Modi's favourite reading. He would just not relate to the appeal's statement: 'We denounce for all time the use of force to achieve political ends.' Turkey's supremo Recep Erdogan, Philippines's Rodrigo Duterte and Australia's Scott Morrison would not either. And Aung San Suu Kyi? Not first State Counsellor of Myanmar, Daw Suu. Mahinda Rajapaksa, standing with chest turned out and stomach tucked in, at power's doorstep in Colombo, would not have time for it at all.

Gandhi is far too idealistic for them all – Hindu, Muslim, Pentecostal, Roman Catholic, Theravada Buddhist. Altogether too humane.

But this is not just about political leaders, or individuals. It is, as I said, about our times. A growing sentiment is responding to majoritarian intolerance of difference, of variation, accommodation, sanctuary. Also, therefore, of indifference to civil liberty, human rights. And it is turning to the supremacist as hero.

Strength, not justice and power, not veracity, are the new gods.

While other books will tell us, for instance, of a typical Gandhi fast by its political or philosophical 'reason', its duration, its agonised inching towards termination, Guha will tell us of the fast's more mundane trigger. For instance, that his 1918 fast for the Ahmedabad mill-workers came after he heard what was literally bazaar gossip to the effect that Gandhi has a car to go about in, eats 'sumptuous food' while the striking mill-hands suffer. And it is this that stung him into the fast. Not an unknown factoid this, but an unnoticed one.

Similarly, great accounts of the Dandi March in 1930, like that vivified in Thomas Weber's *On the Salt March*, have re-enacted that iconic event. But Guha's tracking down 'an eyewitness' account converts the known depiction into some moving footage: 'It was a quick pace between running and walking...The breathless walk made you see how urgent and downright and final was his call...He did not tarry for the roadside honours...He passed on after a lady had placed a kumkum on his forehead...'

Diaries and letters of policemen, civil servants, governors are Guha's preferred sources of insight. And persons like Gandhi's one-time typist, R.P. Parasuram. For Guha, the hero lives in the detail. He has mastered a method, a sociologist's and anthropologist's perhaps. It is this: if you see a document or a photograph, capture its central image but thereafter let its margins, its edges, often frayed and crumpled, open to you another story.

And this is hugely rewarding.

Gandhi's talks with Governor Casey in Calcutta in 1945 are well documented but not quite so the fact that when Gandhi left the governor's mansion, 150 of the liveried attendants, Hindu and Muslim, thronged to salaam him (as recorded by Casey).

The assassination and funeral are, now, lore. Pyarelal has taken us through them in *The Last Phase,* and Rajmohan Gandhi has described them with the deeply moving intonations of a Greek tragedy in his biography, *Mohandas*. From Guha we get not just the burnt crimson of that moment but all the deepening tinctures that drowned with that setting sun. We get the make of the cortège-van, the name of its driver. And a vignette of the assassin in the police station, bleeding from the crowd's spontaneous mauling of him. The best of narrations can sometimes miss a step. Guha has 'Abha' for 'Manu' in his description of the grandniece who was pushed down violently by Godse seconds before he fired from his Beretta. But that does not take away from the magnetic charge of the account.

Guha's word-sketches of the figures, whether famous or scarcely known, with whom Gandhi lived and worked comprise the book's strength. Jinnah and Ambedkar come alive, not at a counter-helm but on the same deck as the main passenger. And with them, the great contestations of Hindustan, no less frenzied now than when Gandhi lived.

And with him gone.

In times such as these, for a new biography of Gandhi to have appeared at all and then to have received discerning appreciation the world over is extraordinary. In fact, it is incredible.

And yet Ramachandra Guha shows in his riveting biography that it is precisely in being out of tune, out of joint, with this 21st century of real and surreal inhumanities, that Gandhi's un-dimming appeal lies. He continues to do in an afterlife opera what he did all his working life: stun by difference.

Guha captures the paradoxical, enigmatic, contrarian Gandhi in his biography brilliantly. And he does so in his own hallmark biographer's style. That is, he goes not by the mastheads of Gandhi's life, not by the 'Gandhi era' headlines, but by the sub-masts, the sub-headers and the fine-font small-typeface details on which the big captions stand.

(*The Telegraph*, October 5, 2018)

47

Message from the Martyrs of Jallianwala Bagh

ONE HUNDRED YEARS AGO, on April 12, a letter dropped into the British Raj's postal system. The writer of the letter was a world-famous poet. That is not the only reason for the letter having been unusual. It was, by the political sights of the government of the times, seditionist. But luminously so.

The Raj's censors must have been greatly tempted to see its contents; perhaps they did, spurred by the ruling 'order' of the day, the Rowlatt Act. Curbing, in the name of war-time discipline, every conceivable civil liberty, the Act enabled stricter control of the press, arrests without warrant, indefinite detention without trial. It empowered the police to search a place and arrest any person they disapproved of without a warrant. Naturally, it outraged India, and both the writer and recipient of the letter.

Written on April 12, 1919, by Rabindranath Tagore to Mohandas K. Gandhi, it was about what its writer called 'the great gift of freedom'. He said: '...India's opportunity for winning it will come to her when she can prove that she is morally superior to the people who rule her by their right of conquest.'

'Faith or the life in death'

Tagore knew, doubtless, that the phrase 'morally superior' would strike a chord in Gandhi. As would the sentence that followed: 'She must willingly accept her penance of suffering, the suffering which is the crown of the great. Armed with her utter faith in goodness, she must stand unabashed before the arrogance that scoffs at the power of spirit.' Tagore ended the letter, as a poet would, with a verse: 'Give me the faith of the life in death, of the victory in defeat, of the power hidden in the frailness of beauty, of the dignity of pain that accepts hurt but disdains to return it.' Prose is ever the 'doer', poetry the 'artist'. And so this letter and the line just cited cannot hope to compete with Tagore's much-quoted poem 'Where the mind is without fear...' But taken for itself, this sentence has to rank among the greatest expressions in prose of truth's protest against power. Certain words, poetic word-images, in that line are scorching: death, defeat, dignity, pain, hurt.

India had, only a few days earlier, seen all those five word-images at play in Delhi. As the scholar-lawyer Anil Nauriya has recently reminded us, on March 30, 1919, the Raj's police fired at a gathering in Delhi protesting the Rowlatt Act on a call by Mahatma Gandhi for a nationwide hartal. Nauriya lists among them Hindus, Sikhs, Muslims.

A sample: Abdul Ghani, b. 1894. Killed in bayonet charge by a British Army unit near the Town Hall, Delhi. Atam Prakash: received bullet wound in firing by the police and died the same day. Chandra Bhan, b. 1889, received bullet wound in firing by an Army unit and died the same day. Chet Ram: received bullet wound in firing by the police and died the same day. Gopi Nath, b. 1889: received bullet wound in firing by an Army unit and died the same day. Hashmatullah Khan: b. 1890: received bullet wound in firing by an Army unit and died the same day. Mam Raj: received bullet wound in firing by the police and died the same day. Radha Saran, b. 1897: received bullet wound in firing by an Army unit and died the same day. Radhey Shyam, b. 1891: received bullet wound in firing by an Army unit and died the same day. Ram Lal, b. 1886: received bullet wound in firing by an Army unit and died the same day. Ram Saroop: received bullet wound in firing by the police and died the same day. Ram Singh: b. 1891: received bullet wound in firing by an Army unit and died the same day. Chander Mal: received bullet wound in firing by the police and died the same day. Seva Ram: received bullet wound in firing by the police and died the same day. Swattin, son of Abdul Karim: received bullet wound in firing by the police and died the same day.

The Delhi firing was, as it were, a macabre rehearsal for what was to follow. And it was doubtless on Tagore's mind when he wrote the letter to Gandhi. It was still in the post's pipelines when, the next day, on April 13, 1919, his poetic vision was to find prescient corroboration. Sikhs, Hindus and Muslims gathered in Jallianwala Bagh, Amritsar, Punjab not to oppose Rowlatt but for a festival that marks the Sikh new year, Baisakhi. Its intent was totally unpolitical. But who is to say how arrogance will work?

On April 13, 1919

What followed is now part of the world's annals of state-led crime. Troops under the command of Brigadier General (temporary rank) Reginald Dyer entered the garden, blocking the main entrance after them, took up position on a raised bank, and on Dyer's orders fired at the crowd for some 10 minutes, minutes that were an eternity. They stopped only when the ammunition supply was almost exhausted. Official sources themselves gave a figure of 379 identified dead, with approximately 1,100 wounded. In those 10 minutes Amritsar became India. It embodied a nation's death-defying dignity in pain, hurt.

Tagore was, at the time of the mowing down, 'Sir' Rabindranath. And he had been a Nobel laureate for Literature for six years. On May 30, 1919, Tagore picked up his pen, this time; not that of a Nobel laureate but of a Knight of the British Empire, to write a letter to the Viceroy, Lord Chelmsford. 'News of the sufferings,' he wrote, had 'trickled through the gagged silence, reaching every corner of India.' He then said: 'The time has come when badges of honour make our shame glaring in their incongruous context of humiliation…I for my part wish to stand, shorn of all special distinctions, by the side of my countrymen who, for their so-called insignificance, are liable to suffer a degradation not fit for human beings.' And he asked of the Viceroy, 'Relieve me of the title of knighthood.'

Solidarity with suffering, especially when it is spontaneous, takes many forms. One is sharing by renunciation. Tagore's self-divestment of the title, then perhaps the most coveted, of 'Sir' was an act of spontaneous solidarity with the suffering of Delhi, of Amritsar. And it was a chastisement, in Tagore's words, of the 'arrogance that scoffs at the power of spirit'.

The martyrs of Jallianwala beckon this generation, all of us, including India and Indians, Pakistan and Pakistanis, Bangladesh and Bangladeshis, Myanmar and Myanmarese, not just Britain, to give human freedom respect, human beings dignity, human rights recognition. Looking around them at those slain – Hindu with Dalit among them, Sikh and Muslim – the martyrs of Jallianwala would want correction and atonement from those on the Indian subcontinent and beyond its boundaries, who today foment division, discord, disunity.

Enduring arrogance

They also beckon us to see that 'arrogance of power' is not a colonial or imperial patent, nor 'the power of spirit' an attribute of liberation struggles alone. Arrogance can occur under post-colonial, post-imperial, 'independent' skies and can – must – summon the power of spirit.

'Rowlatt' is a temperament that seeks domination, control, hegemony. It has the characteristics of the bully – strength and insecurity. Asia, Africa and Latin America have known that temperament in both the hubris of the external ruler, the hauteur of the one within. And they have seen people's power dismantling both. Bowing to public opinion in India and in the UK, the raj repealed the Rowlatt Act, the Press Act, and 22 other laws in March

1922 – a victory of the people. The Rowlatt temperament is not a feature of governments alone. It works in society as well, keeping sections of it in a state of chronic enfeeblement. The Rowlatt temperament is also to be seen in corporate India seeking monopolist domination over its natural resources and public commons.

This centenary of India's rebuffing of the Rowlatt Act's scowl through what Tagore called 'the power of spirit' is one to be cherished, celebrated and be inspired by.

(*The Hindu*, April 13, 2019)

48

Sardar Patel: Truth and Hype About a Leader

SARDAR VALLABHBHAI PATEL WAS the most powerful man of his time.

The Mahatma was the most respected, Jawaharlal Nehru the most loved and Subhas Bose the most longed-for. But in terms of the iron control he exercised over the largest political apparatus in the country and the grip he had on political currents and cross-currents in virtually every province in India, the power wielded by the Patidar from Karamsad, Gujarat, had no match. No near-match, either. Not by far.

Gandhi loved Jawaharlal, trusted Prasad, admired Rajaji, esteemed Azad. But Patel, he leaned on and laughed with. Patel regarded Gandhi as his mentor, his leader.

And yet he 'owned' an equation with the Mahatma that was special. Everyone laughs differently with different people. What Gandhi and Patel planned together, worked-at together, history has recorded. What they laughed over, only they knew. And Gandhi's secretary, Mahadev Desai.

Here are two samples given by Desai in his diaries:

The year is 1932. They are all three prisoners, at Poona's Yeravada jail.

June 11, 1932.

Gandhi (in a sombre mood, contemplating death): Some day or other one must mount the shoulders of the bearers.

Patel: Bring the ship to shore first and then go where you like.

November 24, 1932.

Gandhi (on reading a hate-letter from a person who says that he, the writer, is unfortunate to be living in the same age as Gandhi): Tell me, what sort of reply should I send him?

Patel: Tell him to poison himself.

The Mahatma could not have guessed then that the man giving him this advice was the future deputy prime minister of India and the Sardar could not have known that he, as deputy prime minister and home minister, would have to answer difficult questions about the assassination of his leader.

Prime Minister Nehru and Home Minister Patel had different perceptions on the role of the RSS in the Gandhi assassination. But, as Rajmohan Gandhi tells us in his epic biography of Patel, Nehru wrote to Patel on February 3, 1948: 'I have been greatly distressed by the persistence of whispers and rumours about you and me…We must put an end to this mischief.'

Patel, addressing the Congress in the Constituent Assembly for the first time after Gandhi's departure, called Nehru 'my leader'. The home minister had no doubt in his mind as to who had conspired to kill Gandhi.

'It was the fanatical wing of the Hindu Mahasabha,' Patel wrote to Nehru, on February 27, 1948, 'that (hatched) the conspiracy and saw it through.' A ban followed.

The country's leading socialists targeted the home minister for his ministry's failure to protect Gandhi and asked him to resign. They did not know that Patel had already sent in his resignation to Nehru who had refused to countenance it.

Patel heard his critics patiently and then said he had had several arguments with the Mahatma to let police be stationed in the house he was staying in, but he had turned the idea down outright. And then Patel told his socialist critics not to 'exploit the greatest misfortune and calamity of the nation for party ends'.

Patel's death stunned the nation, Nehru more than anyone else. He was now all in all but all alone. The BJP's prime ministerial candidate Narendra Modi is reported to have alleged that Nehru did not attend Patel's funeral.

Only the ignorant will believe this. Prime Minister Nehru went to Bombay to attend the last rites of his comrade and before doing so, told Parliament '…he will be remembered as a great captain of our forces in the struggle for freedom and as one who gave us sound advice in times of trouble and in moments of victory, as a friend and a colleague on whom one could invariably rely, as a tower of strength which revived wavering hearts.'

With all their differences of style and temperament, Nehru and Patel would have given the country a balance of leadership styles, Prasad and Rajaji helping to cement the duumvirate. But the Fates willed otherwise.

Patel's death, Prasad's absorption into constitutional propriety and Rajaji's returning to Madras left the Congress a one-tree hill. And despite Nehru's instinctively democratic temper, a slow but steady monoculturism took hold over the party which forgot, surprisingly fast, its most powerful 'captain'.

Does the BJP have any right, political, moral or any other, to appropriate the legacy of Sardar Vallabhbhai Patel? None. But it does have an excuse to do so.

The misuse of Patel is the result of the disuse of Patel, the counterfeiting of Patel is the result of the forfeiting of Patel. The BJP would never have thought of gilding the Sardar's legacy if it had not got dust-laden and cobwebbed in its own home.

Party politics in today's India is a child of political power practices from ancient and medieval times. These, to oversimplify them, have traditionally spun around two cults.

First, the hero-worshipping of a figure who is thought to be half-man and half-lion or tiger. This cult may be called lionism. The second, a sycophantic worshipping of descendants thought to be indestructibly self-perpetuating. This cult may be called scionism.

Both cults operate within and across the main political divide of India, especially in the states where the lion and tiger loom large as symbols, and where dynastic arrangements reign in most parties. Lionism and scionism have sought to perpetuate themselves by propitiating their icons. Both are in tragic error, both futile.

Patel would have told both cults off in no uncertain terms. We must not let the misappropriation of Patel go unchallenged. But we must seek his re-appropriation nationally, for we need his aura and Nehru's to work together again.

The hollow 'hunkar' of a lion's paper mask has tried to blow the dust off Patel's legacy. It has coated it, in the process, with the out-breath of a poor joke.

But the dramatics have done us all an unintended favour. They have jogged our memories of the tower of strength that we, in our troubled times, need so urgently to revive our wavering hearts.

(*Hindustan Times*, November 2, 2013)

49

Only Half Our Story

THE NATION CELEBRATES HIM, celebrates it with him.
A flurry of activity overwhelms Rashtrapati Bhavan, particularly the First Lady. As one on the President's staff, I have seen Janaki Venkataraman and Usha Narayanan interiorise the tensions of that national celebration which has its focus in their house, and maintain the composure required of their role through all the comings and goings, split-second departure and arrival timings, the evening reception arrangements and the one for the banquet in honour of the visiting dignitary from abroad. Since the presidents themselves are preoccupied, First Ladies are besieged by childish importunings from relatives, friends and acquaintances for passes for the parade and cards for the At Home. Tact of the highest order is called for, and all this with gnawing anxieties about things, like security, that can go wrong.

Just as no two presidents are alike, no two First Ladies can be similar either and Shubhra Mukherjee will find her own way of addressing her first Republic Day as First Lady. Those who know her, speak of her deep piety and, despite several tribulations like the denial of good health, an acceptance of all that which the Almighty has chosen for her.

Quiet support from their wives has been the great and wholly unacknowledged privilege of our heads of State. But not all of them had the fortune of living in the palace with their wives beside them.

The first Indian to occupy the palace atop Raisina Hill, C. Rajagopalachari, was a widower. His wife Alarmel Manga had died when he was a 36-year-young lawyer in Salem. In his biography of the only Indian Governor General of India, Rajmohan Gandhi describes a day in February 1915 thus: '...he fell seriously ill...On the 14th his condition was judged critical...Manga herself had high fever that night. Yet determined to pray befittingly for her husband's life, she...supplicated Lord Venkateshwara. If her husband recovered, she would offer...(her) jewels to the Tirupati shrine...That night CR slept surprisingly well...Manga's petition seemed granted...However Manga herself...was declining...Nights without sleep were now frequent for CR... On the afternoon of August 22...she said "...I am such a burden...There must be a limit to the endurance of the greatest love..." "*Manga*," he cried. "*Manga*". There was no response. Over three decades later, on shifting to the palace, one of the first "home" things CR did was to place a picture of Manga on his bedroom wall.'

The second Indian and the first president to live in Rashtrapati Bhavan had the most appropriate name for a Rashtrapati – Rajendra, meaning King of Rajas, or the Head of the Kingdom. But his wife had an even more fortuitously apposite name – Rajbansi, meaning 'of the family of Rajas'. The word 'diminutive' may be said to have been coined for Rajbansi Devi. Four feet nothing, she moved from room to stately room with the same carefree gait with which she might have wandered in a mango grove in Bihar. Rajbansi Devi had a modest wardrobe of khadi saris, but they were simply exquisite. She could spin khadi to perfection. And though she chose not to appear at State banquets, nor accompany the President on his (rare) visits abroad, she would go with him, invariably, to Rajghat on the two annual commemorations, sit beside him and ply the charkha there for a long hour. She had a mind of her own, and on the second and third floors of the presidential residence there was no doubt as to who was in total, audible and visible charge. Rajbansi Devi, unknown outside the Hill and un-recalled outside of her family, was India's first First Lady for 12 long years.

Sarvepalli Radhakrishnan, our second President, should ideally have moved into the House with his wife Sivakamu by his side. They had been married 53 years and she had travelled with him to set up home in places as diverse as Madras, Waltair, Oxford, Moscow and New Delhi. In 1956, while he was vice president, she passed away in their home in Madras. Their son, the historian S. Gopal, writes in his remarkably candid biography of Radhakrishnan: 'He recognised that she was the foundation of his life...and a happy marriage, as he saw it, did not require the husband's monogamous attitude.... She was a devoted wife by any standards; he was a devoted husband according to his lights...' The vice president, who was in Delhi on the day, rushed back to Madras. Gopal: 'To those present it was clear he had been devastated by grief, even at one time sobbing like a child...Doubtless he lived through again in his mind the years when she had supported him and recollected his need for her love at later times even though he had not rejected self-indulgence elsewhere.' Sivakamu Radhakrishnan, as First Lady, would have been a golden buttress to that flagstaff of India's collective consciousness.

Our First Ladies have been taken for granted by the conventions of chronicling. This is in keeping with our mentality that regards wives, especially wives of active and prominent men, as ornamental appendages. Records of the presidencies of the US, for instance, show how deeply impactful were the personalities of the First Ladies on the respective presidents and their presidencies. Why is this not the case with us? Have our First Ladies been any less schooled in life and its trials, any less aware of the pulsations of our land, of the strengths and weaknesses of their husbands? Certainly not. It is just that our minds open the door wide to the man, doormat the woman. This is not a loss to the women concerned as much as it is to ourselves and to our understanding of our history.

Kasturba Gandhi and Kamala Nehru have managed, almost miraculously, to obtain some attention, but we do not even know the names of the wives of several of our great leaders – Maulana Azad's wife, the extraordinary Zuleikha Begum, who died when he was in the Ahmednagar Fort Prison; Sardar Patel's wife Jhaverba, who seems to have been obliterated from all accounts, even his own; or the two women Khan Abdul Ghaffar Khan was married to. We know not nearly enough about the wives of Lokamanya Tilak and Gopal Krishna Gokhale, or of Ramabai, Dr B.R. Ambedkar's first wife, to whom he was married for nearly 30 formative and troubled years until her death.

Prabhavati, wife of the Loknayak Jayaprakash Narayan, is an exception. She has a place of her own in our political history and many believe JP's response to the Emergency would have been less strident had Prabhavati been alive at the time. Whether that would have been good for India or not is of course another matter.

Unseeing eyes and un-recognising minds notice but half our story. And not necessarily the more worthy half.

(*Hindustan Times*, January 26, 2013)

PART V

The Ideas of India

50

Ink That Protects the Sanctity of Elections

On the eve of elections to the Lok Sabha, it is natural – and desirable – to think of the first general elections that took place in India, between October 1951 and February 1952. That election year for the country's 360 million people was the first such in independent India professing no single religion, no single doctrine whether political or ideological. The only qualification for an Indian citizen to vote was age – the person, man or woman, of any or no religious denomination, of any or no caste, educated or not, propertied or not, should be above 21 years of age.

By this calculation, 173 million Indian men and women became entitled to vote and elect their governments and their Opposition. A bigger election had not been held anywhere in the world. India could, and did, take pride in – a global pride – the fact that its suffrage was going to be universal, free and fair.

The year 1951 needs to be remembered by and for, and as many things as one can in the context of that election but also very specially, as the year of an ink – the indelible ink used to mark voters' left forefingers to prevent multiple voting by impersonation. We have moved now from the paper ballot to the EVM but the inking of fingers remains in place. Because the risk of impersonation remains in place!

The inking had to be done before being given the ballot paper. This column today is about the making of that ink, which is a story in itself. It is wrapped around the younger of two brothers from Mirzapur, Khaliquzzaman (1889–1973) and Salimuzzaman Siddiqui (1897–1994). The first of them was a politician, a leading light of the Muslim League who knew well India's political leadership, in both the Congress and Muslim League, and the second, in a very different field – chemistry and chemistry research. Salimuzzaman, who, unlike his brother, kept his family name of Siddiqui, is indelibly linked to the evolution of a feat in chemistry and Indian public life – indelible election ink.

Siddiqui, as a chemist working in the Indian Council for Scientific and Industrial Research in the mid-1940s, was contacted by its director general Shanti Swarup Bhatnagar (1894–1955), who asked him to help with the formulation of an indelible ink, which could be used in the elections that were due to the new Constituent Assembly. Bhatnagar, a distinguished chemist himself, sent to Siddiqui a solution of silver chloride to see if that could be developed into the required ink for use by the Election Commission of India (ECI). I am no chemist and am using these names mechanically, without understanding their chemical properties, only their salience to our elections.

Siddiqui found that silver chloride did not stain well. So, he added silver bromide to it and, I am told, there was an immediate improvement in the staining power. Working on that combination, Siddiqui was able to start the manufacture of the indelible ink for use in the 1951–1952 elections.

An unsubstantiated story has it that Quink, the famous Parker pen ink, owes its name to a Filipino, Francisco Quisumbing, who had made and was propagating an ink called Quisumbing Ink which became Quink. Be that as it may, the ink that Siddiqui developed should really have been unofficially called Siddiquink. The ink was introduced for the 1951–1952 elections and irrespective of who won or lost in that election, Siddiqui's indelible ink was a winner in what it was seeking to win – indelibility and impersonation stalling.

I was six years old at the time and the memory I have of that election – and it is indelible – is of my parents coming back from the polling station and chatting about the new experience of having their fingers marked by the indelible ink. We, their children at home, crowded around them to examine this new curiosity, when an old friend of the family walked in just then, also having just voted. He said to my father that he had heard – typical of our sceptical minds – that the ink was not all that indelible and that impersonation could take place by people removing it with a moistened matchstick tip. What, really! And pronto, a matchbox was obtained from the kitchen, two matchstick tips dipped in water, followed by both gentlemen trying with great seriousness to do the little cosmetic act. But – kudos to Siddiqui and the Election Commission, the ink stain would not go. It became fainter, yes, but disappear it would not. Their fingertip skins smarting under the 'attack', the two gentlemen complimented ECI and started talking about other things which did not interest me.

There is a sequel to this that is of interest.

The Partition of India was only four years old and the newly born country was setting up its political and institutional systems. The first Prime Minister of Pakistan, Nawabzada Liaquat Ali Khan, is believed to have contacted Siddiqui and invited him to migrate to Pakistan and help its chemical enterprises. The story is that, the younger brother of the Muslim League politician Chaudhuri Khaliquzzaman was known to Nehru and went to him for advice. Contrary to what one may imagine, Nehru said to him he could go. And he did rise to some status as a pharmacological chemist, becoming the founder and chairman of the National Science Council of Pakistan. But his ink remained in India, indelibly, on millions of forefingers, resurrecting itself, in election after election, safeguarding the peoples' mandates.

I would like to end this column by saying our elections are, above everything else, a great equaliser, a great leveller. From the President of India down to the most humble voter, all vote equally and are inked by the same ink, exactly like each other.

Could anyone have dared impersonate the President of India?

Of course not.

But President K.R. Narayanan, in the 1999 elections, exercised his franchise. He was what he liked to think himself to be, a citizen President and gladly had his forefinger inked exactly like the voter who went just before him and the one who went just after him, did.

And his vote joined the millions of other votes in the great churn of ballots that make India's electoral democracy what it is – a matter of pride, if also of concern about its 'bio-chemistry' that requires great vigilance against subversions of which voter impersonation is but one.

(*Hindustan Times*, April 14, 2024)

51

A Call to Treat India's Prisoners Fairly and Humanely

IT COULD BE YOU or me. Any of us could find ourselves in any one of the 1,500 or so of our jails, sub-jails, district jails or central jails in India. Just as any of us could find ourselves in any of our hospitals – private, or government-run. Just as illness can come of our own doing, we can fall foul of the law wantonly. But just as hospitalisation can also come of dratted ill-luck, imprisonment can come out of plain horrible mischance. And we would be in utter shock, stunned and speechless, if – God forbid – that happens.

Nearly 5,50,000 of us are 'in' today. I have used the word 'us' advisedly. I could have said 'like us' but 'us' is more like it. I am borrowing the phrase from the remarkable Jacinda Ardern, prime minister of New Zealand, who said of the victims of the Christchurch massacre and their kin: 'They are us.' She did not say 'They are just like us' or 'They are one of us'. She said, 'They are us.' If we think of prisoners as 'us', it would be good for them, but even more so for us, because we could be them. You and I could be reading this where no one would want to be. Nearly 4,25,000 of these 'us' are not convicts. That is to say, they have not yet been found guilty and sentenced to prison terms. They are undertrials and many or most of them are likely to be completely innocent of any crime, or at least innocent of an intent to commit crime. Sheer misfortune has brought these undertrial prisoners to the clink, leaving them and their families shattered, their plans and aspirations in a confused jumble of shock, disbelief, fear, agony and worst of all, utter and miserable uncertainty.

There is no telling when their cases will be heard, finalised, setting them free if innocent, or sentenced if not. Imagine when completely fit, being forced to be in hospital, restrained there, with 'real' patients, many of them suffering from incurable and infective conditions. And with no idea of when, if ever, one will be 'discharged'. Unbearable thought! But that is how it is for undertrials.

Any offence committed, wantonly or unwittingly, that is cognisable can invite arrest without warrant, and lead to the start of investigations by the police without the orders of a magistrate. These cognisable offences can be non-bailable – ranging from heinous crimes such as murder, kidnapping, theft, dowry deaths to some others that enter a very grey zone of interpretation such as sedition and defamation. And then, there are offences that are outside the world of the Criminal Procedure Code and the Indian Penal Code (IPC), residing in various statutes. A glance at the words invoking these crimes can make one say in smug home-based judgment: 'Serves the wretched man right.' But we should remember that at the time of arrest what we are seeing or talking of is not a crime but a suspicion of crime, an imputation or accusation, very likely to be correct, but also likely to not be. And we should remember too that these suspicions or accusations can be the result of malice, vendetta and plain tendentious prejudice.

Bailable cognisable offences, which we can most unwittingly be guilty of, include finding oneself in an 'unlawful' assembly or 'committing affray'. That – affray – is an interesting word of which the IPC says: 'When two or more persons, by fighting in a public place, disturb the public peace, they are said to commit an affray.'

On any normal day, one may witness affrays and even get involved in one.

The simple fact is that we live on the rim of situations that can make any of us one of the 5,50,000 of us who are 'in'. A thin door moving on a very slender hinge separates the 'outs' from the 'ins'.

Since the possibility of arrest – deserved and undeserved – is and will remain an all-time given, the very least one may aspire to is the speedy completion of trials and the institution of humane conditions in all jails. I am aware of the fact – who is not? – that prisoners include hardened criminals who are a menace to society and a threat to fellow prisoners and require to be kept under the tightest surveillance. But that ugly truth is no reason for prisons to respond to the barbarity of a few with brutality in general.

Which is why I brought my palms together in admiration of the Madurai bench of the Madras High Court which on January 2 directed the state to amend its prison rules so as to accord with the Model Prison Manual of 2016 and the United Nations Standard Minimum Rules for the Treatment of Prisoners, also known as the Nelson Mandela Rules. Passing orders on a public interest litigation, Justices R. Mahadevan and Sathya Narayana Prasad directed the government to create a prisoners' rights handbook and distribute copies of it to all inmates. Their lordships also directed the state to ensure an effective functioning of the visitorial system and constitute a board of visitors, including non-official visitors, for all prisons. Other directions included: preventing overcrowding, ensuring the availability of drinking water, hygienic food and medical attention. And most significantly, a grievance redressal mechanism.

The Madurai order quoted Mandela as saying: 'No one truly knows a nation unless one has been inside its jails. A nation should not be judged by how it treats its highest citizens but its lowest ones.'

I must admit I had not heard of the Nelson Mandela Rules until I read reports of this order. It is an amazing document. Its opening rule says: 'All prisoners shall be treated with the respect due to their inherent dignity and value as human beings. No prisoner shall be subject to, and prisoners shall be protected from torture and other cruel, inhuman or degrading treatment or punishment for which no circumstances whatever will be invoked as a justification.'

Answering Question No. 3257 in the Rajya Sabha posed by K.C. Ramamurthy, the Union minister of state for home Kishan Reddy said on March 24 last year that his ministry had circulated the Nelson Mandela Rules to all states and Union territories so as to ensure that they are followed. Now that the Madras High Court has made the matter a judicial imprimatur, the Union and state governments have an opportunity to make the Nelson Mandela Rules an Azadi ka Amrit Mahotsav finale. And thereby make India known as a model in prison administration.

(*Hindustan Times*, January 14, 2023)

52

We Owe Our Freedom to the Salt of Our Earth

THIS, THE 75TH YEAR of India's Independence, is the year of the Tricolour. As our flag unfurls, our minds awaken; as it flutters, our hearts miss or gain a beat. And images come to us of our leaders, the likes of whom the world has not known.

But our leaders could not have led, our movements could not have worked, our struggle for freedom could not have triumphed without the people of India. When, after the success of the South African satyagraha, Gandhi and his wife Kasturba were being felicitated in London on August 4, 1914, he said, 'We...got the limelight in South Africa but if we merited any approbation, how much more did those who went into the struggle with no thought of appreciation! Harbut Singh was 75 when he joined the struggle and entered prison and died there. The young lad Narayanaswami was deported to Madras and on his return, starved and died....And Valliamma, a girl of 18 went to prison and was discharged only when she took very ill and died shortly thereafter. 20 thousand workers had left their tools and work and gone out in faith. Violence was entirely eschewed. We are poor mortals before these heroes and heroines.' And he added, 'It is on these men and women, who are the salt of the earth that the Indian nation will be built.' Among those listening were persons of present and future fame – Lala Lajpat Rai, Sachchinanda Sinha and Bhupendranath Basu, Sarojini Naidu and M.A. Jinnah. To all of them, his message about who the real heroes and heroines of the struggle were, went home.

This jubilee year, this year of collective recalling and celebrating, is, therefore, not just about the leaders but about those who made the leaders, powered the movements, gave the struggle its voltage, velocity and – victory. It is about those heroes and heroines, the salt of the earth to whom we owe our freedom, our opportunities, our achievements in the gift of freedom that they have given us. When we falter, fail and go wrong, when our faith wavers and our covenants with our political conscience fray, we let down not just the great Swami, our beloved Vivekananda, the Lokamanya, our cherished Bal Gangadhar Tilak, our Mahatma, our valiant Jawahar whom Tagore described as '*the tarun tapasvi*', our indomitable and only one such Sardar Patel, the scholar-nationalist Maulana Azad, our immortal Shaheed Bhagat Singh, our brilliant law-giver, Babasaheb Ambedkar, not just them, but we betray the salt of our earth, of India. The salt satyagraha of 1930 along the coast of Gujarat, which shook the British Raj as nothing else had, therefore, more than the accident of a catchy idea – salt. It was a recognition of the metaphoric salt. The salt of our earth, the masses that make the peoplehood of India.

This year is also the 80th anniversary of the Quit India movement of 1942. Just as 1857, the year of the First War of Independence, is an unforgettable year, so is 1942. It was on August 8, that the great call to the Raj to quit India was given by the leaders of India, speaking on behalf of its heroes and heroines. At the iconic meeting held in Bombay, the salt of India's earth spoke through its spokespersons – Gandhi, Nehru, Patel, Azad, Kripalani. And the Raj shook. The entire leadership was arrested overnight. Gandhi, with Kasturba, was jailed in Poona. Nehru, Patel, Azad, Kripalani, Asaf Ali, Gobind Ballabh Pant, Shankarrao Deo, the Oriya leader Harekrushna Mahtab, Pattabhi Sitaramayya were locked up in Ahmednagar Fort. Not for a few days or months but for three years. Kasturba died while in that prison. Azad lost his wife, Zuleikha, while he was in jail.

But these were 'specifics' before the bigger, larger, and overwhelming truth: tens of thousands were arrested, mass fines were levied and innumerable real heroes and heroines subjected to public flogging during that movement. It is their sacrifice, purity and hope that we celebrate this year. Their ardour, their sense of duty to India. This year, therefore, is a year of the Tricolour at its most fluent, its truest vibrancy. How are the people of struggling India to be honoured by the people of liberated India? By seeing this anniversary as more than a celebration of the past. By seeing it, to adapt a phrase from Abraham Lincoln, as a consecration of the present for the greatness of our future – in equity and freedom.

(*Hindustan Times*, June 29, 2022)

53

On Reality of Caste, Bihar Holds a Mirror

THERE IS SOMETHING ABOUT Bihar.

It may be the state where the Buddha attained his enlightenment (Bodh Gaya, c. 450 BCE), where the world's first residential university flourished (5th to 13th century CE), where Guru Gobind Singh, the 10th Sikh Guru, was born (Patna, 1666), Gandhi started his first satyagraha (Champaran, 1917), the state from which India's first President Rajendra Prasad hailed (serving from January 26, 1950), where Jayaprakash Narayan commenced his transformative movement against corruption and misrule (1974). But it remains the state that is the subject of the intensest political speculation, and critical comment.

It gets judged adversely and is derided. Its being the third most populous state in India (after Uttar Pradesh and Maharashtra) with the highest population density in the country (1,102 per sq. km), the lowest literacy rate (61.8 per cent), the worst sex ratio (895 females to 1,000 males) are held up against it, quoted in season and out of season. Twenty-five years is a long time. In the political life of a country, that span is longer than its chronological span. If asked what happened in September/October – around this time – 25 years ago, in 1998, in and around the subject of Bihar, one would have to think very hard.

Yet that was a time when Bihar was the centre of political activity. And not an ordinary one at that, for it involved the then President of India, K.R. Narayanan and the then Government of India, led by Atal Bihari Vajpayee. The government of Bihar was being described as dysfunctional, and 'non-existent'. Bihar being on the defensive in numerous court cases was going against it.

The spirited, now-jocund, now-sombre, never-say-die Lalu Prasad had lost his office as chief minister of Bihar in 1997 amid allegations of corruption. In July of that year, he had stunned the political world of India by seeing to it that if he were to leave, his wife Rabri Devi would succeed him. This was considered a joke, a poor one at that. That she was duly elected leader by the party that held a majority in the Legislative Assembly and was legally and constitutionally entitled to that seat, that office, that position of power, was not taken seriously. That a wife, merely because she was the former chief minister's wife, and not a formally educated woman at that, had become chief minister 'through the back door', was what was being said. And by this time in 1998, Rabri Devi's government was in deep trouble.

The precariousness of her numbers in the House apart, her government was being criticised for its standards of governance. No one spoke up for its palpable under-performance, no one wanted to be seen as a defender of her patently unedifying rule. In September 1998, the Union cabinet recommended to President Narayanan that the government of Rabri Devi be dismissed and President's Rule imposed under Article 356 of the Constitution of India. Crucial to the recommendation was the report of newly appointed BJP-affiliated Governor Sunder Singh Bhandari citing financial mismanagement and poor law and order. Governor Bhandari claimed to have sent a 'fool-proof' case for the government's dismissal.

The governor's assessment may have been 'fool-proof', but it was not Narayanan-proof. The President read the cabinet's recommendation line by line, word by word. Those of us on his staff who had gone over the text and made our own comments on it did what we were meant to do, like fact-checkers in any newspaper office. But the president's appraisal of the recommendation was his own. He studied it and reflected on it, in silence, without anyone butting into the process. He had done the same about a year earlier when former Prime Minister I.K. Gujral's government had recommended the dismissal of the BJP government led by Kalyan Singh in Uttar Pradesh. And just as he did then, so he did now. He returned the recommendation to the government for reconsideration. There was no politics to his decision. There was only fairness, constitutional fairness.

Law-and-order failures, financial mismanagement, and misgovernance are bad. But they do not amount to a constitutional breakdown, the sine qua non for President's Rule. This was his clear, simple reading. There can be political democratic responses to those situations, but Rabri Devi did not call for unseating on the grounds of a failure of the constitutional structure. This was a protection he was giving not to a chief minister but to a constitutional principle, a protection he was duty-bound as President of India to give. And while initially, the Vajpayee cabinet was rattled by his decision, just as Prime Minister Gujral's had been, it decided in its maturity to accept the point. It did not press for the dismissal. It did not repeat the recommendation which the President under the Constitution would then have had to accept. *The Hindu* carried an editorial on September 27, 1998, titled 'Well Done, Mr Narayanan', while *Hindustan Times* titled its editorial 'Not A Snub, A Favour'. How a favour? The editorial said that an eminently dismissable government would have donned the mantle of martyrdom had it been dismissed. In the event, it stayed on until the logic of democracy brought about a change. So the President had done the Union government a favour.

It was not to do a favour to anyone that President Narayanan did what he did. It was to do the right and proper thing without fear or favour. He was undisturbed by the criticism that had briefly come his way from the BJP. He was unelated by the encomiums that came to him from the supporters of Lalu Prasad and Rabri Devi. There is something, as I said, about Bihar. It gave the country a chance to see the Constitution's morality being upheld.

Today, when the state is in the news because of its caste survey, Bihar is giving the nation a chance to see its population's reality being upheld. Everyone came out well in 1998 – President Narayanan for returning the recommendation, and Prime Minister Vajpayee for accepting the President's action. Today, a consensus on the reality of caste being recognised, without fear or favour, would be a favour done to our nationhood.

(*Hindustan Times*, October 17, 2023)

54

Uphold the Lofty Ideals Symbolised by the Tricolour

JULY 22, 1947. INDEPENDENCE was about three weeks away. The Constituent Assembly was in session, with Rajendra Prasad chairing it. The first item on the agenda of the day was the formal adoption of the new nation's new flag. Rajen Babu called upon his fellow fighter for freedom, the prime minister-to-be, Jawaharlal Nehru to move a resolution on it.

Youthful at 58, with a gleam in his eyes, Nehru said, 'Memories crowd upon me. I remember the ups and downs of the great struggle for the freedom of this great nation. I remember and many in this House will remember how we looked up to this flag not only with pride and enthusiasm but with a tingling in our veins; also how, when we were sometimes down and out, then again, the sight of this flag gave us the courage to go on. Then, many who are not present here today, many of our comrades who have passed, held on to this flag, some amongst them even unto death and handed it over as they sank to others to hold it aloft. There is the struggle of the people for freedom with all its ups and downs and trials and disasters and there is, finally today as I move this resolution, a certain triumph about it; a measure of triumph in the conclusion of that struggle.'

He then described the features of the flag in detail and dwelt on the significance of the *Ashoka Chakra* at its centre. 'I am exceedingly happy that in this sense indirectly we have associated with this flag of ours not only this emblem but in a sense the name of Asoka, one of the most magnificent names not only in India's history but in the world history.'

The House was palpably excited. Rajen Babu received requests from 25 members to speak on the adoption for the new flag. Time was short. Among those called were the philosopher, Sarvepalli Radhakrishnan, and nine members who could be said to represent the majority Hindu community from different parts of India – H.V. Kamath, Seth Govind Das, P.S. Deshmukh, R.K. Sidhwa, Bal Krishna Sharma, Jainarayan Vyas, S. Nagappa and Lakshminarayan Sahu; three members from the Muslim community – Saiyid Muhammad Saadulla, Chaudhuri Khaliquzzaman, Mohammed Sheriff; three Christian members – H.C. Mookerjee, Joseph Alban D'Souza and Rev. Jerome D'Souza;

the Anglo-Indian member Frank Anthony; two distinguished members representing the depressed classes, H.J. Khandekar and V.I. Munuswamy Pillai; the Sikh, Giani Gurmukh Singh Musafir; the Adivasi leader Jaipal Singh; a representative of princely India, Mohan Singh Mehta of Udaipur; and finally, as the last speaker, the Bulbul-e-Hind, Sarojini Naidu.

All of them spoke with eloquence and passion about the symbolic voltage of the new flag, and of the importance of upholding its honour. What was notable was that the Ashoka was invoked time and time again. 'Now because I have mentioned the name of Asoka I should like you to think that the Asokan period in Indian history was essentially an international period of Indian history. It was not a narrowly national period. It was a period when India's ambassadors went abroad to far countries and went abroad not in the way of an empire and imperialism but as ambassadors of peace and culture and goodwill,' Nehru said.

'Pandit*ji* told you what a great place Asoka has in our history. After the battle of Kalinga, Asoka tried to unite the whole world with love and he achieved such success that the historians not only of this country but also of the whole world admit that there has been no emperor like Asoka,' Das said.

'The *chakra* of Asoka represents the Indian states, because since the time of Asoka the great, not has the whole country has not been under Indian rule, ruled by Indians for Indians,' said Mehta.

'The *dharma chakra* of Asoka reminds us of the condition of the people at the time of that great Buddhist emperor. He ruled not for his personal aggrandisement but for the contentment, peace and prosperity of the people under his charge,' said Muhammad Saadulla.

'This emblem now embodied in our national flag ought to remind every administrator and every citizen of the federation of India that we should forget the past and look to the future,' he added.

'Asoka from Magadha went over to Kalinga and fought a great battle. After very heavy carnage, he was turned into a gentle being – the gentle Asoka; and it is there that the Kalingas in a way conquered Asoka. When I see this flag here, associated with the name of Asoka and also with Buddha, I am reminded that our country Kalinga after a great battle taught a good lesson to Asoka, a non-violent one,' said Sahu.

In her lyrical speech, Naidu said: 'That wheel, what does it represent? It represents the *dharma chakra* of Asoka the magnificent who sent his message of peace and brotherhood all over the world. Did he not anticipate the modern ideal of fellowship and brotherhood and cooperation? Does not that wheel stand as a symbol for every national interest and national activity? Does it not represent the charkha of my illustrious and beloved leader, Mahatma Gandhi, and the wheel of time that marches and marches and marches without hesitation and without halt?'

As she concluded, she added, 'Rise and salute this flag I bid you, rise and salute the flag.' And the entire House did just that. It adopted the flag, standing on its feet and applauding.

Today, on the anniversary of the adoption of the flag, as we celebrate our flag, we must also turn our thoughts to Ashoka and see how vital his message to us is.

Samavaya eva sadhu – concord alone is meritorious – said he in his famous Edict XII. Ashoka, who was invoked so repeatedly and so fervently by members of the Constituent Assembly drawn from different faiths and backgrounds, seems a distant name today. And the aspirations of the Constituent Assembly are also turning to sepia.

Concord is under strain in our life in India. Manipur is the most searing example. I can imagine the flag, downcast, wanting to lower itself to half-mast in Manipur in agony and shame and grief. But then, listening to what our Chief Justice D.Y. Chandrachud has said about constitutional democracy and wanting to see remedial action taken swiftly, I can see the flag fluttering in new self-confidence that says Ashoka's wheel of law on the central band of white is not dead! It will turn and bring justice and healing.

The flag is telling India today: You unfurl me in vain if you do not furl hate, greed and the lust for power. Unfurl me to unfurl the truth of things, fearlessly.

(*Hindustan Times*, July 22, 2023)

55

Crafting an Ethical Mode of Governance for India

INDIA IN 2047? MANY things may happen between now and then that could make any prognosis seem like a bad joke.

Twenty-five years from now, the world as we know it may not be there.

Nuclear swagger, nuclear terror and nuclear error – each one of these is a distinct probability, especially on our subcontinent – might well have turned our planet into a smoking ball of vapours by then. Global warming may have cooked the Earth beyond retrieval, and the pandemic, which has only changed its stripes to spots, might have mutilated our lives unrecognisably by the time of that *amrit vela*.

India, being part of the globe's imperilled crust, should know these fatal risks to its existence. After all, *vasudhaiva kutumbakam* – all the world is one family – has been a mantra for us in India. But truth be told, we are not '*vasudheivi*' as much as we are '*kutumbaki*', a family-bound people with our immediate kin-group affinities, forming our essential identities. The theme of looking at India in 2047 is narrow in terms of the globe's apparent destiny, but it is psychologically consistent with our favourite preoccupations: ourselves. So, let me, an administrator by training, speculate unreservedly on what we will look like, feel like and deserve in terms of governability when we achieve 100 years of freedom.

We can be sure of one thing. We will look exactly what we will be in 25 years from now: Huge. We would have overtaken China in terms of population by 2027, and two decades later in our centenary year of freedom, we will be 1.64 billion strong and counting. Will that be something to be proud of or embarrassed about? Both, because a runaway population count does not speak well of our prudence. But we are growing not because 'we breed like rabbits', given the slowing birth rate nationally and the near-replacement fertility rate in many big states. We are the numbers we are because we do not 'die like flies' any more, a great reason for being 1.64-billion strong, a great reason to be proud of.

But that achievement of ours will make India@100 an exceptionally difficult country to govern, administer and hold together. With that many more of us swelling our towns that want to be cities, and our cities that want to be metropolises and our megacities that want to be Singapore, Hong Kong or even New York, and so many more millions migrating for work from our crumbling villages to our urban dreamlands, we will be a jumble of cement and a tumble of steel.

Our urban population, nearing the giant figure of 1 billion, will struggle to breathe in air that will be more polluted, drink water that will beg to be called potable, and move through traffic 25 times more chaotic than it is now. Urban India will try to hide its slums that will bulge and groan, and sweep from sight, but not from existence, the mountains of garbage on its streets.

Will there be a vision robust enough, and funds enough, courage enough to cope with this nightmare? And do so ethically?

Why ethics? Governance has to do with civics, with politics, with economics. Also, to an increasing degree now, with histrionics. But ethics? Where does that curious and indefinable 'ics' come in? It comes in like this: if India will, with each passing year, be more and not less difficult to govern, then shortcuts to governance solutions will become attractive via elections. Two foundational weaknesses will compromise our power at the hustings. One, our poverty. Two, our divisions. Both get exploited by those greedy for electoral victories. Ethics will be needed to resist that debasing.

Will we have such leaders in 2047? Dare I hope?

We were told, at the time of Independence, that we will collapse under the debris of our incapacity, our divisions. We have not done so. We cannot, as we turn 100, be a country that worships gods and mammon, but trashes human life, human worth, especially that of its daughters. Urban and industrialised India will, by 2047, have made a powerhouse of our country, likely raising its gross domestic product (GDP) from $3 trillion to $20 trillion.

Our scientific and technological community, working exponentially in digital casements of immeasurable power, will have hurled us into gyres of newer and newer achievements. But will masses of us be living in or alongside mired misery even as many more of us live in wired wealth? Will malnutrition, early marriage, maternal mortality due to post-partum haemorrhage, continue to scar the women of India even as the country worships goddesses of legend and lore?

Will we, rural or urban, rich or poor, lend ourselves 25 years from now, to manipulation by the vendors of sectarian strife, the peddlers of hate, the merchants of communal venom stealing political power when they cannot earn it?

This is where ethics comes in. And courage. The courage to fail in the fight to stay free.

Who displayed these traits in our country last? Those who won the polls?

Jayaprakash Narayan never won a single election in his life.
Nor did Kamaladevi Chattopadhyay.
They did not call themselves Gandhians. They were truer to Jawaharlal Nehru than those who have thrived under his name.
They remain inspirations.
There is something called hope.
And prayer.

(*Hindustan Times*, October 30, 2022)

56

Elusive Value

ONE THING HAS JUST about disappeared in today's India. Respect.

It was everywhere, among all of us, no matter how poor or wealthy we were. No matter how down-and-out or 'up there' among the powerful.

And by 'was' I do not mean some bygone age. I am not thinking of the time when Sri Ramana Maharshi and Sri Aurobindo were among us, or Tagore the Gurudev or Gandhi the Mahatma lived as one of us; I am thinking of more recent times.

Mother Teresa of the Missionaries of Charity and Swami Ranganathananda who headed the Ramakrishna Mission were part of the ecology of respect in Calcutta until just the other day. And, not confining myself to the spiritually elevated, let me invite the reader to look at the world of teachers and academics. We had among us till about a decade or two ago great economists, historians, philosophers and scientists teaching fortunate and grateful students. And in the world of law, likewise, advocates and judges commanded the respect not just of their peers in the Bar and on the Bench but of the general public. Many doctors and surgeons were regarded as being 'legendary'. And public servants whose professional and financial integrity was 'beyond doubt' were held in esteem, which is a close cousin to respect.

And though many readers would disagree with this, let me say we had even among the ranks of politicians not a few but quite a few whom we could speak of with respect. 'All right,' I can hear an imaginary reader interject, 'name one such, just one', and as soon as I say the names of Jayaprakash Narayan, Aruna Asaf Ali and Kamaladevi Chattopadhyay, I am corrected and told, 'No, no…those are long gone…give me one name of a politician you respect who has been around from, say, the year 2000.' And though that makes me pause to think of such examples, I can come up with some names. Sitaram Yechury whom we have just lost being the first among them. Now he was an exact contemporary of ours for whom I had respect, true and real respect, for the honesty of his politics and the ardour of his commitments to socialism, secularism and democracy. But even more for the transparent goodness of his heart. I hate to have to use the word, 'late', to describe that man who had years of work waiting for him. 'Granted,' the questioning reader continues. 'Yechury...yes...but then he is now lost to us...Name any other from among those who are around.' Feeling a tad trapped, I persevere in excavating names from the desert that covers the rare finds of 'respected' names. 'Well, though she is not a typical politician,' I say, 'Aruna Roy enjoys respect, wide respect, for the determination with which she has worked for social justice, for the rights of the rural poor. But for her the National Rural Employment Guarantee Act would not have come about. And but for her again the Right to Information Act would never have been passed. I am one of hundreds who respect her unreservedly.'

'Hmmm...' goes the reader.

And I add more names of men who are political but not politicians, starting with Jean Drèze. The Belgian-born development economist and social scientist has, through research and investigations of ground conditions, pioneered action to ameliorate the human condition in hunger-ridden, health-deprived, gender-unequal rural India. No one who has seen him work can fail to respect him. In the same league is another sharply political activist and writer, P. Sainath, whose bringing to national and international attention the phenomenon of farmer suicides guarantees respect for him, if also controversy fabricated by the complicit. And we have the examples of Chandi Prasad Bhatt and Sonam Wangchuk who have done Himalayan scale work to save the Himalaya in their regions – Uttarakhand and Ladakh, respectively – and beyond, by the force of their example. All these men receive respect un-self-consciously, even unmindfully.

Is Amartya Sen, who enjoys respect in an uncommon degree globally, political? He may not accept that description but would not deny that he has influenced politics.

These and others like them who have worked with politics without being politically partisan are keeping respect alive. And there are many others, on the margins of politics, who work with tireless zeal for the amelioration of the human condition, receiving generous and spontaneous respect from the people they are among. The reader-querist is, I believe, not convinced yet that politics can still be the home for respect. Overarching all these names, is His Holiness the Dalai Lama. He is severely, solemnly and by official arrangement self-proclaimedly non-political. But so hugely impactful is the moral quotient of that great man that he has lent to India's political stature vis-à-vis China its single most potent asset.

But to return to the theme of this column – that respect is now not to be seen in our land. All those I have named have stature which is totally independent of status.

Status has long since ceased to draw respect. By status I mean high office. Incumbents of what is called 'position' command deference but that has little to do with respect which comes from sheer admiration bordering on awe. Skill does command appreciation, even applause, but stops short of what may be called respect, for skill's aim is to show ability, talent, deftness, all of which are scarce and require hard work which commands hearty appreciation. Respect seeks attributes other than adroitness, ability. And it seeks it increasingly in vain.

As with individuals so with institutions. The number of institutions that command automatic and unconditional respect is now small if not absent. Among these, the judiciary stands tall as when it protects the right to privacy and when Justice Indu Malhotra, on September 6, 2018, with four other judges of the apex court, declares that Section 377 of the Indian Penal Code was unconstitutional and says on the occasion memorably: 'History owes LGBT people an apology.' The defence forces, I would say, spontaneously evoke it, so much so that I find it sad that special powers should be so needed for them. As does the nursing profession and – curiously – the fire brigade, all of whose personnel risk their lives for us. And when policemen show heroism of the kind they did on 26/11 2008, they do so at once and for all time.

The public is no fool. It judges. Be it tea-stall owners, vegetable vendors, hairdressers, paanwallas, they know what respect means.

And it really is just this: respect is given to those and to that which occasion trust – *bharosa, vishvas, aitbar* or, in Tamil, *nambikkai*.

Respect rushes to that which can be trusted. It recoils from that which cannot be trusted and even more so from that which has forsaken trust.

If respect is unquantifiable, so is trust. Can anyone define *vishvas*? It is, like respect, either there or is not there. The smallest of persons can say who is trustworthy and who is not. And in doing so will respect a governor or a gardener, chief minister or chiropodist, judge or janitor, atomic scientist or an auto-driver, if that person occasions trust.

Credibility and trustworthiness are in retreat in our land. And that has rendered respect scarce.

The public, as I said, is no fool.

(*The Telegraph*, October 13, 2024)

57

A Unified Field of Pain

THERE IS SUCH A thing as the *rasa* of a place, its *sthala-rasa*. There is also such a thing as the *icchha-rasa* of the *rasika* even as there is such a thing as an *icchha-raga* of any lover of classical music. As a *rasika* of Bengal, I can say that my Bengal, which need not be anyone else's, is not tinged with the colours I see sprayed on Holi here in Calcutta or in Santiniketan. Rather, with those that one sees in Tagore's self-portraits and which Nandalal Bose has applied on the *Halakarshan* fresco at Sriniketan and Benode Behari on the three walls at the Hindi Bhavana there – earth brown, mustard yellow, frank madder. These are the colours of life which can be toned to one side to make them the colours of pain, or toned to the other to make them the colours of joy. You can guess to which side mine turn.

Black and white in photographs are not about black and white but about grey, which is the natural colour of so much in life's anomalies, ambiguities. The Great Bengal Famine of 1943 stimulated Somnath Hore's grey sketches, Sunil Janah's black-and-white photographs and, unfortunately in colour, Ray's *Ashani Sanket* – another Bibhutibhushan–Satyajit Ray pairing. These creations are part of that same unified field which saw the dying of 3 million people and the breakdown of village life in all its departments and individual tragedies all merging into one whole, brilliantly symbolised by the giant trees that recur like a refrain in the film. Scarring episodes like the Great Calcutta Massacre of 1946 and the riots of 1947, of which the killings of Sachin Mitra and Smritish Banerjea, non-violent activists for Gandhi, form part, are another unified field of personal tragedies sublimated into a common experience of pain.

There is in Bengal's sensibility, in its *swabhava*, that which metamorphoses tragic experience, when individual, into the collective and then takes the collective to some form of artistically, politically or institutionally shareable expression. I do not wish to dwell on the politicisation of grief, a phenomenon which can be – to the politics concerned – productive as also totally counterproductive.

A slender isthmus of feeling links the continent of Bengal's emotion to the subcontinent of its intellect. Equally, a narrow strait of sentiment links the ocean of Bengal's subliminal sympathies to the bays of its willed understandings.

Continents are made by the sundials of Time, subcontinents by the clock towers of history, and countries, we might say, by the wristwatches of politicians. Bengal's emotional continent is anterior to its intellectual subordinations. And it is that continent which has determined the shape or the structure and the stability of its objective creations.

Oceans are about aesthetics of creation, bays are about their demarcated interpretations. When oceans heave, bays ripple. An ocean of sentiment has fed, one might even say nourished, Bengal's artistic expression. Creativity and even scholarly academic inquiry move over the strait of sentiment in Bengal.

Sentiment is not the same as sentimentality. Derozio and Derozians like Ramtanu Lahiri and Peary Chand Mitra were not sentimental people. But when opposing 'the hollowness of idolatry, the shames of priesthood' and 'summon(ing) Hinduism to the bar of reason', they were actuating a sentiment which we may call, paradoxically, the sentiment of reason. Bengal, even when it employs the instruments of reason, does so with a passionate intensity. In the winter of 1992–1993, I heard Amartya Sen speak in Cambridge on the shame of the demolition of the Babri Masjid. It was among the most moving speeches I have heard in my life. And he was speaking on the side of reason, and against emotion.

Alongside the isthmus of feeling and the strait of sentiment, there also rises in the Bengal I know, a delicate *char*, sandy, soft and shy, from the riverbed of personal experience, personal inclination, personal bent, to make Bengal's shared creations both narrative and three-dimensionally physical. The *Gitanjali*, I would say, arose thus as did the little clay hut in Santiniketan built, as Rabindranath said, for his '*seshbela*'...*jaar naam 'Shyamali*' where '*maatir kole mishbe maati...*' and which '*birodh korbe na dharani sange...*'

The connecting vestibules – the isthmuses of feeling, the straits of sentiment and the *char* of personally felt experience – have been crucial to my understanding of Bengal. It is those strips of sand or water which, like a hyphen, both connect and keep apart, that make Bengal for me, 'my Bengal'. In the case of Rammohun and Vivekananda, these vestibules work through their letters, which share and not just convey, in the case of Saratchandra through his short stories where he lets the characters play, not preach. In the case of Rabindranath, they work through his paintings and shorter poetic or musical works. In the case of Buddhadeb Bose, through the triptych, *Maner Mata Meye*, which, to my mind, is an isthmus, a strait and a *char* combined, linking the heart and the mind, with love shown in all its dimensions, too serious to be taken lightly, too accessible to be seen as philosophic expressions. And loss, too terrible to bear alone, too private to be understood by anyone but the loved.

I may be permitted to place five summations: 1. Bengal, as I see it ('my Bengal') has been a field of many emotions but, very specially, of pain and of the emotions that accompany pain. 2. Bengal is also the field of an unusual concentration of artistic expressions. 3. Bengal's pain starts or occurs at the point of the personal or individual but soon becomes shared in and through expression in literature and the arts, especially music. 4. Thus sensed, shared, sublimated, it joins, like a river to a floodplain, that field of pain in Bengal which takes the experience of pain into itself and gives it a form that can be deeply fulfilling to the first experience and then to subsequent ones in an almost seamless transmission. 5. This phenomenon is not and cannot be peculiar to Bengal but Bengal is certainly a major theatre for it.

So what then makes up 'my Bengal'?

I have asked myself many times if the Bengal I know, respect, covet, love, is the Bengal of emotional catharsis or of its intellectual musculature, the Bengal of political assertion, or of spiritual redemption, the Bengal of pain felt and sublimated or of *ananda* and joy. To say it is a bit of all these would be to cop out of the question, not answer it.

There are works – literary, artistic, musical, basically, 'creative' works. And there is work – hard work on the field, on the ground of real life.

Bengal has given us both, not always in perfect balance, but still, both, sometimes in combination as in the field work of Nirmal Bose, Mahalanobis, Amartya Sen, Sukhomoy Chakravarty, Mahbub-ul Haq and André Béteille, and sometimes separately. I say this after pondering (which is different from reading) the works of Rammohun, Vivekananda, Aurobindo, Bibhutibhushan, Saratchandra, Rabindranath, Buddhadeb Bose, M.N. Roy, and, in our own times, of pre-eminent academics such as the ones I mentioned and, Ashok Mitra, Mahasweta Devi, Tapan Raychaudhuri, Ranajit Guha, Nabaneeta Dev Sen, Partha Chatterjee, Amiya and Jasodhara Bagchi and Uma Das Gupta and of persons in the field like Ashoka Gupta and Tushar Kanjilal. Letters from some of these distinguished contemporaries of mine are among my most prized possessions. They have, more than books, set me on those narrow but continent-linking and ocean-linking bars of human experience.

A statue of sandstone, three and a half feet high, in the Indian Museum, Calcutta, is of the Buddha. It was discovered, according to one version, in the Gond country on the Narmada. Be that as it may, it was drawn, I am sure, by some unknown master sculptor who had before his real or mental eye a youthful Gond, at one with the earth and its innocents, enlightened without knowing it, smiling at the artist who asked him to tarry for a rough sketch made on wet earth to become, in time, this statue.

I was reminded of him when on the tense day that had Nandigram written over it, at Tamluk, I saw a figure, prone, among a dozen more, awaiting post-mortem. It had no smile on its face, only surprise.

In my journeys across the state I saw many who could be the original of the Gond Buddha, many that of his mother, wife, sister, and, yes, daughter. At the *rajbari* in Cooch Behar, a painting of Maharani Indira Devi rivalled that of her daughter, Gayatri Devi. And both were matched for me by no painting but a living being no goddess can surpass for the grace of her deportment, the magnificence of her generosity, the luminosity that surrounded her. On the day I was driving to Nandigram, I stopped by a village, impromptu. The small group of huts in it were inviting me – '*Esho, esho...amar ghare*' in Iffat Ara's voice. After spending a few minutes among them, as I was leaving, one woman, shall I call her goddess, asked me to step into her hut. Just for a moment, she said. I did. From a shelf, she brought out a brass *thali* with a lamp lit on it. And a dab of red powder. I will not describe the touch of her ring finger on my forehead for I cannot.

I must, as I close, share with you a cameo from my childhood. While at school, at age 13, I think, I chanced upon a set of letters retrieved from their sources and kept carefully by my father in a trunk in our home. These were written by Saraladevi Chaudhurani. Wholly emotional, they were addressed to one she called 'Lawgiver'. No prizes for guessing who the Lawgiver was. Her handwriting was beautiful, the words lyrical. In the bunch there were letters written by the Lawgiver to her as well, in green ink, addressing her as 'Pearl'.

In the set was a letter, a very emotional one, from a person as searingly intellectual as Rajaji. Only Bengal, in the shape of Saraladevi Chaudhurani, could have unlocked the sluices of emotion – the emotion of strong disapproval – from the watertight dam of that mind. Asking his 'Dearest Master' to sever his relationship with Saraladevi forthwith, Rajaji wrote '...as to [comparing Saraladevi to] Mrs Gandhi it is like comparing a kerosene oil Ditmar lamp to the morning sun...' Rajaji's advice was followed. I was consumed by a desire to learn more about Saraladevi (apart from kerosene oil Ditmar lamps) and took the bunch of letters to my recently widowed mother who knew about them but had not really read them. Tears flooding her eyes, she reread them and said (in Hindi), '*Jaise rishi-muniyon ki pariksha hoti thi...Apsaraaon ko bheja jata thaa...us hi tarah hamare Bapuji ki bhi pariksha hui...Aur Bapuji us agni pariksha mein vijayi hue...Saraladevi se humein koyi shikayat nahin...Ve pariksha kii maatra maadhyam theen, bas...*'

In his final letter to Saraladevi (available, god be thanked, and published in the *Collected Works*), Gandhi himself called the closure given 'that perfect coincidence, that perfect merging...self-forgetfulness'. Greek means nothing to me now; it did even less when I was 13. But Bengal became for me, from that time onwards, a universe in which transcendental and sacrificial love – Eros – had a place. Sacred spaces inviolable from the dross of human failings and set apart for the worship of the gods – Temenos – had a place. As did paradoxes or puzzles that come to us as in a heap of occurrences – Soros.

Bengal is unabashedly about love – Eros. Bengal is unembarrassedly worshipful – Temenos. And in its ability to juggle the lyrically emotional with the intellectual, the religious and the secular, the tragic with the joyous, Bengal is wholly paradoxical and puzzling – Soros.

Bengal's gift of love tends towards its making a cult of it. To have and love a hero is one thing, to blindly worship that hero, to idolise and lionise and make an idol or deity of the object of that love is another. There is no disloyalty or disrespect involved in disagreement. One should be able to differ from Swami Vivekananda on some particular statement or view of his and still revere him. One should be able to be out of synch with Mahatma Gandhi in the matter of, say, *brahmacharya* in marriage and still hold him in the bonds of love. One should be able to say about Netaji that his political values were inspirational but his political decisions fallible. One should be able to say Tagore's *Gitanjali* is unparalleled, but his own translations of it unsatisfying.

Amlan Datta once wrote to me about what he called 'the risk of love'. Bengal's loves need to court the risks of love. Equally, love of Bengal needs to risk candour. Eros, Temenos, Soros have a fourth cousin – Pyro or Pyros. In Bengal's propensity to ignite thought, inflame desire and combust emotion it is Fire – Pyro or Pyros.

Uma Dasgupta and one of the most distinguished philosophers of our time, Arindam Chakrabarty, have done me the favour of interpreting *Aguner Paroshmani*. Chakrabarty writes in an informal but deeply thought-out communication:

> Fire, standing for all the trials and tribulations of suffering, bereavement, humiliation, disease, ageing – '*duhkha*' as Buddha would have called it – and Tagore's life starting with loss of mother, favourite sister-in-law, father, son, daughter, wife, on and on was full of this fire (full of) burns. People take it as devastation, burning to ashes. Rabindranath – not just in this song but in many many many songs and poems – expresses his '*anubhav*' that this Fire transforms the 'iron in the soul' to Gold.
>
> Hence 'Fire's *Poroshmon*'…mixing of metaphors. Instead of burning down life, may the Fire of extreme suffering touch my life like a *sparsha-mani* and make it '*punya*' – sacred, holy. *E jibon punya karo, e jibon punya karo, e jibon punya karo.* By what? By the gift of BURNING: *dahan daaney*…

That was Chakrabarty, intense and insightful, in his letter. He will, I hope, expand that letter into a book about how emotion moves to reason, feeling to intellect.

My Bengal knows pain. That is not its weakness. In fact, that can be its strength. It can use its experience of tragedy, like *dahan daaney*, to tell itself and India how to salvage solutions from crises, answers from riddles, not by feeding *agun* but by transforming it. 'I cannot leave Bengal,' Gandhi said. 'And Bengal will not let me go.' I can say the first but will not presume to say the second sentence.

This much I will say: Bengal's legacy of pain, her experience of tragedy, her gift of love, her dower of art distinguish it. Distinction is a form of individualism. And individualism can become a love affair with oneself. A lonely distinction is a form of self-exclusion. My Bengal is distinctive but not lonely, unique but not exclusive and says to its Mother, *Diyechhe joto, niyechhe taar beshi.*

(based on the Kamala Lecture given by the writer, *The Telegraph*, January 15, 2013)

58

Flag of Conscience

ON JULY 22, 1947 – this day tomorrow, 77 years ago – independent India's first identity marker unfurled into our life.

The Constituent Assembly was in session in the round, red-and-pink sandstone building which, until a year ago, housed the Parliament of India in our national capital. The members were seated in the semi-circled seating rows in what then was called the Constitution Assembly Hall and, from 1952, called the Central Hall.

I imagine that the day was as hot and humid, but long, very long, fans whirred above the hugely sagacious heads of the Assembly's members as Dr Rajendra Prasad took his presidential seat as the clock struck 10. The business of the day was listed as 'Resolution regarding the national flag'. Just that, five simple words. But what magnetism was packed into them, what history, what aspirations, what faith!

The flag had evolved from the first design crafted by a now almost-forgotten hero of the freedom struggle, Pingali Venkayya (1878–1963), an agriculturist-educator from Andhra Pradesh, who as a 19-year-old had been a soldier in British India deployed, briefly, to South Africa during the Second Boer War (1899–1902) in which M.K. Gandhi had also served as a non-combatant. Venkayya had, on returning to India, become a nationalist and Congressman who wanted the Grand Old Party to have a flag of its own in place of the Union Jack which it would customarily unfurl at its sessions.

Designing such a flag in red and green, he presented it in 1921 to Gandhi who suggested to Venkayya that he add a third, white. The idea was that the flag should hold a message for all of India. That done, a *charkha*, the spinning wheel, which Gandhi felt would connect India in an artisanal, organic bond with its creative roots, was added.

That original flag had been raised by freedom fighter after freedom fighter all over India, many of its 'raisers' and 'holders' suffering baton charges and even bullets; the immortal Matangini Hazra who, at age 73, fell to the British Raj's bullets in 1942 in Tamluk, Bengal, while holding this very flag, standing tall among them.

This national flag, redesigned to replace the earlier spinning wheel (*charkha*) at the centre by the Ashoka *chakra*, was the subject of the day's work in the Constituent Assembly that day in the shape of a resolution.

Resolutions in legislatures have to be 'moved' by a member and this one was moved by none other than Jawaharlal Nehru, not yet prime minister but about to be. Described in the agenda papers of the day as The Honourable Pandit Jawaharlal Nehru (United Provinces: General), he said: '…when I move this Resolution, I think of this concentrated history through which all of us have passed during the last quarter of a century. Memories crowd upon me. I remember the ups and downs of the great struggle for freedom of this great nation. I remember and many in this House will remember how we looked up to this Flag not only with pride and enthusiasm but with a tingling in our veins; also how, when we were sometimes down and out, then again, the sight of this Flag gave us courage to go on. Then, many who are not present here today, many of our comrades who have passed, held on to this Flag, some amongst them even unto death. and handed it over as they sank, to others to hold it aloft. So, in this simple form of words, there is much more than will be clear on the surface. There is the struggle of the people for freedom with all its ups and downs and trials and disasters and there is, finally today as I move this Resolution, a certain triumph about; it a measure of triumph in the conclusion of that struggle.'

And turning to the problems of the then 'present times' in India, which had just been through the nightmarish trauma and suffering of Partition, he said, '…The problems are not anything new to us. We have faced many disagreeable things in the past. We have not held back. We shall face all the other disagreeable things that face us in the present or may do so in the future and we shall not flinch and we shall not falter and we shall not quit.' And this was greeted by loud applause.

Among those who spoke on July 22, 1947 on the 'Flag Resolution' was, like Venkayya, another Indian of Telugu descent and an internationally respected philosopher and teacher, Sarvepalli Radhakrishnan, who would go on to become India's ambassador to the Soviet Union, India's first vice president and, then, its second president (after Rajendra Prasad, the very first). If Nehru's words had come from a historian and political thinker in the line of Ashoka, Radhakrishnan's came from the mind of a philosopher in the tradition of the Adi Shankara.

Said the sage: 'Times are hard. Everywhere we are consumed by phantasies. Our minds are haunted by myths. The world is full of misunderstandings, suspicions and distrusts. In these difficult days it depends on us under what banner we fight. Here we are putting in the very centre the white, the white of the Sun's rays. The white means the path of light. There is darkness even at noon as some people have urged, but it is necessary for us to dissipate these clouds of darkness and control our conduct — by the ideal light, the light of truth, of transparent simplicity which is illustrated by the colour of white.'

Only a mind steeped in India's spiritual intelligence like Radhakrishnan's could then have added: 'This wheel which is a rotating thing, which is a perpetually revolving thing, indicates to us that there is death in stagnation. There is life in movement. Our Dharma is Sanatana, eternal, not in the sense that it is a fixed deposit but in the sense that it is perpetually changing. Its uninterrupted continuity is its Sanatana character. So even with regard to our social conditions it is essential for us to move forward…The red, the orange, the colour represents the spirit of renunciation it is said: (*Sarve tyage rajadharmesu drsta*)…The green is there our relation to the soil, our relation to the plant life here on which all other life depends. We must build our Paradise here on this green earth. If we are to succeed in this enterprise, we must be guided by truth (white), practise virtue (wheel), adopt the method of self-control and renunciation (saffron). This Flag tells us, "Be ever alert, be ever on the move, go forward, work for a free, flexible, compassionate, decent, democratic, society in which Christians, Sikhs, Moslems, Hindus, Buddhists will all find a safe shelter."'

As we remember July 22, 1947, the saffron of renunciation, the white of purity, and the green of our relation to plant life tell us what India is in dire want of: first, the relinquishing of politics' commonest disease — the lusting after power; second, transparent simplicity among all wielders of office symbolised by the shrill hoot of the *lal batti* and, third, among all of us, leaders and led, a sense of responsibility towards our natural resources under the safety of its common sheltering. The Himalaya, our rivers, forests and coasts do not distinguish between Indian and Indian. We are its equal offspring and wards.

We walk past and pass by the flag every day.

We unfurl it, pull the lanyard to hoist it, by way of rote. Those in transient office fly it on their cars as they cut the traffic signals and screech past others not privileged to do so.

The flag must not become a power-flaunting cloth of clout.

It is the fabric of our Republic's conscience, the keeper of its faith in the manifold *dharma*-s of freedom. It is the mantle of India's selfhood as a just nation.

(*The Telegraph*, July 21, 2024)

59

A Symbol of Kakayuga

SHOULD NUMBERS NOT HAVE something to do with that recognition – 'national'?

The crow abounds, teems, thrives where other birds just about survive.

The kite is demographically strong. The Delhi sky, for instance, has multiple linked-in squadrons of the *cheel* whirling in slow motion.

The pigeon, our grey *gutargu* with its silver specks, is populous too.

And companies of the parakeet fleet between trees, like children darting out of school.

But the corvus splendens beats them. It has the confidence of brute majority and the swagger.

I dislike it with passion.

It is ugly and obnoxious.

'You can't call it ugly,' my birder wife Tara put in. '…You could say it is nothing much to look at…' I found all this courtesy wasted on the brazen bird. Yet, for the sake of objectivity, I asked myself, well, supposing the crow was not as common as it is, and was actually rare, would I have looked at it very differently?

No, I concluded, I would not have. I have no problem with the crow's colours. The koel, the drongo, the darter are, all of them, coloured as the crow is. In fact, the crow's black sheen is perhaps the best thing about its looks. It is its wretched nature that gets me.

'Well,' Tara demurred, 'it has an interesting personality.'

'*Ayyo*! Interesting personality?' Protocol and etiquette may have their due place in the world of bird-scholars and birdwatchers but is this rude, discourteous, arrogant, most appallingly behaved creature to be allowed to get away with crimes ranging from trespass, enfoulment, robbery, cheating, deceit, assault, battery, murder (both individual and mass) and many others listed in the Indian Penal Code?

Dr Salim Ali was not just the world's most distinguished bird-man but also the most civilised human being who would have called a spade a large ladle for uses outside the dining context. Even he, yes sir, even Ali had to say of the common crow in *The Book of Indian Birds*: 'Audacious, cunning and uncannily wary…Will eat almost anything: dead sewer rat, offal, carrion, kitchen scraps and refuse…eggs or fledgling birds pilfered from nests. A useful scavenger but also a great bully and therefore a serious menace to defenceless ornamental bird species…'

I do not know why Salimsahib had to say 'dead sewer rat' and 'ornamental', thereby extenuating the scope of the crow's killing sprees. It kills not just dead but dying beings and does that with undisguised relish It also kills recklessly, mercilessly, fledgling or disabled birds and any other helpless creature be it ornamental or utterly plain-looking and plain-living. Indeed, the crow lacks both the ethics and the aesthetics to tell the difference.

Despite its atrocious record, the crow has managed to fascinate some people. If M.F. Husain was drawn to the horse, R.K. Laxman may be said to be fixated by the crow. He has drawn the crow, not to caricature it but simply out of admiration. The reason? It is an 'intelligent bird'. He should be impressed by the same faculty in the fly, the mosquito, the cockroach and the rat. What these four are in the worlds of the insect and the rodent, the crow is to the avian universe – as a species intelligent, ubiquitous, immortal. The dodo may become a byword for the dead, the pink-headed duck live only on the illustrated plates of books, the great Indian bustard hide for dear life behind scrub, the vulture all but disappear, the sparrow gasp for life but the crow will live for ever.

It must always have been around in huge numbers, regarded through myth as ancestor spirit and fed coloured rice down the ages. Ashoka's famous Pillar Edict V, which reads like an archetypal Wildlife Protection Act, mentions (among birds) the parrot, maina, ruddy goose, swan, partridge, white dove, domestic dove and the water-cock among creatures prohibited from slaughter. What about Mr Corvus? He does not figure in the Emperor's protected list, yet how well he has done for himself! And what terrible news that is for other birds! We rarely see the golden oriole now, the owl or the sun-bird. The crow has edged them all out, violated their nests, beaked open their eggs, pecked their fledglings to a shocked crib death.

I put it to some nature conservationists that we should think of…I used the word with trepidation…'culling' crows, if only to save other bird life. My suggestion was met with horror. 'That would not be right. Besides, that chance will get misused to get at other birds, including protected ones…'

An even wiser response followed my brash idea and I withdrew the suggestion and retracted my intemperate thought.

'Your dislike of the crow,' the wise man continued, 'is nothing but a dislike of our own lifestyles. The crow cannot help doing what it does. It is what it is, does what it does, in the places where it is, in the numbers that it is in, not because it is cunning and gluttonous but because of the way we are living. It is the garbage we generate, the filth we accumulate on our streets, that has made the crow grow to its present numbers. It is because it has swollen to its present strength that its predations on other birds have also increased, not because it is out to decimate other forms of bird life. The crow is callous, cruel and cunning because we are.'

The reasoning made sense and I realised that in shiftiness of gait, rapacity of claws, shining versatility of beak and slyness of rolling eyeballs the crow was, in fact, us. Not our ancestor but us and – our future. It need not be our national bird, but it is a national fact, a symbol and a shameful one at that, of our own Kakayuga.

(*Hindustan Times*, November 2, 2012)

60

At the Heart of the Republic

JANUARY 26, 1950. THE date is 70 years old. And seems to belong not just to a distant age but to another planet.

A statesman stepped down from the office of Head of State that day and another, no less distinguished, stepped into his place. Hours before his departure from the nation's first residence in the national capital for his bare-bones home in Madras, India's last Governor General Chakravarti Rajagopalachari spoke with restrained emotion of Jawaharlal Nehru and Sardar Patel in his parting speech: 'The prime minister and his first colleague the deputy prime minister together make a possession which makes India rich in every sense of the term,' he said. And added: 'The former commands universal love, the latter universal confidence. Not a tear need be shed for anyone going as long as these two stand foursquare against the hard winds to which our country may be exposed.'

Moving that day from a life career of startling austerity to that high domed mansion of great expectations, India's first President Rajendra Prasad said with unrestrained optimism: 'Our Constitution is a democratic instrument seeking to ensure to individual citizens the freedoms which are so invaluable. India has never prescribed or prosecuted opinion or faith and our philosophy has room as much for a devotee of a personal god as for an agnostic or atheist. We shall, therefore, be only implementing in practice under our Constitution what we have inherited from our traditions, namely freedom of opinion and expression. Under the new set-up which we are inaugurating today we hope to live up to the teachings of our Master….'

Seventy years on we are entitled to ask if we have someone or anyone who commands universal love and someone or anyone who commands universal confidence among us, the people of India. The frank answer is, there is none. I say this not to make anyone look smaller than his right size or to diminish anyone's stature below his own natural height. And I also say this with the knowledge that it is quite standard and regular for persons to have non-overpowering attributes. But the fact is that we have today no one in our public life, be it in the ruling dispensation or in the ranks of the Opposition, who may be said to command that purest of sentiments – love, or that truest of offerings – confidence. True, we have loyalists and followers. But loyalty and following come from sources and for reasons, unrelated to the heart of feeling.

Qualities that are missed

The ruling dispensation and its supporters would, as they should, point to the prime minister and the Union minister as an ideal combination though, out of caution, they would refrain from calling this power structure a duumvirate. Those in the Congress and its orbit would, likewise, point to the Congress president, her son and her daughter and find strength in that threesome without calling it a triumvirate. We may not begrudge them their loyalty or their devotion. That is how politics and party politics work. But we must point out to them the difference between a leader whom leadership is seeking and a leader with whom leadership is playing hide-and-seek.

Our prime minister is seen by the faithful as possessing an 'immaculacy' and our home minister as endowed with an immediacy. The two doubtless make for a persuasive mutuality in power that can be the envy of any Number One and Number Two team anywhere. A prime minister should have sheen, a home minister should look tough. India needs those qualities in these two offices. But immaculacy, in the essential sense of that term or concept, is not the prerogative of human flesh, much less of political tissue. It may be claimed only by mythology and folklore, by super-naturals, not in real life.

As for immediacy, it is an admirable trait in one who is responsible for the nation's safety and security. But it is as a trait, the smart cousin of decisiveness and can turn into a power at the service of the nation, yes, but also at the call of power politics. Nehru was honest, he was fallible. Patel was tough, he was human. And so one commanded love, the other confidence.

If the two attributes in our first prime minister and deputy prime minister that Rajagopalachari mentioned are missed today, the invaluable freedoms that Rajendra Prasad spoke of are also under challenge.

A Constitution hewn out of the aspirations of the freedom struggle under Mahatma Gandhi's leadership, crafted by men and women of insight, commitment and reformative zeal, enriched by the experience of the world's great democratic republics, was brought to life by the people of India on that, our first Republic Day. The famous photograph of Jawaharlal Nehru signing the freshly bound and illuminated copy of the Constitution of India is a mural. The one of Sardar Patel signing it along with John Mathai, Rajkumari Amrit Kaur and Jairamdas Daulatram is a mosaic.

For some three years prior to that day, members of the Constituent Assembly, numbering about 300, had met, debated, argued, differed, expressed and overcome doubts, and heard Dr B.R. Ambedkar, as chairman of the Drafting Committee, describe the intent and effect of each draft Article. Then, with a great sense of purpose, they finally put their seal of approval on the document they had cradled. Their work brought our Republic into being, our people – us – into an ownership of our destinies and positioned leaders of outstanding agitational ability in offices of challenging administrative responsibility.

Strong spirit

The still centre of that document is the Preamble to the Constitution. And of that Preamble, to use a phrase associated with Ramana Maharshi, its heart-cave (*hridaya-kuhara-madhya*) is the line that says we are giving to ourselves 'Liberty – of thought, expression, belief, faith and worship'. On this the 70th anniversary of our Republic, we cannot but ask how that pre-ambular, that is, before-you-even-start, attribute of our Republican life, fares.

And what is the answer we hear in that heart-cave?

Contrary to what readers of this column may think, I am going to say it fares well.

Well? Well? A deeply disturbed dissenter may ask: 'With three former chief ministers of Jammu and Kashmir imprisoned, the media wary, the bureaucracy timid, the judiciary cautious, how can you say liberty fares well in India?'

I will accept the earnestness of the question and yet maintain it fares well because, for one, *The Hindu* is publishing this article of mine, and for another that the young in India, students and youth, by their almost entirely peaceful protests over the last few weeks, have vivified youth's hearkening to JP's call in 1974 and to Anna Hazare's in our recent memory. Did those movements not peter out? Yes and no. Those two leaders did not come to hold office but the nefarious 42nd Amendment to the Constitution was to a large extent sanitised, and the fact is that a movement became a party and that party has won a huge mandate.

The democratic spirit of the people of India is strong and if it stays non-violent and refuses to be co-opted by vested interests, it will make a difference that neither the protesting young and not-so-young nor the State can quite visualise.

Meanwhile we have Rajagopalachari's and Rajendra Prasad's sagacious words telling us that India is traditionally, instinctively and irreversibly about love, confidence and – liberty.

(*The Hindu*, January 27, 2020)

61

The Essence of Democracy

WHAT DOES SIR WILLIAM Garrow (1760–1840) have to do with the elections now under way in India? The well-known and much-invoked phrase 'innocent until proven guilty' was coined by that British barrister in the course of a 1791 trial at the Old Bailey. He turned the tables on legal practice at that trial by saying that the accusers, not those accused, must be tested, made to establish and prove their accusation in court. The English Court of Appeal in 1935 described Sir William's concept as the 'golden thread' connecting the burden of proof and the presumption of innocence 'within the web of English criminal law'.

The report card

And that connects Sir William with the Indian polls directly. The National Election Watch is a grouping of NGOs and others working for transparency and accountability in elections. The Association for Democratic Reforms (ADR) is a non-partisan NGO working for electoral and political reforms. They have given us telling statistics for four out of the seven phases of elections that have taken place so far. In the first phase of the elections, 17 per cent of the candidates had criminal cases pending against them. In the second phase, the figure went down marginally to 16 per cent. In the third phase, with the largest number of seats in any phase, the percentage of candidates figuring in criminal cases climbed to 21 per cent. In two-thirds of these, the accused have been charged for serious offences like rape, attempt to murder, and murder. In the fourth phase, the last one held so far, according to ADR, a total of 210 candidates faced criminal charges, with 158 being 'serious'. Five candidates had declared cases related to murder, 24 related to attempt to murder, four to kidnapping, 21 to crimes against women, and 16 candidates to hate speech. The phenomenon is not peculiar to any one party. The BJP, Congress, BSP and the Shiv Sena have fielded criminally charged candidates, the BJP being on top of the scale numerically. Even some independent candidates are criminally charged.

The numbers in the three phases remaining are not likely to be very different. Around 20 per cent of all the candidates in the seven phases, it may be, will be candidates with one criminal charge or another pending against them.

Sir William would have exclaimed, 'That does not matter; they may all be found to be innocent!' They well may. Also, they may be the ones who get defeated. On the other hand, studies have shown that those with criminal records (muscle power) plus a seemingly unlimited power of spending (money power) have a distinctly higher chance of succeeding over those with just one of those 'powers' and over those who have neither. So, some of these this time round may well get elected, their dates in court rubbing shoulders with their dates in and with Parliament. And business will be as usual for them, with Garrowian logic and ethics and the notion that many, if not most, of these cases are 'politically foisted' winning the day. The Election Commission has asked for an amendment to the Representation of the People Act to bar, with some caveats, those charged with criminal offences from contesting. But after hearing the matter, the Supreme Court declined, in 2018, to enter this area, 'leaving the decision on criminal netas on Parliament'.

Illiberal intent

It is precisely this 'liberal' arrangement that the most illiberal take advantage of. It is exactly this democratic legerdemain that the most undemocratic occupy. It is this very legal latitude that the most law-disdaining use, abuse.

Mitesh Patel is perfectly entitled under the law to contest from the Anand seat in Gujarat. And we should grant him the presumption of innocence. Whatever else he may be accused of, he cannot be accused of hiding anything. He has declared in his poll affidavit that he was an accused in the 2002 post-Godhra riots, that an FIR was registered against him in Anand district in 2002 for engaging in arson, rioting, stone-pelting and theft, among other charges. And, he has declared, he was booked under Indian Penal Code Sections 147 (rioting), 148 (rioting, armed with deadly weapon), 436 (arson), 332 (causing hurt to deter public servant), 143 (unlawful assembly) and 380 (theft). He may well be found to be innocent of all these crimes.

The point, however, is not that. The point is that the Anand sessions court acquitted him in 2010. Sir William, there you go! But the matter does not end there. The government of Gujarat, yes, the BJP government of Gujarat, acting with amazing rectitude and objectivity, filed an appeal in 2011 against his acquittal. (We shall not go into how it could not have but done so.) So, the charge has not gone away. On the one hand, the BJP government appeals against his acquittal, on the other the BJP gives him a ticket to contest from Anand. Perfectly legal, of course. Consistent with liberal, democratic nostrums. But what about the ethics of it? Eth...what? What in 'Elections 2019' is that?

The case of Pragya Thakur

As I am sure with millions of others, when I heard of Pragya Singh Thakur's candidature from Bhopal, I had but one thought: Malegaon, 2008. We know she is an accused in the 2008 Malegaon bombings, was granted bail following the dropping of charges by the National Investigation Agency and is currently under trial for multiple charges in terms of the Unlawful Activities (Prevention) Act. Technically, she can contest. Technically, she is as yet 'innocent'. Technically, no one can fault her or the BJP for making her its chosen candidate from Bhopal.

But what does her candidature, of Mitesh Patel, and of others, say of the party that has selected them? Why, from so many hopeful applicants for tickets, have they been favoured? Because they can deliver a very particular electoral product. They can deliver polarised victories. Pragya Singh Thakur's comments on Hemant Karkare, the valiant police officer who was martyred in the Mumbai terror attack known as '26/11', do not bear repetition. They belong to the world of curses, hoodoo, jinxes, 'the evil eye', not to the world of rational humanity. And though the BJP 'has distanced' itself from those comments, it has remained as near as near can be to her candidacy.

Narendra Modi is a candidate from the temple town of Varanasi, Amit Shah from the heart-core of the Gujarat riots, Ahmedabad. One is the BJP's leader, the other its president. Yet, it is not these two leaders but the two candidates 'presumed innocent till proven guilty' who represent the face, mind and heart of the party that seeks India's mandate to govern its 1 billion people. Face, mind and heart are incomplete without a soul.

Where is that to come from? From our deepest feelings as a people. We are not at war. But 20 years ago, in 1999, we were: the Kargil War. Our soldiers became the soul of the country. In any war, they become that. It so happened, by the inexorable calendar of parliamentary democracies, that elections had to be, and were, announced, right in the middle of that war. Then-Prime Minister Atal Bihari Vajpayee kept the war and his election campaign distinct. BJP registers will show anyone interested in history that at a political meeting in Haryana when he noticed photographs of our defence chiefs displayed in the backdrop, he said, 'No, this is not proper.' And the arrangement was rectified.

Not proper, not done. That is what ethics are about. Not presumptions of innocence till proven guilty, but presumptions of intention that need no proving.

(*The Hindu*, May 4, 2019)

62

Such a Long Reckoning

IT WAS A WET and windy September in London. The year was 1931. M.K. Gandhi, almost 62 years old then, was there to attend the Second Round Table Conference (RTC) as the sole representative of the Indian National Congress. Called by the British government to discuss the prospect of political changes in India, the conclave was showing up the fissures in India's polity. In two other Indian barristers – M.A. Jinnah, leading the Muslims at the Conference, and B.R. Ambedkar, the clear leader of the Depressed Classes – the divides stood out.

The only political change Gandhi and the Indian National Congress required was complete independence. Jinnah, Ambedkar and representatives of India's princes, Sikhs, zamindars and other 'minority interests' sought to tear up Gandhi's claim that the Congress represented an inclusive India which wanted nothing more and could do with nothing less than *Swaraj* for all Indians, in equality.

On September 18, he penned a statement for *The Daily Mail* describing the genesis and goal of the Indian National Congress: 'The Indian National Congress is over forty-seven years old. It was conceived by an Englishman, Allan Octavian Hume. It has had, besides Hindus, Mohammedans, Parsi and Christian Presidents. It had two women as Presidents, Dr Annie Besant and Mrs Sarojini Naidu. It has zamindars too, as its members.

'The Indian National Congress...knows no distinction between classes or creeds or sexes. It has always championed the cause of the so-called "untouchables"...

'But the unchallenged and unchallengeable claim of the Indian National Congress consists in its representing the millions of dumb paupers living in the seven hundred thousand Indian villages who constitute over 85% of the population.

'It is in the name of this great organisation that I claim complete independence for India.'

An all-important session of the Minorities Committee was to meet on October 8. Waking up at 3 a.m. that morning, after a very strenuous night and only half an hour's sleep, he wrote out a statement to be read at the Committee: 'The Congress has, since its inception, set up pure nationalism as its ideal. It has endeavoured to break down communal barriers...Congress assures the Sikhs, the Muslims and the other minorities that no solution...in any future constitution will be acceptable to the Congress that does not give full satisfaction to the parties concerned.'

85 years ago

It was a season of excitement. The year was 1937.

In the elections which came about under the Government of India Act, 1935, a fruit of three Round Table Conferences, the Congress won spectacularly in eight provinces on its own or with allies. Independence with minority rights protected was its motto. The Muslim League failed to win any province but it installed Fazlul Huq's Krishak Praja Party at the head of a Muslim coalition in Bengal. It had done well in Muslim seats (reserved for the community) in Hindu-majority provinces. Its plank was: 'Congress domination is Hindu domination.' Likewise, Ambedkar's candidates did well in the Maharashtra region of Bombay. Their plank was: 'Congress domination is Caste Hindu domination.'

In October of that year Jinnah was asking Muslims in Hindu-majority provinces to recognise 'Hindu domination'. The Congress's concept of swaraj and 'minority satisfaction' was under strain.

75 years ago

It was a hot and humid August. The year was 1947.

Amid unparalleled bloodshed, dispossession and tragedy, Jinnah walked away with Pakistan. He had, according to his lights, stopped Hindu domination in its tracks. Ambedkar had reason to be pleased that his supporters had made it to legislatures in good numbers. The Congress, assuming power at the Centre in an independent, if truncated, India, had unveiled a secular democracy and was moving towards becoming a federal Republic, where religion was separated from the State and caste was not going to be an obstacle for democratic representation. Minority satisfaction was to be the new democracy's signature.

Today, this topsy-turvy August of 2022, 75 years after Independence, Jinnah's Pakistan is in an electoral shambles, with Bangladesh having loosened itself out of its untenable yoking to Pakistan. India's Dalits, as the Depressed Classes of Ambedkar's time are now more appropriately called, have won a visible political profile in India, though social and economic deprivations remain a torment.

But what about Gandhi's and the Congress's ideal of pure nationalism, representative democracy and minority satisfaction? That ideal is in trouble, dire trouble. And this is not just because the Congress as a party today is a shadow of its past self, or because Savarkar's 1937 'warning' influences several more now than it did in the past. That ideal of pure nationalism is in trouble because majority domination, with caste domination subtly folded into its vocabulary, is being seen by increasing numbers as natural, proper and wholly unexceptionable. 'If democracy is not majority control, what else is democracy?' seems to be their understanding of the political dynamics of our nation. That a democracy is meant to reassure the smallest, the weakest and the most vulnerable is seen as nursery-rhyme idealism.

But who are 'the minority'? Not just the religious minority but the ecological, ideological, linguistic, ethnic, communities living in the margins of fear, insecurity, uncertainty. But not them alone Also those who are culturally outnumbered, the lifestyle singular, the 'different', the 'distant', the 'dissenting' as well. Those who, for instance, would want parity in matters of gender and make the Indian woman feel she is man's equal, our courts to be completely insulated from executive influence, our media to be free, our economy to be purged of monopolies.

A religious majority is only one among majorities, albeit a politically determining one. India, as Menaka Guruswamy has so memorably put it, is a majority of minorities. India is not about Hindu India and non-Hindu India. It is about the aspirations of peninsular India, Himalayan India, forest India, desert India, littoral India, coastal India. And the India of the two mountain fastnesses that political geography has made distinctive – Kashmiri India and Northeast India.

Gandhi in London in 1931 spoke for all of these Indias. As did his colleagues in the Congress of that time. Can the Congress or any political party make that claim today? We have splintered our thinking, split up our feelings. We have become a fractious family. On this defining anniversary we have to face this searing truth. And retrieve the 'we' in us as in 'we the people of India', the life-stream of the Constitution of India which protects us and is, in turn, preserved by us. We have to retrieve our unity in freedom and justice. The Tricolour being unfurled today on home after home, with its blue in the central wheel of dharma, tells us India is home to all Indians equally. 'But how do we do this?' is the question. 'Who is to guide us, lead us?'

The 'salt of the earth'

I started this article by citing Gandhi in London in 1931. I will close by citing him in London again, in 1914. He and Kasturba Gandhi had come there at the conclusion of the highly successful satyagraha in South Africa, on their way back home. Speaking to a galactic audience which included visiting Indians such as Lala Lajpat Rai, Sarojini Naidu and M.A. Jinnah, he said: 'We had got the limelight in South Africa but if we merited any approbation, how much more did those who went into the struggle with no thought of appreciation! Harbut Singh was 75 years of age when he joined the struggle and entered prison and died there. The young lad, Narayanaswami, was deported to Madras and on his return, starved and died.

'Another Tamil youth, Nagappen, was imprisoned and worked on the African veldt in the bitter cold of winter and died. And Valliamma, a girl of 18, went to prison and was discharged only when she took very ill and died shortly thereafter. 20 thousand workers had left their tools and work and gone out in faith. Violence was entirely eschewed. It is on these men and women, who are the salt of the earth, that the Indian nation that is to be will be built. We are poor mortals before these heroes and heroines.'

Those heroes and heroines have not disappeared. They have only been covered by the dust of neglect and condescension. They are the salt of India's earth we must salute today in hope, faith and solidarity. It is they, as Gandhi said, who got India her freedom. It is they who will keep it free – and just.

(*The Hindu*, August 15, 2022)

63

A Necessary Presence

9 0 IS A GREAT number. And a terrific age.
Having crossed 80, 90 walks with the measured steps of emeriti.
Being at hundred's door, it carries the bounce of penultimacy.
A full decade short of a century, it has a venerable vivacity. It has a certain life to it that previous 'round' numbers do not.

Amartya Kumar Sen, who turned 90 this month, was treated just the other day to a pre-birthday joke by the grace of social media. The Nobel laureate was said to have died. The 'news' zoomed across the globe, not because death makes news but because Amartya Sen does. Newspaper offices went into nervous action, defrosting draft obits of the great man. Editors checked out their 'regular' columnists on who could write fresh tributes fast. Photographs were dug up from their archives for the 'classical young Sen' with enigmatically attractive eyes storing econometric puzzles and also those of the most recent 'Sens' with the same eyes wanting relief from today's horrors. And, indeed, some 'well-known contemporaries' were called up to be given the 'sad and as yet unverified news' and urged to put fingertips to keyboards for a tribute 'while we get confirmation'.

The world's sharpest master of welfare economics and social choice theory would, ordinarily, have laughed the joke out but for the fact that his laptop's inbox and mobile telephone were, within seconds, clogged with incoming messages expressing shock, disbelief, and 'tell-me-its-not-true'. And when before too long the hoax was bluffed, out came the next round of messages including one, I must admit, from me: 'Greatly relieved'. 'Thank God…' and 'Now…for your hundredth…' I do not think the historian of famines was amused and was going to reply to any of these. 'Better ways of using my time…' I could hear him say under his breath.

He would, therefore, be glad that his 90th birthday has gone almost unnoticed. 'Better ways of spending time, mine and others,' I can hear him say, with a cube of ice clinking concurrence in a glass of something choice to mark the day.

Sen is a hundred things but is, in my thinking, above everything else, a great witness to some grotesque things human beings have done to themselves and to planet earth, as well as truly wondrous things.

In the years immediately after 1933 (the year Sen was born), he could follow, with his generation, schooling in Dhaka and then in Santiniketan, the rise of a maniac in Europe unleashing World War II on an innocent world with disastrous consequences: first, the Bengal Famine of 1943 caused, among other factors, by the military policy of the time, panic buying, hoarding, triggered by the war. Second, the manufacture of the atomic bomb and its deployment within months upon a country, Japan, that had ceased to pose any threat to the one that made and dropped two of them on densely populated cities. Third, the grafting of an artificial nation with a translocated population on a tract peopled by its natural inhabitants. Fourth, the rise of nuclear, biological and chemical weapons with unknown furies. Fifth, the commencement of techno-commercial hegemonies that divided the world into new inequalities, dependencies and enervations.

His time in Presidency College in Calcutta and then in Trinity College, Cambridge, England, saw great counters coming to these horrors in terms of the UNO's Declaration of Human Rights, the newly independent India giving to itself a Constitution founded on the principles of secularism, social justice and federal equity, the civil rights movement in the US pioneered by millennial individuals like Martin Luther King Jr and Rosa Parks, and movements of shackled nations starting on the African continent led by men of the stature of Kwame Nkrumah, Jomo Kenyatta, Albert Luthuli and, later, Nelson Mandela. And overarching these healings, arising unmistakably and remarkably, a sense of the importance of the aspirations and entitlements of the individual, especially the traditionally under-acknowledged and marginalised communities.

In the 1970s and the 1980s, came science and technology, transforming life unrecognisably, giving humans a new equation with the resources of the earth and new challenges, leading to Sen's interest in 'real wages and using the entire increase in labour productivity, due to technological change' and saw the appearance of his seminal work, *Poverty and Famines: An Essay on Entitlement and Deprivation*.

The nine decades in which Sen has moved from being a precocious student to a cherished teacher have also seen his country acquire the skills of an electoral democracy conducting elections of mammoth proportions, in almost each of which he has made sure he has voted. The West Bengal constituency where he is a registered voter has seen him take his place in the queue inching its way to the ballot box (now electronic machine) along with fellow citizens who are perfectly at ease with the laureate and Bharat Ratna-awardee being one among them.

But these decades have also seen in India new, dire crises, of which five stand out: one, rank callousness as to the damage industrial and techno-commercial exploitation does to non-renewable resources and fragile ecosystems and that which aggressive cropping does to our depleting topsoil and water tables. Two, the continuing low nutrition and basic health levels of the rural poor, especially those of the prematurely 'married-off' young and lactating mothers and school-age children. Three, the vulnerability of the rural workforce and unavoidable migration to uncertain and often collapsed pathways. Four, the contamination of our democratic, especially electoral, system by what is unambiguously called 'muscle and money power'. Five, the brazen undermining of our secular tradition by violent religious bigotry and the equally violent compromising of the rights of the lower castes by swaggering upper caste machoism.

Brooding over all this is a pall of despondency.

Sen's rigorous examination of what he witnessed and studied has resulted in some of the most defining writing of our time, such as his celebrated article in *The New York Review of Books*, 'More Than 100 Million Women Are Missing', in which he shows the impact of inequality on mortality. His book, *Development as Freedom*, suggests likewise, that 'real freedoms', and not metrics such as GDP or income per capita, are what matter.

The present situation of quandaries and complexity is beyond the capacity or even the comprehension of administrators, politicians and technologists. The wondrous opportunities being opened by Artificial Intelligence and, equally, its mind-numbing potential for harm, for instance, beyond the reach of intellectual or academic intervention. We cannot be so naively aspirational as to wait for 'someone' to emerge and redeem us from our sense of being trapped in a hovel of despair, within a ruin of hopes. We have to seek and find within our own human resources the knowledge, understanding and discrimination that Amartya Sen has shown over these decades. The 'joke' I mentioned evaporated in the fakery it came from. But it did make us see for one shuddering moment what life without Sen can be. It showed up for that 'Oh, no!' moment the drought in our time of social philosophers and generational motivators whose word carries truth, veracity, courage and total objectivity.

Is Sen a Marxist? I do not think he will want to contest that. Is he an atheist? I doubt if he would care to proclaim his thoughts on the matter. A dialectical materialist? I would say he is, above all else, a scholar-witness in the open university of the human condition. And one who sees in music and sculpture, in a great film and a fine piece of writing, the 'click' he can find in any mathematical theorem.

'Valuationally gross' is a phrase he used some years ago to describe India's (then) attitude to the struggle for political rights in Myanmar. It is that unceasing attention to the life-giving and life-taking pulsations of our time that has made Amartya Sen who and what he is.

With two wars of vile ferocity blazing, the world's terror modules plotting the next blow and politics getting drained of principles, we need the statesmanship of this independent scholar-witness more than ever. Speak to your mind's *extremis*, Amartya*babu*. Let your keyboard's letters pale and numerals fade under your moving fingers' scorching veracity.

(*The Telegraph*, November 19, 2023)

64

We, the People; Neither Free of Fear nor Fearless

ARE WE A FEAR-FREE people with some of us who are frightened? Or a fearful people with some of us being unafraid? This is not about statistics. Fever can be read in a thermometer. Fear is not measurable. This is about the way things are. As real as the bolt in our door, the lock in our cell phones, the double-blind password in our laptop. 'Oh,' the reader will rightly say, 'those are universal fears.' So they are. But we have our own variants of that universal phenomenon called fear, our own mutants of human dread.

We are not like those in Israel, afraid of Hamas bomb-showers. Or those in Gaza afraid of Israeli bomb-rain. We are not like Ukrainians fearing the next downpour of Russian fire. We are not like the unfortunates in Iran, Saudi Arabia, the UAE or China who face prosecution today and execution tomorrow.

Many admirable men and women across India are fear-free and speak, write, sing without fear. Does that make us, as a people, fear-free?

If I am a Hindu in the Kashmir Valley, I will dread separatist gunfire, fear plying my trade, going to my office, college, school. I could be gunned down any moment by masked men on motorcycles. If I am a Muslim in Jammu, I will dread a shoot-out in Kashmir that has killed a Hindu for it could lead to an immediate backlash in Jammu making me hide, flee. And even if I am a Muslim in Muslim-majority Kashmir, I will be afraid of menacing separatists who want me to become a separatist as well, a fundamentalist, pro-separation even if not pro-Pakistan. With the bizarre train-terror on Pakistan's Jaffar Express rekindling fear of renewed terror attacks, especially along the Line of Control, that is called a real, hard, threat which must make us hugely vigilant. Not just vigilant about terror but about the possible aftermath of terror, in terms of communal conflagrations.

Riot is a community-neutral word. And it disturbs the memory of almost every religious denomination in India with fear of repetitions.

If I am a cowherd, I am afraid I will be lynched for being a beef-peddling anti-Hindu, no matter that goats are routinely sacrificed at temples in the name of gods and goddesses. If I am a cobbler and a knife grinder, a *razai* maker or cotton-fluffer and also a Muslim, I will practise my profession with tension and uneasiness preying on my mind. If I am not a Muslim but living in certain parts of Aligarh, I could be very, very tense.

If I am a Christian in those parts of India where missionaries have been regarded as converters, I am afraid I will be asked to prove my loyalties to India that is Bharat. News about some people, including some elected representatives, wanting any attempted 'conversion' to be awarded the death penalty no less having reached me, I will shiver as I go to sleep, shudder in nightmares.

If I am a peaceable civilian in parts of tribal India, I will be afraid of the uniformed man who has orders to be alert, watchful, and who mistakes me to be a militant, an ultra, and arrests me. I will be afraid, no less, in fact, more, of that very militant and ultra who is a fact of bitter life and who wants me to join him when I do not want to have anything to do with him.

If I were a Manipuri and tribal, I would be afraid of the tribe I am not a member of. And the non-tribal Manipuri is wary of both of us. If I am a Bangladeshi in Assam, I have reason to be afraid.

Two English words have become frightening in India in recent times. The first is immigrant. To have to prove one's legality for the right to live in a place can be a nightmare, especially if one has a family of young and old to support. The second is goon. Landlords are afraid tenants will get goons to intimidate them; tenants are afraid landlords will do the same. Come elections and voters fear goons and goonery like the devil and pray the agents of the state will keep them at bay.

If I am Dalit and a girl in a village that has known upper caste hubris, I will be afraid of moustachioed males lurking like crocodiles in a lake do where a thirsty calf would go unblinking to its nemesis.

If I am an activist for human rights, afraid or not, I am at risk. If I am a crusader for the right to information, if I am a whistle-blower, if I am an investigative journalist, if I am pursuing mafiosi in illegal mining, in gold smuggling, in drug peddling, I am at risk even though I may be unafraid.

Water and language – beautiful things – can turn belligerent. Vehicle number plates of one state in another state can suddenly look provocative when the water disputes heat up. If I am a non-local language speaker, I better learn my local language.

To go back to the question with which I began, I will say we are neither a fear-free people nor a fearful people. We are a people that can be made to fear, encouraged to hate, provoked to hurt, and to panic, leading many to exit from India. Fear is good business for quite a few. They make us addicts of fear, victims of alarm, innocent carriers of fake documents as well.

It follows that we must get de-addicted. The problem is while there are places where those addicted to alcohol and drugs can go for help, there is no sanctuary for those addicted to fear. Which is why law enforcers have a great and unenviable responsibility. And which is why Rabindranath Tagore's great pre-independence work, *Chitto jetha bhoyshunno* (Where the mind is without fear), today holds hope for us, the brave and good people of India that is Bharat.

(*Hindustan Times*, March 21, 2025)

PART VI

Our Institutions

65

In an Era of Diminishing Expectations, the Judiciary Gives Hope

REVOLUTION OF RISING EXPECTATIONS was a much-used phrase in the India of the 1960s. It was about public aspirations for a better life outstripping the State's ability to match them. But another phrase is waiting to be born — rise of diminishing expectations. It is about the gap between what we expect to be available to us as entitlements and the ability of the State to make it available.

This is, like all generalisations, unfair to many an earnest politician, honest, hard-working official, and worthy institution. Readers of this column will know, admire and respect a number of public servants who work tirelessly in their field of duty. But who can deny that the words politician and bureaucrat are not exactly a compliment today? We expect less from the political class than we did in the early years of our Republic. So also from the class of officials. Institutions have also suffered a similar erosion of public confidence. Hearing our judiciary being criticised is deeply demoralising. It plunges diminishing expectations into a pit of utter despondency, despair.

And this is exactly where in the last few days I have, to my relief, my delight, my, touch wood, elation, found so much that reverses and annuls the cynicism. There is hope.

A fortnight ago, I saw the Tamil feature film *Jai Bhim*, which tells the real story of a tribal from the Irula community having died of torture in police custody, while being interrogated for a theft he did not commit. It ends in the perpetrators being arrested and convicted, the young widow being compensated — all because of the perseverance of a lawyer, K. Chandru, and the Madras High Court (HC)'s sensitivity. Chandru went on to become a judge, retiring with an outstanding reputation for probity. The film about criminal injustice to a tribal being reversed by the house of justice has done more than anything else in recent times to strengthen my faith in our judiciary.

In her eye-opener of a column in *Mint Lounge* on November 18, Gita Aravamudan points out that custodial deaths and torture are an old and die-hard phenomenon in India. And she cites the Chief Justice of India N.V. Ramana's stirring words spoken on August 8: 'The threat to human rights and bodily integrity are the highest in police stations…To keep police excesses in check, dissemination of information about the constitutional right to legal aid and availability of free legal aid services is necessary.'

This holds out hope. India signed the UN Convention Against Torture on October 18, 1997. But a quarter century on, it is yet to ratify its signing. Why? Will the higher judiciary be moved to ask why this hesitancy? It well could.

Recently, the Supreme Court (SC) gave a historic pronouncement in an altogether different field. Quashing the orders of the Bombay HC that had acquitted a man charged with sexual assault on a girl on the grounds that the man had groped her over her clothes without skin-to-skin contact, it said limiting the definition of 'touch' to a narrow and pedantic definition would be an 'absurd interpretation'. Justices U.U. Lalit, Ravindra Bhat and Bela Trivedi said that sexual intent was what mattered. The offender was sentenced to three years rigorous imprisonment. Few things can be more confidence-inspiring for the vulnerable girl child and her carers. Cases under the Protection of Children from Sexual Offences (POCSO), we may note, reached 43,000 this year.

And, crowning this, has come the SC's intervention to protect the investigation into the deaths of farmers in Lakhimpur Kheri. The farmers, the Bench led by CJI Ramana said, were 'rammed from behind' and 'then run over' and this matter deserved an 'impartial, fair, just and thorough investigation'. Few things can be more restorative of our sense of expectation from the most crucial of institutions.

India's judiciary has not always reassured seekers of justice. Judges are human beings placed by their calling. They can miss the chance to intervene decisively. For now, however, the rise in diminishing expectations has been given a pause by the judiciary.

(*Hindustan Times*, November 24, 2021)

66

Three-Letter Status

'At the moment he has a V.I.P. with him'…Miss Glidden seemed to divine his perplexity, for…she turned round and whispered through a pursed up mouth, 'Very Important Personage'.
                                C. Mackenzie, 1933, *Water on the Brain* viii. 111

THE EXCELLENT ONLINE ETYMOLOGY Dictionary gives the above as the first written example of the use of the term VIP. I have not read the comic thriller but now that I have seen this excerpt, I intend to do so asap.

Asap? That unseemly word, now in great use, standing for 'as soon as possible', is slang. Let us use it, if we must, but let us know that it comes from the US army slang dating back to 1954 and the Korean War. Captain Annis G. Thompson's book on that hideous war titled *The Greatest Airlift* says: 'Most drops were made on an ASAP or "as soon as possible" basis.' Without knowing anything about the context for that line, let me say 'most drops' sounds like it is about the US air force's bombing campaigns and it sounds pretty frightful. Today, when 'asap' is employed to convey a request or make a promise in breathless urgency, let us not forget where it comes from – a war that left nearly 3 million dead.

The terms, VIP, standing for Very Important Person, and VVIP, with the Very repeated to raise the VIP to a yet higher plane of importance, are not slang in the same sense as 'asap' but are not 'true' words as words come or go. These two initialisms arose as a convenient and, I think, tongue-in-cheek expression in the 1930s and were later put into common use among the cloudy heights of RAF pilots during World War II.

I can imagine a cockpit conversation:

Pilot 1: Hey, these important guys…We fly for them, die for them…rising and leaving home before the sun rises…'Important people' I told Wifey as I was leaving home today. 'You sure care for 'em more than you do for me and the kids…' she said…'They are more important for you than us…' and I couldn't say no…

Pilot 2:…Yep…they're important all right…very important…you know I've read somewhere of a phrase…VIP…Very Important Person.

Pilot 1: Cool!…VIP! That's high-larious…sky-high-larious…VIP…and…VVIP…Will tell Wifey…'Those guys are VIPs…but you are my one and only VVIP'…Cool…

It will do VIPs great good to know that the expression that confers status (though not stature) on them, that makes people cut pathways for them, rise when they approach, bow when they pass, scurry away from enclosures with signs saying VIP or VVIP on them, groan when stopped on roads for their convoys to materialise, scream silently when they are overtaken in queues by them, has more than a touch of sarcasm in it, a dash of derision.

The innocent organisers of arrangements or events with VIP compliance do not mean to be sarcastic. Good Heavens, No! They are wholly earnest. They mean well. But VIPs and VVIPs should know the truth about their three-letter or four-letter status.

Around this time last March, Bhadra Sinha reported in the *Hindustan Times*:

> The Supreme Court has asked the Centre to 'enlighten' it with the origin of the terms – Very Important Person (VIP) and Very Very Important Person (VVIP). Taking strong exception to the rampant misuse of red-beacon lights, sirens, hooters and security cover, the bench headed by Justice GS Singhvi verbally told additional solicitor general (ASG) Siddhartha Luthra and senior counsel Harish Salve to address the court on the issue of what is meant by the word VIP on April 3. Salve is assisting the court as amicus curiae in the matter… 'Please enlighten us with the origin of the word VIP and VVIP and what its place is in a democratic polity,' the bench said expressing concern at the increasing trend of flashing of beacon lights…The SCI has in the past strongly disapproved of police protection given to 'all and sundry' including MPs and MLAs facing no security threat.

The court had taken note of the VIP issue after a petition challenging Z+ security to a Congress leader in Uttar Pradesh was filed before it.

On December 10, 2013, the Supreme Court passed a very carefully calibrated order in *Abhay Singh vs State of Uttar Pradesh & Ors* which recognised the protocol-related need for differentiation with respect to high dignitaries. But it also made it mandatory for several modifications to be carried out consistently with our democratic status. The court said *inter alia*: '…there has been abysmal failure on the part of the concerned authorities and agencies of various State Governments and the Administration of the Union Territories to check misuse of the vehicles with red lights on their top. So much so that a large number of persons are using red lights on their vehicles for committing crimes in different parts of the country and they do so with impunity because the police officials are mostly scared of checking vehicles with red lights, what to say of imposing fine or penalty.'

I find their lordships' academic interest in the origins of the phrases invaluable not just from the lexical point but from the social and cultural setting in which the phrases are employed. And their asking what place the concepts had in a democratic polity, I regard, as constitutionally pertinent.

The VIP and VVIP nomenclatures are made to work for four objectives that may be called the four S-es in the cause of the VIP or the VVIP: to secure Security, to recognise Status, to augment Speed of Services, and to formalise Social Stratum. Those who are not troubled with a sense of insecurity, or inferiority and do not subscribe to stratified views of hierarchies would not care for the titles of VIP and VVIP. Those would encumber them, embarrass them. They would hold high offices without thinking of VIP and VVIP tags. It is those who suffer the pangs I mention that seek and covet them and end up looking the very opposite of what the initialisms mean.

They also run a risk. By announcing themselves as VIP and VVIP through red lights and hooters and the like, they attract attention, not just of the bored onlooker like R.K. Laxman's Babuji but of the anti-social, the downright criminal and outright terrorist.

There is a great Sanskrit word which must out 'S' the four S-es that I have mentioned – *shobha*, or grace. VIP and VVIP tags get the four S-es but lack the fifth, *shobha*. The Hindi phrase about something that lacks grace – *shobha nahin detaa* – says it all, negatively.

Will the 'high dignitaries' of the Republic of India ever see that the concepts of VIP and VVIP do not fit a democratic republic any more than titles (which have been abolished)? Will they ever want to add to the four S-es, the fifth, *shobha*? Or has all grace fled from us?

(*The Telegraph*, March 24, 2024)

67

The Architecture of India's Governance

THIS IS NOT ABOUT Alapan Bandyopadhyay, whose ability as a classical civil servant I had the pleasure of observing when I was working in West Bengal (2004–2009). Nor is it about the circumstances of his concluding days in service and their getting vestibuled into a post-retirement appointment as adviser to the chief minister of that amazing state.

Enough has been written about that subject and I need not add to the wordage.

What I am concerned here with is the hinterland to those proceedings, where the political and administrative flanks of the government meet. We, the citizens of the country, stand at that joint with, very often, the third flank, namely, the judicial, joining them. An understanding of that hinterland and that intersection is essential to our sense of the citizenship of India.

I will start with a memoir. When, in 1968, I was among those who 'made it' to the Indian Administrative Service (IAS), a communication came to me, as it did to all appointees, from the ministry of home affairs, asking me to confirm, by telegram, that I was accepting the appointment. I do not know if that formality is still in vogue.

Before sending my telegraphic response, I showed the small draft of it to my maternal grandfather, Rajaji (C. Rajagopalachari), whose respect for the civil services was strong, and who had encouraged me to take the examinations for it that year. 'Offer Accepted' is what I had drafted. He pondered the draft briefly and asked me to add a word. 'Say gratefully accepted.' Who, I wondered, in that vast office, is going to notice that word. Reading my thoughts, the just-turned-90 veteran said to me, 'There is such a thing as form.'

Form. The concept was crucial. Rajaji had worked with officials from the higher position of their political head. He had, when he held high office, given instructions, issued orders. He had occasion to pull up the slothful, the errant. An officer, he knew, had to have what used to be called (and I hope still is known by those three letters) OLQ – Officer Like Qualities. These did not include the raised chin, the swaggering gait, the air that says 'I am the sarkar'. These included a sense of what can only be called 'the purpose of public administration' which is, basically, ministration, service, to the people.

When, with my batchmates, I showed up at the National Academy of Administration, I encountered one of the ablest officers I have ever met – T.N. Chaturvedi. TNC, as we knew him, was not the academy's director then, but as number two, he personified for us, what being in the service of the government was all about. It was about respect for the architecture of governance and for the governed. It was about humility before the reality of India, its complexity, its grandeur and, simultaneously, a deep awareness of its multiple immiserations in removing which we were to do our little bit.

And this meant that we had to acknowledge that the political class, which goes through the treadmill of elections, knows the pulse of the people in ways in which we do not. And that the politicians' specialisation in the 'pulse' and our acquired expertise in 'pulse-taking' and 'pulse-treating' must work together, in mutual respect.

Mutual. The concept was crucial. And one person who knew this better than anyone else from among the founders of our Republic was our first home minister, Sardar Vallabhbhai Patel.

The Constitution of India is the product of much deliberation, many perspectives. Patel, in charge as he was of the services, spoke for two articles of the draft Constitution affecting the services. The first of these was Article 311. That formulation protected officials from arbitrary punishment by their political bosses.

Now, Patel, like many of the members of the Constituent Assembly, was a stalwart of the freedom struggle. As such, his stature was peerless. He had known what it meant to be jailed and be treated with harshness by big and small officials. To give it back to officialdom would have been natural in a lesser 'first home minister of free India'. But Patel was Patel. There was to be no vendetta.

On the contrary, there was to be trust. More, there was to be respect. Respect for the civilian's opinion, criticism. 'Today,' the Sardar said in the assembly, 'my Secretary can write a note opposed to my views. I have given that freedom to all my Secretaries. I have told them: "If you do not give me your honest opinion, then please you had better go."

And he said in the course of the same speech to critics of the new guarantees that he was introducing under Article 314 for civil servants: 'If you…decide not to have this Service, I will take the Service with me and go. They will earn their living. They are capable people…. Do not take a lathi and say: "We are a supreme Parliament."

This was not an Indian Civil Service officer speaking. This was Sardar Patel. He knew what respect means, in the giving and receiving of it.

(*Hindustan Times*, June 14, 2021)

68

The Subtle Influence of India's President

INDEPENDENCE DAY IS ABOUT the prime minister. The speech made from the ramparts of the Red Fort that morning marks the day. This is as it should be. And it was so this year too.

But on the eve of every Independence Day and Republic Day, our President addresses the nation through airwaves. That speech does not get the attention it deserves. Our President's address this Independence Day eve, recorded in her study in Rashtrapati Bhavan, was dignified, stately. The words were well chosen, well intoned. She spoke with calm assurance and her statement, 'Each one of us is an equal citizen' was most needed. Equality is, after all, enshrined in the preamble to our Constitution, after justice and liberty. Her words reminded me of the Ashokan edict, the Kalinga Edict, which stands close to Bhubaneswar, in her own state of Odisha, in which the Mauryan says, '*Sabe manuse mama praja*...All my subjects are my children.'

Reflecting on all this I could not but recall the 50th year of our independence in 1998, when neither our present President nor our prime minister were very well known outside their states – a great comment on our electoral democracy, where men and women from among the so-called less-known, less-privileged strata of society can rise to the highest offices in the land.

On Independence Day that year – 1998 – our President was Kocheril Ramana Narayanan. One of India's eminent diplomats who had served as ambassador to China and the United States, had been a minister of state for science and technology under Rajiv Gandhi, and then Vice President of India, he hailed from one of Kerala's Dalit communities. He did not allude to that fact; he did not encourage or stop others from doing so either. Narayanan was respected across the political spectrum for his intellectual sparkle, his calm demeanour, and his singularly judicious mind.

The late economist and Ahmedabad-based management guru G.R. Kulkarni was visiting Delhi at that time. Married to my esteemed cousin Sumitra Gandhi Kulkarni, he came over for a conversation and asked me (I was then working for President Narayanan as his secretary) how the I-Day arrangements were going. 'As well as they should,' I replied. 'The drill is fairly straight-forward.'

That, he said, is what is wrong with our I-Day and Republic Day celebrations. They are just too predictable, too set. Instead of the usual speech, he wondered, why don't you request President Narayanan to do something different? 'Like?' I asked. 'Like coming on TV in a conversation, rather than reading out a speech. In a democracy we should have less formality and more interaction, don't you think?' And Gajananbhai, as I called him, spoke of the impact of the fireside chats of the US President Franklin Roosevelt.

I put the thought to President Narayanan who warmed to it at once and there ensued a delightful conversation with him and senior journalist N. Ram, which was relayed over AIR and Doordarshan, on the eve of Independence Day in place of the customary address. He was not shown the questions earlier, and had not prepared his answers. It was to be and was a spontaneous conversation.

There is neither need (nor space) for me to reproduce chunks of that conversation except for a portion that touched on the role of the President. 'My image of a President before I came here and before I had any hope of coming here,' Narayanan said, 'was that of a rubber-stamp President. I thought I would have a lot of time, and leisure for reading, writing, walking etcetera. But somehow I can't get it now. So, my image of a President is of a working President, not an executive President, but a working President. And working within the four corners of the Constitution.'

Elaborating on this, he said the office held 'very little direct power' and it was only in some very critical situations that the President could do one or two things directly. But, he said, the President did have a subtle influence. And this worked 'on the executive and the other arms of the government and on the public as a whole', especially when the President aligned his thoughts to what was right and perceived by the public to be so. When that happened, he said, such advice that a President gave would be accepted 'with grace'. His returning a recommendation for Article 356 to be applied to Uttar Pradesh, he said, was one such. The government fell in line with his thinking.

Now this is not something he could have said in a formal address. But it emerged seamlessly in the conversation. President Narayanan's views were cherished by both the prime ministers who worked with him, I.K. Gujral and Atal Bihari Vajpayee. That the conversation mode was not continued in subsequent years is another matter.

But it came to be known that unlike the speech made at the opening of Parliament's annual session which has to be the government's speech, President Narayanan's speeches on the eve of I-Day and R-Day were his own, as were, largely, those he made at banquets hosted for visiting heads of State. There was no question of his going against government policy but there was no doubt that he would, from 'within the four corners' that he had mentioned, furnish the space with his own, not someone else's intellectual furniture. Thus arose his famous statement on the eve of Republic Day, 2000: 'One half of our society guzzles aerated beverages, while the other has to make do with palmfuls of muddied water. Our three-way fast-lane of liberalisation, privatisation and globalisation must have safe pedestrian crossings for unempowered India.'

Equality in an unequal society like ours means that at given intervals the car-less, engine-less human population must pass on its two feet as a sovereign, while the machines of jet-set transport pause.

I do not doubt that 'within the four corners of the Constitution', President Droupadi Murmu is already exercising the subtle influence that President Narayanan spoke of. In her 'equality address', Ashoka's Kalinga Edict came with quiet dignity to life.

(*Hindustan Times*, August 21, 2023)

69

Constant Verities

During the weeks when 'election fever' was upon us, we heard it said often and scarily that if, in this election, the ruling National Democratic Alliance (NDA) was not defeated and Narendra Modi came back as prime minister, we will not have another election thereafter. The Congress president, Mallikarjun Kharge, said that repeatedly, as did the political economist, Parakala Prabhakar, persuasively.

Well, the NDA is back in power, Narendra Modi duly sworn in as India's prime minister, for the third time. But no one is saying that we will not have another election again.

And this is where not the NDA but the Indian voter has won. Along with, one must say, Yogendra Yadav and his very carefully worded prognoses.

Yes, the verdicts in Odisha, Gujarat, Madhya Pradesh were emphatic, handing the NDA a triumph, as were those in West Bengal, Tamil Nadu and Maharashtra, handing the NDA a rout. But *kul-milaake*, to use the fantastic Hindi phrase that means 'taking it all in all', what the Indian voter has given to the NDA is not a verdict, but a lesson that says, 'I, the voter, am bigger than your presumptions of a landslide win.' And what the voter has given the INDIA coalition is, again, not a 'good result' but the tuition that says: 'You came to me, the voter, seeking justice and I have given it to you but if you want the "lift", you have got to stay firm, hold it fast with clean hands.'

And reflecting on this amazingly nuanced and astonishingly sobering denouement, I thought of our very first election held over many weeks, in 1951–1952, which saw Jawaharlal Nehru and the Congress swept to power at the Centre, for the first time, through the ballot.

As it played out, independent India's first election was just about less than half an election, for less than half the number of eligible voters voted. And then less than half of those that did vote voted for the Congress, for Nehru. Which meant that a little over half of those who did vote did not vote for the Congress or for Nehru. But in the first-past-the-post system, this vote pattern gave the Congress 364 of the 489 seats (and over four times as many votes as the next largest party, the Communist Party), and Nehru formed the first elected government of India with ease and *éclat*.

That election established five verities.

One, belying the grey prognostications of India-sceptics, it showed that India was in charge of India.

Two, vindicating the pragmatism of independent India's opting for universal adult suffrage, it showed that the 'illiterate' Indian holds a post-doc inside the voting booths of the Republic.

Three, cooperating with the constitutionally empowered independent Election Commission of India, the country showed it knew what its institutions were meant to be.

Four, vindicating India's rejection of the Two-Nation Theory, it saw Hindus and Muslims voting together as one electoral college, as one political entity, and as one republican persona, to choose their legislators in fearless freedom.

Five, it made electoral India an exemplar for the newly decolonising world, so much so that it was to seek out the services of Sukumar Sen (1898–1963) of the ICS, our first chief election commissioner.

But we must also take note, in all fairness, that five other truths about that election also emerged.

One, voter turnout being less than 50 per cent – 45.7 per cent to be precise – the Indian electorate was shown to be liable to democratic ennui, a portentous sign for the future.

Two, with 55 per cent of the votes cast going to non-Congress but disparate candidates, the election signalled the fact that India's Opposition parties, divided, would in all likelihood, *kul-milaake*, face defeat.

Three, among those defeated being two stalwarts who stood in opposition to the Congress – Acharya Kripalani and Babasaheb Ambedkar – in Faizabad (UP) and Bombay North, respectively, by inconsequential Congress candidates, the elections showed that voters often vote out of party loyalty rather than out of reason.

Four, the elections showed that an individual leader – Nehru at that time – exercises, as an icon, great sway over the Indian electorate.

Five, Calcutta, in returning from two segments of its constituent parts two Mukherjees with diametrically opposed ideologies in combat – Syama Prasad Mookerjee from the Bharatiya Jana Sangh and Hiren Mukerjee from the Communist Party of India – the elections showed in a 'trailer', as it were, that the Right and the Left would be in contestation, albeit in different colours, for the future of India.

Ambedkar had stood from Bombay North, a 'reserved' seat under the terms of the Poona Pact, as a Scheduled Castes Federation candidate.

He was defeated by the little-known former associate, the Congress candidate, Narayan Sadoba Kajrolkar, who polled 1,38,137 votes compared to Ambedkar's 1,23,576 votes. The Congress need not have opposed the chairman of the Constituent Assembly's Drafting Committee and India's first law minister. It would have been handsome of it to have said, 'We differ from Dr Ambedkar, but we respect him and hold his presence in our first elected Lok Sabha to be important and will not contest his candidature.' But, no. He was opposed. A herb of inestimable value was smothered by a weed in the garden of India's republic.

As was Kripalani, who had been president of the Congress when India became independent and was the first to be called upon to speak in the Constituent Assembly. We know he could not make it in that first election to the first Lok Sabha. But few remember who defeated him.

All the above-listed 10 verities hold today, none more than the one that shows some truly good candidates can lose, denying Parliament political stature.

The elections just concluded can also be seen as showing the following five major verities.

One, if the height of a candidate's stature is strong it can defeat the weight of money; if not, money and its propaganda power stand to do well.

Two, if a people's collective sense of self-respect is hurt, nothing can win against that hurt.

Three, a woman seen as wronged is a hundred times stronger than the strongest candidate.

Four, the standing of the Election Commission of India, despite several blips, continues to be high.

Five, the Two-Nation Theory continues to be rejected by the Indian voter.

But five other features need to be noted as well.

One, voter ennui is still a factor, depressing voting percentages, making real voter preference unclear.

Two, the phenomenon of the political turncoat, who switches parties and loyalties without embarrassment, is getting accepted as 'normal'.

Three, the language of election campaigning has sunk to the deepest of putrefying sewers.

Four, the naming and co-opting, as also the naming and shaming, of communities has grown.

Five – and this is to be counted a great blessing – neither the third nor the fourth verity stated above has really impacted voter judgment.

So, we may be confident that India will see elections happen regularly, with its weaknesses being overtaken by its strengths. The responsibility on both the winners and near-winners is great, with the need for the two to work with mutual civility being paramount. For this, the new Lok Sabha will need a Speaker selected unanimously for complete freedom from biases, who, on becoming Speaker, will relinquish party affiliations and, reflecting the nuanced verdict of the Indian voter, be a true representative of the *bhagya vidhata* of Bharat's electoral democracy, the post-doc Indian voter.

(*The Telegraph*, June 23, 2024)

70

Flickering Hope

IT WAS EID. FREE India's first. Independence was, on August 18, 1947, four days old.

If Independence was new, Partition was new too. And whatever be the heady aspirations of the new nation, new dilemmas were getting ready to intrigue us, new and knotty conundrums gestating in the womb of *swaraj*.

Places no one in Bengal could think of as belonging to another country were suddenly in Pakistan or in India.

Gandhi was in Calcutta, staying by his choice in a graceful if modest Muslim house in the city's suburb of Beliaghata. The mixed population of the capital of the new state of West Bengal had hailed the dawn of freedom. But the 78-year-old was not taking anything for granted. He was certainly not taking displays of bonhomie for granted.

Though divided on maps, the two regions had not yet become rigid in the matter of cross-border movement.

On the 18th, Eid day, even as many Muslims from the city thronged the Beliaghata home and received some fruit from him, a group of dazed Congress workers from Khulna, now in East Pakistan, came to him. On the 15th, they said, they had hoisted the Indian Tricolour presuming that Khulna would remain in India. But the Boundary Commission, bless its simple soul, had 'awarded' it to East Pakistan. This was one of the anomalies of Partition. 'Anomalies' is just a word. But for those it hits, it is no word but a hatchet. All of Khulna district with a Hindu majority of 52 per cent had 'gone' to East Pakistan in lieu of the much smaller Murshidabad district which had been 'awarded' to India. Result: isolation where home was, alienation where life was. For Hindus 'there', Muslims 'here', Partition came with an edge. A razor's edge – *kshurasya dhara*, to use an Upanishadic phrase of uncertainties.

For Gandhi's Khulna visitors, the immediate 'edge' was: What do we do with the Indian flag we have hoisted in Khulna?

Used as he was to major existential issues posed to him as well as quotidian ones like this, Gandhi pondered their dilemma seriously. And he said, 'There can be no two options, the Union Flag must go, Pakistan's must be hoisted, without demur and with joy if possible. Award is award, good or bad.'

Without demur and with joy! Tall order, that. As tall as the well-known bamboo staff with which he had trudged Noakhali's blood-soaked earth and then Bihar's.

That was, as I said, on August 18, Eid day. Gandhi went later that day with H.S. Suhrawardy, the last premier of undivided Bengal (who would later shift seamlessly to Pakistan, becoming prime minister of that country briefly). The venue was the Mohammedan Sports maidan. It held some 4 to 5 lakh persons, from all communities. Gandhi spoke simply. 'We have to make this unity,' he said, 'a lasting one.'

The next day, August 19, he spoke more pointedly at a gathering in Kanchrapara. The population of this place comprised 25,000 Hindus and 8,000 Muslims. Gandhi got the mixed Hindu–Muslim gathering to take out a joint procession with the Indian national flag. But not before telling them something that was vital then, is vital today: 'The custom of not playing music in front of Masjids was introduced by the British regime. We must stick to the same custom until Jawahar or Liaquat introduce some other custom.'

On August 20 – this day, in 1947 – he held his daily prayer meeting in Calcutta in an open area surrounded by Canning Street, Pollock Street, Murgikhana and Kolutolla. He was seated in a way that he had a temple on one side, a *masjid* on the other and a church on the third. This was the very site where, on November 18 in 1946, a vicious communal riot had broken out. Suhrawardy, who was premier at that time, would not have forgotten that riot. He could not have, if he had a conscience – a big 'if', according to many. Gandhi knew his history, knew when to remind who of what. And so, he said at that meeting that he wanted to go back to Noakhali.

He expected the East Pakistan authorities to take note that he (Gandhi) had not forgotten the plight of Hindus 'there' even as he was being mindful of the plight of Muslims 'here', that he regarded the security of minorities in both sectors as a shared responsibility of the two new countries.

Seventy-six years later, today, when East Pakistan is now not the eastern wing of Pakistan but a country by itself, Bangladesh, is there anyone in the two countries and in Pakistan, a third country, who is speaking like Gandhi did in August 1947?

To be sure, yes. There are brave-hearts who are doing so and are, with guts, facing threats from communal bigots and terrorist ogres. They speak and they listen, just as Gandhi did. But they are not only few in numbers; they also lack the one thing Gandhi had: the unquestioning support of large – huge – sections of society. And that makes their task even more difficult than Gandhi's was. The moral dividend that a fast by Gandhi generated in 1947 and 1948 is not likely to be generated today. District magistrates and superintendents of police may impose Section 144 and immobilise internet connections to help ease tensions. But such peace as was brought to Noakhali and Calcutta and, later, to Delhi, was not the work of the State machinery alone. It was the work of an active social conscience galvanised by one man.

And, apart from the Hindu–Muslim question, we in India are now beset by deep social fissures with razor's edges no less sharp, such as have cut up life in Manipur.

No one in the government or in the Opposition can do what Gandhi tried to do. And there is no Gandhi in civil society today who can try doing that. No Jayaprakash Narayan either. So, what does that leave us with?

Endless strife?

To be sure, no.

We have our Constitution, do we not?

Sure, we do. And that is a huge asset, a huge power.

But a book is ultimately a book. Those who read it are inspired by it. But for us to live by its word, it needs to be constantly activated, brought alive, read to us through pulsating interpretations, timely interventions. It needs to belong to us and we to it.

Who can do that?

Only the judiciary. The High Courts and the Supreme Court of India, not going beyond their jurisdictions, not clutching at roles that are not theirs, not crossing any lines, have played and can continue to play that role.

The courts have disappointed as often as they have shone in the best light. They are working under a crushing workload – in terms of the number of cases they need to handle and public expectations. The infamous Emergency (1975–1977) showed our courts in deeply disappointing and brilliantly elevating facets. So also now, when social tensions and violence are at work brazenly, they can emblazon a new path for the nation by making the safety of the bulk of the people (not litigants) their constitutionally enjoined concern.

If the Constitution needs a pivot and the judiciary is so obviously that, then the judiciary to be not a concept but a palpable, tactile reality needs a persona as well. And the Chief Justice of India is exactly that.

It is not for nothing that the Chief Justice of India is oath-bound to work 'without fear or favour, affection or ill-will' and it is not for nothing again that the President of India is administered the oath to 'devote myself to the service and well-being of the people of the Republic of India' by none other than that Chief Justice of India.

The courts are the keepers of India's conscience not by some obscure stardom but by an unmistakable power placed on them by the Constitution. Gandhi was not 'government', he was not 'the Opposition'. The CJI, who is the crest, or the finial of the judiciary, does not have to be Gandhi. But the CJI is Gandhi's hope for the hopeless and help for the helpless today. And the Supreme Court of India is the judicial equivalent of Beliaghata where choked persons from all communities may come for India's constitutional oxygen.

(*The Telegraph*, August 20, 2023)

71

An Enduring Challenge

BURMA LOOSENED ITSELF FROM India 80 years ago this year. Aden did likewise, to become a Crown Colony. Sind was separated from Bombay Presidency at the same time.

Bihar and Orissa became separate provinces.

A Federal Court, precursor to our Supreme Court, came to be founded in New Delhi.

All these were nation-forming, nation-defining moves.

The year 2015 marks eight decades of that Act of the British Parliament which continues, through its afterlife in the Constitution of India, to affect us, to influence us, in fact, to govern us.

And in its scheme of provincial autonomy, state assemblies as we now know them are elected by a popular vote, from among which ministers with thorough-going powers are appointed by titular governors.

By a new and palpable deepening of franchise, it increased the number of voters – with no gender or property or educational bars – from 7 million to 35 million, who voted new governments into office.

Its provisions for a federation at the Centre did not come to fruit at the time but the principle of India's future republicanism was laid by it, with a bicameral Central legislature giving voice to the states and the codification of the nation's interests into the three lists we now see in the Constitution as lists – Union, state and concurrent.

The Government of India Act, 1935 became the future interim Constitution of both India and Pakistan. But it was by no means an unflawed document. Its reluctance to part with governors' powers was self-evident and its separation of electorates, religion-wise, was an abomination.

The Congress criticised the Act, Nehru being its most vocal opponent. But the party did come into its play and contested the elections under it – with considerable success. It won in eight of the 11 provinces – the three exceptions being Bengal, Punjab and Sind.

The Congress took office. Rajagopalachari became the premier as chief ministers were then called, in Madras, G.B. Pant in Uttar Pradesh, Srikrishna

Sinha in Bihar, N.B. Khare in Central Provinces, Biswanath Das in Orissa, Gopinath Bordoloi in Assam, B.G. Kher in Bombay, Dr Khan Sahib in North West Frontier Province.

This year, therefore, in a very real sense, is the 80th anniversary of an Act that led to the Congress forming ministries for the first time, and assuming representative office in almost all of India, and thereby getting apprenticed for the 'tryst' role that awaited it a decade thence.

The principal architect of the Act was the Conservative Lord Butler, 'RAB' as he was called after his initials, who ought to have become prime minister of Great Britain some years later but did not, as 'good guys generally stay second'. Winding up the debate in the House of Commons on the Government of India Bill, Butler said with prescience if also with some self-congratulation, '...we [have] stumbled on a future line of development in regard both to a Constitution for India and, possibly, a model Constitution for the world... which may also tie together the best in the East and the West.' In his Jawaharlal Nehru Memorial Lecture in 1967, 'RAB' Butler revealed that Nehru had told him in a conversation that the 1935 Act had 'proved to be an organic link between the old and the new'.

All this is history.

Nostalgia apart, does the 80th anniversary of the Government of India Act, 1935, hold any significance for India today?

The 1935 Act was the blueprint for the 'final print' of the Constitution of India in which bicameralism at the Centre and devolution of powers at the states remain pivotal. But the final print was to differ from the blueprint in two critical respects.

In his August 14/15 1947 speech, Nehru spoke of India 'stepping from the old to the new'.

The Constitution of India, as masterminded by B.R. Ambedkar, did away with the 'old' in the 1935 Act's separate electorates on religious lines and brought in the 'new' in terms of reserved constituencies envisaged in the Gandhi–Ambedkar Poona Pact.

Why is this critical?

Separate electorates were the pathway to division and to ultimate Partition.

Reserved constituencies were meant to be a pathway to protection and to ultimate cohesion.

Giving his Nehru Memorial Lecture in London in 1970, V.K. Krishna Menon recalled the 'stepping from the old to the new' imagery used by Nehru and said, 'The stepping has never been completed.'

Today, 80 years after the 1935 Act, we need to reflect on where our steps have brought us.

Our constituencies are no longer separate but what of the electorates?

There is a word Gandhi, Nehru and Ambedkar did not use much or at all. Nor Menon either – 'polarised'.

Our electorates are not separate any longer but who can deny they are getting increasingly polarised? Separatism on religious lines has resurfaced in the 'us' and 'them' rhetoric of our electoral politics, in the vocabulary of our campaign speeches. Not frontally like in the 1935 Act but surreptitiously and that much more dangerously, through side-lanes and back doors. It is a fact, a disturbing one, that the last election, which brought the Bharatiya Janata Party to power at the Centre, also saw the smallest number of Muslim members of Parliament to be elected to the 16th Lok Sabha. The House has only 23 Muslim MPs, the lowest figure since 1952. There are no Muslim MPs from UP, from Maharashtra. What does this indicate? First, that the 'victorious' party, the BJP, fielded almost no Muslim candidate. And the parties that did could not see them through because the vote had been polarised. This is ominous.

The wholly mistimed disclosure of the Census of India's latest tabulations on religious lines on the eve of the elections to Bihar is a pointer. Religious divergences have insinuated themselves into our political consciousness, through an unmistakable enunciation of a new, unwritten code of citizenship: Concord through Conformism, Compliance. Dissent is portrayed as indiscipline, and if that dissent talks of liberalism, of pluralism, of secularism, it is threatened with 'Go To Pakistan'. This code sees criticism as disruption and free expression as an extravagance, something a country 'on the move' can ill afford. Our constituencies are not separate but our electorates are voting separately.

And what of reserved seats for the scheduled castes and scheduled tribes, that salutary and high-minded methodology, that Gandhi and Ambedkar devised in 1932, in Poona to Tagore's celebration of their accord? They have done well, to use a Nehruism, 'in large measure'. I cannot do better than quote from the philosopher-statesman, K.R. Narayanan, who was, incidentally, returned to the Lok Sabha over three successive general elections from a reserved seat in Kerala. 'If an illiterate person,' he said in a G.V. Mavalankar Memorial Lecture in 1993, 'becomes a member of Parliament, he might well prove to be a good member. But the problem comes when his illiteracy has been tampered with partial enlightenment by all kinds of forces.' That 'tampering' is done most damagingly at the time of the selection of the 'reserved' candidates by cabals that comprise powerful persons from the higher castes and by powerful self-serving cabals from within the scheduled castes and tribes themselves. Thus has 'reservation' been distorted, its intent disturbed.

Unseparated but polarised, reserved but manipulated, our electorates and constituencies face a challenge. They ought not to let atavistic recoils into outmoded animosities, rivalries and 'othernesses' deflect the nation's 'stepping from the old into the new'.

The 1935 Act needs to be remembered today and revisited for what its afterlife has done, in the good and the bad, for it will be part of us, our daily hopes and our night-time fears as long as we remain a republic.

(*The Telegraph*, September 6, 2015)

72

Beginning Once Again

IN TIMES WHEN POLITICAL parties are led by supremos for seemingly endless durations, what a welcome contrast the Communist Party of India (Marxist) has provided us!

Prakash Karat's being succeeded by Sitaram Yechury as general secretary of the party should tell all our parties something about the grace in relinquishing control and the solemnity of assuming responsible office within a democratic system. All formalities were gone through at the party congress with due decorum and form as the stewardship passed from one distinguished Marxist to another.

Karat's stewardship of the party from 2005 to 2015 was just a decade long, though it seemed longer. His immediate predecessor, Harkishen Singh Surjeet, had held the office of general secretary for 13 years, and Surjeet's predecessor, E.M.S. Namboodiripad, for 14. And EMS's predecessor, the CPI(M)'s founding general secretary, P. Sundarayya, was at the helm for an identical period. PS was and remains an inspiration for the party as an exemplar of intellectual courage, personal daring and organisational acumen. I know Marxist friends speak of all the party's greats with respect, affection. But when it comes to PS, the emotion is one of an almost un-Marxist reverence.

A generation has passed since then. All three – PS, EMS and HSS – were born in the high noon of empire. When EMS, the oldest of them, arrived in his Brahmin family in Malapuram, Kerala, Queen Victoria's son, King Edward VII, was on the throne. PS and HSS were born in the reign of King George V.

PS and EMS had joined the national movement for independence when Gandhi was its pivot. HSS, drawn by the example of Bhagat Singh, was a nationalist before he became a communist, but by the mid-1930s all three went on via the peasant struggle route and the Kisan Sabha to become the party's general secretary. Karat is the first general secretary of the party to have been born after Independence, the first to have joined the CPI(M) without an incubation in the freedom movement.

Indeed, the year Karat was born – 1948 – was already one year into Independence, seeing India on the cusp of its post-Independence advance towards the becoming of a republic. And more significantly, the Constituent Assembly being encouraged at that point, by the chairman of its drafting committee, B.R. Ambedkar, to make social justice its goal.

I recall a talk at my college in Delhi, in the early 1960s, by V.K. Krishna Menon. Slashing the air four times in a Kathakali-like hand movement, Menon said, 'Our Preamble has of course, Liberty [slash 1], Equality [slash 2] and Fraternity [slash 3]. But it has also above these, something which for us is even more important – Justice [a sharp slash 4]. That is the vision we have given to ourselves.' It was my privilege shortly thereafter to meet K. Prakash, as he was known then, in Madras through the kindness of a common friend – 'Kannan' Tyagarajan – a contemporary of his in Madras Christian College. I had little of politics in me and even less of Marx, though I had been greatly drawn to Marxist friends in college, of whom Prabhat Patnaik was – and is – a figure of great height.

Listening to Prakash giving me a succinct account of the Marxist movements in Kerala for the re-distribution of land to help the landless and agricultural labour was more than an education; it was a revelation. I was three years older, but I heard him as a student would a teacher. There was something of a guru in Prakash already, a pedagogue, an explicator of the complex to the simple of mind and new of experience. I heard from him, for the first time, some altogether new phrases like '*michchabhumi*' (surplus land), and '*samaram*' (struggle). At Prakash's age, young students are generally preoccupied with their own career prospects, not *samarams*.

That initiation into a larger field of thought was hugely helpful as I trained in the paddy-rich Thanjavur district as an IAS probationer in 1969. That was one Tamil Nadu region where agrarian reforms were both difficult and crucial. A few months prior to my 'joining duty', 44 Dalit peasants, including women and children, had been burnt alive in the Thanjavur village of Kizhavenmani. The peasants were demanding higher wages as paddy production had increased greatly following the Green Revolution. The paddy producers association staged this fiery orgy when the peasants withheld produce as a tactic. It is because of Prakash's background 'teaching' that I was able to see Kizhavenmani in its proper light. The chief minister of Tamil Nadu at the time was the charismatic C.N. Annadurai. But he was grievously ill, dying barely six weeks later. I do not know if Sardar Ujjal Singh, the then governor of Tamil Nadu, publicly condemned the massacre but am sure, had he done that, the CPI(M) would have welcomed it.

Life plaits events together, it unravels what held fast before. Four decades later occurred the events at Nandigram, West Bengal, which are now part of recent agrarian history. Kizhavenmani and Nandigram are not to be compared. The issues were different. The first was about wages, the second about land acquisition. And yet, there was something that was common between them: the death of innocent peasants. My condemnation, as governor of West Bengal, of the violence that took place in Nandigram under the watch of the Left Front government led to many in the CPI(M) feeling I had let the Left Front government and the CPI(M) down. This was natural. Without Prakash Karat's endorsement, the chief minister, Buddhadeb Bhattacharjee, would not have requested the prime minister, Manmohan Singh, to appoint me to that office. As I heard CPI(M) stalwart after CPI(M) stalwart in the state berate me over Nandigram, I wondered if they were doing what they were doing with the knowledge of general secretary Karat. And I recalled 'K. Prakash' and conversations that now seemed to belong to another planet.

Of the four general secretaries of the CPI(M), Prakash Karat has held the office at its highest and its lowest ebbs. No general secretary has been as close to mould decision-making in Delhi as he, given the CPI(M)'s powerful presence in the Lok Sabha after 2004. And no general secretary has presided over the reverses his party suffered in the five years that followed. Did power make the party of revolutionary struggle become a party of power stratagems? Did plain hubris cause its distancing from people's struggles and its electoral collapse?

Time will answer those questions. Meanwhile, as Sitaram Yechury assumes responsibility for the party, struggle beckons it again. The CPI(M) today is no longer the party of power that it was for a while after 2004. It is a party of struggle once again, exactly as in the time of general secretary P. Sundarayya, when movements, not doctrine, activated the party. The CPI(M) today has ahead of it the struggle against a majoritarian party in power at the Centre, against a dilution of safeguards for those being dispossessed in the name of 'development'. It will have to struggle to keep the primacy of justice as a preamble goal. And for financial probity, administrative accountability, it will have to struggle against the tyranny of money. Yechury's speech in the Rajya Sabha on the Lokpal bill was powerful. As was his intervention, in 2013, on the Nalanda University bill. Addressing the forces of sectarian hatred he said then: 'Remember the final paragraph of Swami Vivekananda's declaration at Chicago. [Interruptions] "I take pity... on those who believe in the destruction of someone else's religion for the purpose of his own religion."' That struggle for safeguarding our pluralism will need to be redoubled now.

Destiny beckons Sitaram Yechury to intensify and enlarge that struggle to include those not in and of the CPI(M) but in and of that way of thought.

(*The Telegraph*, May 3, 2015)

73

Emergency Medicine

'I CHANGE, BUT I cannot die.' – 'The Cloud' by Percy Bysshe Shelley.
The Congress is not dead. Let its enemies not celebrate, its adherents not despair. Even if it wishes death for itself, the grand old party cannot die. If it had been made of bits and pieces of the soils of India, it could and would have died right on those. But it has arisen from the seas and the skies of India. The two sustain each other in a reciprocity that cannot end.

What are the seas and what, the skies? The seas are, quite simply, the seas of India; the skies their collective aspirations. If the Congress had been made only in and by the Gangetic Plain or the Deccan Plateau, a Rann or a Shola, it would have thrived, survived or died inside those tracts. If it had been populated only by the tufted or the turbaned, the be-capped or the bearded, if it had spoken but one language, worshipped but one god, adhered to but one book or teacher, made a religion of its biases or biases of its religion, totems of its beliefs and mascots of its leaders, it would have lived its life and died its death within those shards.

The Indian National Congress founded 130 years ago this year, set out on a political expedition. As yet unaware of the impact their voyage was to make on the history of India and the colonised world, the founders of the Congress, all English-speaking, urban, upper-class men, mostly Hindu, were almost a club symbolising property and privilege.

Scepticism among Muslims about the Congress becoming dominated by Hindus was instantaneous. It was also salutary. Conscious correction of any tilt within its thinking and organising, sectarian or geopolitical, followed quickly. Venues and incumbencies were made representative. If the first session was presided over by the Bengali Brahmin, Womesh Chandra Bonnerjee, the second, held in Calcutta, was presided over by the Parsi statesman, Dadabhai Naoroji. The third was taken to Madras and presided over by Badruddin Tyabji.

Within its first decade, the Congress became worthy of its two adjectives, Indian and National. Over the next nine decades, that is, until 1975, when the nation saw the first national Emergency and the suspension for two years of all civil rights, the party was to see as many as 81 presidents. In terms of religious groupings, there were among these Congress presidents over 40 Hindus, eight Muslims, three Englishmen and one Irishman all Christians, three Parsis. In terms of a linguistic break-up, Hindi-Hindustani-speaking Congress presidents outnumbered the others, but even there they often spoke dialects of Hindi as in the case of Rajendra Prasad or Jagjivan Ram. There were 10 Bengali-speakers among those Congress presidents, six Gujarati, four Marathi, three Tamil, three Telugu, one each Malayalam and Kannada speaking. Prior to that watershed year, 1975, four women held the office, Annie Besant (1917), Sarojini Naidu (1925), Nellie Sengupta (1933) and Indira Gandhi (1959). As an all-India party, the Congress's representative record could have done better but nevertheless, it did well enough. It remained a vessel of exploration, of venture and of dare. And the 1885 Congress image of a zamindar tea party was dispelled by Gandhi and Nehru.

Consolidating the 'boat' image are Gandhi's 15 voyages, including the last in 1931, when he journeyed to England as the Congress's sole representative. In a short statement that he sent to *The Daily Mail* on September 19, 1931, Gandhi wrote, 'The Indian National Congress is no respecter of persons. It knows no distinction between classes or creeds or the sexes. It has always championed the cause of the so-called untouchables, and has of recent years appointed an anti-untouchability committee for hastening the destruction of untouchability. But the unchallenged and unchallengeable claim of the Indian National Congress consists in its representing the millions of dumb paupers living in the seven hundred thousand Indian villages who constitute over 85 per cent of the population.'

The Congress's 130-year-old history can be divided into two halves: the 90 years preceding the Emergency imposed in 1975, and the 40 years since that traumatic year. The pre-Emergency Congress over its 90 years saw 81 presidencies held by 67 presidents (adjusting repeat terms), including Gandhi himself. Broadly speaking, every second year saw a new Congress president. Outstanding Indians held the office for but one one-year term. These included Gokhale (1905), Chittaranjan Das (1922), Gandhi (1924), Sarojini Naidu (1925), Vallabhbhai Patel (1931) and Rajendra Prasad (1934/35). It is not as if there was no 'cliquism' in the 'old' Congress; there was, but it was seen as aberrant and frowned upon. Broadly, there was trust in the party, there was frank disagreement. There was dissent, but no subversion. There was respect, but no fear. Leaders gave place to followers, becoming followers of those that had followed them.

In the 40 years since the Emergency, the Congress has seen its presidentship held by only six persons. And in the 30 years post-Indira, it has seen only four, of whom two have been from outside Indira Gandhi's family, two from within. Suspicion rules in this Congress, not trust; whispers have replaced frank expression. And fear – fear of rejection, of downgrading, of cold-shouldering and therefore of loss of power – is the ambient emotion. This started in its 90th year, 1975, when the Congress elected as its president, the Assam leader, Devakanta Barooah. He was to go into the political annals as the coiner of the historically embarrassing and politically shameless slogan, 'India is Indira'. To that phase must belong the privilege of ending the Congress's tradition of being 'no respecter of persons' and beginning its practice of sycophancy. Succeeding her protégé in 1978, Indira Gandhi held the office till her assassination in 1984.

We are so influenced by the consanguineous profile of the Congress as we have known it since the post-Emergency and Indira era that we forget that this enclosed pattern is an exception, not the rule. The party has been, and will always be, larger than any individual.

Linked to 'Who heads the Congress?' is the question, 'What is the Congress to do?' Electoral defeat of an unparalleled scale prescribes for Congress a change of guard. More, it prescribes for it a change of gear. Sonia Gandhi has led the party with focus and tenacity. I must own to a feeling of respect for her lonely and thankless leadership of a party that does not share its wisdom with her, only its woes, and does not give her strength, only seeks her protecting or promoting hand. She deserved better than to be counselled by the self-seeking and the self-centred. The Congress must return to a voyage in the seas and skies of India from its stagnation in the dry-berth of dynastic docking. And Sonia Gandhi herself must lead that change, not as one under the shadow of defeat but as the harbinger of a renaissance. She has to ask her party to return from the 40-year-old Congress to the 90-year-old Congress. She must leave Indira and Barooah to history's judgment. She should replace herself, not by an indifferent heir, but by the self-assured heritage of her party.

And replacing sycophancy by democratic trust, she must take the party forward to the role spelt out by M.K. Gandhi of 'representing the millions of dumb paupers living in the seven hundred thousand Indian villages who constitute over 85 per cent of the population'. The numbers and percentages have changed, but the representation has not. That is where the Congress's destiny lies and its indestructibility. And that is where India might let the party change but will not let it die.

(*The Telegraph*, March 8, 2015)

74

Silence Is Not Golden:
On the Importance of Being Shashi Tharoor

I F THE LINE AT the head of this article reminds the reader of *The Importance of Being Earnest*, the association would only be natural. But what has made me use it is not the title of Oscar Wilde's famous play. It is an article written exactly half a century ago, in 1965, for *The Statesman* by the then young columnist, Inder Malhotra. He called his piece, 'The Importance of Being Jaisukhlal Hathi'.

Jai who?

Few, even in the Congress, would remember the Gujarati of that name who had been a member of the Constituent Assembly, then Congress member of the Lok Sabha and Rajya Sabha, a Union minister under the prime minister, Jawaharlal Nehru, and was, when that article appeared, a minister under the prime minister, Lal Bahadur Shastri.

The age of foundational ideals had given over and with his post-1965 war popularity at an unprecedented high, Shastri seemed to have inaugurated a new age of high-minded realism. I do not have the article with me but if I recall its thrust aright, Malhotra wrote to say that the country's first post-Nehru prime minister needed steady hands, not brilliant minds, reliable men and women to serve as self-effacing, industrious ministers who would diligently study files and briefs, ably answer questions in Parliament, be of comfort to the State even if a bit of a bore, perhaps, to the Opposition.

I remembered the good and honest Hathi *saheb* while attending a public meeting organised by the Triplicane Cultural Academy last month in Chennai. The theme was the changing role of parliamentarians. An academic (Sudarshan Padmanabhan), a distinguished civil servant (the former chief election commissioner, N. Gopalaswami) and a politician (the former deputy chairman of the Rajya Sabha, Rahman Khan) spoke well and instructively. The following five broad disappointments with members of Parliament emerged in the discussion:

1. Obstructing, not facilitating, the business of the House.
2. Not maintaining, much less raising, standards of debate.

3. Not speaking their minds.
4. Supporting or opposing the government routinely.
5. Being unable to help, in their daily struggles, the people of their constituencies.

As I was listening to these observations, the figure of Jaisukhlal Hathi kept coming to my mind.

Hathi *saheb* could have never ever dreamed of disrupting the proceedings of the House, even if he had been an Opposition MP. He would have done well by the even tenor of legislative discussions. He would, in other words, have been part of the ballast of the Treasury benches, adding to that vessel's stabilising tonnage, preventing it from being rocked by democratic gales. He would have been part of all that makes a liner cruise. And he would have tried his best to give as much attention as possible to those who voted for him.

What of half a century later, today?

I am not sure, but Inder Malhotra might well write an article today titled, 'The Importance of not being Jaisukhlal Hathi'. The only snag being that few would understand the allusion.

The question, 'Jai…who?' would imperil the article. And the counter-point that needs to be made would be lost.

Sound, reliable, steady on the line, eager-to-not-go-wrong, not-to-let-the team-down ministers are today the rule. Brilliance can be a disqualification, mediocrity a merit. The minister who works without attracting attention is a strength, no doubt, to the captain on deck, to the prime minister in Parliament.

No minister would want to speak his or her mind in the cabinet today. That would be too risky. Better silent than sorry. Collective responsibility today means collective resonating….

This of course is not a BJP thing alone. No MP, whether of the ruling alliance or the Opposition, shows anything like independence of mind. If they have that, as I am sure they do, they choose to keep it chained.

And so Jaisukhlal Hathi is once again important, as an example of what ministers and MPs today should not be. But since no one will quite understand the reference to the good Gujarati, who is the counter Hathi *saheb* who can be cited? Who is the non-Hathisaheb we can turn to?

A more unHathi-like Congressman cannot be imagined than the hon'ble member for Thiruvananthapuram. Another Congress MP of those years, long since forgotten, Savitri Nigam, once mixing up the phrase, spoke of the importance of 'gab of gift'. Master of the spoken word, revelling in public attention, Shashi Tharoor turns mikes and lights to himself almost by instinct. He is, to other politicians' chagrin, sought after even when he is under the shadow of personal crises.

'How?' they ask, 'can someone who has lived abroad for years, nursed ambitions of becoming secretary general of the United Nations, is essentially a columnist, author and a university lecture-circuit "type", suddenly parajump on to our politics, get an "MP ticket" and even become a minister?' So runs the resentment. That Tharoor has a very good opinion of himself does not help him. But it galls others the more.

Perhaps it is because he has been away from Indian politics that he has become what an MP was envisaged by the framers of our Constitution to be – an elected representative of the people, who brings to legislative work a sense of the national weal, the regional good and the local 'touch' beyond party blinkers.

Our Constitution makes no mention of political parties. (Political parties have come to figure in it only tangentially through the 10th Schedule, introduced by the 52nd amendment to curb defections.) As far as the main 'run' of the Constitution is concerned, the entire Lok Sabha could consist wholly of non-party independent MPs elected by a simple majority, any Indian citizen, above 25 years of age, to be its leader and thereby, India's prime minister.

An MP is, essentially, an MP, not a Congress MP or Bharatiya Janata Party MP. True, each parliamentary party has a whip. But is an MP's party affiliation an unbreachable contract? No, the 10th Schedule provides for an MP to vote as per his or her conscience, provided the prior permission of the party has been obtained or a *post-facto* condonation. How many MPs would today seek such a permission or condonation? And how many party leaders would give that latitude? They ought to know that an MP is oath-bound only to bear true faith and allegiance to the Constitution of India, not to any other entity.

I can imagine Shashi Tharoor seeking such a permission. And if he were to, he would not be doing something blasphemous. He would be acting within the Constitution. But he would need to take care to see that the Congress's consequential rebuff does not land him in a BJP embrace. Had even one BJP MP spoken against *ghar wapsi*, the renaming of Aurangzeb Road, the ban on meat, the attempted manipulations of autonomous institutions, the murder of respected dissenters, the image of the NDA would have had some redemption, some change. Likewise, if in United Progressive Alliance times, even one Congress MP had spoken in Parliament, in Feroze Gandhi style, against high-ranking corruption, its fate in the 2014 elections may have been different.

For an Opposition MP to have and to exercise the freedom to appreciate a good thing done by the government and for a ruling party MP to speak and vote against the party line is not just legitimate parliamentary practice, it is the very essence of parliamentary democracy. Shashi Tharoor, from the ranks of the Congress, has tried to do that; there is not one BJP MP who has matched him.

Blind conformism is not loyalty, nor independent thinking, dissent. There is more than ordinary importance in being what quite often, and with much discomfiture to himself, Shashi Tharoor, MP tries to be.

(The Telegraph, October 4, 2015)

75

The Eyes of the Beholder

I WROTE IN THESE columns last month on the holy and the sacred. Prompted by the observations of the judge, Markandey Katju, about some fellow judges, I write today on prestige and respect.

Judges and prestige travel together, with ease. Respect is a more demanding fellow journeyer.

The very moment that a judge enters his or her office under an oath, prestige enters his or her being. It precedes the judge ante-median and dutifully follows, post.

But respect hovers, like a truant halo, now there and now gone.

Prestige is almost part of the terms of engagement, an accoutrement. It is brassy, like a mace or the emblazoned brooch sewn on a liveried sash. It can be shined. Prestige is, in fact, a perquisite.

Respect is 'Nota', none of the above. Respect does not in fact 'lie' in the recipient. It resides in the giver. It is trained at the receiver, invisibly, inaudibly.

Prestige superannuates, respect knows no retirement. Prestige is enjoyed. Respect is earned.

From whom?

Quite simply, from the beholder's saying: 'Here is one I respect.'

I can think of judges, not from the distant past but from our times, the very times Katju is writing about, for whom I have felt exactly that. Three of them happen to be women – Leila Seth, Ruma Pal and Prabha Sridevan, with others in that large circle including V.R. Krishna Iyer, Chittatosh Mukherjee and J.S. Verma, who passed away just a few months ago.

'We the people', have no direct role in the judiciary's composition. Nor are we particularly interested in acquiring such a role. But we do want to be assured that this process is fair so that we can have respect for it. And that – respect for the judiciary – we want to have.

Respect is retractable. It is extended on trust, and maintained in verification. When it comes to elective offices, the system of periodic elections serves as an instrument of respect-revalidation or respect-retraction, faith-reiteration or faith-reversal, trust-reaffirmation or trust-revocation.

But when it comes to institutions like the judiciary, respect for it as an institution or for individual incumbents in judicial office is unaccompanied by the dynamics of periodic reaffirmation or of retraction except when, eroded by palpable misconduct, respect for the institution is sought to be vouchsafed by offloading the errant individual through the constitutionally devised processes of impeachment.

The effect of this cocooning or cloistering is that while the prestige of judges has remained constant, respect for them (including those on judicial and other commissions) has fluctuated. This is unfortunate and I believe this can change if the concern within our courts shifts from questions pertaining to their prestige to questions pertaining to the respect they command.

It is certainly the responsibility of the government to vouchsafe the prestige of judges but vouchsafing the respect that the judiciary commands is its own responsibility, indeed, its own exclusive responsibility.

Prestige is about perquisites and privileges. Respect is about trust. Prestige is self-obsessed, respect unselfconscious.

Prestige comes in the shape of a red lamp atop the car, respect comes from that car not cutting the red traffic light.

People move to a side, often pasting themselves against a wall, unsmiling, to let Prestige pass. People greet, with or without a bow, Respect.

Higher than esteem, beyond regard and ahead of admiration, respect is not the subject of politeness, civility or courtesy. In the phrase 'paying one's respects', the concept has got routinised into a form of idle ceremony. But where it is earned and not extended, where it is offered from one's instinctive appreciation and not from calculation or analysis, where it is given without expectation or conditionalities, it is something sublime.

Prestige is twinned to authority. Respect to trust.

The judges, M.C. Chagla and S.T. Desai inspired trust. Why?

Because while adhering to the law, they appealed to values.

Some senior readers of this column will remember that in 1957, Tata Iron & Steel Co. wanted to change their memoranda of association in order to allow the company to make contributions to political parties. The matter went to court. The judges, Chagla and Desai, ruled in the Bombay High Court allowing the change but with the weight of moral *obiter*. They said: 'The very basis of democracy is the voter and when in India we are dealing with adult suffrage it is even more important than elsewhere that not only the integrity of the representative who is ultimately elected to Parliament is safeguarded, but that the integrity of the voter is also safeguarded, and it may be said that it is difficult to accept the position that the integrity of the voter and of the representative is safeguarded if large industrial concerns are permitted to contribute to political funds to bring about a particular result…(W)e think it our duty to draw the attention of Parliament to the great danger inherent in permitting companies to make contributions to the funds of political parties. It is a danger which may grow apace and which may ultimately overwhelm and even throttle democracy in this country. Therefore, it is desirable for Parliament to consider under what circumstances and under what limitations companies should be permitted to make these contributions.'

Twelve years after those bitter truths were uttered, in 1969, a ban did get to be imposed on corporate contributions to election funds. But not even seven years had elapsed after that ban when rethinking started. A bill was introduced in Parliament in 1976 seeking to give companies the power to donate up to 5 per cent of their profits to political parties. Nine years thereafter, Section 293A came to be recast altogether by the Amendment Act of 1985. And how was the bill's object described? The words used were: 'With a view to permitting the Corporate Sector to play a legitimate role within the defined norms in the functioning of our democracy, it is proposed to substitute a new section for section 293A of the Companies Act.'

With the vice-like grip of money throttling democracy, we know why the judges, Chagla and Desai, commanded the respect and trust they did.

The one flawless thing in the world, I believe, is forgiveness. The only thing priceless, I believe, is trust. And trust is at the core of respect. It is either there, or not there. It cannot be insinuated into anyone or anything. It has, simply, to be.

I would like to think of our judiciary with respect, bearing in mind men of the intellectual courage of Chagla and Desai, not of the examples Katju has spoken of.

But to the extent that he has reminded us of the scope for respect in the judiciary, albeit by showing contrary examples, he has done the nation a service.

(*The Telegraph*, August 3, 2014)

76

Why We Need Governors

There is a disquiet in Raj Nivases and Bhavans today. What does the Constitution Bench's order betoken? Are we, Lieutenant Governors and Governors must be thinking, redundant? Are we a mere ornament, like the chandelier overhead or the carpet underfoot? Is there nothing to our office, to us, than having an ADC escort us, a liveried chaperon wait on us, and callers address us as 'Your Excellency'? Is signing the files that come to us in 'aid and advice' from our chief ministers and ministers, receiving the President and Vice President and prime minister when they arrive at the airport, driving with them into the city, and then, after hosting a banquet for them, seeing them off our sole function?

Message from Bengal

The most telling answer to those questions has been provided by M.K. Gandhi. On October 30, 1946, Gandhi was in Calcutta. Consistently with his sense of etiquette, he called on the Governor. The last Governor of undivided – and communally disturbed – Bengal, Frederick Burrows, asked him, 'What would you like me to do?' A popular government headed by Huseyn Shaheed Suhrawardy had been installed in the state and maintaining peace in the state was now the responsibility of the elected ministry. The answer to 'What would you like me to do?' was courteous, but crisp. 'Nothing, Your Excellency,' Gandhi said. He meant that after the British declaration to quit, the Governor's position in India's provinces was that of a constitutional head of state and he must 'let' the representative government do its duty.

Gandhi's advice was consistent with Walter Bagehot's dictum about the Crown having 'the right to be consulted, the right to encourage, the right to warn' but not to be the engine of government. And it anticipated the Supreme Court's July 4, 2018 order. But did he mean that they should go, their offices and their carpets rolled up?

He did not.

And so, returning to the question posed at the head of this column, are Governors then a mere and rather costly superfluity? Is the Governor then, in a word, just a figurehead?

Certainly not.

Now is that not odd, very odd?

Can someone, something or anyone, anything, that has no 'role' be yet valuable?

Curiously enough, yes.

Constituent Assembly debates

During the Constituent Assembly's deliberations on the office of the Governor, the thoughtful S.N. Agrawal, then Principal of a College at Wardha, later better known as Shriman Narayan, a dedicated Gandhian who was later to be a Governor himself, reflected on it. In the last weeks of 1947 he wrote in an article: 'In my opinion there is no necessity for a Governor. The chief minister should be able to take his place and peoples' money to the tune of Rs 5000 a month for the sinecure of the Governor will be saved.' Gandhi, whose advice to Burrows we have noted, responded to Agrawal in *Harijan* (December 21, 1947) as follows: 'There is much to be said in favour of the argument advanced by Principal Agrawal about the appointment of provincial Governors. I must confess that I have not been able to follow the proceedings of the Constituent Assembly…Much as I would like to spare every pice of the public treasury it would be bad economy to do away with provincial Governors and regard chief ministers as a perfect equivalent. Whilst I would resent much power of interference to be given to Governors, I do not think that they should be mere figureheads. They should have enough power enabling them to influence ministerial policy for the better. In their detached position they would be able to see things in their proper perspective and thus prevent mistakes by their cabinets. Theirs must be an all-pervasive moral influence in their provinces.'

This has to be one of the best summations of the value of that office and, indeed, of the difference between 'interference' and 'influence'.

A look at the attendees at one of the early conferences of Governors on May 8, 1949 would show present in the domed hall an array of Governors, each strong-minded but self-composed, not interested in putting his chief minister in the shade or himself in the limelight: the industrialist Homi Mody (United Provinces), the veteran non-Congress leader M.S. Aney (Bihar), the free-thinking lawyer Asaf Ali (Orissa), the old-time Congressman K.N. Katju (West Bengal), Bhavsinhji, the sagacious Maharaja of Bhavnagar (Madras), the ICS veteran C.M. Trivedi (Punjab). They did not look upon themselves as figureheads who could do nothing, nor as martinets who could do any and everything. They knew that they lacked power, but wielded influence, influence to do good, as the governor general, prime minister and deputy prime minister of the day wanted them to, 'without friction and without prejudice to the march of democracy'.

The key words to be taken away from those are 'interference' versus 'influence', 'detached position' versus 'figurehead', 'perspective' versus 'prejudice' and overarching all this, the key phrase: 'all-pervasive moral influence'.

Vital positions

Governors and, for that matter, the President of India, are vital, not because they can hold up or hold back anything – indeed, they should not and cannot – but because they can and should exert the moral voltage, the sense of the rightness and wrongness of things that would underscore the republican credence and democratic credentials of elected governments.

This is where the choice of the incumbent becomes crucial. I have given a few of the names of the first crop of Governors attending the Governors' Conference in May 1949. 'But,' the despondent cynic may ask, 'do we have such persons in our midst today?' At first pulse, it may seem we do not, and that we are going through a drought in stature. But reflection would correct that thought. Women and men in education, commerce, administration, science, medicine, law and public life within and outside of politics, across parties, can surely be found who, as well-wishers, will strengthen and not threaten elected governments working 'for the better'.

Chief ministers and prime ministers head the government. Governors and presidents head the state. Governments govern, states sustain. And in a democratic republic, the people power both. They do so, wanting the chief minister to act conscientiously and the governor to act constitutionally, to ensure self-government is good government, *swaraj* is also *suraj*.

The country has to congratulate the Aam Aadmi Party and its leader, Delhi Chief Minister Arvind Kejriwal, for having elicited from the Supreme Court a benchmark ruling. But it can do more. It can reflect on how, as a chief minister actuates a popular mandate, the Governor exercises that 'all-pervasive moral influence', both together providing the people in their jurisdiction the assurance that they are in secure and mutually composed, not conflicted, hands.

(*The Hindu*, July 6, 2018)

77

His Excellency the Governor

ONE GOVERNOR IN INDIA is regarded as being 'something' – the Governor of the Reserve Bank of India. This is as it should be. He controls money which controls everything. He holds gold for the country. And gold holds fascination for India; always has. In history, sovereigns mint. In British mints, a gold coin called 'sovereign' has long been minted; still is. The RBI Governor is in a sense, sovereign. Ask anyone – by which I mean anyone with any interest in India's fiscal fortunes – who the first Indian Governor of the RBI was and you will hit 'gold' – C.D. Deshmukh. Ask not just a bank-kind of Indian but any educated Indian a 'quiz' question: 'Did any Governor of the RBI become prime minister of India?' and you will get bullion in the esteemed name of Dr Manmohan Singh. All this, despite the fact that the extraordinary powers of the Governor of the RBI flow from 'a mere Act' – the Reserve Bank of India Act, 1934.

Coming from a much loftier text, the Constitution of India, no less, Governors of India's states are, on the other hand, regarded as being 'virtually nothing'. This is not how it should be. For the Governor has not been created absent-mindedly, extravagantly or redundantly. He or she is there for a reason. In fact, more than one.

'Is that so?' one may ask in barely repressed cynicism, which is understandable for the Governor of an Indian state is, under the terms of the Constitution, a symbol, 'a mere symbol'. Here he or she only mirrors the President of India who in turn reflects the position of the British monarch. The office of Governor, derived as it is from the Constitution of India, is a constitutional office and that very nomenclature – 'constitutional' is seen as an allusion to its titular, symbolic nature.

No surprise, therefore, that in the conversations of the public, Governors occasion little interest and less comment. Except when they do something outrageous, which is rare. Or when they do something remarkable, which is rarer. Ask anyone – by which I mean anyone with elementary interest in modern India's political history – who were the first Indians to be appointed to the office of Governor and you will hit rock. Not many will remember that

Sarojini Naidu, no less, was the first Governor of the United Provinces (now Uttar Pradesh). 'The Nightingale' flew out too soon, alas, from her gilt cage after a mere eight months as Governor, a great loss to poetry and to public life for she would have been an outstanding exemplar of what a 'Constitutional Governor' is meant to be and can be.

Likewise, few will know that the first Indian to be appointed Governor of Assam, which then included all the segments that are now the Northeast's seven states, was the extraordinary ICS officer, Sir Akbar Hydari. Son of the former prime minister of Hyderabad State bearing the same name, Sir Akbar signed a key accord with Naga separatists that could have changed the course of that area's history had it not been spurned by stakeholders. Sir Akbar toured his province extensively, dying of a stroke in the dak bungalow of an obscure village in Manipur's interior.

That the first Indian Governor of Bombay, which comprised the whole of today's Maharashtra and Gujarat states, was the scion of Kapurthala's royal family in its Christian branch, Kanwar Maharaj Singh, too, is not known, a real loss to public awareness for Maharaj Singh was a fascinating man, captaining as Governor, at the age of 72, the Bombay Governor's XI against a touring Commonwealth XI in a match starting in November 1950, making him the oldest cricketer to make his first-class debut.

That C. Rajagopalachari was the first and only Indian to be Governor General of India is a general knowledge factoid. Not so the fact he was, prior to that, the first Indian to be Governor of West Bengal, by Mahatma Gandhi's side in Calcutta, on Independence Day, 1947.

With this history, these beginnings, it is unfortunate that Governors of the day should be widely seen as no more than a costly redundancy. This is not what they were intended to be. This is what they have, unfortunately, become. And the blame does not lie entirely with them, the incumbents. The reason for the bored irritation they generate, as I see it, is the pelf that surrounds a Governor. Gubernatorial pelf is, essentially, an optical phenomenon. They are housed in some splendour – markedly above others in high office. Located in the choicest of venues, such as the fine promontory off Malabar Hill in Mumbai where the Arabian Sea's waves lash its rocky margins or the Guindy forest in Chennai where chital and the now thinning-out black buck graze in somnolent detachment, Raj Bhavans are by any standards, enviable locations. And they do occasion a kind of shallow envy.

Substantial acreages surround a Raj Bhavan, sequestering them and also mystifying them. They have large state rooms and suites where wooden stairways and corniced niches hold secrets beyond fiction's imaging or fact's storage. But then they are not quite the fairy-tale palaces they appear on the outside. Old grace peeling away, new accoutrements step in, most noticeably in the shape of false ceilings to support air conditioning, 'modern' trappings and wires, wires everywhere to back up 'connectivity'. That, for Governors who do not need to connect all that much or fast seems odd, but then there is such a thing as keeping up with the times. This keeping up means really a halfway house adjustment between the old and the new, unconvincing, often unsuccessful. Some colonial-period Raj Bhavans still have, miraculously, period furniture and carpets, the value of which is not always appreciated by their occupants or their staff who seek to replace – 'condemn' or 'write off' are the official phrases – the old pieces for having 'outlived their utility'. Machine-made horrors then take their place to create a new optic, a new avatar in splendour. And the mystique continues.

This surrounds them like an aura, of which the biggest feature is being 'His Excellency', which sounds even grander in its formal Hindi form – Mahamahim and grandest in the informal Hindustani – Lat Sahib. The title is being slowly given up but is still around, in usage. 'H E' is escorted with clicking-heels smartness to events by uniformed officers from the armed forces or the Indian Police Service, waited on at the table by hush-soled liveried staff. Governors' 'movements' are quite simply, processional. They do not 'leave', they 'depart'. They do not 'reach', they 'arrive'. They do not 'meet' visitors, they 'grant audience'. The car they move in being escorted and backed by other vehicles; they move in 'a convoy'.

'And all this', an observer might well say, 'for someone who has virtually nothing to do, no powers, no duties, no responsibilities, no work except to appear at ceremonial events and then disappear into the sylvan hollow of his palace'. The word 'anachronism' can then appear in the analysis to be tossed at Governors. With a prefix added for extra effect – 'costly anachronism'. Another word then drifts into the narrative pairing the residence with the resident – 'relic'. With a cruel paraphrasing – 'relic in age and in function'.

This 'state of affairs' is facilely ascribed to 'the kind of persons who are being appointed Governors', with the corollary being '… the kind of political characters that are made Governors…' A brief examination of the state of the Governor then becomes worthwhile, both as a governance matter and as one of pertinent political science and constitution-study interest.

Governors are meant to be politically unbiased. They are expected to act with impartiality. They may have had and, in fact, they have invariably had, political affiliations. Once sworn in, however, they are supposed to move above and beyond political affinities. But – and this is where the rub is – one cannot get away from the fact that their very appointment is a political act. They are appointed by the President of India in but name. They are, in reality, identified and positioned in Raj Bhavans by the prime minister of the day. He may have been advised or assisted in the process by political advisers, colleagues, coalition partners, but the plain fact is that, from the time of Prime Minister Jawaharlal Nehru down to present times, every Governor has been placed in a Raj Bhavan courtesy the prime minister. And ironically enough the prime minister has done that after making a political assessment of the suitability of that person to hold the apolitical office. So-and-so will be a good governor, an impartial, judicious governor, a constitution-protector, rising above all narrow politics, all regional politics, is a political assessment.

The first clutch of Governors, post-Independence, that Nehru picked included front-ranking Congress politicians, distinguished former Dewans, former princes. Their successors, in the 1950s and early 1960s, were also distinguished, though, it must be admitted, the coffee in the filter was now into its second brewing.

But what could Nehru have possibly done? The brown berry was no longer what it had been. If some of the early Indian Governors had to be persuaded to accept that office, now there were many, too many, who wanted to, even lobbied to get there. And then, by the time Indira Gandhi, Rajiv Gandhi, Atal Bihari Vajpayee, P.V. Narasimha Rao, Manmohan Singh became prime minister, politics had become so overpopulated with aspirants and so fraught with intrigue that Raj Bhavans became good 'railway sidings', where the politically inconvenient could be shunted and more pertinently, where a politically astute Governor – never mind that she was no Nightingale or he played no cricket – could be made to 'keep a sharp eye' on the state's politics. And they also became places where those who had to be 'rewarded' were given five years of arboreal ease.

In other words, with time, the political appointment of Governors became a function in politics, not a function above politics as it was in Nehru's time. Not that all his selections were un-flawed. Little wonder then, that the institution of Governor has suffered a trust deficit, never more starkly than when President's Rule is recommended or when, in a 'hung-result' scene, a person is to be invited to form a government.

But fairness requires it to be said that not all post-Nehru appointments to Raj Bhavans have been 'all politics'. True, politicians have dominated the scene but even with that being the case, one has only to see the larger picture of how Governors have functioned to realise that the constitutional purpose of Governors has managed to more than survive. T.N. Chaturvedi in Karnataka was an NDA appointee. But no one has accused him of having functioned with any bias. In fact, no one saw in him any trace of politics even. His term of office was quintessentially constitutional. The late Ram Kapse was an ardent member of the BJP but as Lieutenant Governor of the Andaman & Nicobar Islands during the time the 2006 tsunami hit, he was a turbine of energy – focused, calm, strong. I have mentioned these two examples because politically they belong to a 'church' entirely different from mine and yet I see in them exemplars of the ideal Governor.

Several other examples can be cited of Governors contemporary to us, having served with diligence and quiet efficacy, fulfilling the constitutional purpose of their office. What is that purpose?

Here an allusion to Mahatma Gandhi would be in order.

Change was in the air when Gandhi called on Bengal's last British Governor, Burrows. The Attlee appointee asked Gandhi on October 30, 1946, 'What would you like me to do?' The question was remarkable and historians would not fail to note it was coming from a direct successor-tenant in that house, of George Nathaniel Curzon who, 48 years earlier, had refused to see Gandhi. The answer Burrows received was terse: 'Nothing, Your Excellency.' Gandhi was indicating that, after the British declaration to quit, the governor's position was to be that of a constitutional head.

Shriman Narayan Agarwal, a dedicated Gandhian and later a follower of Vinoba Bhave, gave Gandhi an occasion to express himself clearly on the subject. In November–December 1947, Agarwal cogitated on the office and role of governor as was being debated in the constituent assembly. He, of course, did not know then that he himself would, some two decades later, be Governor of Gujarat, when he wrote in an article that winter: 'In my opinion there is no necessity for a Governor. The chief minister should be able to take his place and people's money to the tune of Rs 5,500 per month for the sinecure of the Governor will be saved...' Agarwal then went on to make some suggestions regarding the criteria and procedure for the appointment of Governors – if indeed that position was to be retained under the new Constitution.

Responding to Agarwal's comments, the Mahatma wrote in the *Harijan* of December 21, 1947: '...much as I would like to spare every pice of the public treasury, it would be bad economy to do away with provincial governors and regard chief ministers as a perfect equivalent. whilst I would resent much power of interference to be given to governors, I do not think that they should be mere figureheads. They should have enough power enabling them to influence ministerial policy for the better. In their detached position they would be able to see things in their proper perspective and thus prevent mistakes by their cabinets. Theirs must be an all-pervasive moral influence in their provinces.'

So, there we have Gandhi's scarcely improvable concept of the role of a Governor in India: Governors must not interfere with the functioning of the elected ministry but must exert an 'all-pervasive moral influence'. Power is one thing, influence another. And that influence can be wielded, through any amount of or no pelf.

On May 8, 1949, Governor General Rajagopalachari convened a meeting of governors which was also addressed by Prime Minister Jawaharlal Nehru and Deputy Prime Minister Sardar Patel. The word 'figurehead' featured in what Rajaji said to the gathering of Governors. 'You should not imagine that you are just figureheads and can do nothing…Our prime minister and deputy prime minister do not hold that view. They want you to develop your influence for good and they expect you to find means for achieving it without friction and without prejudice to the march of democracy.' The Governors attending included industrialist Homi Mody, the veteran non-Congress political leader M.S. Aney, the free-thinking political leader and barrister Asaf Ali, the Congressman and lawyer K.N. Katju, the Maharaja of Bhavnagar, and ICS officer C.M. Trivedi. All of them took the 'march of democracy' forward. None of them saw their role as being bigger or less than what the Constitution had envisaged. They saw things, to borrow Gandhi's phrase, 'in the proper perspective'.

Speaking for myself, I can never forget an unintentional lesson on a Governor's role that I received from an unknown correspondent in Kolkata. Meaning to give me a sense of gubernatorial grandeur, she managed to do exactly the opposite. She began her letter to me in a beautiful hand with the unforgettable words: 'I am honoured, Sir, to be addressing a letter to the Figurehead of the State.'

Textbook right, that was.

Governors are figureheads in the sense in which the Mahatma explained to Governor Burrows. They are not to try to run the state. That way lies tragicomic failure. But they are not straw-filled scarecrows or brass escutcheons either. They wield an influence that goes beyond all optical value.

And that influence is wielded both on behalf of the Centre with the state and on behalf of the state with the Centre. And on behalf of the Constitution with the people of the state. This tripod of influence is the Governor's sole justification and sole prerogative. In our times when there is a real danger of the Centre wanting to become supremacist and the states wanting to fight that tendency with all their federal might, it will be all too easy for Governors to become part of the 'strong Centre' thesis. They will, if they do that, be short-termist in the extreme for the Constitution of India has a different vision of India – an India that is held together by a democratic respect of difference and a republican regard for mutuality. That may be said to be the un-saleable, un-transferable gold of the Union of India. Seventy and more years into being a Republic, the President of India and the Governors of the states of the Union are custodians of that bullion of a people's trust, their gold standard.

(*Seminar*, May 2019)

78

Rescuing Grace from Disgrace

THE WORDS 'CUSTOMARY', 'CEREMONIAL' and 'ritual' are employed to describe the addresses of the President of India to our Parliament at its opening sessions each year and, likewise, to characterise those of Governors when they address the Legislative Assemblies in their state capitals.

India being the land of largely unquestioned custom, ceremonials and rituals, these addresses of the Head of State have also become part of the life of our polity. The President of India and Governor arrive with 'due' fanfare, perform the ceremony of which the officiating 'priest' is the Speaker or Chairman, and depart feeling greatly relieved that it is over.

The speeches or addresses of the Head of State for these occasions, following British practice, are drafted by the government of the day. They are not written by the President of India or Governor, but only read out by them. The drafts for these are received in their offices generally very close to the event and require them to be gone through against a tight time frame. This in itself makes the suggesting of changes by them difficult.

A thought that was worth pursuing

R. Venkataraman, the President of India from 1987 to 1992, was fond of saying, with his characteristic smile, to staff (I was his Joint Secretary), 'When I am asked to read these Addresses, I feel like saying "Rashtrapati Bhavan" and sitting down!' He went through the drafts of the Addresses he got from the government of the day line by line and word by word. And he – not so much we on his staff – would mark out those he felt needed modification. I do not recall a single occasion when his responses were not accepted in toto. But there was one 'move' of his which did not go through.

He asked us, shortly after he assumed office, to contact the Indian High Commission in London to find out what the form of Her Majesty's 'Throne Speech', delivered at the opening of the sessions of the two Houses each year or immediately after a general election, was like. It was his distinct impression, he said, that the speech prepared by Her Majesty's Government is very brief, merely outlining the outer contours of policy and the legislative business proposed for the session ahead – and nothing more. That, he said, is how it should ideally be with the opening of Parliament in India, in place of the long speech that is read out in extenso to a progressively tired gathering of Hon'ble members of Parliament, followed by an equally long translation into Hindi or English as the case may be. President Venkataraman's chief concern was the saving of time and the avoiding of tedium. But he was also aware of the gain from such a reform in terms of the avoiding of interruptions and the other phenomenon which has come so unfortunately to be associated with legislatures' opening ceremonies – tension between the writer and reader of the speech.

The High Commission was 'duly' approached and specimens of Her Majesty's speeches obtained, all of which went to show President Venkataraman's memory to have been spot on. But, sadly, the suggestion made to the government of the day that the British practice be considered for adoption in New Delhi was not heeded.

President K.R. Narayanan, in office from 1997–2002, was no less painstaking with the drafts. We on his team (I was Secretary to the President) would marvel at his being able to spot phrases with subtle connotations which would be best rectified. It gave me no small happiness to see officers of the government acknowledge the pertinence and propriety of changes that 'KRN' directed us to convey. Needless to say, the changes suggested were so patently unbiased and good that they were accepted not just without demur, but gratefully.

A cameo from Kolkata

In Kolkata, as Governor of West Bengal (2004–2009), it was my privilege to suggest, on a few occasions, some changes to draft Addresses to the Hon'ble Legislative Assembly, and Chief Minister Buddhadeb Bhattacharjee invariably accepted them. On the first such occasion, when he had accepted the suggestion at once, there was a slip. On the night before the ceremony, I noticed, to my dismay, that the printed text which had just come to me had not carried out the change. The matter was important enough for me to bring it to Buddhababu's attention over the telephone. He said to me, 'I am to blame. Let me see what I can do but rest assured it will be done.' Was there enough time to reprint hundreds of copies of the Address? There was not. The chief minister did the next best thing. He had a piece of paper pasted over the paragraph concerned, on each and every copy, overnight.

This, of course, drew more attention to the paragraph than its appearance in print would have done, and Opposition members of the Legislative Assembly found cause to explode. Buddhababu told me later that day, 'If the matter comes up formally in the House I will say frankly that you had suggested an important change, that I had agreed to it, but due entirely to my oversight it could not be carried out in time and the next best thing was done…I will lay the facts on the table.' This was political civility.

Occasion arose for me to officiate as the Governor of Bihar (January to June 2006). Exactly as now, Nitish Kumar was chief minister, heading a coalition of the Janata Dal (United) and the Bharatiya Janata Party, with Rabri Devi being leader of the Opposition. The draft for the Governor's Address was unexceptionable and written in flawless Hindi which was, for me, a pleasure to read out. There was not one interruption (which I was expecting) and I noticed throughout when I looked in her direction that Rabri Devi was listening attentively and with the greatest dignity. After the ceremony was over, Nitishbabu said to me that it was the first time in his experience that a Governor's Address to the Assembly had gone off without a single interruption, and he thanked me for it. 'Why are you thanking me?' I said to him. 'The speech was not mine, it was yours.' I will not detain the reader with his rather overwhelming reply.

To conclude: turbulence in the House is not new. Unseemliness has been seen in them for decades. But controversy over Governors' addresses in Assemblies are now rising in frequency and velocity, with Governors, whose dignity is inseparable from that of the edifice of the state and the government bartering accusations and counter-accusations.

Where the problem lies

The root of the problem lies in the foundational dichotomy of one agency writing the speech and another reading it. Professor A.R. Venkatachalapathy published not long ago a fine book, *Who Owns That Song?* – about the rights to Subramania Bharati's 'nationalised' works. One may, following that, ask of the Governor's Address 'Who Owns That Speech?' The one who writes it or the one who reads it out? Subject to correction by constitutional experts, I believe that the Address of the Head of State to the Legislature is an ornament of convention, not a condition precedent for bills becoming law. If it was, then the business of a House that has not had the Governor's Address read out in full, or in tokenistic part, would become invalid. That is not the case. Address or no Address, the Legislature continues its work.

Since political polarisation between the Centre which appoints Governors and the state which elects the chief minister is, to all appearances, set to accelerate in the visualisable future, a way out has to be found. I believe President Venkataraman's suggested solution gives us that way out. If all concerned agree that the Head of State need read out just the bare outline of the legislative business ahead, the Address will then belong to neither its drafter nor its reader but to its rightful owner-listener, namely, the collective body of Legislators. Presidents and Governors will, I think, be relieved with such a rearrangement.

But what of the governments? Will they be ready to forego the chance to air their accomplishments and plans? They would need convincing that the Motion of Thanks that follows the Address is where that airing is best done – as it is, in British Parliament.

It will take an innovative and self-denying chief minister to start the reform to rescue a custom, ceremony and ritual of grace from disgrace.

(*The Hindu*, February 15, 2024)

79

Delimitation Fallout Needs No Political Forecasting

THERE WAS A TIME, not all that long ago, when English speakers in the south of India routinely referred to our north as 'Upper India'. This sense of the north's upper-ness included, somewhere in its folds, a sense of the north having the upper hand in the affairs of the nation, of being bigger, more populous and, therefore, the more dominant of the two. Being 'upper' also encased within its meaning the fact of the nation's capital, Calcutta and later Delhi, being 'up' there, with Simla as the nation's summer capital 'up above the world so high like a diamond in the sky'.

The political summit

The Imperial Legislative Council, with its Central Legislative Assembly as the Lower House and the Council of State as the Upper House, being located in Delhi pushed that upperness further up. Seeing persons of the eminence of Muhammad Habibullah, A. Rangaswami Iyengar, S. Srinivasa Iyengar, Omandur Ramaswami Reddiar, Arcot Ramasamy Mudaliar, Tanguturi Prakasam, Ananthasayanam Ayyangar, T.S. Avinashilingam Chettiar, V.V. Giri, S. Satyamurti, N.G. Ranga, C.N. Muthuranga Mudaliar, T.S.S. Rajan, K. Santhanam, M.C. Rajah, the Raja of Bobbili and N. Sivaraj 'move' diligently to Delhi by up-bound trains, for legislative sessions, could not but reinforce the perceived image of India's north as India's political summit. Later, the Constituent Assembly with N. Gopalaswami Ayyangar, Alladi Krishnaswami Iyer, Rajaji, Jerome D' Souza, K. Kamaraj, O.V. Alagesan, C. Subramaniam, V.I. Munuswamy Pillai, in it, and some remarkable south Indian women – Ammu Swaminathan, G. Durgabai, Annie Mascarene, Dakshayani Velayudham – and successive Lok Sabhas and the Rajya Sabha drawing members of Parliament of the stature of A.K. Gopalan, T. Nagi Reddy, C.N. Annadurai, P. Sundarayya, Panampilly Govinda Menon, C.H. Mohammed Koya, M. Ruthnaswamy, K.T.K. Thangamani and Era Sezhiyan, going to Delhi, by air rather than by rail, of course, continued the 'India's north as India's peak' image. Needless to say, that 'peak' was scaled in terms of outstanding legislative performance by these men and women.

Congress and left symmetry

The Indian National Congress, however, it needs to be noted, was from the very start, aware of the need for India's regions to be seen as equal, bereft of any asymmetry. Its very third session after Bombay (1885) and Calcutta (1886) was held in Madras (1887, and many times later), followed by several Congress sessions of note taking place in the south – Amaravati/Amraoti (1897), Coconada (1923), Belgaum (1924), and the seminal one, at Avadi (Madras) in 1955, attended by Yugoslavia's President Marshal Josip Broz Tito, where the party adopted 'a socialistic pattern of society' as its avowed objective.

The All India Kisan Sabha, the peasant wing of the Communist Party of India, likewise, which had first met in a 'founder-conference' in Lucknow in 1936, met at its fifth session in 1940 in Palasa, Srikakulam, then in Madras Presidency and now in Andhra, under the chairmanship of Rahul Sankrityayan. It has, since, met very pointedly in southern venues as much as in northern.

These considered arrangements embody the opening Article 1 of our Constitution: India, that is Bharat.

That phrase makes India, Bharat and Bharat, India – one belonging to and in fact, being the other.

But the question needs to be asked, today: What makes India, 'India', or Bharat, Bharat?

And why, today?

Impact of delimitation

Because four years from now, India's electoral democracy will stand on an existential crossroads. A delimitation of the constituencies that will elect members of the Lok Sabha, following the population figures returned by the next decennial Census, is to take place in 2026.

A good thing! We cannot have, should not have, the same number of members of Parliament – 543 – representing a vastly increased population in the Lok Sabha. Mathematically speaking, the higher the number of people per constituency, the lower the impact each voter has on parliamentary representation – clearly an undesirable situation. The Constitution of India recognised this and provided for a periodic, Census-linked rearrangement of constituencies to make their representation in Parliament tenable. More people should mean more MPs. Simple, sound logic. But simple, sound politics also? No.

A population-based marking out or rearrangement of constituencies, as envisaged in Article 82 of the Constitution, will have the effect of giving more MPs to the states and Union territories that have let their numbers grow, and will give markedly less MPs to those that have held their numbers in some check. Realising the anomaly that a delimitation based on Census data would cause, a delimitation freeze was put in position by Prime Minister Indira Gandhi through the 42nd Amendment of the Constitution in 1976. This was extended by Prime Minister Atal Bihari Vajpayee through the 84th Amendment. It is this extension that is to end in 2026, placing us at a crossroads.

What the data show

What is the way forward?

Considering the Census data for 2011, almost half (48.6 per cent) of our population (of approximately 1.38 billion) is contributed by the states of Uttar Pradesh, Maharashtra, Bihar, West Bengal and Madhya Pradesh. According to the projections made by the Technical Group formed by the National Commission on Population, ministry of health and family welfare for 2011–2036, Uttar Pradesh's share in India's population would see an increase by 1.74 percentage points (from 15.30 per cent in 1971 to a projected 17.03 per cent in 2026), Bihar's by 1.59 percentage points (from 7.69 per cent in 1971 to a projected 9.28 per cent in 2026) and Rajasthan's by 1.17 percentage points (from 4.70 per cent in 1971 to a projected 5.87 per cent in 2026).

Tamil Nadu's share in India's population would see a decline by 2.08 percentage points (from 7.52 per cent in 1971 to a projected 5.44 per cent in 2026), undivided Andhra's by 1.46 percentage points (from 7.94 per cent in 1971 to a projected 6.48 per cent in 2026), and Kerala's by 1.36 percentage points (from 3.89 per cent in 1971 to a projected 2.54 per cent in 2026). Interestingly, West Bengal's will also decline by 1.03 percentage points (from 8.08 per cent in 1971 to a projected 7.05 per cent in 2026).

Rearranging and standardising the number of people per constituency through the scheduled delimitation exercise will inevitably lead to a reduced representation for states that have managed to stabilise their populations, and to a higher representation for states that have not stabilised their populations.

It needs no political forecasting to see that emotions will be strained by a delimitation exercise that adds electoral sinew to one set of states, while depleting representative muscle to another. The upperness syndrome, which has now become a thing of the past, should not come back in the guise of delimitation. We cannot afford a tension on the north-south front in addition to those we already have.

There are alternatives

There are two alternatives before us: one, we go in for another freeze, this time not for any specific period but until all states have achieved population stabilisation. Two, we request demographic and statistical experts to devise a mathematical model along the lines of the 'Cambridge Compromise' based on a mathematically equitable 'formula' for the apportionment of the seats of the European Parliament between the member-states. That formula cannot be applied to our situation as such but needs to be studied so as to customise it for our needs.

Given the complications of the Indian demographic scene, and the distorting shadow that Census data may cast on the delimitation process, I would say the first option is the more persuasive one. The population-stabilising states of India that is Bharat, which include all the southern states, must continue to enrich our legislative and parliamentary processes as they have been doing since the time of the Imperial Legislative Council, with no penalties having to be paid for their sense of responsibility. We need to limit population, not representation.

(*The Hindu*, May 19, 2022)

PART VII

TROUBLE IN PARADISE

80

National Blind Spot

GOING DOWN ONE OF Chennai's busy roads on a blazingly hot afternoon two weeks ago, my car stopped at a traffic signal. This was the alms-seekers' moment. A man in his early forties, accompanied by a girl in her early teens who looked like she could be his daughter, materialised from nowhere. I saw, as they approached, that he was totally blind. He was holding a tin can with a slit just wide enough for coins or currency notes if folded twice over. He did not say anything, nor his daughter. They just stood under the scalding sun as I dropped all the coins I had into his tin box. And as I rolled up the window to shut the heat out, I heard him say in a clear voice, '*nannri*'. Just that. I have never heard the Tamil equivalent of 'thank you' said with such quiet dignity, elegance. It was not said mechanically, or casually. It was said like the sayer knew the word's core. The daughter then gently nudged him towards the kerb where, as the light turned green and my car moved, they became invisible.

Moving on in my air-conditioned Estilo, I recalled a 'born-blind' boy of about 10 I was introduced to in Calcutta by an NGO working for the sightless nearly two decades ago. He was the very embodiment of cheer and a cricket fan, besides. 'Who is your cricket hero?' I asked the tiny Calcuttan, assuming that he would say 'Sourav'. But no, he surprised me by his choice. He said with a smile: 'Shocheen'. How he had made that choice I could not fathom. There is no way he could have seen the player playing on screen. Or read about him in the papers. He should be in his 30s now. He is perhaps employed, married, a father. Wherever he is, he is bound to have something if not all of the cheer he showed when he was just 10.

And I thought of another, older boy, gentle, looking like he could be a poet, I met in a home for the blind with other boys and their carers. There was no cheer in him. When I took his hands in mine and said some inanities, he heard me in silence and said nothing (he could speak). He just smiled in his own, very hesitant, way but tightened his hold of my hands and by not releasing them for some long seconds seemed to say, as I imagined, something. What could that be? Later, I fantasised that he wanted to say: 'I need to talk…to convey many things...just to you but I know we are not alone...I never know when I am alone and when I am not...Never alone to know...or for natural needs...feeling my privacy is mine...without wondering who is watching me...and when certain other things happen to my body...like...I will not describe it...I do not want anyone looking but I know they are and perhaps sniggering...This is one great loss for us the blind...everything is clothed in blindness and everything is naked...everything is private and nothing is private...But I am detaining you...*Namaskar Rajyapalshaheb...Namaskar...Aabaar aashun...*come again...But why would you? No need for you to return...'

This conversation took place in my imagination. But I know it to have been more real than any I have heard with my ears. I have not even been dimly aware of, even vaguely concerned about, what goes on in the 'talkie' of the blind one's screen. If I was able to see it, it would be something no Censor Board would allow, no film screen would endure.

Most of us are not even aware that India heads the world's chart in the number of the blind, the vision-impaired. According to the 2020 figures of the International Agency for the Prevention of Blindness, India has 9.2 million blind persons, followed by China at 8.9 million and Indonesia at third place with 3.7 million.

The percentage of females in the Indian population being around 48 per cent, there are about 4.5 million blind women and girls in India. A mortifying thought! And no less mortifying is the fact that of the 9.2 million blind Indians, 5 million live in extreme poverty, that is to say are poor, wretchedly poor.

The *nannri* came to me from one of those 5 million.

Given that, on an average, a member of the Lok Sabha represents 1.5 million persons, India's blind at 9.2 million can be taken to constitute the equivalent of six Lok Sabha constituencies and India's-blind-plus-poor three Lok Sabha constituencies. Being scattered throughout the length and breadth of India, they do not have a single person, blind or sighted, to represent them collectively. And here I am speaking of the blind, not the visually impaired. If those were to be included in the count, the size of the non-representation of vision-impaired India would become staggering.

Representation apart, the subject of blindness and the needs of the blind itself have, to the best of my knowledge, not occupied sufficient attention of our Parliament and legislatures. What are the major causes of blindness in India and are they being addressed? Is there a plan to increase the infrastructure for eye care in terms of the number of eye doctors and eye hospitals? Is stem cell research being explored to see if that transplant pathway will work for retina-related blindness?

Blindness occupied Parliament's attention in a way it should not have had to. This was after the diabolic 1980 episode of policemen blinding

31 undertrials in Bhagalpur, Bihar. The event was ghastly. That policemen could pin down the prisoners, gouge their eyes out with bicycle spokes, and then pour sulphuric acid on the hollow sockets was beyond belief, beyond acceptability. The statement by Prime Minister Indira Gandhi in Parliament on December 1 about the happening befitted her station. 'What are we coming to in this country?' she said and continued, 'That anybody can do this is beyond my comprehension…I am not able to say anything more…' She broke down while admitting to feeling 'physically sick'.

But the 'Bhagalpur' day in Parliament was carried by Atal Bihari Vajpayee who said in an unusual 'take' that he offered to share the blame for the malaise in society, prompting the then home minister, Zail Singh, to say he too did the same. This was not just unusual but unprecedented. 'I share the blame…' Who says that today?

Bhagalpur was a crime perpetrated by perverts. *Slumdog Millionaire* and Jayamohan's Tamil works show us that streak of perversity, the malaise in our society, that can inflict blindness. Even the policemen who did what they did were policemen only in a manner of speaking. They were males, the dominant species, exercising brute power not so much as policemen but as dominant males. Caste was involved, class was involved, but above all god-damned insolence was involved. And the apathy of us, Indians, to such happenings was involved. And do we take responsibility? Atalji was exceptional. The malaise he spoke of includes a passive condition, no less corrosive for being passive – our indifference to the condition, so real, so tormenting. Will the new Lok Sabha, whatever its composition, spare a moment to see what India can do to live down its dubious distinction of being the nation with the world's Number One Blind population?

Amazing initiatives have been made to give encouragement and assistance to the blind in sports and in the arts by official agencies and NGOs. Salutations to them and their initiators! But the Calcutta boy who said 'Shocheen' with enchantment and the Chennai man who said '*nannri*' with grace demand of the metaphoric blind in the generality of us that we open our eyes and, withal, our purses to their need and their hope.

(*The Telegraph,* May 19, 2024)

81

Gone Girls and Boys

THE LATEST REPORT OF the National Crime Records Bureau tells us that in 2022 India has experienced a surge in kidnapping and abduction cases, with over 1 lakh reported incidents across the country. It happened some six years ago in a 'posh' residential colony in New Delhi. Kanha (name changed) was the seven- or eight-year-old son of a woman who is by current norms of upper-middle-class etiquette called 'a domestic'. She would sweep and swab and mind various chores in the house. Kanha had gone that day, after his regular school hours, to a tutor for extra classes. Tuition over, he stepped out and was seen by a few to move towards what was assumed to be his home. He did not reach home. He has not been seen since. Frantic searches and inquiries by the mother and her shocked employers yielded no information, no clues, no hypotheses either. Vendors who are regulars in the area were asked if they had seen him around that day. All said, '*Nahin…nahin dekha…nahin malum.*' The phrase, '*pata nahin*', cut a gash in the mother's heart every time she heard it. Pilgrimages were suggested, to shrines of different faiths. They were undertaken, the deities propitiated. Astrologers were recommended. They were met, paid. No Kanha.

The police were sensitive enough to take down the complaint but could make no headway. Dark hints were then thrown to say it must be an 'inside' affair, an act of family spite. 'But we have no family enmities, no property disputes…' was met by other 'domestics' with scepticism. 'If someone has carried him away for ransom, we would be contacted wouldn't we…?' the family asked. 'Besides, what money do we have to part with?'

The boy's family has resigned itself to Kanha having been lost. There is a faint hope in the parents that he will one day return, a grown man, declining to talk about what happened, where he was taken, but laden with silent gifts, even money…a dream.

The above is what may be called a 'real, personally known occurrence'.

Faint memories were stirred of 'famous' kidnappings by this real-life story. In 1966 occurred the kidnapping in Australia of three siblings in what is known as the Beaumont Kidnappings. Jane Beaumont, Arnna Beaumont and Grant Beaumont disappeared from Glenelg Beach near Adelaide, South Australia, on January 26 that year. Many people had seen the three children on and near that beach in the company of 'a tall man with fairish to light-brown hair and a thin face with a sun-tanned complexion and medium build, aged in his mid-thirties.' That is all. They have not been seen or heard of since. The Beaumont kidnappings are 'big' torments.

But apart from 'big and famous' kidnappings, there are hundreds upon hundreds in our own country that we just do not know of.

The latest report of the National Crime Records Bureau (NCRB) tells us that in 2022 India has experienced a surge in kidnapping and abduction cases, with over 1 lakh reported incidents across the country. Surge in kidnappings? Why? How? This figure comes to an average of more than 294 cases per day or over 12 every hour. In 2022, from the reported 1,07,588 kidnapping and abduction cases, no less than 76,069 cases were of children, the equivalents of Kanha and the Beaumont children. This disturbingly high number of cases highlights the vulnerability of children to such criminal activities.

The NCRB has cautioned against assuming an 'increase in crime' as opposed to an 'increase in registration of crime by police'. The report tells us quite rightly that effective police action can and has led to an increase in reported cases.

But it would not be wrong to assume that if there are 12 registered kidnappings of children every hour, the number of those actually being kidnapped every hour is bound to be more. By how many, I dare not speculate.

True, kidnappings and abductions are only one among a plethora of crimes. But the fact that they involve children, including (and mainly) girl children, must make us, well, scream. William Blake's lines come to mind: 'A Robin Red breast in a Cage/ Puts all Heaven in a Rage.'

This is no ordinary crime that we are living with. This is not just a crime against humanity but an outrage against humanity. And, yet, barring one or two media reports, no one has howled in protest. Not politicians, not civil society, if it can be called that.

I can hear cracked old voices say, 'Kidnappings are as old as the hills…They have always happened, always will…' Maybe, but then I would like to say, 'Would you like it if your child or grandchild was among the 12 children and more kidnapped every hour and say, this is an old phenomenon…' Would you?

We can imagine what must be happening to the kidnapped children if they have not been murdered. They would be abused. Just that. Abused.

And there is without doubt a class aspect here. The majority of those kidnapped children belong to what may be called 'India's poor'. If any of the 12 children per hour belonged to an upper-middle-class or well-to-do urban family, not to speak of a celebrity family, the whole country would have been shaken up. The unknown becoming invisible is not news.

No police establishment is unaware of the sites of trafficking and prostitution. No institution can be without the knowledge of the ways in which child labour – forced, violent and bizarre – is practised.

I believe something like a Mission: Rescue Kidnapped Children is imperative. We simply cannot live with the fact that every single hour a dozen or so or more of India's children are getting abducted. The following thoughts are shared for what they are worth with the ardent hope that they can be read and improved upon.

Kidnappings can hardly ever be individual enterprises. They have to be carried out by a gang or a group. This must make their operation easier to unravel. Awards for information and for 'insider' revelations should be announced. Again, one can hear the objection, 'Will this not lead to fake kidnappings for the sake of the award money?' Of course, it will. But it will take no missile technology to ascertain the fake from the real kidnapping.

I would also suggest an amnesty scheme under which kidnappers are encouraged to come clean against non-punitive arrangements. This would require some careful fine-tuning of rules but should be tried, at least experimentally.

Finally, an all-India conference over two or three days should be called by the Union government in the department of child welfare to be attended by families of kidnapped children selected by state commissions for the welfare of women and children based on registered cases. This will be an eye-opener to all of us about the society we are living in – blinkered. The deliberations will also be therapeutic for the parents or guardians as they hear each other. And I believe constructive suggestions will emerge from them for the detection of and reunification with the kidnapped children.

I have two other post-final suggestions: surely there are cases of 'genuine' kidnapped children having been found and returned to their families. They should be central to the conference, describing their experiences. And to give the entire exercise meaning, the conference should be inaugurated not by a VVIP from the government but by a 'kidnapped returnee'. And I would suggest that the conference be co-chaired by a panel of the following strong women: Maneka Gandhi (who has headed the ministry of women and child development), the relentless crusader for social justice and gender rights, Brinda Karat, 'top-cop' Kiran Bedi, Shabana Azmi, and Kanimozhi, the Tamil Nadu MP who has pioneered bold legislative measures in the private members' bills mode.

I will conclude with another Blake quote: 'Some to Misery are Born/ Every Morn and every Night/ Some are Born to sweet delight/ Some are Born to sweet delight/ Some are Born to Endless Night.'

Can the new year dawn in light for these children in darkness?

(*The Telegraph*, December 24, 2023)

82

Righteous Paths

MANY OPPOSITION PARTIES, INCLUDING the Indian National Congress, the Trinamool Congress, the Communist Party of India (Marxist) and the Communist Party of India, asked for the resignation of the Railway Minister, Ashwini Vaishnaw.

Nothing can be more predictable or niggling than the responses excerpted above of some Opposition parties to the grim tragedy of the triple rail collision in Balasore district of Odisha on June 2, 2023.

Could a train accident of this kind not have happened when the railway minister of the day was from any of these parties? Or when the Railway Board of the day was one set up by the government of the day? And would not the Opposition at that time – including the Bharatiya Janata Party – demanding the resignation of such a railway minister or the Railway Board, have seemed unfair to the man or woman running that ministry or serving on the Railway Board of the day?

Resignations, like apologies, are routinely demanded by those who are lucky enough to be on the right side of the incident. But a resignation or apology so demanded is not a resignation or contrition. It is an extraction, a toll or a levy made by the contextually strong from the situationally weakened. And, therefore, morally, not the gold of a heart's mint but the small change of a niggard smeltery.

I do not know if, at the time of writing, the Railway Minister, Vaishnaw, has indeed offered to resign or, in fact, has resigned and whether his resignation has been accepted. If he has done so, or does so after this has been written, all honour to his sense of accountability, his own personal code of ethics. If he has not, no discredit to him, no minus marks, for he has his own sense of his *dharma*, his *karma*, and his perception of where his duty lies.

But before I dwell on the duty-sense of another Railway Minister – Lal Bahadur Shastri – a brief discussion of history in the Odisha region.

Did anyone ask the emperor, Ashoka, for his abdication or apology after the Kalinga war, which must have played out not far from the scene of this collision? Doubtful. In fact, no. None is known to have done so, unless it was someone in his immediate circle among his kin or his advisers who advised him in his royal chambers and has left no record of such a conversation. From all we know, Ashoka felt his agony, atoned, and announced his remorse, all in the solitude of his lonely contemplation and entirely of his own accord. He had his anguish and apology carved on stone-faces in places as far removed from Kalinga as the north-west of the Indian land mass and in the far south.

Again, in the temple town of Puri in 1938, there occurred another act of contrition. With his wife, Kasturba, his secretary, Mahadev Desai, and Desai's wife, Durga, Gandhi had gone to Puri at the end of March, 1938. Kasturba did what many Hindu pilgrims at Puri do. Along with Durga Desai and another associate, she visited the Puri temple. This upset Gandhi who had declared day in and day out that whoever believed in the removal of untouchability should shun temples which were not open to Harijans. Gandhi writes: 'The agony was enough to precipitate a collapse. I turned pale. The machine recorded an alarmingly high blood pressure, but I knew better than the machine. I was in a worse condition than the machine could show. The three who went there were the least to blame. They went in ignorance. But I was to blame, and Mahadev was more to blame in that he did not tell them what their dharma was and how any breach would shake me. He ought to have thought also of its social repercussions.' Mahadev, when he came to know of Gandhi's pain, cried and, starting a fast, said he would like to leave Gandhi's service. That is, he offered to resign. But Gandhi, who had been furious with Desai, refused to consider his secretary's offer to leave.

Odisha has been the scene of great churnings of the human spirit.

To now return to rail accidents and railway ministers. The year, 1956, had not been an easy one for the then Railway Minister, Lal Bahadur Shastri. In August, a major railway accident in Mahbubnagar, Andhra Pradesh, killed 112 people. Owning moral responsibility for the accident, Shastri tendered his resignation to Prime Minister Jawaharlal Nehru who persuaded Shastri to withdraw it. On November 23, a worse railway accident occurred in Ariyalur, in what was then the state of Madras, involving the Madras-Tuticorin Express, causing 142 deaths. The engine and the first seven bogies had plunged into the Marudaiyar river while crossing the bridge over it in torrential rain, hurtling its passengers into the swollen waters. Shastri submitted his resignation, once again; this time, non-negotiably. In his resignation letter, Shastri said that 'it will be good for me and the Government as a whole, if I quietly quit the office I hold'. The use of the word, 'quietly', by Shastri invested it with a meaning all its own.

Nehru was in a dilemma. He went on to say in the Lok Sabha that he had the highest regard for Shastri but 'from the broader point of view of constitutional propriety' he was accepting his resignation so 'that...no man should think that whatever might happen, we carry on without being affected by it'.

Those in the Opposition, no less than those on the Treasury Benches, were flabbergasted by the resignation. Such was the esteem in which Shastri was held. But some people will never be satisfied. And skirmishing is always attractive, especially when the receiving party is in the dock. A member of the Lok Sabha from the region, K.M. Vallatharas, of the Krishak Mazdoor Praja Party, in a rasping speech, said Shastri's resignation was of no use when the deputy minister and local officials did not resign. Vallatharas singled out the Railway Board for special attention, calling it 'a lethargic organisation'. Shastri's response has to go down as something of a classic: 'I am perhaps small in size and perhaps soft in tongue and people are apt to believe that I have not been firm with the Railway Board. Though not physically very strong I think I am internally not so weak. There are different ways of doing things…'

O.V. Alagesan, the MP for Chingleput, was in a dilemma of his own. He was from the state – Madras – where the accident had occurred and was then the Union deputy minister for railways under Shastri. Alagesan, in Madras on the day, hearing the news of the accident over the radio, rushed to the site with officials for an immediate assessment. Shortly thereafter, calling on Nehru, he said he would like to quit as well. Panditji refused to accept the resignation and saying, 'Don't be silly,' he advised the only minister now left for Railways: 'You take charge of the ministry and continue the good work both of you have been doing.' Alagesan's family cherishes his staying on the burning deck, an act no less exacting than leaving it.

Accountability is best determined by the accountable, not others. And one's own sense of accountability can include resigning and not resigning. And accepting or not accepting another's resignation. Gandhi's 'collapse' in Puri, Desai's wanting to leave and Gandhi's asking him, nonetheless, to stay, Shastri's 'different ways of doing things', Alagesan's responses and Nehru's direction are about conscience's working for one's own inner peace, not another's outer skirmishing. One's own moral acknowledgement, not another's admonitory judgment.

Dharma is about being accountable to one's own self but in the daylight of the world's gaze.

The Balasore train accident has shown the perilous vulnerability of poor passengers in 'unreserved' bogeys which, if battered in an accident, make identification of the nameless dead virtually impossible. Packed into the bogeys their journeys, even when uneventful, are a nightmare. When exposed to an accident, the nightmare turns into a tragedy. How is this problem to be addressed and by whom? Until that is done and train travel made equally safe for all passengers, accountability rests not just on a minister or a board but on the entire system of railway travelling in India.

(*The Telegraph*, June 18, 2023)

83
Different Challenges

THE YEAR, 1963 – a Bollywood film could be made on it with the title, *Saath Saal Pehle* – was a droll sort of year. Recovering from the lashing received by us from the Sino-Indian war in the dying months of the previous year, India amounted to little for itself and accounted for less in the world that year.

It had one major accomplishment to its credit, though, and one major embarrassment to its debit that year.

The accomplishment was technological: it launched its first-ever rocket from a small fishing village near Trivandrum, as the town was then called. Sharp-brained and sharp-eyed technologists and rocket engineers, including A.P.J. Abdul Kalam, accomplished the successful launch with the help of three persons whose knowledge of rocket technology was zero but whose minds and hearts were as pioneering as those who had chosen the site for its atmospheric and ionospheric suitability (as well as its ideal distance from both China and Pakistan). Of these, two were bishops – the 'local' bishop, Rev. Peter Bernard Periera, and the bishop of Trivandrum, Vincent Victor Dereere, incidentally, a Belgian. The third was an administrator, the district collector, Madhavan Nair. These three busied themselves in acquiring 600 acres from the coastal community for the Thumba Equatorial Rocket Launching Station. India hailed the launch and the technologists behind it, as it should have done. But the two priests and the collector are not remembered quite as much as they deserve to be for what they did to make India the space major it is today.

The embarrassment was part-religious, part-political, for it took place in Kashmir where those two – religion and politics – are inextricably wound together. On December 27, 1963, news broke out that the *Moi-e-Muqqadas*, believed to be a strand from the beard of the Holy Prophet, had gone missing – stolen, it was said – from the Hazratbal shrine around 2 a.m. when the custodians of the shrine were, like anyone else at that hour of the night, asleep. The chief minister of the state at the time was the little-known Khwaja Shamsuddin: he announced an award of 1,00,000 rupees to anyone providing information regarding the theft. Communal tension rose like a freak fever. Three days later, Prime Minister Jawaharlal Nehru sent the head of the Intelligence Bureau (IB), B.N. Mullik, to Kashmir to investigate the crime. Much more than a theft was at stake. On January 4, 1964, Mullik informed Nehru that the relic had been recovered. A relieved prime minister said to Mullik, 'You have saved Kashmir for India.' Not much or everything is known about the details of the recovery but after Kashani, a Sufi poet and Sunni leader, identified it as the original and genuine relic, matters quietened down. A few arrests were made but some people we do not know of need to be thanked for having averted a major communal catastrophe in India that year. Like the two priests and the collector in Trivandrum, they are not remembered or even known very clearly.

A sophisticated space probe and a crude crime made news that year for India. The first soon passed out of public memory, but the second has stayed.

What is it about events that makes some of them liable to be forgotten and some not? I am unsure.

Saath saal baad, I must confess I did not recall the space launch. It is only recourse to the marvels of digital sources and resources that refreshed the event for me.

But I remember the theft of the relic vividly and the relief that its recovery brought. Is it because it was, after all, a crime and, like all crimes of note, was something of a thriller for an 18-year-old? Or because it was about religious belief, religious bonds, and religious susceptibilities? News of refugees fleeing what was then East Pakistan into West Bengal, as a direct result of the Hazratbal theft, worried us to no end at that time.

Fast forwarding to *saath saal baad*, India has, just the other day, announced the Indian Space Policy 2023 with the 'Vision' to 'enable, encourage and develop a flourishing commercial presence in space' and it speaks of its role in India's 'socio-economic development and security, protection of environment and lives, pursuing peaceful exploration of outer space, stimulation of public awareness and scientific quest'. This is no ordinary venture, no simple plan, but an audacious strategy that will make the Indian Space Research Organisation propel us towards what may be called the *Chandrayaan* and *Gaganyaan* age. Are there equivalents of Bishops Periera and Dereere and Collector Madhavan today, somewhere, to thank for this great stride? They have to be there, for there is no such thing as a space programme without ground support.

But there is another, bigger, issue.

While we have zoomed ahead in space, we still lack public awareness and public interest in the subject, not just to know and appreciate but also to ask, interrogate, the space programme and the policy. How much of the programme is beneficial to the quality of life in India? How much of it is just clubbist – designed to keep us in the high company of space majors? How much of it is actuated by supremacist pride?

And, parallelly, we need to know that the hold of religion in India, the grip of totems, taboos and tradition, is exactly where it was, if it is not even more menacing. India in 1963 saw a pioneering venture into space take place as also, alongside it, a religion-related theft that brought us to the brink of a communal meltdown. India in 2023, which has just seen a major Space Policy launched, is as prone as it was *saath saal pehle* to traumas caused by religious frenzies unleashed by terrorist crimes and reactions to those. And, in the 'normal' rhythms of life, religious icons are invoked with fervour in election campaigns.

The sacral and the secular coexist co-extensively in India. Ironies have been India's signature.

The present occupant of B.N. Mullik's position in the Intelligence Bureau (IB) is, I am sure, aware that saving communal peace for India will have to be a priority. And that Mullik-type swiftness and intelligence need to be his aim and accomplishment. And just as a Sufi poet and spiritual leader in Kashmir joined in the process of normalisation *saath saal pehle*, so too now it will be essential for lawmakers and law enforcers to work in tandem with civil society to ensure that religious suspicion, intolerance and bigotry are not allowed to stymie us as a modern nation. A policy for India's skies will have little meaning if India's cities, towns and villages remain the playground of religious sensitivities, caste and community strife and, worse, the plaything of sectarian crime. Manipur's example is there for all to see.

Every region in India has places of worship, objects of reverence, relics. Which means every place in India needs to be, in Nehru's words to Mullik used for the Hazratbal relic, 'saved for India'. An onerous task, yes. But less expensive perhaps than our space missions. And more directly connected to the quality of our life. While *Chandrayaan* and *Gaganyaan* are launched for India, *Jivanyaan* has to be saved for India.

This is the lesson 1963 holds for India in 2023.

(*The Telegraph*, May 21, 2023)

84

Seismic Traumas

THE PARISH REGISTER AT the Holy Trinity Church in Stratford-upon-Avon says William Shakespeare was baptised there on April 26, 1564. It is surmised, thereby, that he was born three or four days prior to that date, which makes today or tomorrow – April 23 or 24 – his birthday. It is known, more precisely, that he died on April 23, 1616, making him one of those – not all that few, given that humans are self-renewing and calendar dates are not – who have a birthday and a death day in common.

I was not thinking of the great playwright and sonneteer, much less of his birthday or death day, when, last week, I was listening to a remarkable workshop on earthquakes. India International Centre (IIC) in New Delhi had organised this most purposeful event, in the wake of the February 6, 2023 earthquakes in Turkey and Syria which left some 60,000 dead and 1.5 million homeless, with a view to alerting India and the surrounding regions to the seismic threats they face and the right responses to those – *in good time*.

But what on earth do quakes have to do with Shakespeare? Just this, that the Bard has interesting things to say in the most unexpected ways on just about everything. And in ways that go beyond his wit to his wisdom. And so many of his phrases have got embedded in our minds that we do not even know we are using Shakespeare when we are saying them, like 'cruel to be kind', 'the be-all and end-all', 'foregone conclusion', 'wild goose chase' and, when we are shocked by someone or something, 'Et tu Brute…'

So…did Shakespeare have something to say on earthquakes? This was the thought that occurred to me while reflecting on IIC's timely deliberations. I had a faint recollection of such a reference in one of his plays, which one I could not remember. Blaming, in Shakespeare's words again, my 'crabbed age' for not remembering the reference, I did the next most natural thing, namely, turn to Google and lo! came the reference. It occurs in *Romeo and Juliet*. The Nurse, trying to remember Juliet's age, pegs it to her memory of an earthquake.

'On Lammas-eve at night shall she be fourteen;/ That shall she, marry; I remember it well./ 'Tis since the earthquake now eleven years;/ And she was wean'd, – I never shall forget it, –'

That reference has led some scholars, perhaps inaccurately, to date the play to 1591, since there was an earthquake in England on April 6, 1580. Known as the Dover Straits earthquake, so severe was the shaking that it toppled part of the gables of St. Paul's Cathedral in London and led Thomas Deloney, a balladeer, to write a tract titled, 'Awake, Awake'.

Some 6,000 kilometres due east of England, the earth had shook much more menacingly and murderously only 25 years earlier, in 1555. This was in the Kashmir Valley. This was around midnight in the month of September, the exact day of occurrence not being known. That Kashmir earthquake was of 7.6 to 8.0 moment magnitude and had a Modified Mercalli intensity of XII (*Extreme*). It mauled not just the Kashmir Valley but much of north-western India, killing an estimated 600–60,000 individuals. In the Valley's legend and lore, the experience has remained vivid, despite the many tribulations, natural and man-made, that have followed in the five centuries. There is no one now who can say in the Nurse's words, 'I remember it well,' or 'I never shall forget it,' but the genetic memory of the people of the Valley remembers it and will always.

There is a more earthy reason for it to do so as well.

An earthquake occurred, while everyone there slept, in the wee hours of May 31, 1935 at Quetta, Balochistan (now part of Pakistan). The earthquake had a magnitude of 7.7 and it is estimated that anywhere between 30,000 and 60,000 people were killed. One of the most intensively photographed experiences, the Quetta earthquake is a permanent seismic marker in the subcontinent's memory.

The earth's crust is oblivious to political and national calendars. It has its own calendar.

On August 15, 1950, our Independence Day, occurred the first major earthquake in independent India. It occurred in the rugged mountainous areas just south of the McMahon Line between India and Tibet, and had devastating effects. I am no seismologist, nor do I have even basic understanding of tectonics, but I can understand, in broad terms, what is meant by: 'It was the sixth largest earthquake of the 20th century. It is also the largest known earthquake to have not been caused by an oceanic subduction. Instead, this quake was caused by two continental plates colliding.'

On January 26, 2001, our Republic Day, occurred the Gujarat earthquake, more precisely known as the Bhuj earthquake, at the very time that we were witnessing pageants and parades marking that major anniversary. With a maximum felt intensity of X (*Extreme*) on the Modified Mercalli intensity scale, the earthquake killed about 20,000 and injured some 1,70,000. *Science* is a great journal. In a response to the Bhuj earthquake of January 26, 2001, it is believed that 70 per cent of the Himalayas could experience an extremely powerful earthquake because since the 1950 earthquake enough slippage has taken place for a large earthquake to occur.

I am not going to detail here the tsunami that mutilated life on the coasts of 14 countries on December 26, 2004 because that is about a very different order of catastrophes but will round off my sequence of seismic traumas with some more. On October 8, 2005, an earthquake occurred around 9 in the morning, centred near the city of Muzaffarabad, affecting nearby Balakot in Khyber Pakhtunkhwa and areas of Jammu and Kashmir. The numbers killed are staggering – 86,000 – with an equal number injured and countless millions displaced. It is regarded as one of the deadliest earthquakes in South Asia. The Valley shook again on May 1, 2013. On April 25, two days from today, it will be eight years since Nepal was jolted as no jolt has jolted it since the 1934 earthquake, which we know of as the Bihar earthquake. In a space of 30 seconds, Kathmandu shifted 10 feet southwards. Some 9,000 persons were crushed to death in those seconds. Within five months of that, Afghanistan was shaken by what is called the Hindukush earthquake, killing 400 people.

Earthquakes, we know, can never be prevented; they cannot be predicted (as of now). But we can prepare for them. They are contingencies that can be planned for only in the most general terms, being beyond exact or even approximate measuring. But in all rational calculation, they are contingencies that must be provided for because of (i) high probability; (ii) high financial and physical cost if provided for and incalculably higher if not provided for.

The principle is the same as in any insurance arrangement: the higher the risk, the higher the premium.

We need State interventions and outlays on:
1. Foreclosing and rolling back engineering enterprises that weaken the earth's crust, especially rocky terrain, in the high-seismic risk zones 2, 3, 4 and 5.
2. Superimposing on the existing seismic zonation maps which are really X-ray plates, new, carefully drawn mapped plans for the protection (which can include evacuations, demolitions and rebuilding) of highly vulnerable structures, and assessing the seismic status of high follow-on secondary risk structures like hydel projects and atomic reactors.
3. Setting up a seismic building insurance scheme wherein premiums for insuring against collapse can be offered and encouraged.
4. Unveil a bold and creative architectural norm that makes earthquake proofing in the vulnerable areas a desideratum.
5. Do an assessment of the costs of rescue, temporary sheltering and rehabilitation zone-wise, of dislocated populations.

6. Fast-forward collaboration with countries like Japan and Chile that are experts in the field on earthquake anticipation through sensors and viable architecture nostrums. This would involve expenses on hiring consultants.

The speed with which we rushed relief to Turkey augurs well for our planning betimes for our own seismic safety.

As does the most welcome news that a forthcoming satellite, NISAR, jointly developed by our Indian Space Research Organisation and National Aeronautics and Space Administration of the US, is going to map the earthquake-prone Himalayas 'with unprecedented regularity' and in a way that will not be obstructed by cloudy conditions, thereby giving potential warnings of likely seismic threats.

The Nurse in *Romeo and Juliet* remembers.

Her alter egos in the devastated terrains remember.

But most of us do not.

This amnesia is suicidal.

Anyone looking at the perilously teetering constructions in our Himalayan towns, many of them multi-tiered on stilts, will see in a trice how susceptible they are to collapse in even a 'mild' seismic occurrence. But if anything like what hit Nepal eight years ago were to visit us, god forbid, the consequences would be too terrible to contemplate.

I would like to believe that the IIC's initiative, which had participants from the Government of India's ministry of earth sciences and many young interested seminarists, and the new possibilities opened by NISAR will be an equivalent of Deloney's 'Awake, Awake'.

(*The Telegraph*, April 23, 2023)

85

Gross Valuation

On November 15, according to a subtle calculation, the world's population touched 8 billion. And who was the largest contributor to this figure? Who but…India, adding 177 million people out of the last billion born in the world. This 'contribution' would have been a matter of some embarrassment were it not for some good news that came alongside. The United Nations – no less – said on that day that India's population growth appeared to be stabilising, adding that this showed that India's national policies and health systems, including access to family planning services, were 'working'.

India's population growth is indeed stabilising, with the Total Fertility Rate, which is about the average number of children born per woman in India, having declined from 2.2 to 2.0 – taking India as a whole.

India 'as a whole' stands complimented.

But is India an un-differentiated 'whole'? All of us know it is not. As does the world. The United Nations Population Fund has said 31 of India's states and Union territories (comprising 69.7 per cent of the population) have achieved fertility rates below the replacement level of 2.1 – a good statistic, showing the increased adoption of modern family planning methods. 'This indicates,' the UN organisation has said, 'significant improvements in access to family planning related information and services.' To that we must add, 'in the states and Union territories where the stabilisation has been established'.

The National Family Health Survey-5 tells us that Bihar, Uttar Pradesh, Jharkhand, Manipur and Meghalaya are above the replacement level, that is, they have not done that well. Madhya Pradesh, Rajasthan, Assam, Gujarat, Haryana. Mizoram, Uttarakhand, Arunachal, Chhattisgarh, D&N Haveli, Kerala, Odisha, Telangana and Tamil Nadu are below 2.1 but above 1.7. They may be said to have done quite well. Andhra Pradesh, Himachal Pradesh, Karnataka, Maharashtra, Nagaland, Tripura, Delhi, Punjab, West Bengal and Puducherry are below 1.7 but above 1.4. They may be said to have done very well. Chandigarh, J&K, Lakshadweep, A&N Islands, Goa, Ladakh and Sikkim are below 1.4. They have done extremely well. These 'not that well', 'quite well', 'very well', 'extremely well', are my expressions, not the NFHS's. And a more scientifically calibrated description might be more appropriate.

But this column is not about our family planning performance as such. It is about something that comes from it, something that is worrisome.

Most political watchers are training their eyes on India two years from now – 2024 – when the next general elections are due. But population watchers are looking at four years from now – 2026 – when India's electoral democracy is going to do a 'handhold' with India's demography. A delimitation of the constituencies that will elect members of the Lok Sabha, following the population figures returned by the next decennial census, is to take place in 2026, as envisaged in Article 82 of our Constitution.

More people, the Constitution noted, should mean more MPs. This is sound logic. We ought not to have the same number of MPs – 543 – representing a vastly increased population in the Lok Sabha. Right. 'Higher the number of people per constituency, lower the impact each voter has on Parliamentary representation'. Right. But life moves without the permission of logic.

And so…? A new nationwide delimitation based on the latest population figures.

Such a population-based marking out or rearrangement of constituencies will have the effect it is meant to have: giving more MPs to the states and Union territories that have that many people more. But the same exercise will give markedly less MPs to those that have held their numbers in some check. The word, 'anomaly', seems to have been made for this situation. 'Piquant', as well. Seeing that a delimitation based on census data would create a political anomaly and a civilisational piquancy, Prime Minister Indira Gandhi, through the 42nd Amendment of the Constitution in 1976, froze the process. Prime Minister Vajpayee, through the 84th Amendment, froze it yet again. They were pragmatic. They had a sense that the India that is Bharat is about Bharat, not its most populous chunks. It is this double extension that is to end in 2026.

Going by the census data for 2011 and projections made by the Technical Group formed by the National Commission on Population, ministry of health and family welfare for 2011– 2036, Uttar Pradesh's share in India's population would see an increase by 1.74 percentage points, Bihar's by 1.59 and Rajasthan's by 1.17. Tamil Nadu's share in India's population would see a decline by 2.08 percentage points, undivided Andhra's by 1.46 percentage points, Kerala's by 1.36 percentage points, West Bengal's by 1.03 percentage points.

Broadly speaking, the South, the East and Northeast will have lesser MPs in the Lok Sabha as a result of the 2026 delimitation than they have now. So will Maharashtra, Punjab, Delhi, among others, from the West and North. All of them for the reason that their awareness of the importance of family planning and access to methods for it have been good – an achievement of people-policy-partnership, verily a joint venture.

A delimitation exercise that adds electoral value to one set of states while depleting representative value to another is, to use a phrase coined by Amartya Sen in another context, 'valuationally gross'. It cannot but be seen as an unfair punishment where there should be a deserved reward.

Demography and democracy must go hand in hand in a country which takes electoral representation seriously. In a Republic which sets store by federal principles, this becomes even more important.

There is another dimension to this, as pointed out in a recent symposium called in Delhi by the eminent media personality, author and family welfare communicator par excellence, Rami Chhabra. The delimitation exercise is also going to, ipso facto, deepen the representational disadvantage faced by women, because it so happens that the population-controlling states are also those where the women of India have played a decisive role in that achievement and where their role in the process of elections and representation has been critical.

Delimitation is due; democracy calls for it.

Delimitation must not become debilitation; demography calls out to it.

Two alternatives are available to us:

One, another freeze, this time not for any specific period but till such time as all states achieve population stabilisation.

Two, demographic and statistical experts devise a mathematical model along the lines of the 'Cambridge Compromise' based on a mathematically equitable 'formula' for the apportionment of the seats of the European Parliament among the member states. That formula cannot be applied to our situation as such but needs to be studied so as to customise it for our needs. A fascinating new proposal made by Rami Chhabra is for the reintroduction of double-member constituencies which, if twinned to the proposals for a percentage increase in reservation of seats for women, will give us two 'hits' – no loss of MP numbers plus gain in women's representation.

The population-stabilising states of India that is Bharat must continue to enrich our legislative and parliamentary processes as they have been doing with no penalties having to be paid for their sense of responsibility as to population prudence. And with the Indian woman's voice being heard loud and clear, not above but on a par with the others.

(*The Telegraph*, November 20, 2022)

86

Double Whammy

CHENNAI, BENGALURU AND DELHI are the three cities in which I spend most of my time. So, what happens in them affects me. It becomes part of me. Over June, the sun scorched Chennai. The temperature hovered around 38 degrees Celsius, touching and crossing 40 degrees Celsius on certain days. And in Nature's response to this, the skies above the city rained. At 44.98 mm on June 21, the city recorded its heaviest rainfall in 10 years. Memories of the 2015 floods were disturbingly stoked but to the city's relief, the waters stopped short of touching that dangerous watermark.

June this year was the wettest June Bengaluru has known in full 10 years. At 198.5 mm for the month as a whole, the city was soaking wet. There was a pattern to this: it rained, generally, in the evenings and through much of the night, the slush making it impossible for seniors to go for their walks in the pleasant pre-twilight or in the early morning.

This summer, Delhi went through as many as six heatwaves, the sizzler being in mid-May, when the temperature touched 49 degrees Celsius. On June 8, Delhi's temperature stood at 44 degrees Celsius, described as 'four notches above the season's average'. The city was officially declared as passing through a heatwave.

'We, the people' of Chennai, Bengaluru and Delhi mopped our brows and pitied our collective fates.

But is that all that we should be doing? The climate changes, we do not. I speak of most of us, ensconced in cities.

Climate change has lost no time; climate-change warriors in the shape of whistle-blowers have not either, but 'we the people' have lost time, though we do not quite understand how, by our 'couldn't be bothered' ness.

And through this all, COVID-19 in its new variants, best known by the one called Omicron, quietly, almost sneakily, continued to spread across the country with a never-say-die determination. Chennai and Delhi had more active cases on July 1 this year, 2022, than they did last year at the same time. (The Bengaluru and all-India figures show us being better off this year than last year.) 'The virus is not over', we were told. But underlying that was a subtext that said, 'It is not like what it was, not so widespread or so virulent, but it is there…' The virus's present avatar is a moderate-sounding member of what is essentially a dangerously fundamentalist outfit – the coronavirus. Fewer hospitalisations and fewer deaths due to the 'mild' variant do not mean that the virus has decided to turn soft for all time or that it is not going to be joined by other diseases, including vector-borne ones, triggered by climate change, to swipe us and the rest of the world in ways unbeknown to us now.

Percy Bysshe Shelley has a poem called 'The Cloud', with a famous line in the voice of the cloud: 'I change, but I cannot die.' The novel coronavirus changes but does not die. At least it has not, so far. It is mild, it was said this summer. You get a passing fever, and before you have as much as felt it, the thing has gone. The rate of vaccination-seeking dropped, and manufacturers were left with unlifted stocks. And, most tellingly, the price of masks per piece, fell. We flocked everywhere, mixing and milling as ever, the high and mighty among us, no less than us, ourselves. And did not have any use for the mask.

So, we have before us this phenomenon of bizarre weather patterns and the weird virus acting like allies in a war game against us, the childlike authors and victims of our own ways, lifestyles. While the knowledgeable sensed the danger, knew the glaring truth, did anyone, anywhere in India, speak out about this situation, its portent? By 'anyone', I mean someone in a high seat in India. And by 'anywhere', I mean not in webinars organised by the earnest for the innocent but in national platforms addressed by the powerful for us, the peoplehood of India. Has anyone in authority said to fellow Indians that this 'double whammy' of climate change and the pandemic holds danger, that we better do something about that danger, together, and fast?

One person has been doing that consistently – Dr K. Srinath Reddy, president of the Public Health Foundation of India. In a recent article (*The New Indian Express*, July 8, 2022), he says: '…humanity does not have the luxury of time to deal with these two threats separately and sequentially. It is no mere coincidence that these two mainly anthropogenic disasters are simultaneously demonstrating their sinister strengths through the prolonged Covid pandemic and unprecedented levels of global temperature rise, noted since 2020.'

He ends by sounding a warning: 'The clock is ticking fast on the climate front. COVID-19 has sounded the alarm that many dangers created or accelerated by human folly need a determined response to reduce their impact.'

Wiser words have not been spoken in our pandemic and climate-change times. Nor more timely ones. But when have wise words been heeded by the unwise? Or timely warnings been acted upon by the self-deluded?

So, are we self-condemned to more agonies, more disease and death?

Are the games of power, of wealth and of giddy competition going to absorb us so completely as to make us the chess players of the Oudh of 1857 that Munshi Premchand wrote of in his timeless novella, *Shatranj Ke Khilari*, and Satyajit Ray turned into a great film with the eponymous title? Are we going to go cavorting mindlessly to utter grief?

I await a strong and caring voice that tells us the bitter truth that Dr Reddy has spoken, but this time from the authority of what is called 'Public Office', and corresponding action like, for instance, that of the late Rajkumari Amrit Kaur who, as Union health minister, launched the BCG vaccination programme and initiated the nation's first major mass immunisation programme. Or the late C. Subramaniam who, as Union minister for agriculture, told us that we were living 'ship-to-mouth' and must become self-sufficient in foodgrain production superfast or – starve. The late V.K. Krishna Menon has been seen as the Union defence minister who failed us in the 1962 Sino-Indian war. But as closer observers tell us, it was his tireless work in making India self-sufficient in defence production that helped us get, under Prime Minister Lal Bahadur Shastri, our victory in 1965. Menon was not in office then to receive credit.

We miss such a voice, such an example. Climate change and COVID-19 are dangers that demand of us, the people of India, certain hard self-regulations. Asking those from us is difficult. But explaining why they were not asked of us, when it is too late, will be much more so.

A great song of Elton John's is: 'Sorry seems to be the hardest word'. It should not become the word our generation will hear in a howling desert of futility.

(*The Telegraph*, July 24, 2022)

87

Locked Lives

WE DO NOT – cannot – imagine life in prison. By 'we', I mean those who have not been in prison. Jails, we believe, are for others. A moment's reflection will tell us how short-sighted that is; how self-centred, wrong.

Speaking of India and Indians, the number of offences listed in the Indian Penal Code for which the punishment is imprisonment for life or for different terms, under 'simple' or 'rigorous' categories, is huge. The number and nature of enactments outside the IPC for which arrest and imprisonment are envisaged is also large. For us to have a sense of what life in jail means is eminent good sense. Exactly as it is for us to know what it feels like to be in hospital. Rightly or wrongly, for a real or wrongly suspected condition, or just unwittingly, one could find oneself in prison.

How is one to acquire that '*gyan*' of prison life?

A visit would, of course, be the best method. But jails are not public spaces where one may saunter in and out. One has to have credentials to visit a jail – as I did. The then prime minister, Manmohan Singh, had advised governors to visit 'Correctional Homes' (as jails have very appropriately been renamed) to see if their conditions were aligned with basic human dignity and decency. Visiting the one at Alipore, Calcutta, my first and most unforgettable '*gyan*' came from a sound – the cold and steely clang of the bolt that shut the barred prison gate behind me. I was a privileged visitor and the guards performed that duty with many salutes but I can never forget that sound which said in every language on earth: 'You are now "inside"; the world and everything in it like loved ones' laughter, the aromas of freedom, the taste of options, the invitation to do as you please, is now "outside".'

The detenus, undertrials and convicts I met in different Correctional Homes were interested, of course, in improvements in their conditions. One of them, as I was leaving the one in Alipore, came running to me with what I thought must be a mundane complaint. It was not. He asked me if the prison library could not get a better range of books. Chastened, I told myself, that is Bengal. Bankim's, Rabindranath's, Sarat's, Mahasweta's Bengal. And I was not surprised to see that 'prison reform' in the state of West Bengal had gone to the extent of getting prisoners to take part in staging Tagore's plays, a production of *Tasher Desh* travelling to Delhi and being staged in the capital's Siri Fort auditorium.

But while every inmate of a jail would want better books, better food, better treatment, what she or he really craves for is to be out, to be released, to get *mukti*. And that is what a convict just cannot get, pre-term. An undertrial, however, can, if qualified for it under a provision introduced in the Criminal Procedure Code – Section 436A – by an ordinance in 2005. This basically says that if any prisoner being tried, in other words, an undertrial prisoner, a 'UTP', for an offence not punishable by death has undergone detention up to one-half of the maximum period of imprisonment specified for that offence, that undertrial prisoner shall be released by the court on a personal bond with or without sureties. And, further, that no undertrial prisoner shall be detained for more than the maximum period provided for that offence.

Section 436A is an extraordinarily mitigative instrument in the hands of the justice system. It is a sagacious provision that humanises penology, sends a beam of hope into the grey dank of a prison cell.

As on January 1, 2021, there were 3,71,848 UTPs in India's 36 states and Union territories, amounting to more than 75 per cent of the total number of human beings in Indian prisons. The numbers today are unlikely to be very different. Of these, those 'eligible' for 'premature' release under the 'one-half of the maximum period of imprisonment' is very small. Those actually released, even smaller.

The 'beam' of hope is slender and weak. The intention behind the 2005 ordinance has not been served. Where is the snag? It is for state governments, being in charge of prisons, to act on S.436A in their wisdom. But there has to be such a thing as a national propulsion for action for implementing the spirit of the new Section. Is that propulsion there? Are punitive instincts stronger than human ones?

On this Amrit Mahotsav of India's freedom, a relook at the scope of S.436A would be apposite. I would urge that 'one-half of the maximum period' be modified by a new yardstick to the advantage of the UTPs. And advisories be issued to state governments to ensure that not a single UTP eligible for 'premature' release is denied that release. S.436A is meant to be celebrated, not deflated, activated, not frustrated.

This is also the occasion to celebrate another exceptional arrangement pertaining to prisoners. In 2008, India and Pakistan agreed to exchange lists twice every year, on January 1 and July 1, of civilian prisoners in each other's custody. This came from the fourth round of 'composite dialogues' then in progress between the two governments. The late Pranab Mukherjee was our minister for external affairs then and his Pakistani counterpart was Shah Mahmood Qureshi. Our then high commissioner to Pakistan, the late and absolutely brilliant Satyabrata Pal, signed the agreement for India while the then Pakistan high commissioner to India, Shahid Malik, signed for his country.

The exchange of lists has been happening regularly despite all the fluctuations in our bilateral ties, including the deep lows caused by terrorism. On January 1, this year, India and Pakistan exchanged, through diplomatic channels, simultaneously at New Delhi and Islamabad, the lists of civilian prisoners and fishermen in their custody under the provisions of the 2008 Agreement. India handed over a list of 282 Pakistan civilian prisoners and 73 fishermen in India's custody to Pakistan and Pakistan shared a list of 51 civilian prisoners and 577 fishermen in its custody who are Indians or are believed to be Indians. The next exchange is due on July 1.

The assumption of office by a new government in Pakistan coinciding with the 75th anniversary of Independence in both countries gives them an opportunity to infuse a new energy into this essentially humanitarian situation and exchange more than lists – exchange prisoners. And, withal, in the course of this salutary process, vouchsafe the long overdue return to India of Kulbhushan Jadhav.

Going a step further, a similar exercise done between India and Bangladesh as well would make the Amrit Mahotsav live up to its name.

Age-senior readers of this column will recall the 1961 Hindi film, *Kabuliwala*, based on Tagore's great story (1892) of that name. Manna Dey sings hauntingly in it Prem Dhawan's song – 'Ay mere pyare watan…Ay mere bichhare chaman…' – for Balraj Sahni. The India–Pakistan Agreement of 2008 is the diplomatic embodiment of that *arazu*, that *abaru*. It must come alive this year.

(*The Telegraph*, April 24, 2022)

88

Honouring the Word

NO TEACHER TEACHES BUT learns so much more in the process. My students had been tasked to write essays on the broad subject of India's nationhood. There was not a single essay from which I did not learn something. One of them, on tribal India, contained a memorable quote from a speech given in the Constituent Assembly on December 19, 1946 by the Munda leader, Jaipal Singh. 'I rise,' he said, 'to speak on behalf of… the original people of India…As a jungli…The whole history of my people is one of continuous exploitation and dispossession by the non-aboriginals of India punctuated by rebellions and disorder, and yet I take Pandit Jawaharlal Nehru at his word. I take you all at your word that now we are going to start a new chapter, a new chapter of Independent India where there is equality of opportunity, where no one would be neglected…'

What I was moved most by in that deeply affecting quotation was the faith, the simple honest trust, reposed by the tribal leader in one man's word – Jawaharlal Nehru's word: 'I take Pandit Jawaharlal Nehru at his word.' And then, broadening his faith, 'I take you all at your word…' The essay made me reflect on 'the word' today, the value, traction, worth of a word that is given by the authority of the State.

The Ayodhya Canto in Tulsidas's *Ramacharitamanas* has the line spoken by Dasarath: '*Raghukula riti sada chali ayi, prana jahu baru bachanu na jayi.*' Translated by A.G. Atkins, it means: 'Tis a known rule in Raghu's line, one naught can shake; Life may go, but his word a man may never break.'

Three instances of 'the word' given by the Indian State, post-Independence, came to mind. In two of these the word was kept and one in which it was not.

In the first instance, the word was almost betrayed. It occurred in 1948 when the question arose of the division of the cash balance between India and Pakistan. India was required to and bound itself to pay a sum of Rs 75 crore to Pakistan as its proportionate cash asset. India had paid Rs 20 crore in the first instalment and was set to pay the second instalment of Rs 55 crore when Pakistan invaded Kashmir. Nehru and Patel favoured holding the amount back. Would Pakistan not use the money to purchase arms to use against

India? The Governor General, Mountbatten, and Gandhi, both prevailed on the government to make good the payment. Imprudent idealism? Inviting the smirk of the cynic and the snarl of the jingoist, one should say honour won. The honour of the plighted word. And India has a huge moral advantage logged there, in its book of accounts with Pakistan.

The second major word of honour was given by the prime minister, Nehru, on the floor of the Lok Sabha on August 7, 1959. This was on the subject of India's official language. The south, Tamil Nadu in particular, had been disturbed at what seemed to it like Hindi imperialism. Nehru said: '...for an indefinite period – I do not know how long – I should have, I would have, English as an associate, additional language...as an alternative language as long as people require it and the decision for that I would leave not to the Hindi-knowing people, but to the non-Hindi-knowing people.' This was the polar opposite of majoritarianism and Madras was assuaged. A year after Nehru's death, in 1965, suspicions of Hindi imposition rose again and riots broke out in Madras. The prime minister, Lal Bahadur Shastri, reiterated the assurance. English, he said, would continue as the second official language as long as non-Hindi-speaking people wanted it. This Nehru–Shastri word of honour is cited every time there is apprehension in Tamil Nadu over the intentions of Hindi enthusiasts. And Delhi is obliged to say there is no change in the assurance given. The Nehru–Shastri word has not only thereby served to keep Tamil Nadu reassured but has in fact blunted the resistance of the people of the state towards Hindi as a language per se.

The third major instance of the word and its honour arose over the princely states of India which covered 48 per cent of the area of undivided India and nearly 30 per cent of its population. Defending the privy purse, the author of the integration of the states, Vallabhbhai Patel, said in the Constituent Assembly: 'Let us do justice to them...The rulers have now discharged their part of the obligations by transferring all ruling powers...The main part of our obligation under these agreements is to ensure that the guarantee given by us in respect of privy purses are fully implemented. Our failure to do so would be a breach of faith and seriously prejudice the stabilisation of the new order.' Whatever the socialist in Nehru may have felt about the princely order, the man of honour in him did not cavil at the purses. But the prime minister, Indira Gandhi, clearly displeased by the princes' rallying round the Swatantra Party, abolished the privy purses in 1970. The total amount payable to the princes at the time was only 4 crore rupees a year. Patel's word of honour was relinquished at the altar of political hubris in the garb of democratic equity.

The State's 'word' keeps being given.

Addressing a gathering of Christian leaders at Vigyan Bhavan, New Delhi, in February 2015, the prime minister, Narendra Modi, extolled the 2008 inter-faith 'Hague Declaration' on human rights and announced: '[S]peaking for India, and for my government, I declare that my government stands by every word of the above declaration. My government will ensure that there is complete freedom of faith and that everyone has the undeniable right to retain or adopt the religion of his or her choice without coercion or undue influence. My government will not allow any religious group, belonging to the majority or the minority, to incite hatred against others, overtly or covertly. Mine will be a government that gives equal respect to all religions.'

A 'tweet' is hardly the vehicle for a word of honour but if the prime minister tweets a word of honour, the word becomes more important than its vehicle. On World Press Freedom Day, last May, Modi tweeted, 'Our unwavering support towards a free and vibrant press, which is vital in a democracy.'

Both these – guaranteeing freedom of faith and freedom of speech – are our prime minister's words of honour. They are words of honour in the highest Jaipal Singh sense of the term. Our prime minister knows more than anyone else that many things have happened, deeply troubling and shameful, that have belied his words of honour. Is it too late, even futile, to say, like the Munda leader did to Nehru, '…and yet I take Prime Minister Narendra Modi at his word'? His word of honour needs to be recognised for what it is. That, in his own words, is 'vital in a democracy'.

If not in the Jaipal Singh–Nehru sense of honour, for Nehru is outside his mind's chemistry, then in Sardar Patel's sense of honour, can our prime minister be mindful of the moral vacuity of a 'breach of faith'? And can he reflect on Tulsidas's lines: '…*prana jahu baru bachanu na jayi*?

(*The Telegraph*, July 2, 2017)

89

Time for Caution

THIS DAY – NOVEMBER 1, 2015 – marks the 80th anniversary of the first staging in London of T.S. Eliot's *Murder in the Cathedral*.

Perhaps the best-known English play post-Shakespeare, it was written in early 1935 when fear, a sickening fear, of single-leader absolutism hung over the world.

A paranoid and power-drunk Stalin had begun his brutal purges in Russia. With thousands being killed and transported to labour camps, Russia was acrid with the blood of imaginary and real opponents spilt by his manic dictatorship. Unable, it is said, to live with this reality, Stalin's wife committed suicide.

Likewise, the ghoulishness of Hitler's Germany was revealing itself. Anti-Jewish riots occurred in Berlin that summer, in which several Jews were severely beaten. And on September 15 and November 14, 1935, the infamous Nuremberg Laws defined Reich citizenship in terms of 'blood', like this:

1. A person belongs to Germany only if of 'kindred blood'.
2. Jews are not of German blood.

Eliot wrote *Murder* in dramatic verse that intolerant year.

The protagonist of the play, Thomas À Becket, Archbishop of Canterbury, was murdered four days after Christmas inside the cathedral in Canterbury in 1170. Historical accounts of the growing rift between King Henry II and his once-favoured Archbishop point to the growing unease of the monarch with the priest's independence and the priest's disapproval of the monarch's authoritarian rule. Hilaire Belloc has described their rift as 'the quarrel between the Soul and the State'. There are many variations of a rhetorical line attributed to Henry II that are said to have prompted four of his Knights to go to Canterbury and kill Becket. The best known of these is 'Who will rid me of this troublesome priest?' Others have 'meddlesome' and 'pestilential' instead of 'troublesome'. But all attributions suggest Henry's intention. They do not reflect a direct command.

The Knights were not praised by the King, nor were they punished. Becket, on the other hand, was not only canonised a couple of years later but, more importantly, went on to become a legend and a martyr in popular lore. That he was no unblemished 'soul', having wielded with seeming enjoyment official power as chancellor himself, is no longer of any relevance. The fact of his murder is what has remained alive and has made him the symbol of an individual's opposition to authority, of courageous dissent.

Eliot's own move to Roman Catholicism was, doubtless, at the heart of his turning to the Becket theme. But there can also be no doubt that the rise of two forms of authoritarianism in Europe during the early and mid-1930s gave Eliot the contextual stimulus for writing this play.

There were in the original draft of *Murder* some lines which the producer felt would not work on stage. Dropping them, Eliot incorporated some of them in 'Burnt Norton', one of the Four Quartets. This has the famous Eliot lines on 'Time present and time past', one of which is: 'Time past and time future/ What might have been and what has been/ Point to one end, which is always present.'

Becket was. Becket is. Becket will always be.

Dissent was, dissent is and dissent will always be unwelcome to a majoritarian State. And when that State becomes intolerant, it becomes authoritarian.

We are not there yet. Not yet.

And, *inshAllah*, may we never get there.

But there are on the terraced palate of dictatorial appetites gradients where foretaste lies, where aftertaste finds rest. And there are cooks around the royal table, cook-mates and waiters, waiting to produce, to proffer and to please with *Voila*! what they believe is, 'in his mind', the chosen dish.

Either impunity or immunity, real or perceived, has parasolled events such as the Ghar Wapsi movement, Christmas re-christened Governance Day, broadsides against Vice President Hamid Ansari for not attending the prime minister's yoga rally, more vituperative attacks on him for his alleged 'communalism' in supporting reservation for Muslims, Aurangzeb Road's renaming, demands for banning beef, meat-sales suspension on certain days, the murder of rationalist writers, the Dadri lynching, the clamour against the book launch of the Pakistani political writer, Khurshid Kasuri, the ink-blackening of Sudheendra Kulkarni and of the Jammu and Kashmir independent MLA, Engineer Rashid, the blocking of Ghulam Ali's recital in Mumbai, the agitation against BCCI's discussions with its Pakistan counterparts, and the steady and subtle redirections being attempted in cultural and academic institutions that are meant to be autonomous.

The list given above is far from exhaustive.

It does not include the relentless harassing of individual dissenters through the social media and, more directly and invasively, through e-mail and even telephones. 'Go to Pakistan' is the common mantra, accompanied by abuse that belongs to the world of obscene speech, with a super-speciality in the invoking of parentage abuse, incest and sexually transmitted diseases.

What is deeply troublesome about this 'Becketising' of dissent is not just its traceless patronage but its endless fallout. In other words, the unending spiral of a minority backlash. Intolerance is not a majoritarian monopoly. Patience has its limits everywhere. And goodness knows there is more than one kind of mischief-maker and potential disrupter of the peace among India's diverse and complex Muslim communities. And who can afford to underestimate the propensity of India-haters in Pakistan and Bangladesh to arm disaffection in India with the technologies of chaos and death?

The murder of an 'anti-beef' activist from the Bajrang Dal runs to a script.

It can duplicate and replicate itself everywhere, without limit, without remorse.

What we are really staring at in India is the prospect of communal tensions boiling over and becoming communal riots in which violent bloodthirsty minds that direct the deeds stay unknown and unseen. Let there be no mistake about this: the inciters of communal frenzies in India are in a partnership. They are allies, friends, bosom friends. One may sport a tuft and a *tilak*, the other a flowing beard. One may chant the Vedas, the other intone the Quran. But both extremists, in moving farther and farther from each other, actually end up bumping each other's back and, turning, embrace in a common cause: hatred. And the power that hatred gives them over the hating flock.

I may also be permitted a visual imagining.

So easy it is, so utterly simple, to create a rumour, and a little tremor even by means of a blast or a knife-cut in a place of religious voltage during a season of festivities, that the vendors of hate will not want to deny themselves the pleasure. The abscess has never been as distended as now, for the slightest graze, to open it.

And if, *na karey Narayan*, that misery of miseries were to happen, the chain of reprisals will require superhuman power to control.

And who will be responsible, who?

The unspoken word when speech was needed.

The un-extended arm when help was needed.

The un-shed tear when grief was needed.

More than even these, what will be responsible is the howling absence of reprimand, uttered loud for all to hear, that India is not to be trifled with, her fragile calm not to be tampered with, her privacies are to be respected, her fevers becalmed, her fires to be put out, not fanned.

But if 'liberal India' were to merely wait for that word, that High Reprimand, and it never comes, it will be responsible as well, for not having seen the danger and done what we could have, betimes to caution, to warn and to strive.

(*The Telegraph*, November 1, 2015)

90

There Is Struggle Ahead

A.K. Ramanujan ends his poem titled 'Prayers to Lord Murugan' with these lines: 'Lord of answers, / cure us at once / of prayers.'

India's conscience-stricken pluralists have a secular equivalent of prayers – faith in 'good sense prevailing over the communal virus'. The time has come for them to cure themselves at once of this naive faith. The virus has no intention of letting itself being prevailed upon.

The same year that Ramanujan's publisher stopped selling his thought-churning essay 'Three Hundred Ramayanas' – 2011 – the Delhi-based Shiksha Bachao Andolan Committee went to court against the publisher of Wendy Doniger's acclaimed work *The Hindus: An Alternative History*. The grounds were similar to those advanced against Ramanujan: Hindus felt 'humiliated' by the book, which 'denigrated Hindu traditions'. A little over two years later, in an out-of-court settlement, the publisher has withdrawn the book from the Indian market.

Book-bullies are a major strain of the communal virus. They go for the authors, publishers, book-stores and galleries with the glee and rapacity of a conquering horde. In likening Doniger's detractors to the Taliban and describing the out-of-court settlement as 'atrocious', the Union minister Jairam Ramesh did show a backbone, but one that is rare in politics and becoming rarer. The historian Ramachandra Guha has done what was expected of him. He has said that Doniger's publisher should have taken the matter on appeal to the next higher court. It chose not to do so. Why? Because, like everyone else, publishers too are 'adjusting' to the tyranny of perceived hurt, feigned injury. They are submitting, like most of us, to the 'inevitable' of a denominational take-over of India. A spine can be faulted for turning noodle only if the rest of society is vertebral.

So the loss of this individual battle against the 'virus' can be said to have been lost. Scholars of Indian history – its sociology, its faith traditions, its liberal instincts – will take the Doniger episode as a sign that the epidemic is spreading, getting stronger; also, that the virus is now being described as something that is not only not to be resisted but as something to be embraced. A self-styled Shiksha Bachao Andolan calls *The Hindus* a bad book, and so it becomes a bad book. Calling it a bad book becomes good nationalism, calling it an anti-India book becomes a pro-India position, calling it 'denigrating' of Hinduism amounts to valorising Hinduism.

Dubbing a work, any work, as derogatory of Hinduism or subversive of national pride serves three purposes. First, it stokes the fire at the Hindutva *havan*. Second, it bonds those who take the objectors at their word with the Hindutva priesthood. Third, and most important, it takes attention away from issues of criticality like gender justice, domestic violence, *khap* tyranny, honour killings, malnutrition, migrant-labour exploitation, the loot of natural resources and corruption. The Doniger episode, like the Ramanujan one before it, is about more than a publisher's acceptance of the subversion of domain integrity. It is yet another indication of Indian society's innocent neglect of the subversion of its genetic integrity.

For these many decades since Independence, the communal rhetoric has been negative – the Congress is pseudo-secular, the Left is disconnected, Trinamul is opportunistic; all of them appease the Muslim minority, flatter the Christian minority, use the Sikh, Dalit-Buddhist and other minorities to keep 'us', the real sons and daughters of Bharat Mata, down. Now that communal rhetoric has turned 'positive' – forget all the others, they do not count. India is Hindu, we are Hindu, we are India. And we now have a leader of leaders who is what we are: Hindu, Hindu Indian. He is the turban on our head, the tilak on our forehead, the string on our wrist, the ring on our finger. To the jargon of 'Bharat Mata in danger' (in the hands, among others, of writers like Ramanujan and Doniger) is now added a fatherland vocabulary, where a leader is being fantasised in the shape of all that Nehru was not, and his Congress successors have not, and can never be. He is Maharana Pratap, Chhatrapati Shivaji, Krishna Deva Raya.

He is also Swami Vivekananda, he is Sardar Patel. He is more. He knows his technology. He knows his commerce. He either dams rivers or bridges them. He is going to propel us into superpowerhood.

Max Mueller has said in his essay 'The Movement for Religious Reform in India Inaugurated by Raja Rammohun Roy': '[The Indian] people are ready to be led, but they expect a leader to lead them.' Our agitations, protests and rallies are populated by people not just 'ready' but wanting, eager and, in fact, impatient to be led. And since the people in their different pockets expect a leader to lead them, they will find them, not always wisely, but always earnestly, sometimes worshipfully.

The challenge lies in what Babasaheb Ambedkar said. 'You must know,' he said with his extraordinary perspicacity, 'that your man is really great before you start worshipping him.' And he added, 'This, unfortunately, is not an easy task. For these days, with the Press in hand, it is easy to manufacture great men. Carlyle used a happy phrase when he described the great men of history as so many Bank Notes. Like Bank Notes they represent gold. What we have to see is that they are not forged notes.'

A relentless exposure of air-pumped masculinity is what is now needed, and alternatives found, according to one's best lights. The electoral choice is one choice ahead of us. The larger choice, which is linked to the electoral choice, is that of our unhappy land's goals for its joint peoplehood. I cannot subscribe to the view that, like all viruses, let the Hindutva virus have its five-day (read five-year) run, and it will exhaust itself. This is the Ramanujan 'prayer', which we must cure ourselves of at once. For the slouch towards the Bethlehem of our unique peoplehood is not just electoral or even political. It is cultural in a very deep sense. It seeks to change the axis of our national identity, converting a society that is inherently plural and therefore co-existentially accommodative into one that is essentially intolerant, punitive and non-inclusively authoritarian. The Ramanujan and Doniger cases are signposts to the path of determined resistance for those who look upon the Indian republic as a home to its people of varying strengths, not a gymnasium for its six-ab obsessors.

There is struggle ahead.

(*The Telegraph*, February 19, 2014)

91

Ill Fares the Land

AND TREMBLING, SHRINKING FROM the spoiler's hand, / Far, far away thy children leave the land. / Ill fares the land, to hastening ills a prey, / Where wealth accumulates, and men decay.

Oliver Goldsmith's knowledge of India must have been less than minimal. And he was certainly not thinking of a future Hindostan when he wrote those lines in 'The Deserted Village'. But I have often thought of his depiction as made for our times, our Indian times.

Near the flat my wife and I have rented in Chennai, three 'independent' houses have been given over to high-rise. They were not old patrician buildings whose demise is to be regretted aesthetically. The new ones coming in their places are not hideously ugly, either, as they could well have been. A lovely copper-pod tree in one of those houses which could have yielded to built-up square footage has been spared the axe, an incredible thing. So there is nothing remarkable about this landscape morphing, and certainly nothing to be very regretful about.

But this construction triplet has brought something else to the suburb which is new. It has brought unheard-of dialects of Hindi to a part of Chennai where only Tamil and English held sway. Construction workers from the coal-mining tracts of central and eastern India have set up camp in Tiruvanmiyur and, with seemingly effortless ease, are raising buildings, floor by floor, for people with whom they do not have even a language in common.

These are the migrant workers we speak and write about, the flotsam of India's booming construction industry and the jetsam of India's urban sprawl.

In Coonoor, the lovely little hill town in the Nilgiris, where we own a cottage, I can hear the same east India dialects being spoken alongside Tamil and the languages that the local Badaga and Toda speak. If the Roerichs could paint as they did in the Himalaya, an Elwin could study and write as he did in the Northeast, a Ruskin Bond be as brilliantly prodigious in fiction as he is from Mussoorie, why should the daughter or son of a migrant from Chhattisgarh in the cool climes of the Nilgiris one day not attain artistic renown? Why not?

It is not just an east to south thing. Palagummi Sainath recently told a Chennai audience that labourers from Tiruchengode in Tamil Nadu are working in deep-bore well projects in Maharashtra.

In far-off Dandi, Gujarat where I was visiting not long ago, I asked a question in Gujarati of some people sitting by the beachfront. They did not answer and said, instead, in broken Hindi that they were from literally the other end of the country, Odisha, brought there by 'builders'. That was a stand-alone English word they used.

'Builders of Modern India' is the name of a very good series of books launched by the publications division of the Government of India. They were written by well-known writers about some great Indians, foundationally great figures from history.

The phrase's initiators would not have thought that the metaphorical 'builder' which they had in mind would be recognised by a progressively regressing number of readers and that the word would be famous in a very different, very literal context in 21st-century India. They would not have expected the word to be used in its original English form domiciled in dialects spoken across the country to mean the man who buys up houses, rents steel jaws to crunch them down, human hands to pile brick on brick, shoulders to move rod on iron rod, heads to cart bag on cement bag, engages architects and engineers to raise in their place tall, vertical structures that resemble a many-eyed, many-eared, many-mouthed mammoth, or winding roads, looping bridges or whatever. For those who, by the motion of their limbs, actually make these structures, as opposed to those who finance them, 'builder' also means the man who transports them from their villages, with no contractual agreements, some hundreds of railway track miles away, as in an earlier era, men and women were shipped under indenture or similar systems to Ceylon, Mauritius, South Africa, Fiji among other destinations.

What links today's migrant workers to those early *girmitiya* (Indian workers translocating under 'agreements' to work on mines and plantations overseas) is that their move is voluntarily involuntary. It has a very willed fatalism to it, a collaborative self-trapping.

At one level we can celebrate the linguistic bouquet that has formed of itself in these places. Just as Tamil, Telugu and Bhojpuri came to be heard on far-off shores as early as the 19th century, eastern dialects of Hindi being heard in Chennai, Coonoor and Dandi or Tamil being heard in Maharashtra in our times can be a happy thing. Perhaps, as in those lands, many a patois will grow out of the cross-pollinating contact between the arriving language with the host language. As could a new and lively English. I can, in fact, envision a novel in English written by a descendent of Chhattisgarhi migrants, titled *Builder*. These very migrants could well throw up a V.S. Naipaul.

But before that happens and as wealth changes hands from seller to buyer to builder to broker, and accumulates in all these hands, many persons and many lives, many traditions and many skills will decay beyond recognition. That the population of farmers is going down alarmingly is now too well known to be reiterated. But 'and men decay' happening to thousands upon thousands of workers moving from one part of India to another, one form of life and livelihood to another, is no less appalling than what happened to *girmitiya* two centuries ago. The only saving grace is that there are no 'deaths on voyage'.

At a superficial level, there is a kind of cheerfulness about the translocated workers, as might be expected in an army garrison going to battle, but underlying all that, especially in the disoriented mothers and infant children, there is a wan dazedness, a sense of deprivation so deep and encompassing as to resemble bereavement. In the criss-cross of an impoverished humanity searching for what is called 'hand-cash', a great upheaval of life is taking place.

Pather Panchali is being re-enacted every day, with this difference – that the families leaving their homesteads are not going to find a Bibhutibhushan to write about them, though a wannabe Satyajit Ray may well try making a film out of their misery, as part of the same accumulation of wealth.

Will this large slice of India have Aadhaar cards? More pertinently for 2014, will it have the vote? Energetic administrations might accomplish the near-impossible and swing into action to provide it with one. But who will the decaying vote for? The 'builder', with a freebie thrown in? Fortunately or unfortunately for them, migrant workers are not vote banks. Whose loss is that? Not theirs. But as to what they are banks of, in terms of craft traditions, farming skills, agricultural, fishing and climate knowledge, music and dance heritage, we are neither aware of nor concerned about. And this is a national decay to which the accumulations of the nation's (read 'builder's') wealth will bear rich testimony.

(*The Telegraph*, November 3, 2013)

92

Totem and Taboo

IN NOVEMBER 1948, A debate of some moment took place in our Constituent Assembly. It was on a name for the new India, the Republic of India, that was to come into being on January 26, 1950. The occasion for the debate was provided by the draft for the first article of our Constitution – Article 1(1), which defined India. B.R. Ambedkar, as chairman of the drafting committee had proposed, 'India, that is Bharat, shall be a Union of States.'

The erudite professor, Shibbanlal Saksena, suggested on November 15, 1948, that Part I should say, 'The name of the Union shall be BHARAT.' Meeting again almost a year later, on September 18, 1949, the Constituent Assembly took up H.V. Kamath's new amendment proposing that 'Bharat or, in the English language, India, shall be a Union of States.' 'Is it necessary to have all this?' Ambedkar asked, 'I do not understand the purpose of it…' Kamath's amendment putting 'Bharat' before 'India' was then put to vote. The assembly divided by a show of hands. Kamath's amendment was lost, 38 supporting Kamath, 51 supporting Ambedkar's formulation. A difference of 13 hands gave us 'India, that is Bharat', rather than 'Bharat, that is India'.

The difference was vital. India was the reality that subsumed Bharat, its dream. We live in the real even as we conjure the ideal. India was about life where the common man and woman – Hindu, Muslim, Sikh, Buddhist, Christian, agnostic – face inflation with poverty, extravagance with squalor, corruption with defeat and where he and she have to be hassled at each step, whether it is for an electric connection, a change of name in the electric meter, a birth certificate, a land-mutation, a driving licence, by men with the authority to delay if not deny what is due and where men and women have to face cheats and conmen posing as facilitators. That is where rage resides. Bharat is where the affluent and privileged – the two going together – open the doors of malls and multiplexes, where bullet trains link the rich with the richer, where spaceships are launched from, missiles tested, submarines built, and also where yogic asanas are taught, indigenous noodles made to substitute ones with 'foreign'-sounding names, where methods of attaining bliss and calm are prescribed.

Ambedkar's formulation adopted by the Constituent Assembly is being questioned today, nearly 70 years later, by those who want to rewire the reality of India and Hindustan using the leaden batteries of a spurious 'Bharat'. Saying or not saying '*Vande Mataram*' and '*Bharat Mata Ki Jai*' is being made a test of patriotism. Who is anyone to test anyone else's patriotism in a republic? '*Agar Bharat mein rehna hoga to Vande Mataram kahna hoga*' is a form of bullying alien to the spirit of our Constitution and wholly unworthy of the values of a republic.

'*Bharat Mata Ki Jai!*' intoned from the fullness of one's free heart is one thing, but when made to lobotomise Article 1 of the Constitution, drop 'India', banish 'Hind', it becomes menacing. No Indian can menace another Indian in India's name. No one can choreograph Bharat into a goddess figure with 'fierce aspects' in order to turn the Republic of India into a theocratic nation state.

Bharat resonates with every fibre of our being in Lata Mangeshkar's words: '*Koyi Sikh koyi Jaat Marathal koyi Gurkha koyi Madaraasil Sarahad pe maranewalal har veer thaa Bhaaratavaasi.*' Bharat Mata resonates no less in Atal Bihari Vajpayee's tribute to Nehru on the great leader's death: '*Bharat Mata aaj shok magnaa hai – uskaa sabse laadlaa rajkumar so gayaa…surya ast ho gayaa, taaron kii chhayaa mein humen apna marg dhundhna hai.*'

But it does *not*, and should never, resonate with all Indians when some hate-filled goon demands that another Indian must say Bharat, not Hind or India and, foaming at his mouth, asks her or him to declaim '*Bharat Mata Ki Jai*' when she or he believes equally and interchangeably in '*Jai Hind*'. It not only does not resonate with them, but it also positively raises the gall in them. They will not abandon Bharat, Bharat Mata or Vande Mataram to be abducted.

Nations, great and small, have anthems, emblems, mottos, flags. States that slip under a supremo's clawed clasp or the vice-like grip of a 'supremo ideology', a 'supremo-ism', a 'supremo cult' including a fake 'supremo goal' to be a superpower or a regional power or, if not even that, at the very least, an internal gas chamber, add to those symbols of State another – a national totem. We who have grown with Bharat and Bharat Mata alongside Hindustan *Zindabad* and *Jai Hind* cannot allow *Bharat Mata* to become a totem, cannot allow that golden heritage to be reduced to a blade of the cheapest tin. Our forebears could be slapped with sedition for saying '*Bharat Mata Ki Jai*'. We cannot be slapped with sedition for not saying it.

Also, let us not forget that totems and taboos go together. When something prescribes, lays down at the cost of dire consequences, that 'something' also forbids. What do the *Bol Bharat Mata Ki Jai* prescribers taboo? They taboo sharing the spaces of democratic choice, republican optionality, national liberties. In the name of order, they prescribe conformism and taboo individuality. In the name of nationalism, they prescribe jingoism and taboo self-criticism. In the name of the nation, they prescribe allegiance and taboo thought. They are not nationalists, they are tattooists. They want to scald and brand humans into herds. In the name of statesmanship, they want helmsmanship. In the name of a leader, they want a herder.

If we look closely at the person wanting Bharat and Bharat Mata to become a pair of totems and tattoos, we will find, first of all, that the person is a he, a man singularly un-agonised about caste oppression, the grim future of India's politically organised but socially and economically discriminated Dalits, her politically orphaned and socially un-understood tribals, about human rights, civil liberties, the rule of law. The question does not even arise of the *Bol Bharat Mata Ki Jai* man worrying about global warming, about the fragility of our water aquifers and wetlands. But most important of all, the '*Bol Bharat Mata Ki Jai Varnaa...Dekh...*' man is not going to be concerned about the torments of '*Bharat Mata Ki Beti*'. He would not want Manna Dey's '*Ay merey pyare vatan*' to be invoked because it sings not of 'his' kind of *mata* but the *ma* whose ocean heart clasps the *nanhi si beti*. He will not want Mehboob Khan's immortal film, *Mother India*, to be screened afresh because that is about a Mother *India*, played by someone named Nargis.

The game plan is simple: let the hired or wired hotheads put the fear of the bully into the dissenter, make her or him cower under the filth of abuse, the sludge of calumny, the scare of 'action'. And why? So that via the headiness of religious frenzy, a power cabal gets established in the nation state and a fanned-up fanaticism keeps age-old oppressions unchecked - caste oppression, religious oppression, class oppression and above all, male oppression of not just the female but of the dissenting Indian, female and male.

Making '*Bharat Mata Ki Jai*' a 'safety password' is about road-rolling diversity, opiating discontent, anaesthetising misery. It is about robotising a people that are, by instinct and temperament, open to charismatic leadership, so that they listen and obey, act and react to signals and slogans, signs and signage like so many digits. To make 'Bharat' an escutcheon and '*Bharat Mata Ki Jai*' a compulsory battle cry is to make Bharat an eternal zone of combat where there is always 'the Other', that being of course the one who is discontented with the prevailing order, dissimilar and dissenting.

Bharat Mata is far too valuable a concept, too valuable, to be turned into something that excludes and threatens huge chunks, large glacial masses, massive tectons of her offspring, the Peoplehood of India. We cannot let a fatherland schemata of pernicious biases stage a coup in our motherland. We whose national motto has come from the Upanishads, whose emblem from Ashoka, whose anthem from Tagore and whose Constitution have risen, after careful labour, from the integrated will of a people, cannot be doped into becoming a totem raj.

(*The Telegraph*, April 3, 2016)

93

Civilised Killing

IS ANYTHING NEW ABOUT this 'new' year for us? Not in our way of punishing the guilty, or those thought to be guilty. Death has been ordered by the Ruler of India, over centuries. The way of executing has changed, but executing stays. As we enter 2016, it is instructive to see how and where the death penalty stood in 1516, 1616, 1716, 1816 and 1916. And where it stands, or how it drops into the scaffold's dark well, in 2016.

1516

Sikandar Lodi is enthroned in Delhi. A Persian scholar, he attempts versifications under the effete pen name of Gulrukhi, 'Of Flower-like Countenance'. He is fond of creating gardens, beautiful buildings. But he is a bigot and inflicts bigoted punishments. Notoriously, he has a sadhu called Bodhan burnt alive for saying Islam and Hindu dharma are equally acceptable to the creator.

Krishnadevaraya is king of Vijayanagara. A strong administrator, he is proud to be personally and politically tough. He believes his task is to preserve the *dharma*. But he 'maintains the dharma by killing'. Fernao Nuniz, a Portuguese traveller, says of Krishnadevaraya's punishments: 'Nobles who become traitors are sent to be impaled alive on a wooden stake thrust through the belly…'

Hundred years on, in 1616

The Mughal emperor, Jahangir, loves the arts, miniature painting, animals and birds. Mansur, the greatest of miniaturists, paints Jahangir's birds including the rare dodo. Jahangir's court dazzles. But he shows nothing of his father's – the great Akbar's – pluralism when he orders Guru Arjan Dev, the fifth Sikh Guru, to be executed. The Guru is tortured before being killed. Jahangir has earlier had his rebellious son, Khusrau, blinded. A painting of great sadness shows Khusrau being taken on elephant back past a row of his friends and followers impaled on stakes.

Vijayanagara is in its last gasp. The new king Sriranga II, in a palace coup led by Jagga Raya, is thrown into Vellore Fort prison with his entire family and put to death. The practice of royalty murdering its own kind is now established in India's north and south as a form of political power-games. Capital punishment is the preferred weapon.

Another hundred years later, by 1716

The Mughal Empire is in decline. It has not forgotten – how can it? – Aurangzeb's executions of his brothers, nephew, of Sarmad the Sufi saint, of Guru Teg Bahadur, of Sambhaji, head of the Maratha Confederacy. A grandson of Aurangzeb, Farrukhsiyar, is on the shaky throne. His grandfather's example before him, he has the incumbent Mughal vizier and several nobles executed in mere whimsy. And he orders the execution of the poet laureate Jafar Zattalli, on the assumption that he had composed poems critical of his regime. Banda Singh Bahadur, a Sikh leader of great courage and charisma, has established his authority in Punjab and won great renown as an abolisher of the *zamindari* and one who gave tillers proprietary rights. In 1716, Farrukhsiyar moves against Banda, captures him after a grim battle in Gurdaspur, brings him to Delhi, tortures and then executes him.

In the south, Vijayanagara has disintegrated and the Marathas are down. But the Peshwas are rising to the fore. There is something elevated about the Peshwa mind, but this does not redeem the Peshwa system of punishment which is carried out either by hanging the condemned man, cutting him to pieces or decapacitation. A further refinement includes breaking the skull under mallets. But Brahmins, if sentenced to death, are to be poisoned.

A further century on, by 1816

On the relics of a vanished Vijayanagara, a debilitated Mughal Empire and a directionless Maratha conglomerate, India's new guest, Britain's East India Company, makes determining inroads. In 1799, the collector of Tinnevelly gives mouth-foaming chase to Kattabomman, the defiant ruler of Panchalankurichi and on capturing him, has him hanged from a tamarind tree. Several of Kattabomman's associates are also executed. 20 years on, in 1816, the example is still strong on every colonial and colonised mind.

Lord Hastings, as Governor General of India by 1816, wants to be different. In the Maratha war that he wages, he exacts heavy casualties yet eschews bloody reprisals, retributive hangings and decapitations. But this is just for the now. A mere 40 years later, no more, after the Great Rebellion of 1857, the British Raj is also going to become merciless as a punisher. Savage, in fact, with the death penalty being its absolute favourite.

By 1916

The need to protect the colony from insurrection is seen as paramount. But the Raj's brutality, post-1857, has raised such a stench that the mood in London is for punishment to be awarded lawfully, under a law, not capriciously or whimsically. The Indian Penal Code has come into effect in 1860, listing a number of 'capital offences' which include 'waging war against the State'. The Partition of Bengal and its reversal have seen a great new energy unleashed that threatens the Raj with home-devised bombs and bullets. A Defence of India Act is brought into being in 1915. Hangings and firings are back. In London, Curzon Wyllie, the political aide-de-camp to the secretary of state for India, Lord George Hamilton, is assassinated on July 1, 1909, by the Indian revolutionary, Madan Lal Dhingra. And after a trial in the Old Bailey, an unrepentant Dhingra is hanged on August 19, 1909.

And, now, in 2016

Independent India has inherited capital punishment from its blood-smeared history. Its emancipating founders do not dispense with that 'king' of punishments. The first to be hanged in free India, within months of freedom, is Nathuram Godse, assassin of the Father of the Nation. The threat to 'high functionaries' remains great. Hangings have made no difference to that form of privileged crime, not to speak of humbler murders. Thanks to the Supreme Court's mature orders the death penalty is now ordered only in 'the rarest of rare' cases. Rajiv Gandhi's family saying that it does not believe in the death penalty has been hugely civilising, as is the Indian Left's consistent support for its abolition. The forward logic of all this points to its abolition. But public opinion in India remains 'death-penalty minded'. Terrorism and the deaths of innocents at the hands of cynical cabals entrench that opinion, as does the brutal rape and murder, in Delhi, of Nirbhaya. The present Parliament of India too is similarly minded.

Many, very many, outside the State's anatomy but within its embrace, also want the death penalty to stay. Not just stay but stay tight and get tighter. They are like the *ulema* who goaded and then applauded medieval executions of 'unbelievers'. Bodhan, Sarmad and Zattalli were all killed by the Lodi and Mughal states for something like un-belief. Today's India is divided into 'believers' in bhakti and shakti on the one hand and those who believe in a liberal State on the other.

A wise and brave law commission, headed by the perspicacious judge, A.P. Shah, has recommended doing away with the death penalty. But it has said also that acts against the State, in other words, terrorists, should remain visitable by death. Terrorism has weighed on its recommendation.

In the three years of his incumbency, President Pranab Mukherjee has brought a glitter of his own to Rashtrapati Bhavan. Like Jahangir's menagerie, he has had the birds of his garden documented in a book, *Winged Wonders of Rashtrapati Bhavan*. And like that great Mughal, he has had to deal with, and deal, the death penalty. Three persons found guilty of terrorist acts have gone to the gallows under the ink of his pen. More await his decision.

The law does not, will not, tolerate acts against the State. But will the Indian State let go of the death penalty, a grand perquisite of authority, be it imperial, colonial or republican? Unlikely. We may not burn, decapitate, crush heads under mallets as before but we will 'hang by the neck till death'. We may not put needles through eyes; we will use other means of the third degree in *thanas*. We are not uncivilised.

What, then, is new about 2016?

Nothing?

Not so.

Over the frenzy and the froth, there are those, neither insignificant in numbers nor in stature, who are thinking what Amartya Sen said in Delhi just the other day to a hall packed to overflowing: 'Killing for killing is like the market economy – a system of exchange. We are under a market economy; we need not be under a market scaffold.'

(*The Telegraph*, January 3, 2016)

94

Restore India's Heritage of a Shared Peoplehood

THE GLADSTONIAN LIBERAL, JOHN Morley (1838-1923), opposed imperialism and supported Irish Home Rule. But he had a dim view of India's aspirations for freedom. 'There is, I know,' wrote Morley, 'a school of thought who say that we might wisely walk out of India and that Indians can manage their own affairs better than we can. Anyone who pictures for himself the anarchy, the bloody chaos that would follow, might shrink from that sinister decision.' Disapproving of reformist enlargements to Indian franchise and representation, he rebuked the 'reformers' with searing words: 'When across the dark distances you hear the sullen roar and scream of carnage and confusion, your hearts will reproach you with what you have done.'

Quoting these two observations of Morley's in an essay on the man, Winston S. Churchill wrote (in his *Great Contemporaries*), ominously: 'Only time can show whether his fears were groundless.'

Prognoses, right or wrong

Today as we approach the 75th anniversary of India's freedom, we may ask if time has disproved those grim prognoses contained in Morley's keywords.

Is there 'anarchy' in India?

Absolutely not. Ours may be called by observers a turbulent democracy. True, some of our leaders often forget the laws, forget that there is such a thing as the Constitution of India. And many politicians speak with hatred in their minds and poison on their tongues with impunity. That does not make India a lawless desert.

Is there 'bloody chaos'?

Of course not. Yes, there are moments of mayhem, hours of bedlam, days of havoc. Our legislatures know pandemonium. Our government offices know disarray. But bloody chaos? No way! Our chaotic moments can be bad; they are not bloody.

Is there 'confusion'?

Yes, there is. It is something new. And it has been deliberately sown, assiduously nurtured. It is about what our national identity is, what we as a people are in our core beings. India has been, through the ages, about three 'C's – caste, creed and country. The first is a matter of kinship, the second about worship, the third about citizenship. The first two are about high sentiment, the third about a high ideal. Leaders of India's renaissance did not want the first two to engulf the third. They wanted the first to become irrelevant, the second to become a private matter, the third to engage us. Today, caste and, more to the point, religion, are engulfing the country. The Hindu–Muslim divide is at its sharpest ever since Independence.

And do we hear the 'sullen roar and scream of carnage'?

One has to be where, in W.B. Yeats' words, 'the blood-dimmed tide is loosed, and…the ceremony of innocence is drowned' to hear that roar and scream. If these two fearsome sounds had been heard for the first and last time when India was partitioned, one might have let the horrible trauma recede in our collective memories. But no, just as it had happened many times before India became independent, and happened at the hour of freedom, it has happened afterwards again and over again. When did it happen last? One can say 'yesterday'. One can say 'yesterday' every day, knowing that the 'yesterday' can spew into 'today', any day.

Diminishing India

The Hindu–Muslim divides growing to a new and menacing proportion diminishes our country, debases its greatness, destroys its heritage of a shared Peoplehood.

Riots have invariably started over flimsy incidents, like fires generally are, but Hindu–Muslim riots have got quickly co-opted by other entities, with the help of mercenaries to serve sinister purposes. 'Entities' is a euphemism; we know who those are. They belong to both denominations.

Who started the disturbances on Ram Navami day? We are unlikely to ever know. Who gained, we will and already do know – nameless, faceless, soulless manipulators. Who lost, who suffered, is tragically known as well – Hindu and Muslim innocents. But more, beyond those innocents, who bleeds? Our country, its cohesion, its coherence, its conscience.

Social media spread the news of early incidents with the speed of light. District authorities in Madhya Pradesh, according to reports, had houses of some of those implicated in the rioting demolished. They acted surgically. Who came under the 'blade'? Destroyers of public property being made to pay for that destruction is sound, but is it sound to make the wives and children of the accused also pay by being rendered roofless?

Gandhi's fast

In 1924, terrible Hindu–Muslim riots scarred the Muslim-majority district of Kohat, in the North-West Frontier Province. Gandhi went on a 21-day fast in Delhi by way of penance. Emerging from it, greatly weakened, he said in a feeble voice to those gathered around him: 'We ought to be able to live together. The Hindus must be able to offer their worship in perfect freedom in their temples, and so should Musalmans be able to say their azan and prayer with equal freedom in their mosques. If we cannot ensure this elemental freedom of worship, then neither Hinduism nor Islam have any meaning.'

'There is no point citing Gandhi today; he is ancient history', I can hear the dejected reader say and my first instinct would be to say, 'I know.' But there are many, many of them wielding great influence, who would demur. The stand on secularism taken by the chief minister of Tamil Nadu, M.K. Stalin, in recent policy pronouncements, citing Gandhi and Bhagat Singh, has been exemplary. The statements of the Communist Party of India (Marxist) in its just concluded conclaves in Kannur, have been salutary. These complement the traditionally strong positions on secularism taken by the Indian National Congress and many other political parties across the country. Very significant has been the statement of the former chief minister of Karnataka, B.S. Yediyurappa on the Ram Navami violence: 'It is our desire that both Hindus and Muslims should live like children of the same mother.'

Courts must step in

It is time now for the courts of the land to take a stand, with the National Human Rights Commission and the National Commission for Minorities as their thought-partners, to uphold the Preamble and Article 25 of our Constitution. In *S.R. Bommai vs Union of India* (1994), the Supreme Court of India held that secularism is one of the basic features of the Constitution. To weaken the freedom of conscience is to weaken a fundamental freedom. The spewing of hatred by inflammatory words and any abetting of those by elements in power belittle the Constitution and betray the people of India. It cannot be permitted. Communalism inverts our citizenship, perverts our humanity, subverts our Constitution.

Very recently, as many as 100 Muslim residents of Dalvana, a village in Gujarat's Vadgam taluka, were invited to offer Maghrib Namaz and break their fast during the Ramzan month on the premises of its Vir Maharaj Mandir, a 1,200-year-old temple. 'When the heart is hard and parched up, come upon me with a shower of mercy…' wrote Tagore.

In the prevailing aridity, Gujarat has shown that grace has not been lost.

We do not have to disprove Morley and Churchill. We have to prove ourselves to the conscience of our Republic.

(*The Hindu*, April 15, 2022)

95

Bengal Needs No Radcliffe Line of Hatred

ELECTION TIME IN WEST Bengal has, for decades now, meant violent time.

There is violence during the campaigning, violence during the polling, violence during and after the counting of votes. The level of election-related violence and its duration vary but it is there.

So, what does that fact show? What does it establish?

That Bengal is a violent state and Bengalis are a violent people?

Certainly not.

Not just Bengal-centric

They are no more violent than any other part of India or section of Indian society when provoked, instigated, manipulated to think, speak and act violently. One has to only refer to the speeches made on the eve of Direct Action Day in 1946 at the Maidan, in Calcutta, to understand what I mean. Within hours of those incendiary speeches the city was bleeding. An estimated 4,000 people were killed. Very shortly thereafter, incitement and instigation doing their worst, the Noakhali region of East Pakistan saw appalling violence perpetrated on the Hindu minority there, with an estimated 5,000 killed. Bihar responded with matching fury, killing, according to information given to the British Parliament, an equal number of its Muslim minority and, according to *The Statesman*, twice as many. A peace-cherishing province was leveraged thus into peace-shattering violence.

Battered as it was, Bengal was 'bettered' by other areas. The worst instance of Partition-time violence among all regions, took place in Punjab. 'Virtually,' says Wikipedia, 'no Muslim survived in East Punjab (except in Malerkotla) and virtually no Hindu or Sikh survived in West Punjab.' All this was around the partitioning of India. Much later, in the anti-Sikh riots in 1984 an estimated 2,800 were killed in Delhi, and another 3,350 nationwide. These are official figures. The actual numbers are likely to have been much higher.

In the Gujarat riots of 2002, official estimates put the toll at 1,044. The actual numbers, again, are perhaps much higher.

So, let no one tar Bengal and Bengalis with the sweeping description of 'violent'. They are only as violent or non-violent as any other part of India or its people, not a whit more. Maoist violence, the other ogre that has menaced life in Bengal, is not by any means confined to the state where Naxalbari lies but is spread across over 200 districts across nine states.

Spreading hate

The violence that marred phase four of the eight-phase elections now being held in the state is most unfortunate and to be bemoaned. But our distress over it misses another far more important, much more serious and infinitely more dangerous form of violence that is accompanying the elections in West Bengal.

That violence is being done to the mind of Bengal, to its thinking wires, its feeling nerves, to its very soul. It is being done by the unrelenting spread of the virus of communal hate, of sectarian animosity of the 'line' that Hindus and Muslims are different breeds of human species. Whichever side of the communal divide it comes from, hatred as an idea and a strategy is no less violent than 'plain' violence. Once planted, it incubates in the minds and hearts of people, like a virus, and then erupts with an uncontrollable febrile frenzy.

The Partition years

The then Muslim League premier of undivided Bengal, H.S. Suhrawardy, had much to explain for the violence that disfigured Bengal in 1946 and 1947. On Suhrawardy's last day in that office, August 14, 1947, he had on his hands a challenging 'guest' – Gandhi, who was staying in Hydari Manzil, at the Muslim quarter of Beliaghata in Calcutta. At his prayer meeting that evening, over 10,000 people gathered in the grounds around that house to hear him. It was the month of Ramzan. Pyarelal records in his iconic biography (*Mahatma Gandhi: The Last Phase*, Navajivan, pp. 368–69), that some in the congregation shouted, 'Where is Suhrawardy?' Suhrawardy was inside that house at the time, engaged in *namaz*. Gandhi told them that. After the prayer meeting gave over and Gandhi returned to the house, there was an uproar. Many had surrounded the house, which at Gandhi's behest was un-policed, and demanded that Suhrawardy appear. Gandhi opened a window and got Suhrawardy to stand beside him, resting one hand on the outgoing premier's shoulder.

One of the crowd to the premier: 'Are you not responsible for the Great Calcutta Killing?'

Suhrawardy: 'Yes, we all are.'

'Will you answer my question, please?'

'Yes, it was my responsibility.'

Pyarelal writes: 'This unequivocal, straight and candid answer by one who had made arrogance and haughtiness his badge and never known humility had a profound effect on the crowd.' But the incubating virus was working still. Riots broke out within days in Calcutta, viciously. Two young men, Sachindranath Mitra, 37, and Smritish Banerjea, 28, interposing between rioting mobs, were killed on the spot. On hearing that a truck carrying Muslim labourers had a bomb thrown on it in the same area – Beliaghata – killing two of them, Gandhi went to the scene. A four *anna* piece was lying near one of them that had rolled out of the daily wager's waistband. Gandhi started a defining fast. It was in complete and exact harmony with the mind and soul of Ramakrishna's, Vivekananda's and Tagore's Bengal. And equally, with the stoic Bengal of the two simple, humble but absolutely true Bengalis, Sachindranath and Smritish.

'There should no longer be any more Hindu–Muslim riots in Calcutta…' the fasting Gandhi told Bengal's leaders who implored him not to fast. 'I shall terminate my fast if all of you accept this responsibility.' Seventy or so hours after his fast had begun, a group of leaders came to him to report that the innate good sense of the majority of the people of the city had prevailed over the furies let loose by the rioters. The mob that killed and burnt was not Bengal. The majority that stilled the mayhem, was.

'We the undersigned,' the leaders said in a paper they gave to him, 'promise to Gandhiji that peace and quiet have been restored in Calcutta once again. We shall never again allow communal strife in the city. And shall strive unto death to prevent it.' Among the signatories were Suhrawardy and N.C. Chatterjee, the Hindu Mahasabha leader. Netaji's elder brother, Sarat Chandra Bose, was a third.

Bengal then and now

That was and is Bengal. Its antibodies against the virus are strong. Its immune system is active. But if the load of the viral inoculum is huge, the balance can get affected. It can collapse.

Beliaghata 1947, representing Bengal's immune system, checked the virus. It has, by and large, remained in check. In 1971, 50 years ago, the virus all but disappeared, with the state hailing the return of Bangabandhu Sheikh Mujib Rahman to Dhaka and the birth of Bangladesh, even as another Tagore composition – '*Amar Sonar Bangla*' – became the national anthem of the new nation.

Bengal's immune system should be spared the challenge of an overload of the communal virus. It is one thing to go through an election that seeks to win its favour; quite another to have a Radcliffe Line of hatred cut through its mind and torment its soul.

Beliaghata 1947, Bangladesh 1971 and the ballot for Bengal 2021 bear witness to its covenants with life unto death.

(*The Hindu*, April 14, 2021)

96

When Brecht Speaks as Ambedkar

POLICEMEN AND POLICEWOMEN ARE not mindless digits in khaki. They have all been to school. Many of them are MAs, some PhDs. And they have families, friends just like anyone else who has not been clad in hide-tough uniforms the whole day. When at the end of duty hours they return home, get back to home-clothes, settle down to a tired day's evening, like anyone else, they talk of all they went through during the day, good and bad, honest and wicked, how they had to respond to political orders, 'high' influence, low intrigue. They laugh then at the ways of the cunning world of which they have become part, and feel sometimes proud of what they did and sometimes not. And then turn on their television sets to watch not news – of which they have had enough and more – but, to lighten their minds, old and new cinema, hear Lata Mangeshkar singing through the lips of Meena Kumari, or Asha Bhosle through those of Madhubala. In states like West Bengal and Maharashtra, with their strong traditions of theatre and musical arts, they can well go to see a play, 'with family', based on old epics or written by bold new playwrights staged in theatre-houses invariably named after Tagore, in his grey-flowing beard, or the great Chhatrapati Shivaji in his sharp-pointed black one.

Brecht at Bhima–Koregaon

Yet, Bertolt Brecht's is not a name all policemen on duty in Maharashtra's Bhima–Koregaon village on January 1, 2018 are likely to have known. The great German playwright is, sadly, 'niche'. Why sadly? Because he is bound to have amused, inspired, delighted, enthralled the non-*kitabi*, the not-a-bookworm-at-all as much as the bespectacled 'intel'. And because Brecht speaks the truth and doesn't care a hoot whether his truth is seen as the truth or is not. And Brecht's truth, rather like truth itself, is non-denominational, non-sectarian. The Marathi translation of his timeless play *The Good Person of Szechwan* is more than likely to have passed by the police force on duty at the village celebrating, as it has done for decades, on that day the great

Dalit-Mahar battalion's vanquishing – disputed by some – of the much stronger army of the Peshwa order known for its rough-handling of Dalits. Only, this year the celebration was the more celebratory, being the centenary year of that 1818 victory. And since one group's celebration is seen as another group's lamentation, 'law and order' was a concern. And rightly so. Violence and counter-violence saw 'the law' swing into action, 'order' asserting itself. And months later, arrests are still being made. Has all this been without 'fear or favour'? The courts will, without doubt, tell us.

Those who know Brecht's play laugh at lines in it like these:

'I am afraid of making enemies of other mighty men if I favour one of them in particular. Few people can help us, you see, but almost everyone can hurt us.'

'Stomachs rumble even on the emperor's birthday.'

'The First God: Do people have a hard time here?'

'Wang the water-seller: Good people do.'

'The First God to Shen Te the prostitute: Above all, be good, Shen Te, Farewell!'

'Shen Te: But I am not sure of myself, Illustrious Ones! How can I be good when everything is so expensive?'

'The Second God: We can't do anything about that. We mustn't meddle with economics!'

And they would have understood, with a sigh, the line: 'No one can be good for long when goodness is not in demand.'

The same play, one of the funniest, wittiest, most profoundly thoughtful and mind-rinsingly disturbing in that genre, has the woman prostitute-protagonist burst out with the words: 'Unhappy men! Your brother is assaulted and you shut your eyes! He is hit and assaulted and you are silent!...What sort of a city is this? What sort of people are you? When injustice is done there should be a revolt in the city. And if there is no revolt, it were better that the city should perish in fire before the night falls...'

In Ambedkar's words

In words that powerfully echo Brecht's, the architect of our Constitution, Babasaheb Bhimrao Ambedkar, said in the Constituent Assembly: 'How long shall we continue to live this life of contradictions? How long shall we continue to deny equality in our social and economic life? If we continue to deny it for long, we will do so only by putting our political democracy in peril. We must remove this contradiction at the earliest possible moment or else those who suffer from inequality will blow up the structure of political democracy which this Assembly has so laboriously built up.'

Here is a great, perhaps the greatest, German writer of our times, using a Chinese parable to give the world a touch of truth about the human condition, the human propensity for domination and the human impulse for freedom, justice. And when on January 1, 2018, in the Bhima–Koregaon event these lines with a timeless and location-free message were recited in their Marathi rendering, they were seen as 'an incitement to violence'. If, instead of Brecht's the reciter had cited Babasaheb's words, would he have been charged with incitement to violence? Today, who can tell?

Mohandas Gandhi was charged, likewise, in the spring of 1922 'for inciting disaffection towards His Majesty's government' for articles by him published in *Young India*. In one of them, titled 'Shaking the Manes', he used a phrase from then current political discourse and 'shook' the Raj. The accused said in his famous trial: 'I have no personal ill-will against any single administrator, much less can I have any disaffection towards the King's person. But I hold it to be a virtue to be disaffected towards a government which in its totality has done more harm to India than any previous system.'

We have our own Brechts.

Just before the declaration of the national emergency in 1975, Jayaprakash Narayan had, before a massive rally in Delhi, quoted the great Hindi poet Ramdhari Singh Dinkar's lines: '*Singhasan khali karo ki janata aati hai* (vacate your throne, here come the people).' We know what happened thereafter to JP, to India. Also, what happened subsequently to the system that imprisoned him.

We shall see

Faiz Ahmad Faiz's poem *Hum Dekhenge* (We Shall See) is a classic in the same vein, quoted time and again as a call against oppression.

Citing literary sources, turning to parables, prose, plays, poetry is the wherewithal of political discourse. Our prime minister has in a Dinkar commemoration cited the same line with pride.

Just as policemen on duty are only human beings in uniform, so are lawyers in black silk. They know true from false, fact from fiction.

India, the theatre from time immemorial of a hundred injustices, a thousand oppressions is also the site of a million awakenings. Therein lies its strength.

Kuchh baat hai (there is that something), as Iqbal sang, about Hindustan that cannot let its self-hood fade.

(*The Hindu*, September 21, 2018)

97

India Stares at Water Scarcity

BUT SOMETHING ELSE, SOMETHING urgent, something is already upon us. And something that is going to coincide with the elections. A drought.

The rains have failed us. Nothing new, one might say. True, except that the rains' letdown this time comes on top of an already low-rain and, in many places, no-rain ground situation. And the next nearest rains are six months away. The cruelly blue, cloudless skies over much of India, north, central, eastern and peninsular India, say it all. And there is no guarantee that June will see the onset of a normal monsoon.

What the sky says

Does anyone care? Does the political class? The prime minister and chief ministers are not unaware of the situation. They cannot be. The India Meteorological Department (IMD) has given them enough data. But when droughts and elections intersect, it is extremely uncomfortable for leaders. It is inconvenient to dwell on the skies' tidings. Which government would like to tell farmers that suffering lies at their threshold? Who would like to tell them that water will be scarcer than before, that aquifers will plummet, crops wither, livestock go thirsty? Which government would, just weeks before the elections, tell us that with reservoirs drying up taps will sputter to a stop and that we may well be looking at water rationing? The truth is, none of them will say that. This is where, as Amartya Sen has told us time and again, the media comes in, and comes in redemptively. It is India's great good luck that public awareness, nudged and prodded by public discussions on meteorological data and media reportage, has kept droughts from deepening into famines in our country.

The IMD report on scant rains has received scant attention so far, with exceptions being provided by P. Sainath's relentless warnings and observations of experts of the calibre and veracity of Ramchandra Sable, agro-meteorologist, and D.M. More, secretary of the Second Maharashtra Irrigation Commission, reported in the *Hindustan Times* (January 6, 2019).

Rain deficit facts

To turn to the facts. The actual deficit last monsoon was modest – barely 10 per cent. But the post-monsoon rainfall (October to December, 2018) or PMR as it is called by meteorologists, has registered a 44 per cent deficit. This national average deficit conceals shortages in some regions where it is much higher. In Marathwada, according to the IMD, the deficit is 84 per cent, in Vidarbha, 88 per cent.

Why should we worry, more than before, this time? For the reason that this low-rain and no-rain situation is going to aggravate the water crisis that we have brought upon ourselves without the 'help' of a dry sky. Years of policy-driven, corporate-driven water transfers from rural to urban, agriculture to industry, poor to rich, and so on, have made our countryside chronically water-scarce. Urban India does not realise this fast enough or well enough. It will, when there are power outages and air conditioners do not work! 'By April–May,' Sainath said to me, 'this drought could be tormenting millions in several States.' And that is when election campaigning will be at its peak.

The pre-election mood 'yesterday' was all about agrarian distress, farm-loan waivers. Will the pre-election mood 'tomorrow' be even thinking of, leave alone talking of, drought and what can be done to address it beyond loan waivers?

Though our major leaders deny it, *Kaun Banega Pradhan Mantri* – KBPM – is what occupies the high seat in their thinking today. They seem to be in aphasia if not amnesia about the massive waterlessness that has hit us already. If they see the parched ponds, the sharded earth, the leaf-shedding trees, panting crops, drooping livestock, they do not talk about it.

That is how politics is. And yet that is not how politics should be and that is not how the rural Indian voter is going to allow politics to be. Not any more. And good for that voter that it be so. Anti-incumbency may take five years in electoral politics to mature into an ouster. It does not take more than one failed farming season to turn to impatience and then to rage. No politician in office or aspiring to it today can ignore the drought. It is going to be the biggest and immediate test for the new governments in Karnataka, Rajasthan, Madhya Pradesh, Chhattisgarh. Somewhere in her hurt ego, a 'relieved' Vasundhara Raje must be glad she is not going to have to fight the drought. Likewise, Shivraj Singh Chouhan and Raman Singh. Not the Bharatiya Janata Party, not the NDA, not Narendra Modi but the drought is going to be the real challenge to the 'collective opposition' as it seeks to and could well manage to, oust the present regime.

Let there be no doubt that the prime minister of India 2019 will have to be India's Drought Commissioner.

And let her or him face the challenge four-square and render a national service.

Time and money are short

There is a prequel to this.

For the NDA, time is short, money is not. For the Opposition, time is short, money shorter. What is short for both, equally, is credibility. It is critically short. The voter, especially the rural voter, has no illusions. A government either helps it overcome its life-and-death problems or does not. The 'Delhi Government' will be tested in 2019 for its credibility on many issues, among which certainly l'affaire Rafale is now top of the list, followed by the Reserve Bank of India and the Central Bureau of Investigation mess-ups. But the elections in 2019 will test its credibility by what it does and says it will do for water-starved, food-short, livelihood-broken, rural India's agrarian distress. And in states where the NDA is not in power – and now the states in which it is not exceeds the number of States in which it is – the rural voter will vote against whoever is in office unless the 'government party' makes drought relief, water use, food security and massive earth-related programmes its absolute priority. In other words, unless it makes agrarian distress, now aggravated by the drought, its priority.

The failure of rains this time is so serious that 'Drought' now means not just a farm crisis but a national crisis that will affect towns and cities no less than villages. 'Agrarian crisis' appears to urban India as something 'out there'. No longer true. It is only a matter of time when the 'taken-for-granted' piped water supply will falter and when water cans will cost even more than they do, today.

Whoever becomes prime minister will do well to appoint a commission like the Farmers' Commission, which Dr M.S. Swaminathan headed, to advise him or her on how water-scarce India, all of India, needs to face drought. And give that Commission just one month to complete its study, make its recommendations not just to government but to all Indians, to us, who have become so used to water-access imbalance, water-use lopsidedness, water prodigality in the midst of water poverty that we just do not care. And this time, not advisories or appeals but penalties will be needed.

Addressing the deepening drought, agrarian distress and water management are critical not just for our governments to survive but for us to survive our governments.

(*The Hindu*, December 4, 2021)

98

Heed This 67-Year-Old Tryst

DEAR PRIME MINISTER

Warmest greetings to you on Republic Day.

You were born the same year as our Republic was. So, as the Republic turns 67, you do too. Twinned, by birth, to the Constitution, you have with it another bond. As prime minister of India you have taken an oath, in the name of God, to 'bear true faith and allegiance to the Constitution of India'. And from that great position, you have called it India's holy book. You are therefore, a Constitution-person twice over, by birth and by oath.

Two and a half years after taking that oath, on this anniversary day, how do you see yourself in that bond?

You could, of course, say, 'Ask the people of India, they will tell you if I have or have not been true to it.' If I were to do that, I know, there would be a torrent of appreciation for you. Not just the appreciation of your admirers but appreciation from objective observers as well.

No one can deny the fact that between 2014 and 2017 your appeal has grown. It has grown for three reasons. First, you have been seen as decisive, a 'doer'. Second, you are perceived as having 'taken on' corruption. Third, you are regarded as being tough, tougher than all your predecessors, on terror. There is a fourth image that must also be placed on the table, though it is not exactly complimentary. You are believed to be clever, *hushiar*. And your 'at midnight tonight' announcement on demonetisation has been seen as *hushiari*. 'Good for the country, no?' people said while queueing up the next morning in front of ATMs.

The important question

But does being all those three – decisive, hard on corruption, tough on terror – translate into 'bearing true faith and allegiance to the Constitution'? Today, on Republic Day, it is important that we reflect on that question.

Prime Minister Indira Gandhi was a decisive woman. Between 1975 and 1977 she was even more decisive than her usual decisive self. Having declared a national emergency, she came down with an iron hand on people she portrayed as criminals, black-marketers, hoarders, corrupt. And terrorism, as we now know it, was absent during that period. But was Indira Gandhi true to her oath? You were 25 years old at the time, Mr prime minister. You will remember how when she reneged on the Constitution, betrayed her oath, she was thrown out of power – lock, stock and barrel.

Indira was not India. No prime minister can be India. India alone is India.

An impression prevails that you want to be seen as India, that criticism of you therefore amounts to criticism of India, tantamount to treason. Questioning demonetisation becomes, in one flowing sequence, validating black money, going soft on terror and questioning your judgment – all anti-national. An immaculacy surrounds you, an assumption of infallibility imbues your pronouncements. And hence an aura of unquestionability.

No one who is accountable to Parliament, which represents all the people of India, can be a dictator or even a supremacist in the sense in which the word is normally used for one who wants to establish the superiority of a particular ethnicity, class or culture. But, Mr prime minister, you are a supremacist for your vision of India. You want your India, the India you are prime minister of, to do things that will be hailed as exceptional, unprecedented, unparalleled. You want India to reach, go beyond, Mars, an Indian land on the moon. You want to send more Indian missiles hissing into the light blue skies than your predecessors did, more Indian submarines to plumb noiselessly into the deep blue sea than your predecessors would have dreamt of. There is, at one level, something quite natural and admirable about a prime minister being ambitious for his or her country, to think big, bigger, biggest for his or her people. Except when a nation's leader believes in personal supremacism.

Sardar Patel was not such a supremacist. He was a supreme realist.

Isolated power

While supremacists love their own very particular crowds and those crowds love them, they are, as persons, very lonely. And loneliness finds two friends: secrecy and arbitrariness. A mist of trail-less circumstances surrounds a supremacist's decisions. And these decisions come to be taken impulsively, whimsically. Sometimes they can be inspired, but on most occasions they create more problems than they solve and can also cause havoc. Isolated power is isolated from the advantages of consultation, from the benefit of an equal colleagueship. It is isolated, therefore, from the great bonus of republican partnership. So fond does he become of the dulcet tones of his own voice, that his auditory powers atrophy. Even when he seems to be listening to others, the personal supremacist is, in fact, listening to his own voice reacting to what he is hearing. He is his own singer, his own song and his own listener. The self-centrism of an elected leader is, in democratic terms, an irony. In republican terms, an anomaly. It scarred the period 1975–1977. It must not, in the same or modified form, in de jure fact or in de facto spirit, be readmitted into our polity, our political culture.

There are signs of it wanting to.

Abolishing the Union Planning Commission, replacing independent heads of autonomous academic institutions by persons of known bias, the stalling of judges' appointments, the superseding of generals in Army promotions, of diplomats and bureaucrats in other elevations, the dangling in the air of the Lokpal, the undermining of the RTI Act, blacklisting NGOs, demonetisation, all come from the conviction, 'I am the Alpha and the Omega, the Indus and the Ganga' of India. That, Mr prime minister, is an uninsured journey into Great Unknowns on a gilded *ratha* with mini-supremacists scrambling atop it.

A political leader may, for all his egotism, be highly knowledgeable about certain things on his home ground. Much more so than, for instance, his officers. No diplomat could have matched Jawaharlal Nehru's understanding of international affairs. No officer, ICS, IAS, IPS, could have matched Patel's knowledge of political psychology, Chief Minister Pant's understanding of rural politics, Chief Minister Namboodiripad's sense of rural and urban economics, Chief Minister Kamaraj's mastery of Tamil Nadu's complex politics. But there are areas where others, experts, officers and NGOs, know better, remember more than a politician. As, for instance, in fiscal planning, foreign relations, defence strategy, science and environment policy and, above all, in 'real-life' issues like unofficial 'official' extortions, job insecurity, health non-coverage, the absence of insurance and pension cover. The deference by non-expertise to experience becomes a leader.

The way forward

You advise us to make do with less and less cash. Are you teaching us how to make do with less and less water? Let ATMs run out of money, use cards, you tell us, use digi-*dhan*. What about when our lakes go dry? Can we live with digi-*jal*? You are not warning the country of the known and unknown horrors of climate change, the power and fuel crises that await us, the pandemics, air-borne, water-borne and vector-borne, that are whirling overhead. You are telling us to be *swachh* but what of that behemoth source of *aswachhata*, our plastic lobby? You are teaching us the merits of yoga, but you are not disabling the fountainheads of ill-being in our gutka lobby, tobacco lobby. The control over our land commons, mines, forests by mafiosi, middlemen and mega 'developers' continues unchallenged.

And then, there is Kashmir. The team which, led by Yashwant Sinha and catalysed by Wajahat Habibullah, went to the Valley has made searingly honest findings, vital recommendations. Heed, Mr prime minister, their clear voice. Had Jayaprakash Narayan's warnings and guidance been heeded in the 1960s, Kashmir would have been spared the agonies it is going through today. The Constitution has not intended that part of our country for ceaseless bloodletting. History is giving us another chance for a bold new initiative that makes the most beautiful part of our nation its most peaceful.

I said at the start that your appeal has grown. So has, in typical Indian contrariness, your dis-appeal. Those who believe in the core values of our Constitution, though they are not bound to it by birth or oath, are deeply disturbed, dismayed, by the growing intolerance of dissent and the misrepresentation of criticism as anti-national.

You may have seen, at Girnar, Ashoka's famous Edict VI which says 'I am never completely satisfied with my work of wakefulness or despatch of business.' Remember, please, Ashoka's admission and his remorse which he called, in Magadhi Prakrit, *anusaya*. Your own exquisite language, Gujarati, has another sublime word for it, *anutaapa*. Atonement and compassion do not betoken weakness, they betoken nobility which is a leader's sign.

With pride in our Republic, and faith in its ability to reclaim hope from despair,

Your fellow citizen.

(*The Hindu*, January 30, 2017)

99

Spread Thin and Wide

'WHEN AN OLD WOMAN hears the dance she knows,' writes Chinua Achebe, 'her old age deserts her.' Seeing tribal India today the Nigerian novelist could well have said, 'When a tribal hears the order "Dance", dance deserts her.'

'Tribal India'?

That is how non-tribal India calls the universe of the 100-million-strong 'scheduled' by the Constitution and the laws of India. Numbering about 700, they are spread across more than 500 districts in 34 of our states and Union territories. How do those tribes define, describe non-tribal India? Do they have names for un-scheduled India?

Some choice epithets, one can be sure, are current in the vocabulary of the Bhil, drawn from the same Indo-European group of languages, or of the Gond, Khond, Oraon and Toda, who use derivations of the Dravidian group of India's many tongues. Absolutely scalding names for non-tribal India must be vivifying the everyday Tibeto-Burman speech of the tribes of north-eastern and Himalayan India. If they are compiled and published, they will do India's ego a world of good.

India's tribal population is spread dew-thin across its length and breadth and its islands in the Arabian Sea and the Bay of Bengal. Had it been concentrated instead, in its three most 'tribal' states, Madhya Pradesh, Maharashtra and Odisha, and not been as varied in modes of living and livelihood as it is, India would have had a different political ecology. We would have had, even if as a compromise name, at least one prime minister from one of our major tribal communities – Bhil, Gond, Santhal, Mina, Naikda, Oraon. Each of those is populous, ranging from 3 million to 10 million, but they are scattered over several states.

India's tribes are as ancient as the 'dancing girl' of Mohenjodaro, who is at once 12 and 5,000 years old. They are old, they are young. They are wise, they are strong but being far too finely spread out, they fail to count. In a democracy numbers count, size works, bulk matters. Those can be mobilised. But as we are also a republic we have found in India's strong-limbed and handsome tribes a distinct use. They give our republic its most vivid colours. They are symbols of our 'diversity' that can be used on national days for spectacle, at sport meets for the gold, silver and bronze. We like them to dance, sing. We celebrate their 'colourfulness', their 'grace', their crafts. Dancing to their own rhythms but at our bidding, in their speeds but to our tunes. In their zest but for our shows.

Hansda Sowvendra Shekhar, the Jharkhand-based government doctor and author of *The Mysterious Ailment of Rupi Baskey* (Aleph), has a powerful short story 'The Adivasi Will Not Dance'. It is about a visit to Jharkhand by the President of India to inaugurate a thermal power station that is coming up on land from which Santhals have been evicted. The ceremony will of course include 'customary' Santhal dancing. '...We Adivasis,' says the protagonist, 'will not dance anymore...We are like toys – someone presses our "ON" button, or turns a key in our backsides, and we Santhals start beating rhythms on our *tamak* and *tumdak* or start blowing tunes on our *tiriyo* while someone snatches away our very dancing grounds.'

The 33-year-old doctor–author posted in a Jharkhand outpost has written about a matter of vital concern to fellow Jharkhandis, to *adivasi* kin and to all those who cherish India's republican spirit. Should a government servant express personal opinions on policy matters in public? Is that not 'playing politics'? What Shekhar has written about is political to the extent that it concerns a political decision to regularise the domicile of massive numbers of non-Jharkhandis in the state. It is social, cultural, civilisational to the extent that it concerns displacement, dispossession, destitution. And that of a people, namely tribals, who are recognised by the Constitution of India as being vulnerable and in need of protection. Turning the 'adivasi dance' into a political metaphor is not 'taking part in politics'; it is expressing the deepest possible anguish that a whole community is feeling and which by a writer is best expressed through writing. This has been said by others in different ways and in varying contexts that apply to all our tribes who suffer one or the other form of the acutest neglect, exploitation and oppression, to which has been added the spectre of Maoist violence.

Most significantly, there was the report of the high-level committee that was appointed by the United Progressive Alliance II government 'to examine the socio-economic, educational and health status of tribal communities and recommend appropriate interventional measures to improve the same...' A stellar cast comprising its membership, the committee has said in its report (still 'under examination') on the subject of domicile: '...there has been considerable in-migration of non-tribals to Scheduled Areas as well as non-Scheduled areas with large tribal populations. This influx has changed the relative population of tribal and non-tribal communities in the area, often worsening the disparity between the two groups.'

The report needs to be read by as many Indians as possible for it tells us as much about non-tribal India as it does about tribal India. It tells India that non-tribal India's non-comprehension of tribal India may or may not be a loss to the tribals; it certainly is a loss to India. Their being unique, being themselves, being different makes them invaluable to India. Being un-typical of India's 'mainstream', for instance, in gender equity, holds a lesson for the country. The sex ratio of tribal India is 990 females to 1,000 males, against the all-India figure of 940 to 1,000. And then in the matter of equating with nature's cycles, tribal India can be a national professor. It holds a key both to our genetic past and to our ecological future.

The Indian establishment is sceptical of non-governmental organisations working with tribals, looking for Maoist links in them. The report advises the State to not conflate all NGOs with the cult of violence; that is un-wisdom. Do not, in some thumb-rule fashion, suspect them, seek to crush them.

Fifty years ago this year, an infamous 'crushing' took place in Bastar. On March 25, 1966, Pravir Chandra Bhanj Deo, the 37-year-old former Maharaja of Bastar state, was killed by police fire, opened at the steps of his palace at Jagdalpur. Pravir symbolised his tribal ex-subjects' fight against the exploitation of natural resources in the region. He bore no firearms, only bows and arrows, as he emerged from his rooms to face the police. With 12 others, he was gunned down. He received 13 bullets. Acharya Kripalani termed the outrage 'another Jallianwala Bagh'. In an impassioned speech in Parliament, Atal Bihari Vajpayee, expressed astonishment over the haste with which Pravir was cremated, without even his wife being allowed to see the remains. M.N. Govindan Nair, Communist Party of India member of Parliament and son-in-law of the historian, Sardar K.M. Panikkar, made (for a Marxist) an unexpected point. 'During the time of the raja,' said Nair, 'they could move about from one part of the forest to the other, they could collect forest wealth and somehow exist…Now you are not allowing them to do so.'

Had Jawaharlal Nehru or Lal Bahadur Shastri been prime minister, I do not think the tragedy would have occurred. Or if it had, would have occasioned a scandalised condemnation. But this was the Indira era. A probe by a Supreme Court judge was asked for, to no avail. On the seedbed of callousness has the poison tree of Naxalism grown. State personnel on duty die at Maoist hands. But the ones to suffer most are tribal innocents.

A pivotal recommendation in the Tribal Committee's Report says: 'Large numbers of tribals, men and women, are in jails…a Judicial Commission needs to be appointed to investigate cases filed against tribals and their supporters; only this will allay the concerns that have risen about the misuse of criminal law by the state.'

Can we expect the National Democratic Alliance government, on the 50th anniversary of the Jagdalpur manslaughter, to act on this recommendation? We cannot let Chinua Achebe's line in *Things Fall Apart* describe the Republic of India's response to its tribal heritage: 'The Pacification of the Primitive Tribes of the Lower Niger'.

(*The Telegraph*, July 3, 2016)

100

Mirrors of India

I AM NOT IMAGINING THIS, not conjuring it up. Those familiar with Gujarat, the history of India's freedom struggle know it. They know it well.

And yet today it sounds like a fairy tale. A dream-sequence, unreal, incredible, an operatic passage of the most utopian imagination. And yet it is not. It is a 'real thing', as real as today's news, or – tomorrow's in the making.

One hundred years ago, in 1917, in this very month of November, there took place a momentous event in Godhra, Gujarat – yes, Godhra, the Godhra of the burning train carriages where 'Gujarat 2002' started. The event was a conference that took place, the like of which had not been convened earlier and was not to be repeated.

Called, in English, the Gujarat Political Conference, it was better known and hailed at the time as the Gujarat Rajkiya Parishad. It was the first of its kind and in many ways was to be the only one of its kind. Attended as it was by 'cultivators, petty traders and small cultivators', it became an all-India conference, a renaissance conference.

The deeply compartmentalised society of those times must have seen the four leading lights of the conference, Tilak, Gandhi, Jinnah and Patel, like this: one Maharashtrian, three Gujarati; one Muslim, three Hindu; one 'Indian lawyer', three barristers. The first named was the most famous of them all, the tallest Indian leader, acclaimed as a Chitpavan Brahmin scholar, teacher, editor, social reformer and chapter-turner, who had declared *swaraj* to be his, and by extension his fellow Indians', birthright. Of the three Gujaratis, Gandhi at the 'happening' age of 48 was most surely identified by that Gujarati congregation as a Modh Bania barrister, not yet the Mahatma. Jinnah at a very contemplative 41 must have been 'noted' by the gathering as an Ismaili barrister from the vicinity of Karachi, nowhere near being the future Quaid-e-Azam. And Vallabhbhai Patel, raring to go at 42, seen, with just pride, as a sturdy barrister from the Patidar community yet to be embraced by a future generation as 'the Sardar'.

There was no representative of India's Depressed Classes among them. Bhimrao Ambedkar, the future Babasaheb, 26 years young then, had just returned to India from New York with an MA degree from Columbia, yet to begin work. But the problem of that community was to be placed by Gandhi at the heart of the Godhra proceedings.

And there was no woman on the podium, not one. But the Congress's president of that year, Annie Besant, was an unseen presence. 'It is due to Mrs Besant,' Gandhi said in his opening address, 'that Swaraj is on the lips of hundreds of thousands of men and women.'

With his South Africa reputation aglow and fresh from his victorious indigo satyagraha in Champaran, Gandhi made the Godhra conference an all-India, pan-India, conference heralding swaraj, no less. And he made Patel its organisational kingpin.

'This conference,' Gandhi declared, 'is in the nature of a foundation. And if it is well and truly laid, we need have no anxiety as to the superstructure.' He added, poignantly, 'The time is most critical for the whole of India.'

But why of all places was Godhra, a small and little-known town in north Gujarat's Panchmahal, selected for the conference?

For the reason, one may infer, that Godhra held within it all the promises and all the problems that confronted Indian society and all the opportunities and all the challenges as well. It had, aside from its diverse and un-cohesive Hindu population, an equally diverse and un-cohesive Muslim population and a sizeable, deeply depressed, oppressed, suppressed 'untouchable' community. And though a town, yet surrounded by the distresses of rural India, peasant India, again divided by its own traditions, totems and taboos but 'united' by misfortunes, natural ones like droughts and floods and man-made. All of them, in separate boxes, with separate prides, prejudices and poverties, stark poverties. Godhra was India in miniature.

'I am but a baby of two and a half years in Indian politics,' said Gandhi at the beginning of his written presidential address, 'I cannot trade here on my experience in South Africa. I know that in these circumstances, acceptance of this position is to a certain extent an impertinence.' But that modest gesture made, the 'two-and-a-half-year-old' took off. In an epic speech in Gujarati, he dealt with local Godhra-specific issues like a Bakr Id riot that had blazed across the town, provincial issues, national issues, social, economic and political. 'Throughout my wanderings in India,' he said, 'I have rarely seen a face exuding strength and joy. The middle classes are groaning under the weight of awful distress. The lowest orders have nothing but the earth below and the sky above. They do not know a bright day.' Disputing the Raj's claim that the wealth of India was growing, he said: 'It is only too true that statistics can be made to prove anything. The economists deduce India's prosperity from statistics. People like me who follow rough and ready methods of reckoning shake their heads over Blue-book statistics. If the Gods were to come down and testify otherwise, I would insist on saying that I see India growing poorer.'

But the Raj was not his only target. Indian society – we, as a people – were the subject of his and the conference's critical gaze, no less. 'Protecting the cows,' he said, 'seems to be an ancient practice. It originated in the special needs of this country. Protection of its cows is incumbent on a country 90 per cent of whose population lives upon agriculture and needs bullocks for it…But here we have to face a peculiar situation. The chief meaning of cow-protection seems to be to prevent cows from falling into the hands of our Muslim brethren and being used as food…It is not religion but want of it to kill a Muslim brother to save a cow. I feel sure that if we were to discuss the matter with our Muslim brethren in the spirit of love, they would appreciate the peculiar condition of India and readily cooperate with us in the protection of cows…' Gandhi had a joint 'Hindu–Muslim' resolution readied on political reforms, including elections, to be presented to the secretary of state, Edwin S. Montagu. And he got Jinnah to move it for adoption in the conference. Gandhi insisted that Jinnah move the resolution in Gujarati and Jinnah agreed.

The community of the Dhed, long regarded as 'untouchable', was brought to the delegates' special notice at a special meeting with them. 'We, Hindus and Muslims have become one,' Gandhi said at the Dhed gathering. A Bombay police report noted: 'Mr Gandhi asked the upper classes to convert their theoretical sympathy for the Dheds into a practical one and to subscribe towards opening and maintaining a school for Dhed children. Rupees 1653 were subscribed on the spot.'

Godhra was an India in miniature for the Gujarat Political Conference of 1917 working for *swaraj*.

Gujarat 2017 is India in miniature. And it is telling us: 'The time is most critical for the whole of India.'

(*The Telegraph*, November 26, 2017)

Acknowledgements

MOST OF THE PIECES of writing in this volume have appeared as columns in *Hindustan Times* (New Delhi), *The Telegraph* (Kolkata) and *The Hindu* (Chennai).

I am grateful to those eminent newspapers for, first, carrying them and, second, for signalling no objection to their republication in this volume.

To *The Statesman* and *The Indian Express* from which also more slender borrowings have been made, I record my thanks.

No venture in writing for newspapers commences or thrives without some individual in those houses of inked thought taking an interest in the ecology of the contributor's mind.

In 2009, when I had just returned to 'private station' after five eventful years in Kolkata's Raj Bhavan, Indrajit Hazra, who was then with *Hindustan Times*, asked me to write for that newspaper – a bond that continues to this day.

That was an honour and a 'command' since my father had been its editor for nearly two decades.

An earlier generation would have described Aveek Sarkar as 'a newspaper baron'. We know better than to fall for such clichés, but he was helming *The Telegraph* then with flair. He and his senior colleague, the historian Rudrangshu Mukherjee, asked me to do the same for that ace newspaper in Kolkata, a generosity which Arup Sarkar and Atideb Sarkar have continued.

N. Ram, who is indistinguishable from *The Hindu*'s calibre and its values, encouraged me to write for it. This was a great privilege as Ram is a thinker and journalist of the highest order whose tireless work for the first freedom of expression and the physical safety of media persons is something India can be proud of.

To all of them and their successors and colleagues, in particular Lalita Panicker, Prashant Jha and Amrith Lal in *Hindustan Times*, Leo Uddalak in *The Telegraph* and Suresh Nambath, Mini Kapoor, Srinivas Venmani and Narayan Lakshman in *The Hindu*, I offer personal thanks.

To *The Hindu*'s current chairperson Nirmala Lakshman I convey appreciation and thanks for her unfailing editorial welcome.

Finally, to Chirag Thakkar, the initiator, curator and hands-on organiser of this Bloomsbury idea, I tender my sincerest thanks.

Index

Aadhaar cards, 335
Aam Aadmi Party, 282
Abbas, Khwaja Ahmed, 142
abduction, 302–304. *see also* kidnapping and abduction
Abdullah, Sheikh, 20
Abhay Singh vs State of Uttar Pradesh & Ors, 248
Abraham, Meera, 95
Abraham, Thomas, 95
accountability, 305–307
Achebe, Chinua, 361, 364
Addison, Joseph, xv
administrative-diplomatic services, 18, 20
Advani, L.K., 83, 85
aesthetic and moral faculties, man and animals, 52
affray, 197
Afghanistan, 7, 35, 72, 149, 313
Afghan refugees, 7
Africa, 31–34, 236
    gain for G21 by AU joining, 32–34
    inclusion of African Union in G21, 31, 32
    inter-country conflict resolution, 32
    nuclear-free zone, 32–33
    peace-keeping operations, 32
    Pelindaba Treaty, 32–33
African Nuclear-Weapon-Free Zone Treaty, 32–33
Agni (missile), 66
agrarian crisis, 356
Agrawal, Shriman Narayan, 281, 287
Ahmedabad, 99, 102, 134, 172, 230, 252
Ahmedabad Textile Industry's Research Association, 134
Ahmednagar, 153
Aiyar, Mani Shankar, 3, 5
Ajmer Sharif, 171
Akhtar, Javed, 150
Alagesan, O.V., 55–57, 307
Alam, Mir, 157
al-Assad, Bashar, 41
Alexander, Horace, 50
Ali, Aruna Asaf, 69, 210
Ali, Asaf, 200, 281, 288

Aligarh, 240
Aligarh Muslim University, 142
Ali, Ghulam, 328
Ali, Hamid, 50
Alipore, Calcutta, 321
Ali, Rajab, 172
Ali, Sadiq, 101
Ali, Salim, 49–52 142, 222–223
Allende, Salvador, 41
All India Handicrafts Board, 94
All India Kisan Sabha, 294
All India Majlis-e-Ittehadul Muslimeen, 18
All You Who Sleep Tonight (Vikram Seth), 152
al-Zahar, Mahmoud, 28, 29
Ambedkar, B.R., 158, 166, 189, 200, 227, 231, 232, 256–257, 264, 265, 268, 332, 336, 352, 366
Amritsar, 181, 182
Amundsen, Roald, 42
anachronism, 285
Ananda Vikatan, 107
An Autobiography (Jawaharlal Nehru), 132
Andaman and Nicobar Islands, 286
Andhra Pradesh, 55, 219, 295, 316
Andrews, C.F., 74, 162
Aney, M.S., 281, 288
Annadurai, C.N., 268
Ansari, Hamid, 328
Antarctica, 32, 42, 43
    Antarctic territories, 43
    atomic explosions in, 43
    monitoring of activities, 44
    peaceful use of continent, 43
    scientific research in, 43
    scientific stations in, 43, 44
    territorial claims over, 43
    treaty on space, 43–44
Antarctic Treaty, 43–44
Anthony, Frank, 56, 205
anti-Sikh riots, 1984, 347
anti-untouchability committee, 271
anutaapa, 360
Ape Super Ape (film), 51
Aravamudan, Gita, 245

archaism, 168
Ardern, Jacinda, 196
Argentina, 43
Ariel, M., 73
Ariyalur train accident, 55–56
arrogance of power, 182
Article 356 of the Constitution, 202
artificial intelligence (AI), 29, 237
    coders and jobs, 29
    earthquake-prediction tool, 30
    global war, use in, 29
    Sri Lanka's plantation workers and, 16
Asad Sud, 172
Asaf Ali, Aruna, 95, 96
'asap,' use of, 247
Ashani Sanket (Satyajit Ray), 213
Ashoka (or Asoka, emperor), 137, 205, 305–306, 338
Ashoka chakra, 204–206, 220
Ashram Bhajanavali (Sabarmati Ashram), 157
ashraya (refuge), 7–8
Asokan period, in Indian history, 205
Assam, 264, 284
    Bangladeshi in, 240
    Association for Democratic Reforms (ADR), 228
Atkins, A.G., 324
atomic bomb, 236
atomic reactors, 4
audi alteram partem, principle of, 164
Aurangzeb, 340
Aurobindo, Sri, 215
Australia, 43, 81
authoritarian State, 328
Azad, Maulana, 101, 184, 189, 200
Azmi, Shabana, 304

Bachchan, Harivansh Rai, xiv, 129
Bacon, Francis, xv
Badshah of the Pathans, 143
Bagchi, Amiya, 215
Bagchi, Jasodhara, 215
Bagehot, Walter, 280
Bahadur, Banda Singh, 340
Bailey, Wellesley, 162
Bainbridge, Kenneth, 66
Bajaj, Kamal Nayan, 148
Bajrang Dal, 329
Balasore train accident, 55, 305, 307
Baloch political dissidents, 7
Bandyopadhyay, Alapan, 250
Banerjea, Smritish, 117, 172, 213

Bangalore, 72
Bangladesh, 10, 11, 129, 155, 232, 260, 323, 329
Baranwal, V.K., 154
Barooah, Devakanta, 272
Bastar killing, 363
Basu, Bhupendranath, 199
Basu, Jyoti, 69
BCG vaccination programme, 320
Beaumont kidnappings, Australia, 302–303
Becketising of dissent, 329
Behari, Benode, 213
Belgaum, 153
Belgium, 43
Beliaghata, 76, 158, 259
Bengal, 213–218, 232, 259, 280
    char of personally felt experience, 214
    creativity and artistic expression, 214–215
    emotional continent, 214
    Eros, Temenos, Soros and Pyro, 217
    experience of pain, 213, 215, 217
    gift of love, 217–218
    isthmus of feeling, 214
    sentiment of reason, 214
    strait of sentiment, 214
Bengal Famine of 1943, 236
Bengaluru, 318
Bengal, violence in, 347–350
    Beliaghata 1947, 348
    election-related, 347, 348, 350
    Partition years, 348–349
    speeches on Direct Action Day in 1946, 347
Besant, Annie, 231, 271, 366
Beschi, Costanzo Giuseppe, 73
Béteille, André, 215
Bhabha Atomic Research Centre reactor, Bombay, 3
Bhagalpur, Bihar, 301
Bhalla, M.M., xiv
Bhandari, Sunder Singh, 202
Bharat, 336
Bharati, Subramania, 107
Bharatiya Jana Sangh (BJS), 113, 256
Bharatiya Janata Party (BJP), 113, 163, 176, 185–186, 202, 228–230, 265, 274, 291, 305, 355
Bharatiya Nagarik Suraksha Sanhita, Section 479 of, 85
Bharat Mata, 337–338
Bharatpur Waterbird Sanctuary, 50
Bharat Ratna, 167–169

Chakravarti Rajagopalachari, 167
C.V. Raman, 167, 168
Mother Teresa, 170
posthumous conferrings of, 135–138
Sarvepalli Radhakrishnan, 167–168
Bhatia, Kishan, xvi
Bhatnagar, Shanti Swarup, 193–194
Bhat, Ravindra, 246
Bhattacharjee, Buddhadeb, 40, 41, 58–60, 269, 290–291
Bhatt, Chandi Prasad, 211
Bhave, Vinoba, 287
Bhavsinhji, 281
Bhima-Koregaon event, 2018, 351–353
Bhopal, 230
Bhosle, Asha, 351
Bhubaneswar, 129, 252
Bhuj earthquake, 312
Bhutto, Benazir, 3, 4
Bhutto, Zulfikar Ali, 3, 10
Bibhutibhusan, 215
Bigelow, Albert, 65
Bihar, 101, 147, 201–203, 263, 264, 265, 281, 291, 295, 315, 316, 347
  caste survey in, 203
  no constitutional breakdown, 202
  populous state, 201
  Rabri Devi's government in, 201–202
  recommendation to President for government's dismissal, 202
  return of recommendation for reconsideration, 202
  upheld of Constitution's morality, 203
Bihar earthquake, 313
Bindal, M.K., 30
biological weapons, 236
Birla House, 109, 159
Birla Mandir, New Delhi, 65
birth control, 37
Biswas, Anil, 60
Blake, William, 8, 38, 303, 304
blind persons, in India, 299–301
  Bhagalpur incident, 301
  initiatives by official agencies and NGOs, 301
  non-representation in Lok Sabha, 300
  number of, 300
  Parliament's attention to, 300–301
  and poverty, 300
  women and girls, 300
Blondie (fictional woman), 36
Bolivar, Simon, 41

Bolpur, 61, 62
Bombay, 104, 200, 264, 284
Bond, Ruskin, 139, xiii
Bonnerjee, Womesh Chandra, 270
book-bullies, 330
The Book of Indian Birds (Salim Ali), 223
Booth, John Wilkes, 165
Border, Peace and Tranquility Agreement with China, 137
Bordoloi, Gopinath, 264
Bose, Buddhadeb, 214, 215
Bose, Nandalal, 213
Bose, Netaji Subhas, 101, 166, 184
Bose, Nirmal, 215
Boundary Commission, 259
Bourke-White, Margaret, 20
Bower Birds, Australian, 52
Brasília, 160
Brecht, Bertolt, 351–352
Britain, 43, 65, 68, 69, 120
British Raj, xvii, 153, 155, 340–341
BSP, 228
Buck, Pearl S., 37–38
Buddha, 137, 201, 205, 215, 217
Buddha Jayanti, nuclear test on, 64
builder, 334–335
Builders of Modern India (book), 334
burden of proof, 228
Burma, 263
Burman, S.D., 132
Burrows, Frederick, 280, 287
Butler, 'RAB,' 264

Calcutta, 39–41, 51, 63, 72, 75, 134, 158, 160, 167, 172, 178, 210, 213, 256, 259–261, 270, 280, 284, 299, 347
CANDU reactor, Karachi, 3–4
canonisation, 160–163
capital offences, 341
capital punishment, 340
Carson, Clayborne, 82
caste and religion, in India, 344
Central Cottage Industries Emporium, 94
Central Hall, 219
Central Provinces, 264
Ceylon, 14
Chagla, M.C., 273, 279
Chakrabarty, Arindam, 217
Chakravarty, Sukhomoy, 215
Chamber of Princes of India, 69
Chanda Sahib, 73
Chandrachud, D.Y., 61, 206

Index

Chandrayaan-3 (India), 44, 45
Chatterjee, Nirmal Chandra, 62
Chatterjee, Partha, 215
Chatterjee, Somnath, 61–63
Chatterjee, Sunil, 134
Chattopadhyay, Harindranath, 90–91, 133
Chattopadhyay, Kamaladevi, 89–97, 105, 133, 209, 210
  care for individuals, 96–97
  Civil Disobedience movement, 92
  Congress Socialist Party, 92
  crafts, attention to, 94–95
  early life/childhood, 89–90
  equality/support for womankind, 91, 93, 97
  friends in outside world, 95
  Gandhiji and, 90–94, 97
  Inner Recesses Outer Spaces (memoir), 89
  no to office and power, 94
  political participation, 90–94
  Quit India movement, 94
  remarriage with Harindranath, 90
  salt satyagraha, 89, 91–92
  Sangeet Natak Akademi, 95, 96
Chaturvedi, T.N., 251, 286
Chaudhry, Kamala, 133–134
Chaudhry, Khem, 134
Chaudhurani, Saraladevi, 216
Chavez, Hugo, 39–41, 58–59
chawls (Bombay), 37
chemical weapons, 236
Chennai, 299, 318, 333
Chhabra, Rami, 317
Chhattisgarh, 355
Chicago, 171
Chief Justice of India, 261–262
child labour, 304
The Child Marriage Restraint Act 1929 (Sarda Act), 36–37
Chile, 39, 314
China, 3, 37, 80, 94, 151, 170, 207, 211, 239, 252, 308
  AI-driven tool for earthquakes prediction, 30
Chitrasena (Sri Lankan dancer), 95
Chitto jetha bhoyshunno (Rabindranath Tagore), 241
Chomsky, Noam, 41
Chopra, Neeraj, 18, 20
Chopra, Pran, xvi
Chouhan, Shivraj Singh, 355
Christian India, 161

Christianity, 163
Christian missionary, in Tamil-speaking world, 72–74
Christians in India, 162
Churchill, Winston S., 343, 346
Civil Disobedience movement, 1932, 92
civil rights movement, US, 236
civil warriors, 18–21
classism, 81
climate change, 318, 359
  action from Public Office, 320
  and COVID-19, 318–320
  danger from double whammy, 319
  self-regulations, need of, 320
climate crisis, 115
Clinton, Hillary, 35
The Cloud (poem), 319
Clyde, S.S., 156
Collected Works, 216
collective responsibility, 274
communal frenzies, inciters of, 329
communalism, 165, 345
communal peace, 310
communal rhetoric, 331
communal riots, 260, 329
communal tension, 309, 329
communal violence, 147, 171–172
communal virus, 330–332
The Communist Manifesto, 39, 41
Communist Party of India, 61, 68, 69, 256, 294, 305
Communist Party of India (Marxist), 267–269, 305, 345
communists, 69
Companies Act, Section 293A of, 279
conflict-free environment, sustainable development in, 32
Congress, 113, 126, 146, 172, 173–174, 176, 226, 228, 231–233, 255, 257, 263, 270–272, 273, 276, 294, 305
  as all-India party, 271
  change in, need of, 272
  destiny, 272
  founders of, 270
  Gandhiji on, 271
  history, 271
  post-Indira, 271–272
  pre-Emergency, 271
  presidents, 271
  sessions in south, 294
  Sonia Gandhi and, 272
  suspicion/fear in, 272

Index

40 years since Emergency, 271–272
Congress Socialist Party, 92
Constituent Assembly, 18, 163, 167, 185, 219, 227, 251, 257, 281, 336, 352
Constitutional fairness, 202
Constitutional Governor, 284
Constitution of India, 225–227, 251, 261, 264, 275, 283, 337, 338, 343
   1935 Act and, 263–265
   Article 1, 336, 337
   Article 25, 345
   Article 82, 295
   Article 311, 251
   Article 314, 251
   Census-linked re-arrangement of constituencies, 294–295
   drafting of, 227
   first Republic Day, 225, 226
   freedom of opinion and expression on, 225
   Lok Sabha, 275
   42nd Amendment to, 227, 295, 316
   Preamble to, 227
   rights of minorities, 163
   secularism as basic feature of, 345
   84th Amendment of, 295, 316
   three lists, 263
   10th Schedule, 275
   on tribals, 361, 362
construction workers, 333–335
conversions, Christian, 162
Cook, Frederick, 42
Coonoor, the Nilgiris, 333
COP27 summit, in Sharm el-Sheikh, 121
corporate contributions, to election funds, 278–279
correctional homes, 84, 321
corruption, 167, 168, 201, 331, 357
Cousins, James, 91
Cousins, Margaret, 91
COVID-19 pandemic, 79
   Indian Tamils of Sri Lanka and, 16
   lockdown, 80–81
   Omicron, 318–319
   spread of, 29
crafts and handweaves traditions, 104, 105
crime against humanity, 303. *see also* kidnapping and abduction
criminally charged candidates, 228–230
Criminal Procedure Code
   Section 108, 153
   Section 436A, 322
cross-border terrorism, 10

crow, cruel and cunning bird, 222–224
3 'C's, India and, 344
cultural czarina, 104
Curzon, George Nathaniel, 287
custodial deaths and torture, 245
cyber terror, 115

Dadabhai Naoroji: Pioneer of Indian Nationalism (Dinyar Patel), 120
The Daily Mail, 271
Dakshineshwar, 61
Dalai Lama, 103, 104, 170–172, 211
Dalal, Rusi, 120
dalits, 232, 240
Dandi March, 178
Dange, S.A., 69
Das, Biswanath, 264
Das, Chittaranjan, 271
Dasgupta, Uma, 217
Das, Seth Govind, 204, 205
Datta, Amlan, 217
Daulatram, Jairamdas, 226
death of innocent peasants, 268–269
death penalty, 339–342
   in 1516, 339
   in 1616, 339–340
   in 1716, 340
   in 1816, 340–341
   in 1916, 341
   abolition of, 341, 342
   acts against the State, 342
   after Independence, 341–342
   historical perspective, 339–341
   public opinion, 341
   rape and murder cases, 341
   terrorism and deaths of innocents, 341, 342
   in 'the rarest of rare' cases, 341
de Cuellar, Javier Pérez, 116
defence forces, 19, 20, 212
Defence of India Act, 83, 341
Delhi, 30, 76, 103, 158–159, 188, 252, 261, 268, 269, 293, 317, 318, 339, 347, 353
Delhi firing, on Rowlatt Act protestors, 181
Delhi to Chungking (K.P.S. Menon), 49
delimitation, 294, 316–317
   on 2026 census data, 316
   census data and, 295–296
   of constituencies in 2026, 294
   freeze, 295, 316
   impact of, 294–295

political anomaly and civilisational
    piquancy, 316
population-stabilising States, 295
States with increase in population, 295
valuationally gross, 317
women, representational disadvantage to,
    317
Deloney, Thomas, 312
demonetisation, 357, 358
Deo, Pravir Chandra Bhanj, 363
Deo, Shankarrao, 200
Dereere, Vincent Victor, 308
Desai, Anita, 150
Desai, Durga, 306
Desai, Mahadev, 144, 184, 306
Desai, Morarji, 7, 83
Desai, S.T., 278, 279
Deshmukh, C.D., 283
Deshmukh, P.S., 204
De Silva, Minnette, 95
Development as Freedom (Amartya Sen), 237
Dev, Guru Arjan, 339
Devi, Gayatri, 133, 216
Devi, Indira, 216
Devi, Krishna, 112
Devi, Mahasweta, 215
Devi, Rabri, 201–203, 291
Devi, Rajbansi, 188
Devi, Rukmini, 105
Dey, Manna, 323, 338
Dhaka, 236
Dhanammal, Veena, 106
dharma, 305, 307, 339
dharma chakra of Asoka, 205
dharmaguru, 171
Dhebar, Uchharangrai Navalshankar, 57
Dhed community, 367
Dhingra, Madan Lal, 341
digi-dhan, 359
Dinkar, Ramdhari Singh, 353
disarmament, 66–67
distinction, 218
Doctrine of Lapse (Dalhousie), 73
Doke, Joseph J., 157
Donne, John, 74
Doraiswamy, G., 56
Doraswami, Anand, 36
double-member constituencies, 317
Dover Straits earthquake, 312
Drèze, Jean, 211
Dronning Maud Land/Queen Maud Land,
    42–43

drought
    agrarian distress, 356
    and elections, 354–356
    national crisis, 356
    rain deficit, 355, 356
D'Souza, Jerome, 161, 162, 204
D'Souza, Joseph Alban, 204
Durban, 157
Duterte, Rodrigo, 177
Dutt, Subimal, 129, 131
duumvirate, 226
Dyer, Reginald, 181

earthquakes
    AI-driven tool for prediction of, 30
    anticipation, 314
    Bhuj earthquake, 312
    Bihar earthquake, 313
    Dover Straits earthquake, London, 312
    earthquake-prone Himalayas, 314
    frequency in higher seismic zones, 30
    high-risk zones, 27
    Hindukush earthquake, 313
    human activities and, 30
    India and Tibet, 1950, 312
    Kashmir Valley, 1555, 312
    kshurasya dhara, 25, 27
    Nepal earthquake, 313
    NISAR (satellite), use of, 314
    preparations for, 313
    public participation/backing for earthquake
        preparedness, 26
    Quetta, Balochistan, 1935, 312
    seismic mapping of risk factors, 26–27
    South Asia, 2005, 313
    State interventions, need of, 313–314
    tectonic plates and fault lines of India,
        25–26
    Turkey and Syria, 2023, 25–27, 311
    in Uttarakhand and Himalayan arc, 25–26
    warnings of likely seismic threats, 314
    workshop at India International Centre,
        311, 314
East India Company, 340
East Pakistan, 7, 10, 259, 260, 347
Eden, Emily, 72, 74
Eden, Fanny, 72, 74
Eden, George (Earl of Auckland), 72
Edict VI of Ashoka, 360
Edict V of Asoka, 223
Edict XII, 206
Einstein, Albert, 66, xvii

Eisenhower, Dwight D., 43
election campaigning language, 257
Election Commission of India (ECI), 194, 229, 256, 257
election-related violence, in West Bengal, 347–350
elections, in India
    ADR statistics on, 228
    candidates with criminal charge, 228–230
    elections just concluded, 255, 257
    first election to first Lok Sabha, 255–257
    inking of fingers in, 193–195
    Sir William Garrow's concept and, 228–230
electoral democracy, 236, 252, 258, 294
electoral politics, 265
electorates, polarised, 265
Eliot, T.S., 327–328
Elphinstone, Mountstuart, 73
Elwin, Verrier, 74, 162
Em and the Big Hoom (Jerry Pinto), 141
emergency, 83–85, 105, 173, 261, 270, 358
    horrors of, 83–84
    India as vast prison house during, 83–84
    radical reform, need of, 85
    50th anniversary of, 83
Emperor versus Bal Gangadhar Tilak, 154
Engels, Friedrich, 39, 69
England, 68, 72, 81, 90, 142, 271, 312
English Court of Appeal, 1935, 228
English fiction, Indian writers of, 140–141
An Equal Music (Vikram Seth), 140
Erdogan, Recep, 177
Essays of Elia, xv
eternal verities, 137
ethics
    in governance, 208–209
    for human activity in outer space, 42–45
Europe, 236, 328
European Union, 31
expectations, diminishing, 245

Faiz, Faiz Ahmad, 150, 152, 353, xiv
family planning, 162
    importance of, 315, 316
Farmers' Commission, 356
farmers death, in Lakhimpur Kheri, 246
Farrukhsiyar, 340
Farsakh, Nebal, 28
fascism, 169
The Fate of Butterflies (Nayantara Sahgal), 140
fear
    addiction to, 239–241
    law-enforcers responsibility, 241
    variants of, 239–240
fear-free people/fearful people, 239–241
Fernandes, George, 83
fictional veracity, 150
The Final Century (Martin Rees), 66
Finsbury, 120, 121
First Ladies, 187–189
First War of Independence, 1857, 200
flag of India
    adoption of, by Constituent Assembly, 204–206
    anniversary of adoption of, 204, 206
    Ashoka Chakra in, 204–206
    features of flag explained by Nehru, 204–205
    Resolution regarding, 219–221
    speakers on motion of new flag, 204–205
Flather, Shreela, 124
Floyd, George, 80, 81
fractious family, 233
France, 43
freedom of faith, 326
freedom of speech, 326
free will and destiny, 52
From Fear Set Free (Nayantara Sahgal), 140
From Heaven Lake (Vikram Seth), 140, 151

Gaddafi, Muammar, 41
Gadgil, N.V., 175
Gandhi 1914-1948 (Ramachandra Guha), 177–179
Gandhi, Abha, 76
Gandhi-Ambedkar Poona Pact, 264
Gandhi Ashram, Meerut, 101
Gandhi, Indira, xvii, 3, 7, 9–12, 103, 105, 126, 127, 133, 271–272, 286, 301, 316, 325, 357–358
    assassination anniversary, 173
    delimitation freeze, 295
    national emergency, 173
    nature and environment, 51
    Pokhran I, 64
Gandhi, Karamchand 'Kaba', 156
Gandhi, Kasturba, 53–54, 132, 189, 199, 200, 233, 306
Gandhi, Mahatma, xviii, 36, 50, 52, 53–54, 79–81, 90, 104, 109, 110, 115–117, 132, 145, 156, 164–165, 172, 180, 184, 199, 200, 201, 216–219, 231, 233–234, 271, 272, 280, 284, 287,

378 Index

325, 353, 365
assassination, 119, 164
in Beliaghata, 76, 259
in Calcutta on eve of Independence, 75
collapse in Puri, 306
engagements with music, 156–159
fast for Ahmedabad mill-workers, 177
fast in Delhi, Hindu-Muslim riots and, 345
Godhra conference, 366–367
Hindu-Muslim peace, 177
on Indian National Congress, 231, 271
Sabarmati Ashram, 157
Second Round Table Conference, 231
security of minorities, 260
Gandhi, Maneka, 304
Gandhi, Manu, 158
Gandhi, Rajiv, 3–5, 7, 252, 286, 341
Khan–Menon Agreement, 4–5
1988 visit to Islamabad, 4
Gandhi, Rajmohan, xviii, 81, 174, 178, 185, 187
Gandhi, Ramchandra, 119
Gandhi, Sonia, 174, 272
Ganguly, Nishat, 124
Garrow, William, 228, 229
Gaza, 239
gender justice, 37
Gengan, David, 82
Germany, 67, 327
Gharana Maryada, 113
Ghosh, Amitav, xiii, 140–141
girmitiya, 334, 335
Gitanjali (Tagore), 153, 214, 217
global warming, 207
gluttony of civilisation, 79–80
Godhra, Gujarat, 365–367
Godse, Nathuram, 164–165, 341
Gokhale, Gopal Krishna, 189, 271
The Golden Gate (Vikram Seth), 140, 151
Goldsmith, Oliver, 333
The Good Earth (Pearl S. Buck), 37
The Good Person of Szechwan, 351
goons, 240
Gopalan, A.K., 56, 69
Gopalaswami, N., 273
Gopal, S., 127, 130, 135, 188
Gorky, Maxim, xvi
'Go to Pakistan,' 328
governance, architecture of, 250–251
Government of India Act, 1935, 232, 263–266
Governor of the Reserve Bank of India, 283

governor(s), 280, 283–288
address to Legislative Assembly, 289–292
all-pervasive moral influence, 281–282, 287
appointment, 285–286
constitutional head of state, 280, 282
exemplars of ideal Governor, 286–287
hung-result scene, 286
march of democracy, 288
movements, 285
need of, 280–282, 287–288
political assessment by Prime Minister, 286
politically un-biased, 285
post-Nehru appointments, 286
President's Rule, 286
Raj Bhavans, 284–285
Gowda, Deve, 7, 65
Great Bengal Famine of 1943, 213
Great Calcutta Massacre of 1946, 213
Great Contemporaries (Winston S. Churchill), 343
The Greatest Airlift (Annis G. Thompson), 247
Great Revolt of 1857, 73, 340
Greenpeace, 65
Green Revolution, 268
G20 Summit, New Delhi, 31
Africa gain by AU joining G20, 32
African Union (AU) in, 31, 32
gain for G21 by AU joining, 32–34
Guantanamo's concentration camp, 35
gubernatorial pelf, 284
Guevara, Che, 41
Guha, Ramachandra, 177–179, 330
Guha, Ranajit, 215
Gujarat, 184, 200, 229, 255, 287, 334, 345, 346, 365
Gujarat Political Conference of 1917, Godhra, 365–367
Gujarat riots of 2002, 348
Gujarat Vidyapith, Ahmedabad, 100
Gujral, I.K., 7, 11, 65, 202, 253
Gulzar, 150
Gupta, Ashoka, 215
Gupta, Indrajit, 68–71
Gupta, Uma Das, 215
Guruswamy, Menaka, 233
Guterres, Antonio, 115, 116
G.V. Mavalankar Memorial Lecture, 1993, 265
Gwalior, 112

Habibullah, Wajahat, 360
Hague Declaration, 326

Index

Haksar, P.N., 105
Hamilton, George, 341
Hansard, 56
Hanuman Chalisa, 118
Haq, Mahbub-ul, 215
harmony, inter-community, 171
Harris, Kamala, 121, 132
Harrison, George, 124
Hasina, Sheikh, 7
hate and violence, dislike of, 119
Hathi, Jaisukhlal, 273, 274
hatriotism, fuelling of, 12
Hazare, Anna, 227
Hazra, Matangini, 219
Hazratbal relic theft, 308–309
Hegiste, Vasantrao, 172
heritage of a shared Peoplehood, destruction of, 343–346
High Courts, 261
Hindu domination, 232
Hinduism, denigrating of, 330, 331
Hindukush earthquake, 313
Hindu Mahasabha, 77, 146, 185
Hindu-Muslim divide, 344
Hindu-Muslim riots, 344, 345
Hindu Rashtra, 77
The Hindus: An Alternative History (Wendy Doniger), 330, 331
Hindustan Times, 248
Hindutva, 12
Hindutva virus, 332
Hiroshima, 79
Hitler, 69
Holborn (London, Great Britain), 120
Hore, Somnath, 62–63, 213
House of Commons, 53–54, 120, 121
human rights activist, 240
Hum Dekhenge (poem), 353
Hume, Allan Octavian, 231
Huq, Fazlul, 232
Husain, Dr Zakir, 126, 144
Husain, M.F., 223
Hydari, Akbar, 284
Hyderabad, 18

identity-clustering, 14
illness/death, of Indian prisoners, 53–54
immaculacy, 226
immediacy, 226
immigrant, 240
Imperial Legislative Council, 293, 296
imprisonment, 196
for life, 321
In Custody (film), 150
independence of India
 1947 and, 75
 Hindu Rashtra, idea of, 77
 new generation of Indians, 77–78
 partition and, 75
 plural society with secular government, 77
 75th year of, 199–200
 two nation theory, 77
 violence and riots after, 75–76
India and Bharat, 336
India, as majority of minorities, 233
INDIA coalition, 255
India in 2047, 207–209
 ethics in governance, 208–209
 gross domestic product (GDP), 208
 population growth, 207
 risks to existence, 207
 urban population, 208
India International Centre, New Delhi, 96, 311
India Meteorological Department (IMD), 354
Indian Administrative Service (IAS), 250
Indian Council of Scientific and Industrial Research, 193
Indian High Commission, London, 289
Indian liberalism, voice of, 152
Indian Museum, Calcutta, 215
Indian National Congress, 120, 231, 270, 345. *see also* Congress
Indian Penal Code (IPC), 197, 229, 321, 341
 Section 124 A, 153
Indian Space Policy 2023, 309, 310
Indian Space Research Organisation, 310, 314
Indian Tamils, in Sri Lanka, 14–16
India–Pakistan Agreement of 2008, 322–323
 lists of civilian prisoners, exchange of, 322–323
India–Pakistan wars, 9
 1947–48, 9, 10
 1965, 9, 10, 127
 1971, 9, 10
 1999, 10
India-Pak war of 1965, 127
India's north as India's political summit, 293–294
individualism, 218
Indore, 175
inking of fingers, in elections, 193–195
 first general elections, 193
 making of ink, 193–194
 to prevent multiple voting by

impersonation, 193
  Siddiqui's indelible ink, 194
Intelligence Bureau, 309
International Agency for the Prevention of Blindness, 300
International Geophysical Year (IGY), 1958, 43
intolerance, 169
Iran, 239
Iraq, 35
Isal, Shireen, 124
Isha Upanishad, 167
Islam, 163
Islamabad, 3, 4, 323
  Rajiv's 1988 visit to, 4
Israel, 239
Israel–Palestine war, 28
  air attacks on Gaza, 28
  number of causalties, 28
  UN warning to Israel, 28
Iyer, V.R. Krishna, 277

Jadhav, Kulbhushan, 323
Jagdalpur manslaughter, 363, 364
Jahangir (Mughal emperor), 339
Jai Bhim (film), 245
jail, life in, 321–322. *see also* prisoners, in jail
Jain, L.C., 95
Jaishankar, S., 115
Jaitley, Arun, 83
Jallianwala Bagh massacre, 181–182
Jammu and Kashmir, 227, 239
Janah, Sunil, 213
Janata Dal, 291
Japan, 43, 67, 94, 236, 314
Jarvis, Rev., xiv–xvi
Jawaharlal Nehru Memorial Lecture, 1967, 264
Jayakar, Pupul, 96, 103–105
Jefferson, Thomas, 77
Jharkhand, 315, 362
Jinnah: Ek Punardrishti (V.K. Baranwal), 154
Jinnah, M. A., 77, 121, 147, 154, 155, 177, 199, 231, 232, 234, 365, 367
John, Elton, 320
Jorasanko, 58
Joseph, George, 161
judges. *see also* judiciary
  and prestige, 277–278
  respect and trust on, 277–279
judiciary
  Chief Justice of India, 261–262
  Constitution and role of, 261–262
  High Courts and Supreme Court, 261–262
  hope from, 245–246
  respect in, 277–279
  respect to, 212

Kabuliwala (film), 323
Kajrolkar, Narayan Sadoba, 257
Kakayuga, 222–224
Kalam, A.P.J. Abdul, 308
Kalinga, 205
Kalinga Edict, 252, 254
Kalinga war, 305–306
Kamala (name), 132–134
Kamaladevi. *see* Chattopadhyay, Kamaladevi
Kamaraj, K., 94, 126, 130, 359
Kamath, H.V., 204, 336
Kanimozhi, 304
Kanjilal, Tushar, 215
Kannur, 345
Kanpur, 171
Kapse, Ram, 286
Kapurthala, 161
Karat, Brinda, 304
Karat, Prakash, 83, 267–269
Kargil war, 10, 230
Karkare, Hemant, 230
Karnataka, 286, 345, 355
Kashani, Sufi poet, 309
Kashmir, 20, 239, 308–309, 360
Kashmir earthquake, 1555, 312
Kashmiri India, 233
Kasturba Gandhi memorial fund, 104
Kasuri, Khurshid, 328
Katju, K.N., 281, 288
Katju, Markandey, 277, 279
Kattabomman (ruler of Panchalankurichi), 340
Katugastota-based Institute of Social Development, 15
Kaur, Rajkumari Amrit, 161, 226, 320
Kaushal, Abhishek, 125
Kejriwal, Arvind, 282
Kenyatta, Jomo, 236
Kerala, 252, 265, 267, 295, 316
Khaliquzzaman, Chaudhuri, 193, 194, 204
Khan, Ayub, 10
Khandekar, H.J., 205
Khan, Khan Abdul Ghaffar, 142–149
  appellation of Badshah (king), 143
  champion of non-violence, 145
  Congress in NWFP, 146
  Congress session, Nagpur, 143
  early life, 142
  education, interest in, 142–143

Index

formation of Pakistan, 147
freedom struggle, 143–146
Gandhiji and, 145–147
khilafat movement, 143
Khudai Khidmatgars' campaign, 145
life after Partition, 148–149
life in Gandhiji's movement, 146
meeting at Utmanzai, 143
meeting with Jinnah, 147
model prisoner, 144–145
national movement, 144
non-violent direct action, 144
NWFP to Pakistan, 148
Pathan leader, 143
'Red-Shirts,' 146
religious faith, 144–145
Sarhad-e-Gandhi (Frontier Gandhi), 145
satyagraha, 144–145
two-nation theory, 147
Khan, Humayun, 4
Khan, Liaquat Ali, 194
Khan, Mehboob, 150, 338
Khan–Menon Agreement, 4–5
Khan, Nishat, 124
Khan, Rahman, 273
Khan Saheb, Dr, 142, 143, 146, 264
Khan, Ustad Vilayat, 140
Khare, N.B., 264
Kharge, Mallikarjun, 255
Kher, B.G., 264
khilafat movement, 143
Khudai Khidmatgars, 145
Khulna, 259
Khusrau, 339
kidnapping and abduction, 302–304
    award money for information, 304
    of children/girl-children, 303, 304
    class aspect, 303
    by gang or group, 304
    Mission: Rescue Kidnapped Children, 304
    murder/abuse of kidnapped children, 303
    NCRB report, 2022, 302, 303
    outrage against humanity, 303
    real-life stories, 302–303
    reported cases, increase in, 303
    sharing experiences of kidnapped returnee, 304
    suggestions for prevention, 304
    surge in cases, 302, 303
killing for killing, 342
King Haakon VII's Plateau, 42
King, Martin Luther, 236

Kisan Mazdoor Praja Party, 101
Kisan Sabha, 267
Kishoreji, Awadh, xiii–xiv
Kizhavenmani, Tamil Nadu, 268
Kolkata, 58, 283, 290
Kothandapani, A., 56
Kripalani, Acharya, 98–102, 145, 200, 256, 257, 363
    Champaran campaign, 99, 100
    contribution to education, 100–101
    first meeting with Gandhiji, 98
    freedom struggle, 99–101
    Gandhi and, 98–101
    general secretary of Congress, 101
    rebel in college time, 98
    retirement from public life, 102
    roots in Sindh, 98
    teacher of history, 98, 100
Krishak Mazdoor Praja Party, 307
Krishak Praja Party, 232
Krishnadevaraya (king of Vijayanagara), 339
Krishnamachari, T.T., 107
Krishnamurti Foundation's Rishi Valley school, 104
Krishnamurti, J., 103, 110
Krishnaswamy, N., 102
Krishna, T.M., 156
Ku Klux Klan, 165
Kulkarni, G.F., 252–253
Kulkarni, Sudheendra, 154, 328
Kulkarni, Sumitra Gandhi, 252
Kumarappa brothers, J.C. and Bharatan, 161
Kumari, Kamala, 134
Kumar, Nitish, 291
Kural, the (Tirukkural of Tiruvalluvar), 73

Ladakh, 211
Lahiri, Ramtanu, 214
Lahore, 10
Lakhimpur Kheri, deaths of farmers in, 246
Lalit, U.U., 246
Lal, Sham, xvi
Lama, Dalai, 7
Lamb, Charles, xv, xvi
language speaker, non-local, 240
Lanka Sama Samaj Party, 95
The Last Phase (Pyarelal), 21, 178
Lawrence Dana Pinkham Memorial Lecture, Chennai, 155
Laxman, Kamala, 134
Laxman, R.K., 134, 223, 249
Left Front government, 269

Index

legal aid, right to, 246
Lenin, 69
The Leprosy Mission, 162
Libya, 35
Lincoln, Abraham, 80, 165, 200
Line of Control (LoC), 10, 11
lionism, 186
Li Wenliang, 81
lockdown, 80
    migrant workers and, 80–81
    upper class of society and, 80, 81
Lodi, Sikandar, 339
Lokpal bill, the, 269
London, 133, 151, 156, 199, 231, 233, 327, 341
Lord Chelmsford, 182
Lord Hastings, 340
Lord Mountbatten, 147
Luna-25 lander (Russia), 44
Luther, Martin, 79–81
Luthra, Siddhartha, 248
Luthuli, Albert, 80, 236
Iyer, Musiri Subramania, 109

Maclellan, Nic, 65
Madhushala (Harivansh Rai Bachchan), 129
Madhya Pradesh, 19, 255, 295, 344, 355, 361
Madkam, Jamlo, 81
Madras, 70, 73, 90, 92, 102, 104, 109, 110, 126, 127, 188, 225, 263, 268, 270, 281, 307, 325
Madras high court, Madurai bench, 197–198
The Madras Music Academy, 107
Madurai, 106
Madura Mission, 73
Maghrib Namaz, 345
Mahabharata, 330
Mahabubnagar rail accident, 55, 56
Mahadevan, R., 197
Mahalanobis, P.C., 215
Maharaja of Mysore, 68, 70
Maharashtra, 255, 265, 295, 334, 351, 361
Maharshi, Ramana, 227
Mahatab, Harekrushna, 200
Mahatma Gandhi - The Last Phase, Navajivan (Pyarelal)
Maintenance of Internal Security Act, 83
majoritarian State, 328
majority domination, 233
'Malaiyaham200' event, 15
Malaviya, Madan Mohan, 98
2008 Malegaon bombings, 230

male oppression, 338
Malhotra, Inder, xvi, 273, 274
Malhotra, Indu, 212
Malik, Shahid, 323
Mandela, Ndileka, 82
Mandela, Nelson, 32, 79–81, 236
Manga, Alarmel, 187
Mangalore, 89, 163
Mangeshkar, Lata, 337, 351
Manila, 160
Manipur, 206, 240, 261, 284, 310, 315
Manjusri (Sri Lankan artist), 95
Maoist violence, 348, 362
Mao Zedong, 69
Mappings (Vikram Seth), 151
Markandaya, Kamala, 133, 141
market economy, 342
martyrs of Jallianwala, 181–182
Marxist movements, in Kerala, 268
Marx, Karl, 39, 59, 69
Mascarenhas, Adrian, 160
mass extinction, 66
mass immunisation, 162, 320
Mathai, John, 226
Mathur, Anandi Prasad, 171
Mayo, Katherine, 36–37
medical aid, to sick detainee, 54
Medtner, Nikolai, 69
Medtner Society, London, 69
Meeradebi, 60
Meghalaya, 315
Mehta, Mohan Singh, 205
Mehta, Tushar, 6
Member of parliament (MP), 275
    BJP MP, 275
    Congress MP, 275
    disappointments with, 273–274
    independence of mind, 274
    opposition MP, 275
    ruling party MP, 275
    10th Schedule, 275
Menon, K.P.S., 4
Menon, Narayana, 107
Menon, V.K. Krishna, 102, 123, 264, 268, 320
Midnight's Children (Salman Rushdie), 118
migrant workers, 80–81, 333–335
militant/ultra, 240
Minorities Committee session, 231–232
minorities, rights of, 163
minority backlash, 329
minority, in India, 233
minority satisfaction, 232

Mint Lounge, 245
Minty, Abdul S., 33
Misri, Vikram, 18–19
missionaries, as converters, 240
Missionaries of Charity, 160, 210
Mitra, Ashok, 215
Mitra, Peary Chand, 214
Mitra, Sachin, 117, 172, 213
M.N. Roy Memorial Lecture, New Delhi, 155
Model Prison Manual of 2016, 197
Modern India (Sumit Sarkar), 145
Modified Mercalli intensity scale, 312
Modi, Narendra, 4, 5, 10, 45, 135, 137, 170, 174, 177, 185, 230, 255, 325, 355
   Chandrayaan 3 success, 45
   inclusion of AU in G21, 31, 32
Mody, Homi, 281, 288
Mohammed, Dost, 72
Mohandas (Rajmohan Gandhi), 178
Montagu, Edwin S., 367
Mookerjee, Asutosh, 134
Mookerjee, Harendra C., 163
Mookerjee, H.C., 204
Mookerjee, Syama Prasad, 256
Moon Agreement, 44, 45
Moore, Samuel, 39, 41
More, D.M., 354
Morley, John, 343, 346
Morrison, Scott, 177
Moscow, 68–69
Mother India (film), 150, 338
Mother India (Katherine Mayo), 36
Mother Teresa, 160–163, 170, 210
Mountbatten, Lord, 325
Mozumdar, Sucheta, 101
Mueller, Max, 331
Mughal Gardens, 64
Muhammad Saadulla, Saiyid, 204, 205
Mukherjee, Chittatosh, 277
Mukherjee, Hiren, 62, 256
Mukherjee, Pranab, 322, 342
Mulgaokar, S., xvi
Mullik, B.N., 309, 310
Muniswami, M., 56
Muralitharan, Muthiah, 14
Murder in the Cathedral (play), 327–328
Murmu, Droupadi, 137, 252, 254
Murshidabad, 259
Musafir, Giani Gurmukh Singh, 205
muscle and money power, 237
Muslim League, 77, 147, 193, 232
Muslim members of parliament, 265

Mussoorie, 50
mutual respect, 251
Myanmar, 237
The Mysterious Ailment of Rupi Baskey (Hansda Sowvendra Shekhar), 362

Nagappa, S., 204
Nagappen, Sammy, 53, 234
Nagasaki, 79
Naga separatists, 284
Naidu, Sarojini, 90, 92, 109, 199, 205–206, 231, 234, 271, 284
Naipaul, V.S., 334
Nair, Madhavan, 308
Nair, M.N. Govindan, 363
Nalanda University bill, 269
Namboodiripad, E.M.S., 69, 267, 359
Nanda, Gulzarilal, 130, 135
Nandigram, 59, 60, 216, 268, 269
Naoroji, Dadabhai, 120–122, 270
Narayanan, K.R., 58, 64–65, 195, 201–203, 252–254, 265, 290
Narayanan, M.K., 12
Narayanan, Usha, 187
Narayanaswami (satyagrahi in South Africa), 199, 234
Narayan, Jayaprakash, 54, 83, 97, 132, 133, 189, 201, 209, 210, 261, 353, 360, xvii
Narayan, Prabhavati, 132–133, 189
Narayan, R.K., 70–71, 141
Narwal, Himanshi, 19
Narwal, Vinay, 19
Nasik, 175
Nasreen, Taslima, 7
National Academy of Administration, Mussoorie, 251
National Aeronautics and Space Administration, US, 314
National Commission for Minorities, 345
National Commission on Population, 295
National Crime Records Bureau (report), 302
National Democratic Alliance (NDA), 170, 174, 255, 275, 355, 356, 364
National Disaster Management Authority, India, 26
The National Election Watch, 228
National Human Rights Commission, 345
National Institute of Disaster Management, 30
National Investigation Agency, 230
nationalism, 163, 337
National Rural Employment Guarantee Act, 211
National Science Council of Pakistan, 194

national totem, 337
nature, 80
Nauriya, Anil, 181
Nayar, Kuldip, xvi
Nayyar, Pyarelal, 147, 148, 159, 178
Nazir, 159, 175
Nectar in a Sieve (Kamala Markandaya), 133
Needham, Jospeh, 52
Nehru, Jawaharlal, 4, 7, 9–11, 14, 15, 19, 49–52, 56, 64, 65, 76, 92, 94, 95, 101, 102, 110, 113, 119, 123, 127, 129–131, 132, 135, 146, 163, 167, 170, 176, 184, 185, 194, 199, 200, 204, 205, 209, 220, 225, 226, 255, 264, 271, 273, 286, 288, 306, 307, 309, 324, 325, 337, 359, 363
    first election, 255–256
    Patel and, 175, 176
    on satyagraha, 144, 145
    wildlife and birds, interest in, 49–52
Nehru, Kamala, 95, 132–133, 189
Nehru Memorial Lecture in London, 1970, 264
Nelson Mandela Rules, 197–198
Nepal, 314
Nepal earthquake, 313
The New York Review of Books, 237
New Zealand, 43, 196
Nigam, Savitri, 274
Nilgiris, 73, 74, 333
NISAR (satellite), 314
Nkrumah, Kwame, 236
Noakhali, 76, 147, 260, 261
non-militarisation, of outer space, 43, 45
non-tribal India, 361
Non-Violence (artwork), 115–116
non-violence of brave, 116
Noorani, A.G., 154
Northeast India, Christianity in, 162
Northeast India, 233
North Pole, 42
North-West Frontier Province (NWFP), 142–149, 264
Norway, 42, 43
nuclear bomb, 3
    testing at Pokhran, 64
nuclear devastation, 66
nuclear disarmament, 33
nuclear explosions, 4
nuclear installation/facilities, prevention of attack on, 4
nuclear restraint, 3–5

nuclear site lists exchange, 4, 5
nuclear terror, 207
nuclear threat, no voices from civil society on, 66
nuclear war, 3, 4
nuclear weaponisation programme, 64–67
nuclear weapons, xvii, 3, 5, 32–33, 115, 137, 236
    countries, 3–5
nuclear winter (sculpture), 62, 63
Number Fifty Four (Earl Grant), 160
Nuniz, Fernao, 339
Nuremberg Laws, 327
nursing profession, 212

Obama, Barack, 35, 79
Odisha, 252, 255, 305, 306, 334, 361
OLQ (Officer Like Qualities), 250
Omicron, 318–319
On the Salt March (Thomas Weber), 178
Operation Hardtack, 65
Oppenheimer, J.R., 66
Orissa, 263, 264, 281
Orwell, George, xvii
Outer Space Treaty, 44, 45
Owaisi, Asaduddin, 18, 19

Pacific Islands, 65
paddy producers association, 268
Padmanabhan, Sudarshan, 273
Pahalgam shootout, 19
Pahwa, Madanlal, 76
Painkra, Kamlesh, 81
Pakistan, 18, 77–78, 135–137, 147, 152, 154, 155, 165, 194, 232, 260, 308, 322, 323, 324, 329
    formation of, 75, 77
    nuclear weapons, 3
    two nations theory, 77
    wars with India, 9–10
Palme Dutt, Rajani, 68
Pal, Ruma, 277
Pal, Satyabrata, 323
pandemics, climate change and, 318–320
Pandit, Vijaya Lakshmi, 140
Panikkar, K.M., 363
Pant, G.B., 200, 263, 359
Parasuram, R.P., 178
Parks, Rosa, 236
parliamentary democracy, 276
Parthasarathi, G., 105
partition, 20, 75–78, 194, 259, 264

Index

anniversary of Independence and, 75, 78
  bloody mess and refugees, 75
  consequences, 75
  day of rejoicing and of mourning, 75
  with razor's edge, 259
  and refugees, 7
  violence and riots, 75–76, 119, 347
party politics, in today's India, 186
Patel, Mitesh, 229
Patel, Sardar Vallabhbhai, 18, 19, 21, 69, 173–176, 184–186, 200, 225, 226, 251, 271, 288, 324, 325, 358, 359, 365
  birth anniversary, 173
  Congress and, 173–176
  death of, 175, 185
  Gandhi and, 184
  integration policy, 174
  iron control over political apparatus, 184
  Nehru and, 175, 176, 185
  use/owning of, 174
Pather Panchali, 38, 335
Patnaik, Prabhat, 268
patriotism, test of, 337
Peary, Robert, 42
peasants, death of
  Kizhavenmani, 268
  Nandigram, 268, 269
Pelindaba Treaty, 32–33
Peradeniya, 49
Periera, Peter Bernard, 308
Perkovich, George, 12
Peshawar, 142, 149
Peshawar school, shooting at, 164
Peshwa system of punishment, 340
Peter I Island, 43
Picasso's *Guernica*, 62
Pietermaritzburg, 80
Pillai, V. I. Munuswamy, 205
Pinto, Jerry, xiii, 141
plebiscite, 148
point blank range, 164–166
Pokhran I, 64
Pokhran II, 64, 66
Polak, Henry S.L., 53
policemen, respect to, 212
political detenus, 84, 85
political pansy, 169
political turncoat, phenomenon of, 257
politicisation of grief, 213
politics and party politics, 226
Poona jail, 200
Poona Pact, 158, 256

Pope, George Uglow, 72–74
population of India
  on 2026 census data, 316
  fertility rates, 315
  National Family Health Survey-5, 315
  population-stabilising states, 315
  stabilisation in growth, 315
  United Nations on, 315
Poverty and Famines: An Essay on Entitlement and Deprivation (Amartya Sen), 236
Poverty and Un-British Rule, 121
power, isolated, 358–359
Prabhakar, Parakala, 255
Praja Socialist Party, 56, 101
Prasad, H.Y. Sharada, 105
Prasad, Lalu, 201, 203
Prasad, Rajendra, 101, 175, 184, 188, 201, 204, 219, 225, 226, 271
Prasad, Sathya Narayana, 197
Premchand, Murshi, xvi, 320
Presidency College, Calcutta, 236
President of India, 282
  address to Parliament, 289–292
  equality in speech of, 252, 254
  influence of, 253
  Parliament's annual session, speech on, 253
  speech on eve of I-Day and R-Day, 252–254
President's Rule, 202
Press Act, 182
presumption of innocence, 228–230
presumptions of intention, 230
Pretoria, 31
Prison and Chocolate Cake (Nayantara Sahgal), 140
prisoners, in jail, 196
  affrays, 197
  arrest on suspicion of crime, 197
  bailable cognisable offences, 197
  cognisable offences, non-bailable, 196–197
  exchange of, 323
  grievance redressal mechanism, 197
  hardened criminals, 197
  illness and death of, 53–54
  improvements in inmates conditions, 321–322
  life in prison, 321–322
  Madras High Court on, 197–198
  Nelson Mandela Rules, 197–198
  premature release, 322
  prisoners' rights handbook, 197
  Section 436A of CrPC, 322

treatment of, 196–198
undertrials, 196, 322
visitorial system, 197
prisoner's rights handbook, 197
prison, life in, 321–322. *see also* prisoners, in jail
Pritam, Amrita, 134
Prithvi (missile), 66
privacy, as fundamental right, 152
process of natural selection (Darwin), 51
Protection of Children from Sexual Offences (POCSO), 246
public awareness of space programme, 309
public confidence, erosion of, 245
Public Health Foundation of India, 319
public involvement, in earthquake preparedness, 26–27
Pugwash conferences, 138
Pugwash Movement, 66
Punjab, 281
    partition-time violence in, 347
pure nationalism, ideal of, 232, 233
Puri temple, 306
'the purpose of public administration,' 250

Queen Victoria, 72, 73
Quetta earthquake, 312
Quink (Quisumbing Ink), 194
Quisumbing, Francisco, 194
Quit India movement, 1942, 69, 94, 200
Qureshi, Shah Mahmood, 323
Qureshi, Sofiya, 19

Rabindra Sarovar Stadium, Calcutta, 40
racism, in US, 165
Radhakrishnan, S., 126–128, 130, 131, 135–137, 167, 188, 204, 220–221
    on eve of Independence, 167–168
Radhakrishnan, Sivakamu, 188
Radice, William, 124
Rahman, Sheikh Mujib

Rai, Lala Lajpat, 199, 234, xiv
railway accidents, 55–57
Rainbow nation, 162
Raine, Kathleen, 124
Rajagopalachari, C. (Rajaji), xviii, 127, 184, 187–188, 225, 226, 250, 263, 284, 288
Rajan, P., 84
Rajapaksa, Mahinda, 177
Rajasthan, 295, 316, 355
Raj Bhavans, 284–285

Rajendran, Vijaya, 109
Raje, Vasundhara, 355
The Rajiv I Knew (Mani Shankar Aiyar), 3
Rajpal, W.S., xiv–xv
Ramabai, Pandita, 161, 189
Ramacharitamanas (Tulsidas), 324
Ramakrishna Mission, 210
Ramamurthy, K.C., 198
Ramana, N.V., 246
Raman, C.V., 167, 168
Ramanujan, A.K., 330
Ramasamy, Periyar E.V., 166
Ramayana, 330
Ramesh, Jairam, 330
Ram, Jagjivan, 271
Ram, N., 253
Ram Navami violence, 344, 345
Ranadive, B.T., 69
Ranganathananda, Swami, 210
Rao, P.V. Narasimha, 4, 7, 135, 137, 286
Rashtrapati Bhavan, 129, 161, 187, 252, 342
Rashtriya Swayamsevak Sangh (RSS), 112
Raya, Jagga, 340
Raychaudhuri, Tapan, 215
Rayner, Angela, 121
Ray, Satyajit, 320, 335
Reddy, Kishan, 198
Reddy, K. Srinath, 319, 320
Reddy, Snehalatha, 84
red lights on vehicles, 248
Rees, Martin, 66
refugees in India, 6–8
release of sick detainee, 54
relic, theft of, 308–309
religion in India, hold of, 310
religious divergences in political consciousness, 265
religious intolerance, 310
religious majority, 233
religious minority, 233
Representation of the People Act, 229
Republic of India, 261, 336–338
    70th anniversary of, 225–227
Reserve Bank of India Act, 1934, 283
reserved constituencies, 264
respect, in today's India, 210–212
Reuterswärd, Carl Fredrik, 115
Reynolds, Earle, 65
Right to Information Act, 211
right to life, sick detainee and, 54
riots, 239, 344
rishta (relationships), 134

Index

robotic malevolence, 115
rocket launch, first, 308
Rohingya refugees, 6
Rolland, Romain, 157
Roman Catholics, 160
Romeo and Juliet (Shakespeare), 311
Roosevelt, Franklin, 253
Rotblat, Joseph, 66
Round Table Conference (RTC), 231, 232
Rowlatt Act, 143, 180–183
Rowlatt temperament, 182–183
Roy, Aruna, 211
Roy, Juthika, 158
Roy, M.N., 69, 215
Roy, Raja Rammohun, 161, 214, 215
RSS, 12
Rumi, Jalalud-din, 99
rural poor/workforce, 237
rural voter, 355, 356
Rushdie, Salman, 118–119
Russell, Bertrand, 66, xvii
Russell-Einstein Manifesto, 1955, 66, xvii
Russia, 239, 327
Russia–Ukraine war, 28
    civilian deaths/injuries, 28

Sabarmati Ashram, 157
Sable, Ramchandra, 354
Sadasivam, T., 108
Saheb, Aziz Ahmad, 123
Sahgal, Lakshmi, 69
Sahgal, Nayantara, 140
Sahu, Lakshminarayan, 204, 205
Sainath, P., 81, 211, 334, 354, 355
Saint of Kalighat, 170
Saksena, Shibbanlal, 336
salt of the earth, 199–200, 233–234
salt satyagraha of 1930, 200
Salve, Harish, 248
Sangeet Natak Akademi, 95, 96
Sanger, Margaret, 37
Sankrityayan, Rahul, xiii, 294
Santiniketan, 61, 62, 90, 98, 134, 213, 236
Sarabhai, Mrinalini, 134
Sarabhai, Vikram, 134
Saratchandra, 214, 215
Sarda, Harbilas, 36, 37
Sarkar, Sumit, 145
satyagraha, 53, 144, 145, 199
Saudi Arabia, 239
Savarkar, Vinayak Damodar, 77, 165
Saxena, Anshu, 96, 97

scholarship, 72–74
Scindias, 112
scionism, 186
Scott, Robert, 42
Scudder, Ida, 162
Second Boer War, 219
Second Round Table Conference, London, 157
Section 144, 261
Section 479 of Bharatiya Nagarik Suraksha Sanhita, 85
Section 377, of the Indian Penal Code, 212
secular democracy, 232
secular intelligence, 13
secularism, 345
sedition, 153–155
seismic building insurance scheme, 313
seismic safety, 26–27
seismic traumas, 311–314. *see also* Earthquakes
seismic zoning map, 26, 313
seismologists, 26
self-centrism of elected leader, 359
self-effacement, 57
self-exclusion, 218
The Self and The World (Rupert Snell), 133–134
Sen, Amartya, 62, 211, 214, 215, 235–238, 317, 342, 354
Sengupta, Nellie, 271
Sen, Nabaneeta Dev, 215
Sen, Sukumar, 256

separatism on religious lines, 265
Sethi, Rajeev, 104
Seth, Leila, 277
Seth, Vikram, 140, 150–152
Sevasadan (film by K. Subrahmanyam), 108
sexual intent, 246
The Shadow Lines (Amitav Ghosh), 140
Shah, Ajit Prakash, 155
Shah, Amit, 230
Shah, A.P., 342
Shakespeare, William, 39, 311
Shamsuddin, Khwaja, 308
Shankar, Pandit Ravi, 123–125, 140
Shanmukhavadivu, Veena, 106
Sharif, Nawaz, 137
Sharma, Bal Krishna, 204
Sharma, O.P., 89
Shastri, Lal Bahadur, 7, 9–12, 55–57, 127, 130, 131, 135–137, 273, 305–307, 320, 363
    moral responsibility for rail accident, 306
Shaw, George Bernard, 14
Shekhar, Chandra, 4, 7, 83

Shekhar, Hansda Sowvendra, 362
Shelley, Percy Bysshe, xiii, 270, 319
Shelvankar, K.S., 105
Sheriff, Mohammed, 204
Sherwani, Maqbool, 20–21
Shiksha Bachao Andolan, 330, 331
Shivaji, Chhatrapati, 351
Shiv Sena, 228
Siachen Glacier, Jammu and Kashmir, 11
Siddiqui, Salimuzzaman, 193–195
Sidhwa, RK, 204
A Silence of Desire (Kamala Markandaya), 133
Simla, 3
Simla Agreement, 10, 11
Sind, 263
Singh, Bhagat, xiv, 166, 200, 267, 345
Singh, Charan, 83, 135
Singh, Guru Gobind, 201
Singh, Harbut, 53, 199, 234
Singh, Jaipal, 205, 324, 326
Singh, Kalyan, 202
Singh, Kanwar Maharaj, 284
Singh, Karni, 56
Singh, Khushwant, xvi, 141
Singh, Manmohan, 4, 11, 58, 62, 84, 137, 174, 269, 283, 286, 321
Singh, Martand, 104
Singh, Natwar, 63
Singh, Raman, 355
Singh, S. Nihal, xvi
Singh, Surinder, 123
Singh, Ujjal, 268
Singhvi, G.S., 248
Singh, V.P., 4, 7
Singh, Vyomika, 19
Singh, Zail, 301
Sinha, Bhadra, 248
Sinha, Sachchidananda, 199
Sinha, Srikrishna, 263–264
Sinha, Yashwant, 360
Sinnasamy, Periasamy, 14
Sino-Indian war, 127, 308, 320
Sirimavo–Indira Gandhi Pact of 1974, 15
Sirimavo–Shastri Pact of 1964, 15
Sitaramayya, Pattabhi, 200
Skopje, 160
Slumdog Millionaire, 301
Snell, Rupert, 124, 133
social distancing, 81
social justice, 268
social media, 152, 235, 328, 344
solidarity with suffering, 182

Sombre, David Ochterlony Dyce, 121
Somnath temple, Gujarat, 61
Soundarya Mahal, Madras, 107
South Africa, 31–32, 41, 43, 50, 67, 79, 80, 115, 157, 162, 199, 219, 234, 366
South African satyagraha, 199
South Asian Association for Regional Cooperation (SAARC) summit, Islamabad, 4
South Pole, 42–44
South Sea House (Charles Lamb), xv
sovereigns mint, 283
Soviet Union, 43, 68, 69
space missions, ethics for human activity in, 44–45
Speaker, Lok Sabha, 62, 258
S.R. Bommai vs Union of India, 345
Sridevan, Prabha, 277
Sri Lanka, 7, 95
    ethnic groups in, 14
Sri Lankan Moors, 14
Sri Lanka's plantations, Indian Tamils on, 14–17
Srinivasier, Semmangudi, 109
Sri Ramcharitmanas (Tulsidas), 118
Staines, Gladys, 162
Staines, Graham, 162
Stalin, Josef, 69
Stalin, M.K., 345
state assemblies, 263
'statue for Godse,' 165, 166
Steele, Harold, 65
Stevenson, Robert Louis, xv
Subbulakshmi, M.S., 106–111, 118, 159
    awards, 109
    bhajans in major Indian languages, 109
    magical influence on listeners, 107
    Meera bhajans, 109
    music and concerts, 109–110
    music talent from childhood, 106–107
    role in films, 108–109
    as social exemplar, 109
    voice and stage presence, 107
Subrahamanyam, K., 108
Subramaniam, C., 320
Suhrawardy, H.S., 158, 260, 280
A Suitable Boy (Vikram Seth), 140, 150, 151
Sunak, Rishi, 120–122
Sundarayya, P., 69, 267, 269
supremacism, personal, 358
supremacists, 358

Index

Supreme Court (SC), 6, 152, 229, 246, 249, 261, 262, 282, 341, 345
surgical strikes, 12
Surjeet, Harkishen Singh, 69, 267
sustainable development, 32, 33
Suu, Daw, 177
Suu Kyi, Aung San, 177
Swaminathan, M.S., 66, 135, 138, 356
Swarajya, 153–155
Syria, 311
    earthquakes in, 25–27

Tagore, Rabindranath, 40, 41, 58, 61, 80, 90, 134, 153, 158, 180–181, 199, 214, 215, 241, 338, 345, 351
    letter to Gandhi, 180–181
    self-divestment of title, 182
Taliban, 164
Tamil Nadu, 49, 83, 255, 268, 295, 316, 325, 334, 345, 359
Tanjore (Thanjavur), 106
Tansen, 112
Tashkent, 135, 137
Tashkent Declaration, 10, 11
Tata Iron and Steel Co., 278
tattooists, 337
teachers' day, 126
Teen Murti, New Delhi, 129
Templeton prize for Progress in Religion, 127
Tenth Schedule, 275
terror, 11–12
terror attacks, 239
terrorism, 19, 137, 341, 342, 358
Thakur, Pragya Singh, 230
Thakur, Purusottam, 81
Thanjavur village of Kizhavenmani, Dalit peasants death at, 268
Tharoor, Shashi, 274–276
The Hindu View of Life (Sarvepalli Radhakrishnan), 130
theocratic nation-state, 337
Theosophical Society, Chennai, 118
Things Fall Apart, 364
Thondaman, S., 15
Thoreau, Henry David, 177
Thrown to the Wolves (Pyarelal), 146
Thumba Equatorial Rocket Launching Station, 308
Tibet, 170
Tigers, Durbars and Kings (Fanny Eden), 72
Tilak, Lokamanya, 153–155, 189, 199, 365
Tirukkural Book III, 74

Tiruvalluvar, 73–74
Tiruvanmiyur, 353
Tito, Marshal Josip Broz, 294
Tolstoy, Count Leo, 9–10
topsoil and water tables, depletion of, 237
Topsy (fictional woman), 35–36
Total Fertility Rate, 315
totem raj, 338
totems and taboos, 336–338
trafficking and prostitution, 304
train accidents, 305–307
    accountability for, 307
    in Ariyalur, 306
    in Balasore district of Odisha, 305, 307
    in Mahbubnagar, Andhra Pradesh, 306
    resignation of railway ministers, 305–307
translocated workers, 334–335
tribal India, 240, 361–364
    cases against tribals, 363
    in-migration of non-tribals to tribal populations areas, 362
    Jagdalpur manslaughter, 363, 364
    Maoist violence, 362
    neglect and exploitation, 362
    NGOs working with tribals, 363
    report of high level committee, 362
    sex ratio, 363
    symbols of diversity, 362
tribal communities, 361
tribal population spread, 361
Trinamool Congress, 305
Trinity College, Cambridge, 236
Triplicane Cultural Academy, Chennai, 273
triumvirate, 226
Trivandrum (Thiruvananthapuram), 308
Trivedi, Bela, 246
Trivedi, C.M., 281, 288
Trotsky, 69
Trump, Donald, 177
trustworthiness, 212
tsunami, 313
turbulent democracy, 343
Turkey, 311, 314
    earthquakes in, 25–27
Two-Nation Theory, 11, 77, 147, 256, 257
Tyabji, Abbas, 50
Tyabji, Badruddin, 270
Tyagarajan, Kannan, 268

UAE, 239
Ukraine, 239
Uncle Tom's Cabin (Harriet Beecher Stowe), 35

UN Convention Against Torture, 246
undertrials, 196, 322
    in correctional homes, 85
    release on bail, 85
    Section 436A, 322
Union Planning Commission, 359
United Kingdom, 43
United Nations (UN), 115, 116, 163
    moon agreement, 44
United Nations Convention Against Torture, 80
United Nations Population Fund, 315
United Progressive Alliance, 170, 275
United Provinces, 281, 284
United States (US), 35, 43, 65, 79, 81, 94, 121, 134, 165, 188, 252
University of Calcutta, 167
University of Texas (US), 30
Unlawful Activities (Prevention) Act, 230
unlawful assembly, 197
UNO's Declaration of Human Rights, 236
U Nu, 7
Upanishads, 338
upperness syndrome, 295–296
Usendi-Rokade, Pushpa, 81
USSR, 65
Uttarakhand, 25, 211
Uttar Pradesh, 172, 253, 263, 265, 295, 315, 316

Vaishnaw, Ashwini, 305
Vajpayee, Atal Bihari, 4, 7, 10, 11, 64, 83, 112–114, 131, 137, 201, 203, 230, 253, 286, 295, 301, 316, 337, 363
Vajpayee, Krishna Bihari, 112
Vallatharas, K.M., 56, 307
Valliamma, 53, 199, 234
'valuationally gross' (Amartya Sen), 237
Varanasi, 171, 230
vasudhaiva kutumbakam, 207
Vedvyasji, xiii
vehicles with red lights, 248
Venezuela, 39, 53
Venkatachalam, G., 94
Venkatachalapathy, A.R., 291
Venkataraman, Janaki, 187
Venkataraman, R., 97, 103, 289–290
Venkayya, Pingali, 219
Verma, J.S., 277
VHP, 12
Vidyarthi, Ganesh Shankar, xvi, 117, 171–172
Vigyan Bhavan, New Delhi, 325
Vijayanagara, 339, 340

violence
    anti-Sikh riots, 1984, 347
    in Bengal, 347–350
    Gujarat riots, 2002, 348
    Partition-time, 347
    speeches on Direct Action Day in 1946, Calcutta, 347
VIP and VVIP nomenclatures, 247–249
Vir Maharaj Mandir, 345
vision-impaired. *see* blind persons, in India
Viswanathan, Radha, 109
Viswanathan, V., 129, 131
Vivekananda, Swami, 171, 199, 214, 215, 217
voter ennui, 256, 257
voter impersonation, 193–195
Vyas, Jainarayan, 204

Walden (Henry David Thoreau), 177
Walls, Laura Dassow, 177
Wangchuk, Sonam, 211
war against war-mongering, 13
War and Peace, in the Union List, 9–13
war for justice, 21
war-mindedness, 12
war-psychosis, 12
wartime duty, 19
Watan-e-Aziz, 18, 19
water crisis, 355
water disputes, 240
water scarcity, 354–356
weaver bird, black-throated, 52
West Bengal, 40, 58, 84, 167, 236, 250, 255, 259, 268, 269, 281, 284, 290, 295, 316, 322, 351
wild life and birds, 49–52
The Wild Life of India (E.P. Gee), 49
Williams, Harold, 50
Winged Wonders of Rashtrapati Bhavan (Pranab Mukherjee), 342
Wodeyar, Jayachamarajendra, 68–71
words of honour, 324–326
    cash payment to Pakistan, 324–325
    by prime minister, 326
    privy purses, 325
work ethic, 168, 169
World Crafts Council, 95
World Parliament of Religions, 171
World Press Freedom Day, 326
World War II, 93, 236, 247
Wyllie, Curzon, 341

Yadav, Yogendra, 255

year of Tricolour, 199–200
Yeats, W.B., 344
Yechury, Sitaram, 83, 210–211, 267, 269
Yediyurappa, B.S., 345
Yeravada jail, Poona, 184
Young, Chic, 36
Young India, 172, 353

Zamir, Eyal, 29

Zardari, Asif Ali, 3
Zattalli, Jafar, 340
Zhou Enlai, 69
Zia ul Haq, 96
Zoonotic pandemics, 80
Zuleikha Begum, 189, 200

About the Author

A diplomat and renowned academic, Gopalkrishna Gandhi is the grandson of Mahatma Gandhi and C. Rajagopalachari. He is Distinguished Professor of History and Politics at Ashoka University. Gandhi has previously served as Secretary to the Vice President of India; Joint Secretary to the President of India; High Commissioner of India to South Africa and Lesotho; High Commissioner of India to Sri Lanka; Ambassador of India to Norway and Iceland; Governor of West Bengal; and Governor of Bihar, among other positions. Gandhi also set up the Nehru Centre in London and was its founding director.

An independent thinker, prolific writer and translator, Gopalkrishna Gandhi has authored several books including his recent memoir, *The Undying Light*, the novel *Saranam (Refuge)* and the play *Dara Shukoh*. He is also the author of *Abolishing the Death Penalty* and the editor of *Gandhi: Essential Writings*. He has translated Vikram Seth's *A Suitable Boy* into Hindi as *Koi Achchha Sa Ladka* and writes regularly for *Hindustan Times* and *The Telegraph*.